D0982868

CHIEF MODERN POETS
OF ENGLAND AND AMERICA

Selected and Edited by
GERALD DEWITT SANDERS
and
JOHN HERBERT NELSON

NEW YORK
THE MACMILLAN COMPANY
1929

Set up and electrotyped. Published April, 1929.

Set up and electrotyped in the United States of America by
J. J. LITTLE AND IVES COMPANY, NEW YORK
Printed by Berwick & Smith Co., Norwood, Mass.

CHIEF MODERN POETS
OF ENGLAND AND AMERICA

THE MACMILLAN COMPANY
NEW YORK · BOSTON · CHICAGO · DALLAS
ATLANTA · SAN FRANCISCO

MACMILLAN & CO., Limited
LONDON · BOMBAY · CALCUTTA
MELBOURNE

THE MACMILLAN COMPANY
OF CANADA, Limited
TORONTO

PREFACE

If the only reason for the publication of this volume were simply to add another to the many collections of modern poetry now in print, no apology would justify its appearance,—for besides the great number of compilations which seem to exist chiefly to reflect the editors' private preferences in verse, there are already enough good anthologies which, attempting to treat the modern movement as a whole, include a few selections by each of a large number of authors, or which sufficiently illustrate the work of poets of certain sections, classes, sects, movements, and nationalities. Our aim, however, has been to prepare a book different in several ways from any of these—to represent but a limited number of the important recent poets writing in English, yet to give enough of the work of each to allow the student to judge the poet as an individual rather than as a mere participant in a general movement; and while suppressing all criticism of our own, to offer enough biographical and bibliographical helps to enable those interested to find easily what is being thought and said of the different poets whose work is included.

The need of such a volume has been long felt, but the difficulty of securing material held in copyright has up to now stood in the way. Through the kind indulgence, however, of poets and publishers, some of whom so far recognized the needs set forth by the editors as to depart from long established customs in the matter of permitting the use of selections, we have succeeded in producing much the sort of book we envisioned at starting. One important poet, we regret to say, refused us any of his poems, and three others felt unable to allow the use of as many as requested; but in the main the book is as we hoped to have it.

The choice of poets was made after reading the works to date of upward of two hundred authors, and representative selections from numerous others; and though we are far from asserting that those selected are the only significant ones, we have, with the one exception noted, omitted no name and included none without reasons which to us seemed valid. We regret, for instance, not being able to represent two poets whose reputations rest upon long works; but to reprint their shorter pieces would impair the worth of this book; whereas to take excerpts from the long works would be unfair to the poets themselves. Naturally no two sets of editors would hold exactly the same opinions of their contemporaries; yet that we have found no conflict of opinion over the worth of at least a score of those included, and little disagreement over the rank of any omitted—with the exceptions already noted—indicates perhaps that the time has come when most persons well versed in the works of the modern poets are able to agree upon who best will repay a careful study upon the part of readers not so familiar with the whole field.

For various reasons we have omitted from this volume critical material dealing with individuals and with modern poetry as a whole. If on no other account, deference to teachers who may use the book, and who have opinions of their own which they will wish to offer, would prevent our giving critical estimates of the poets and their accomplishments; moreover, any introduction attempting to explain all the manifestations in the field of English poetry during the last half century, if it meant to do more than scratch the surface, would exceed reasonable limits—and of the articles scarcely scratching the surface there are plenty already. We have, however, by giving short biographical sketches, appending full bibliographies of the poetical works of the authors represented, and giving a list of some of the more important critical books and articles, shown the way to such students as wish a greater knowledge of the poets than the selections alone furnish.

We wish to express our gratitude to the librarians of the University of Arizona, the University of Chicago, the University of Kansas, and the Michigan State Normal College for various courtesies shown us while we were selecting the material used; to Mr. Kendall B. Taft and Mr. John F. McDermott, of Washington University, and Miss Lois Whitney, of Vassar College, for criticism of the selections made; to Mr. R. R. Smith, of the Macmillan Company, for his kind interest in helping secure copyright privileges and for his aid in other directions; to Mrs. Florence Sanders and Miss Amy Carson for help in preparing the manuscript; and to Professors Martin W. Sampson, of Cornell University, William S. Johnson, of the University of Kansas, Sidney F. Pattison, of the University of Arizona, Millett Henshaw, of St. Louis University, Dr. Charles W. Everett, of Columbia University, and Dr. Walter H. French, of Cornell University, for helping us in a number of ways while the volume was in preparation.

G. D. S.
J. H. N.

CHICAGO, ILLINOIS.
February 18, 1929.

ACKNOWLEDGMENTS

The appreciative thanks of the editors are tendered to the following publishers, who have generously consented to the reprinting of the material indicated, which they control as holders of the copyright, or authorized publishers, or both:

D. APPLETON AND COMPANY, New York: For "The Comet of Going-to-the-Sun" from *Going-to-the-Sun* (copyright 1923), and "Rain" and "Nancy Hanks, Mother of Abraham Lincoln" from *Going-to-the-Stars* (copyright 1926) by Vachel Lindsay.

CHATTO AND WINDUS, London: For selections from *The Earth for Sale* by Harold Monro.

E. P. DUTTON AND COMPANY, New York: The selections from *The Old Huntsman, Counter-Attack,* and *Picture-Show* by Siegfried Sassoon are used by permission of E. P. Dutton and Co., Ltd., New York.

THE FOUR SEAS COMPANY, Boston: For "White Nocturne" from *Nocturne of Remembered Spring* (copyright 1917), "Morning Song of Senlin" and "Wind in the Old Trees" from *The Charnel Rose* (copyright 1918), and "Portrait of One Dead" and "Palimpsest" from *The House of Dust* (copyright 1920) by Conrad Aiken; and "Court Lady Standing Under a Cherry Tree," "Two Ways of Love," "A Woman Standing by a Gate with an Umbrella," "Spring Love," "A Life," "Mutability," and "Fugitive Beauty" from *Japanese Prints* (copyright 1918) by John Gould Fletcher.

HARCOURT, BRACE AND COMPANY, New York: For selections from *Secrets* by W. H. Davies; and from *Smoke and Steel* (copyright, 1920, Harcourt, Brace and Howe, Inc.), *Slabs of the Sunburnt West* (copyright, 1922, Harcourt, Brace and Company, Inc.), and *Good Morning, America* (copyright, 1928, by Carl Sandburg; reprinted by permission of the publishers, Harcourt, Brace and Company, Inc.) by Carl Sandburg.

HARPER AND BROTHERS, New York: For "Renascence" and "Thou Art Not Lovelier Than Lilacs" from *Renascence and Other Poems,* published by Harper and Brothers (copyright, 1917, by Edna St. Vincent Millay); "Oh, Think Not I Am Faithful to a Vow" from *A Few Figs from Thistles,* published by Harper and Brothers (copyright, 1922, by Edna St. Vincent Millay); and "I Know I Am but Summer to Your Heart" and "Euclid Alone Has Looked on Beauty Bare" from *The Harp Weaver and Other Poems,* published by Harper and Brothers (copyright, 1920, 1921, 1922, 1923, by Edna St. Vincent Millay) by Edna St. Vincent Millay; and for selections from *Collected Poems, Second Series* by W. H. Davies.

HENRY HOLT AND COMPANY, New York: For selections from *Collected Poems, Down-adown-Derry, The Veil,* and *Peacock Pie* by Walter de la Mare; from *North of Boston, Mountain Interval,* and *New Hampshire* by Robert Frost; from *Last Poems* by A. E. Housman; and from *Chicago Poems* and *Cornhuskers* by Carl Sandburg.

HOUGHTON MIFFLIN COMPANY, Boston: The selections from *Irradiations—Sand and Spray* and *Goblins and Pagodas* by John Gould Fletcher; and from *Sword Blades and Poppy Seeds, Men, Women, and Ghosts, Pictures of the Floating World, Legends, What's O'Clock?, East Wind,* and *Ballads for Sale* by Amy Lowell are used by permission of, and by arrangement with, Houghton Mifflin Company.

ALFRED A. KNOPF, INC., New York: For selections from *October and Other Poems* by Robert Bridges; from *Collected Poems, First Series* by W. H. Davies; and from *Fairies and Fusiliers, Country Sentiment, The Pier-Glass,* and *Whipperginny* by Robert Graves.

HORACE LIVERIGHT, INC., New York: For selections from *Priapus and the Pool and Other Poems* by Conrad Aiken; from *Collected Poems* by H. D.; and from *Personae* by Ezra Pound.

THE MACMILLAN COMPANY, New York: For selections from *The Tree of Life* (copyright 1918) and *Breakers and Granite* (copyright 1921) by John Gould Fletcher; from *The Stonefolds* (copyright 1907), *Daily Bread* (copyright 1912), *Fires* (copyright 1912), *Borderlands and Thoroughfares* (copyright 1914), *Battle* (copyright 1915), *Livelihood* (copyright 1917), *Hill-Tracks* (copyright 1918), *Neighbors* (copyright 1920), and *I Heard a Sailor* (copyright 1925) by Wilfred Wilson Gibson; from *Wessex Poems* (copyright 1898), *Poems of the Past and Present* (copyright 1902), *Time's Laughingstocks* (copyright 1909), *Satires of Circumstance* (copyright 1914), *Moments of Vision* (copyright 1917), *Late Lyrics and Earlier* (copyright 1922), *Human Shows—Far Phantasies* (copyright 1925), and *Winter Words in Various Moods and Metres* (copyright, 1928, by Florence E. Hardy and Sydney E. Cockerell) by Thomas Hardy; from *The Last Blackbird* (copyright 1907) and *Poems* (copyright 1917) by Ralph Hodgson; from *General William Booth Enters into Heaven* (copyright 1913), *The Congo* (copyright 1914), *The Chinese Nightingale* (copyright 1917), *The Golden Whales of California* (copyright 1920), and *Collected Poems* (copyright 1913, 1914, 1916, 1917, 1919, 1920, 1923, 1925) by Vachel Lindsay; from *Salt Water Ballads* (copyright 1902), *The Story of a Round-House and Other Poems* (copyright 1912), *Dauber* (copyright 1913), *Reynard the Fox* (copyright 1919), *Enslaved and Other Poems* (copyright 1920), and *Collected Poems* (copyright 1912, 1913, and 1914 by The Macmillan Company, and 1916, 1919, 1920, 1921, 1922, 1923, and 1925 by John Masefield) by John Masefield; from *Real Property* (copyright 1922) by Harold Monro; from *Captain Craig* (copyright 1902), *The Man Against the Sky* (copyright 1916), *The Three Taverns* (copyright 1920), *Avon's Harvest* (copyright 1921), *Dionysus in Doubt* (copyright 1925), and *Collected Poems* (copyright 1916, 1917, 1920, 1921) by Edwin

Arlington Robinson; from *Homeward, Songs by the Way* (copyright 1894), *The Earth Breath* (copyright 1897), *The Divine Vision* (copyright 1904), *Voices of the Stones* (copyright 1925), and *Collected Poems* (copyright 1913, 1919, 1926) by George W. Russell ("Æ"); from *Insurrections* (copyright 1909), *The Hill of Vision* (copyright 1912), *The Rocky Road to Dublin* (copyright 1915), *Songs from the Clay* (copyright 1915), *Reincarnations* (copyright 1918), and *Collected Poems* (copyright 1909, 1912, 1915, 1918, 1925, 1926) by James Stephens; from *Helen of Troy* (copyright 1911), *Rivers to the Sea* (copyright 1915), *Love Songs* (copyright 1917), *Flame and Shadow* (copyright 1920), and *Dark of the Moon* (copyright 1926) by Sara Teasdale; and from *In the Seven Woods* (copyright 1903), *Responsibilities and Other Poems* (copyright 1916), *Lyric Poems* (copyright 1916), *The Wild Swans at Coole* (copyright 1917), *Later Poems* (copyright 1922), *Early Poems and Stories* (copyright 1925), and *The Tower* (copyright 1928) by William Butler Yeats.

JOHN MURRAY, London: For selections from *Poetical Works* by Robert Bridges.

THE POETRY BOOKSHOP, London: For selections from *Children of Love* and *Strange Meetings* by Harold Monro.

CHARLES SCRIBNER'S SONS, New York: For selections from *The Children of the Night* and *The Town Down the River* by Edwin Arlington Robinson.

FREDERICK A. STOKES COMPANY, New York: For "The Barrel-Organ" (copyright 1906), "Forty Singing Seamen" (copyright 1906), "The Highwayman" (copyright 1906), and "Song—Let Not Love Go Too" from "Drake" (copyright 1909), from *Collected Poems,* Volume I; "Seven Wise Men" from "A Coiner of Angels" (copyright 1913), from *Collected Poems,* Volume II; and *The Silver Crook* (copyright 1920), from *Collected Poems,* Volume III, by Alfred Noyes.

THE VIKING PRESS, INC., New York: For "On Reading the War Diary of a Defunct Ambassador" and "An Old World Effect" from *Satirical Poems* (copyright 1926) by Siegfried Sassoon.

The editors wish also to express their grateful obligation for special courtesies shown them by Mr. Conrad Aiken, Mr. A. E. Housman, and Mr. Harold Monro.

CONTENTS

PART ONE

THE ENGLISH AND IRISH POETS

PART TWO

THE AMERICAN POETS

CHIEF MODERN POETS
OF ENGLAND AND AMERICA

PART ONE

THE ENGLISH AND IRISH POETS

THOMAS HARDY

Thomas Hardy, novelist, short story writer, dramatist, and poet, was born June 2, 1840, on the border of Bockhampton Heath, about three miles from Dorchester, in a house which he described as "low, but rambling and spacious, with a paddock and large stablings." His father and mother were Thomas and Jemima Hardy: the former, a master-builder by trade, traced his ancestry back to a Norman gentleman, named Le Hardy, who with his brother settled in the island of Jersey about 1360; the latter came of a long line of English yeomanry.

At the age of eight young Hardy, who until then had been taught by his mother, registered at the Dorchester Primary School, which he attended for six years, his training there being supplemented later by a year's study with a French governess. At sixteen he entered the office of John Hicks, a Dorchester architect, under whom he served for five years, in his spare time pursuing studies in classical and modern literature with a fellow pupil. Upon reaching twenty-one Hardy left Dorchester for London, where for the next five years he was assistant to Sir Arthur Blomfield, an architect of prominence. During his stay in London he attended evening classes at King's College, where he completed his formal education.

As early as 1860, Hardy began writing verse, and though none of this was published, he continued the practice during his years of association with Blomfield. In 1867 he moved from London to Weymouth. By this time he had decided to become a writer, but failing to obtain an audience for his poetry, he turned his attention instead to prose, and started his first novel. This work failed of publication, but his second one, *Desperate Remedies,* appeared in 1871 after Hardy had advanced £75 to insure the publishers, Tinsley Brothers, against loss. Other novels followed quickly, the next being *Under the Greenwood Tree* (1872) and *A Pair of Blue Eyes* (1873). With the appearance of the latter, Hardy definitely gave up the profession of architecture, which he had continued to practice desultorily after leaving London, and began to devote himself exclusively to writing. During the next twenty-two years he wrote eleven novels, many of them of first importance in English literature, three volumes of short stories, and a number of essays and articles. The appearance in 1895 of *Jude the Obscure* evoked such a storm of criticism, however, that Hardy formally renounced the writing of fiction, and turned his attention again to poetry.

In 1898 he published *Wessex Poems,* his first volume of poetry, and thereafter, except for a volume of short stories and an occasional short article, he devoted himself to this form of expression. In the thirty years following the appearance of *Wessex Poems,* he published six volumes of lyric poetry and two dramatic poems, one of the latter, *The Dynasts,* being his most ambitious work.

Hardy was twice married, first in 1874 to Emma Lavinia Gifford, who died in November, 1912. On February 11, 1914, he married Florence Emily Dugdale, his secretary, an author of children's books and magazine articles. Following his first marriage, the Hardys lived at Stourminster-Newton, then for a time in London, and later at Wimborne. After 1885 they lived near Dorchester, in a house called Max Gate, which Hardy himself designed.

In his later years numerous honors were showered upon Hardy. In 1910 the Order of Merit was bestowed upon him; in 1912 he received the Gold Medal of the Royal Society of Literature; he was given the honorary degree of Doctor of Laws by Aberdeen, Bristol, and St. Andrews, and of Doctor of Literature by Cambridge and Oxford Universities; and was made honorary fellow of Magdalene College, Cambridge, and of Queen's College, Oxford.

He died at Max Gate on January 11, 1928. On January 14th the body was taken to Woking, where the heart was removed, placed in an urn, and taken to the village church of Stinsford, where it was placed in the grave of his first wife. The rest of the body was cremated, and the ashes buried in the Poets' Corner in Westminster Abbey.

FIRST OR LAST

(SONG)

If grief come early
Joy comes late,
If joy come early
Grief will wait;
Aye, my dear and tender!

Wise ones joy them early
While the cheeks are red,
Banish grief till surly
Time has dulled their dread.

And joy being ours
Ere youth has flown,
The later hours
May find us gone;
Aye, my dear and tender!

"THE CURTAINS NOW ARE DRAWN"

(SONG)

I

The curtains now are drawn,
And the spindrift strikes the glass,
Blown up the jaggèd pass
By the surly salt sou'-west,
And the sneering glare is gone
Behind the yonder crest,
While she sings to me:
"O the dream that thou art my Love, be it thine,
And the dream that I am thy Love, be it mine,
And death may come, but loving is divine."

II

I stand here in the rain,
With its smite upon her stone,
And the grasses that have grown
Over women, children, men,
And their texts that "Life is vain";
But I hear the notes as when
    Once she sang to me:
"O the dream that thou art my Love, be it thine,
And the dream that I am thy Love, be it mine,
And death may come, but loving is divine."

HE INADVERTENTLY CURES HIS LOVE-PAINS

(SONG)

I said: "O let me sing the praise
Of her who sweetly racks my days,—
    Her I adore;
Her lips, her eyes, her moods, her ways!"

In miseries of pulse and pang
I strung my harp, and straightway sang
    As none before:—
To wondrous words my quavers rang!

Thus I let heartaches lilt my verse,
Which suaged and soothed, and made disperse
    The smarts I bore
To quiet like a sepulchre's.

But, eased, the days that thrilled ere then
Lost value; and I ask, O when,
    And how, restore
Those old sweet agonies again!

FAINTHEART IN A RAILWAY TRAIN

At nine in the morning there passed a church,
At ten there passed me by the sea,
At twelve a town of smoke and smirch,
At two a forest of oak and birch,
And then, on a platform, she:

A radiant stranger, who saw not me.
I said, "Get out to her do I dare?"
But I kept my seat in my search for a plea,
And the wheels moved on. O could it but be
That I had alighted there!

A THUNDERSTORM IN TOWN

(A REMINISCENCE: 1893)

She wore a new "terra-cotta" dress,
And we stayed, because of the pelting storm,
Within the hansom's dry recess,
Though the horse had stopped; yea, motionless
We sat on, snug and warm.

Then the downpour ceased, to my sharp sad pain,
And the glass that had screened our forms before
Flew up, and out she sprang to her door:
I should have kissed her if the rain
Had lasted a minute more.

"I NEED NOT GO"

I need not go
Through sleet and snow
To where I know
She waits for me;
She will tarry me there

Till I find it fair,
And have time to spare
From company.

When I've overgot
The world somewhat,
When things cost not
Such stress and strain,
Is soon enough
By cypress sough
To tell my Love
I am come again.

And if some day,
When none cries nay,
I still delay
To seek her side
(Though ample measure
Of fitting leisure
Await my pleasure),
She will not chide.

What—not upbraid me
That I delayed me,
Nor ask what stayed me
So long? Ah, no!—
New cares may claim me,
New loves inflame me,
She will not blame me,
But suffer it so.

THE SIGH

Little head against my shoulder,
Shy at first, then somewhat bolder,
And up-eyed;
Till she, with a timid quaver,
Yielded to the kiss I gave her;
But, she sighed.

That there mingled with her feeling
Some sad thought she was concealing
It implied.
—Not that she had ceased to love me,
None on earth she set above me;
But she sighed.

She could not disguise a passion,
Dread, or doubt, in weakest fashion
If she tried:
Nothing seemed to hold us sundered,
Hearts were victors; so I wondered
Why she sighed.

Afterwards I knew her throughly,
And she loved me staunchly, truly,
Till she died;
But she never made confession
Why, at that first sweet concession,
She had sighed.

It was in our May, remember;
And though now I near November,
And abide
Till my appointed change, unfretting,
Sometimes I sit half regretting
That she sighed.

ON THE DEPARTURE PLATFORM

We kissed at the barrier; and passing through
She left me, and moment by moment got
Smaller and smaller, until to my view
She was but a spot;

A wee white spot of muslin fluff
That down the diminishing platform bore
Through hustling crowds of gentle and rough
To the carriage door.

Under the lamplight's fitful glowers,
Behind dark groups from far and near,
Whose interests were apart from ours,
She would disappear,

Then show again, till I ceased to see
That flexible form, that nebulous white;
And she who was more than my life to me
Had vanished quite. . . .

We have penned new plans since that fair fond day,
And in season she will appear again—
Perhaps in the same soft white array—
But never as then!

—"And why, young man, must eternally fly
A joy you'll repeat, if you love her well?"
—O friend, nought happens twice thus; why,
I cannot tell!

THE CONTRETEMPS

A forward rush by the lamp in the gloom,
And we clasped, and almost kissed;
But she was not the woman whom
I had promised to meet in the thawing brume
On that harbor-bridge; nor was I he of her tryst.

So loosening from me swift she said:
"O why, why feign to be
The one I had meant!—to whom I have sped
To fly with, being so sorrily wed!"
—'Twas thus and thus that she upbraided me.

My assignation had struck upon
Some others' like it, I found.
And her lover rose on the night anon;
And then her husband entered on
The lamplit, snowflaked, sloppiness around.

"Take her and welcome, man!" he cried:
"I wash my hands of her.
I'll find me twice as good a bride!"
—All this to me, whom he had eyed,
Plainly, as his wife's planned deliverer.

And next the lover: "Little I knew,
Madam, you had a third!
Kissing here in my very view!"
—Husband and lover then withdrew.
I let them; and I told them not they erred.

Why not? Well, there faced she and I—
Two strangers who'd kissed, or near,
Chancewise. To see stand weeping by
A woman once embraced, will try
The tension of a man the most austere.

So it began; and I was young,
She pretty, by the lamp,
As flakes came waltzing down among
The waves of her clinging hair, that hung
Heavily on her temples, dark and damp.

And there alone still stood we two;
She one cast off for me,
Or so it seemed: while night ondrew,
Forcing a parley what should do
We twain hearts caught in one catastrophe.

In stranded souls a common strait
Wakes latencies unknown,
Whose impulse may precipitate
A life-long leap. The hour was late,
And there was the Jersey boat with its funnel agroan.

"Is wary walking worth much pother?"
It grunted, as still it stayed.
"One pairing is as good as another
Where all is venture! Take each other,
And scrap the oaths that you have aforetime made." . . .

—Of the four involved there walks but one
On earth at this late day.
And what of the chapter so begun?
In that odd complex what was done?
Well; happiness comes in full to none:
Let peace lie on lulled lips: I will not say.

THE DAME OF ATHELHALL

I

"Dear! Shall I see thy face," she said,
"In one brief hour?
And away with thee from a loveless bed
To a far-off sun, to a vine-wrapt bower,
And be thine own unseparated,
And challenge the world's white glower?"

II

She quickened her feet, and met him where
They had predesigned:
And they clasped, and mounted, and cleft the air
Upon whirling wheels; till the will to bind
Her life with his made the moments there
Efface the years behind.

III

Miles slid, and the port uprose to view
As they sped on;
When slipping its bond the bracelet flew
From her fondled arm. Replaced anon,
Its cameo of the abjured one drew
Her musings thereupon.

IV

The gaud with his image once had been
A gift from him:
And so it was that its carving keen
Refurbished memories wearing dim,
Which set in her soul a twinge of teen,
And a tear on her lashes' brim.

V

"I may not go!" she at length outspake,
"Thoughts call me back—
I would still lose all for your dear, true sake;
My heart is thine, friend! But my track
Home, home to Athelhall I must take
To hinder household wrack!"

VI

He was wroth. And they parted, weak and wan;
And he left the shore;
His ship diminished, was low, was gone;
And she heard in the waves as the daytide wore,
And read in the leer of the sun that shone,
That they parted for evermore.

VII

She homed as she came, at the dip of eve
On Athel Coomb
Regaining the Hall she had sworn to leave.
The house was soundless as a tomb,
And she stole to her chamber, there to grieve
Lone, kneeling, in the gloom.

VIII

From the lawn without rose her husband's voice
To one his friend:
"Another her Love, another my choice,
Her going is good. Our conditions mend;
In a change of mates we shall both rejoice;
I hoped that it thus might end!

IX

"A quick divorce; she will make him hers,
And I wed mine.
So Time rights all things in long, long years—
Or rather she, by her bold design!
I admire a woman no balk deters:
She has blessed my life, in fine.

X

"I shall build new rooms for my new true bride,
Let the bygone be:
By now, no doubt, she has crossed the tide
With the man to her mind. Far happier she
In some warm vineland by his side
Than ever she was with me."

THE LAST LEAF

"The leaves throng thick above:—
Well, I'll come back, dear Love,
When they all are down!"

She watched that August tree,
(None now scorned summer as she),
Till it broidered it brown.

And then October came blowing,
And the leaves showed signs they were going,
And she saw up through them.

O how she counted them then!
—November left her but ten,
And started to strew them.

"Ah, when they all are gone,
And the skeleton-time comes on,
Whom shall I see!"

—When the fifteenth spread its sky
That month, her upturned eye
Could count but three.

And at the close of the week
A flush flapped over her cheek:
The last one fell.

But—he did not come. And, at length,
Her hope of him lost all strength,
And it was as a knell. . . .

When he did come again,
Years later, a husband then,
Heavy somewhat,

With a smile she reminded him:
And he cried: "Ah, that vow of our whim!—
Which I forgot,

"As one does!—And was that the tree?
So it was!—Dear me, dear me:
Yes: I forgot."

THE CURATE'S KINDNESS

(A WORKHOUSE IRONY)

I

I thought they'd be strangers aroun' me,
But she's to be there!
Let me jump out o' waggon and go back and drown me
At Pummery or Ten-Hatches Weir.

II

I thought: "Well, I've come to the Union—
The workhouse at last—
After honest hard work all the week, and Communion
O' Zundays, these fifty years past.

III

" 'Tis hard; but," I thought, "never mind it:
There's gain in the end:
And when I get used to the place I shall find it
A home, and may find there a friend.

IV

"Life there will be better than t'other,
For peace is assured.
The men in one wing and their wives in another
Is strictly the rule of the Board."

V

Just then one young Pa'son arriving
Steps up out of breath
To the side o' the waggon wherein we were driving
To Union; and calls out and saith:

VI

"Old folks, that harsh order is altered,
Be not sick of heart!
The Guardians they poohed and they pished and they paltered
When urged not to keep you apart.

VII

" 'It is wrong,' I maintained, 'to divide them,
Near forty years wed.'
'Very well, sir. We promise, then, they shall abide them
In one wing together,' they said."

VIII

Then I sank—knew 'twas quite a foredone thing
That misery should be
To the end! . . . To get freed of her there was the one thing
Had made the change welcome to me.

IX

To go there was ending but badly;
'Twas shame and 'twas pain;
"But anyhow," thought I, "thereby I shall gladly
Get free of this forty years' chain."

X

I thought they'd be strangers aroun' me,
But she's to be there!
Let me jump out o' waggon and go back and drown me
At Pummery or Ten-Hatches Weir.

AFTER THE FAIR

[*From* AT CASTERBRIDGE FAIR]

The singers are gone from the Cornmarket-place
With their broadsheets of rhymes,
The street rings no longer in treble and bass
With their skits on the times,
And the Cross, lately thronged, is a dim naked space
That but echoes the stammering chimes.

From Clock-corner steps, as each quarter ding-dongs,
Away the folk roam
By the "Hart" and Grey's Bridge into byways and "drongs,"
Or across the ridged loam;
The younger ones shrilling the lately heard songs,
The old saying, "Would we were home."

The shy-seeming maiden so mute in the fair
Now rattles and talks,
And that one who looked the most swaggering there
Grows sad as she walks,
And she who seemed eaten by cankering care
In statuesque sturdiness stalks.

And midnight clears High Street of all but the ghosts
Of its buried burghees,
From the latest far back to those old Roman hosts
Whose remains one yet sees,
Who loved, laughed, and fought, hailed their friends, drank their toasts
At their meeting-times here, just as these!

THE DARKLING THRUSH

I leant upon a coppice gate
When Frost was spectre-gray,
And Winter's dregs made desolate
The weakening eye of day.
The tangled bine-stems scored the sky
Like strings of broken lyres,
And all mankind that haunted nigh
Had sought their household fires.

The land's sharp features seemed to be
The Century's corpse outleant,
His crypt the cloudy canopy,
The wind his death-lament.
The ancient pulse of germ and birth
Was shrunken hard and dry,
And every spirit upon earth
Seemed fervorless as I.

At once a voice arose among
The bleak twigs overhead
In a full-hearted evensong
Of joy illimited;
An aged thrush, frail, gaunt, and small,
In blast-beruffled plume,
Had chosen thus to fling his soul
Upon the growing gloom.

So little cause for carolings
Of such ecstatic sound
Was written on terrestrial things
Afar or nigh around,
That I could think there trembled through
His happy good-night air
Some blessed Hope, whereof he knew
And I was unaware.

THE LAST CHRYSANTHEMUM

Why should this flower delay so long
To show its tremulous plumes?
Now is the time of plaintive robin-song,
When flowers are in their tombs.

Through the slow summer, when the sun
Called to each frond and whorl
That all he could for flowers was being done,
Why did it not uncurl?

It must have felt that fervid call
Although it took no heed,
Waking but now, when leaves like corpses fall,
And saps all retrocede.

Too late its beauty, lonely thing,
The season's shine is spent,
Nothing remains for it but shivering
In tempests turbulent.

Had it a reason for delay,
Dreaming in witlessness
That for a bloom so delicately gay
Winter would stay its stress?

—I talk as if the thing were born
With sense to work its mind;
Yet it is but one mask of many worn
By the Great Face behind.

TRANSFORMATIONS

Portion of this yew
Is a man my grandsire knew,
Bosomed here at its foot:
This branch may be his wife,
A ruddy human life
Now turned to a green shoot.

These grasses must be made
Of her who often prayed,
Last century, for repose;
And the fair girl long ago
Whom I often tried to know
May be entering this rose.

So, they are not underground,
But as nerves and veins abound
In the growths of upper air,
And they feel the sun and rain,
And the energy again
That made them what they were!

THE BLINDED BIRD

So zestfully canst thou sing?
And all this indignity,
With God's consent, on thee!
Blinded ere yet a-wing
By the red-hot needle thou,
I stand and wonder how
So zestfully thou canst sing!

Resenting not such wrong,
Thy grievous pain forgot,
Eternal dark thy lot,
Groping thy whole life long,
After that stab of fire;
Enjailed in pitiless wire;
Resenting not such wrong!

Who hath charity? This bird.
Who suffereth long and is kind,
Is not provoked, though blind
And alive ensepulchred?
Who hopeth, endureth all things?
Who thinketh no evil, but sings?
Who is divine? This bird.

THE REMINDER

While I watch the Christmas blaze
Paint the room with ruddy rays,
Something makes my vision glide
To the frosty scene outside.

There, to reach a rotting berry,
Toils a thrush,—constrained to very
Dregs of food by sharp distress,
Taking such with thankfulness.

Why, O starving bird, when I
One day's joy would justify,
And put misery out of view,
Do you make me notice you!

SNOW IN THE SUBURBS

Every branch big with it,
Bent every twig with it;
Every fork like a white web-foot;
Every street and pavement mute:
Some flakes have lost their way, and grope back upward, when
Meeting those meandering down they turn and descend again.
The palings are glued together like a wall,
And there is no waft of wind with the fleecy fall.

A sparrow enters the tree,
Whereon immediately
A snow-lump thrice his own slight size
Descends on him and showers his head and eyes,
And overturns him,
And near inurns him,
And lights on a nether twig, when its brush
Starts off a volley of other lodging lumps with a rush.

The steps are a blanched slope,
Up which, with feeble hope,
A black cat comes, wide-eyed and thin;
And we take him in.

A PLAINT TO MAN

When you slowly emerged from the den of Time,
And gained percipiènce as you grew,
And fleshed you fair out of shapeless slime,

Wherefore, O Man, did there come to you
The unhappy need of creating me—
A form like your own—for praying to?

My virtue, power, utility,
Within my maker must all abide,
Since none in myself can ever be,

One thin as a phasm on a lantern-slide
Shown forth in the dark upon some dim sheet,
And by none but its showman vivified.

"Such a forced device," you may say, "is meet
For easing a loaded heart at whiles:
Man needs to conceive of a mercy-seat

Somewhere above the gloomy aisles
Of this wailful world, or he could not bear
The irk no local hope beguiles."

—But since I was framed in your first despair
The doing without me has had no play
In the minds of men when shadows scare;

And now that I dwindle day by day
Beneath the deicide eyes of seers
In a light that will not let me stay,

And to-morrow the whole of me disappears,
The truth should be told, and the fact be faced
That had best been faced in earlier years:

The fact of life with dependence placed
On the human heart's resource alone,
In brotherhood bonded close and graced

With loving-kindness fully blown,
And visioned help unsought, unknown.

ON THE PORTRAIT OF A WOMAN ABOUT TO BE HANGED

Comely and capable one of our race,
Posing there in your gown of grace,
Plain, yet becoming;
Could subtlest breast
Ever have guessed
What was behind that innocent face,
Drumming, drumming!

Would that your Causer, ere knoll your knell
For this riot of passion, might deign to tell
Why, since It made you
Sound in the germ,
It sent a worm
To madden Its handiwork, when It might well
Not have assayed you,

Not have implanted, to your deep rue,
The Clytæmnestra spirit in you,
And with purblind vision
Sowed a tare
In a field so fair,
And a thing of symmetry, seemly to view,
Brought to derision!

TO LIFE

O Life with the sad seared face,
I weary of seeing thee,
And thy draggled cloak, and thy hobbling pace,
And thy too-forced pleasantry!

I know what thou would'st tell
Of Death, Time, Destiny—
I have known it long, and know, too, well
What it all means for me.

But canst thou not array
Thyself in rare disguise,
And feign like truth, for one mad day,
That Earth is Paradise?

I'll tune me to the mood,
And mumm with thee till eve;
And maybe what as interlude
I feign, I shall believe!

"LET ME ENJOY"

(MINOR KEY)

I

Let me enjoy the earth no less
Because the all-enacting Might
That fashioned forth its loveliness
Had other aims than my delight.

II

About my path there flits a Fair,
Who throws me not a word or sign;
I'll charm me with her ignoring air,
And laud the lips not meant for mine.

III

From manuscripts of moving song
Inspired by scenes and dreams unknown,
I'll pour out raptures that belong
To others, as they were my own.

IV

And some day hence, towards Paradise
And all its blest—if such should be—
I will lift glad, afar-off eyes,
Though it contain no place for me.

THE IMPERCIPIENT

(AT A CATHEDRAL SERVICE)

That with this bright believing band
  I have no claim to be,
That faiths by which my comrades stand
  Seem fantasies to me,
And mirage-mists their Shining Land,
  Is a strange destiny.

Why thus my soul should be consigned
  To infelicity,
Why always I must feel as blind
  To sights my brethren see,
Why joys they've found I cannot find,
  Abides a mystery.

Since heart of mine knows not that ease
  Which they know; since it be
That He who breathes All's Well to these
  Breathes no All's-Well to me,
My lack might move their sympathies
  And Christian charity!

I am like a gazer who should mark
An inland company
Standing upfingered, with, "Hark! hark!
The glorious distant sea!"
And feel, "Alas, 'tis but yon dark
And wind-swept pine to me!"

Yet I would bear my shortcomings
With meet tranquillity,
But for the charge that blessed things
I'd liefer not have be.
O doth a bird deprived of wings
Go earth-bound wilfully!

. . . . .

Enough. As yet disquiet clings
About us. Rest shall we.

THE OXEN

Christmas Eve, and twelve of the clock.
"Now they are all on their knees,"
An elder said as we sat in a flock
By the embers in hearthside ease.

We pictured the meek mild creatures where
They dwelt in their strawy pen,
Nor did it occur to one of us there
To doubt they were kneeling then.

So fair a fancy few would weave
In these years! Yet, I feel,
If someone said on Christmas Eve,
"Come; see the oxen kneel,

"In the lonely barton by yonder coomb
Our childhood used to know,"
I should go with him in the gloom,
Hoping it might be so.

"THERE SEEMED A STRANGENESS"

(A PHANTASY)

There seemed a strangeness in the air,
Vermilion light on the land's lean face;
I heard a Voice from I knew not where:—
"The Great Adjustment is taking place!

"I set thick darkness over you,
And fogged you all your years therein;
At last I uncloud your view,
Which I am weary of holding in.

"Men have not heard, men have not seen
Since the beginning of the world
What earth and heaven mean;
But now their curtains shall be furled,

"And they shall see what is, ere long,
Not through a glass, but face to face;
And Right shall disestablish Wrong:
The Great Adjustment is taking place."

THE MAN HE KILLED

"Had he and I but met
By some old ancient inn,
We should have sat us down to wet
Right many a nipperkin!

"But ranged as infantry,
And staring face to face,
I shot at him as he at me,
And killed him in his place.

"I shot him dead because—
Because he was my foe,
Just so: my foe of course he was;
That's clear enough; although

"He thought he'd 'list, perhaps,
Offhand like—just as I—
Was out of work—had sold his traps—
No other reason why.

"Yes; quaint and curious war is!
You shoot a fellow down
You'd treat if met where any bar is,
Or help to half-a-crown."

THE PITY OF IT

I walked in loamy Wessex lanes, afar
From rail-track and from highway, and I heard
In field and farmstead many an ancient word
Of local lineage like "Thu bist," "Er war,"
"Ich woll," "Er sholl," and by-talk similar,
Nigh as they speak who in this month's moon gird
At England's very loins, thereunto spurred
By gangs whose glory threats and slaughters are.

Then seemed a Heart crying: "Whosoever they be
At root and bottom of this, who flung this flame
Between kin folk kin tongued even as are we,
Sinister, ugly, lurid, be their fame;
May their familiars grow to shun their name,
And their brood perish everlastingly."

IN TENEBRIS

II

Considerabam ad dexteram, et videbam; et non erat qui cognosceret me. . . . Non est qui requirat animam meam.

Psalm CXLII.

When the clouds' swoln bosoms echo back the shouts of the many and strong
That things are all as they best may be, save a few to be right ere long,

And my eyes have not the vision in them to discern what to these is so clear,
The blot seems straightway in me alone; one better he were not here.

The stout upstanders say, All's well with us: ruers have nought to rue!
And what the potent say so oft, can it fail to be somewhat true?
Breezily go they, breezily come; their dust smokes around their career,
Till I think I am one born out of due time, who has no calling here.

Their dawns bring lusty joys, it seems; their evenings all that is sweet;
Our times are blessed times, they cry: Life shapes it as is most meet,
And nothing is much the matter; there are many smiles to a tear;
Then what is the matter is I, I say. Why should such an one be here? . . .

Let him in whose ears the low-voiced Best is killed by the clash of the First,
Who holds that if way to the Better there be, it exacts a full look at the Worst,
Who feels that delight is a delicate growth cramped by crookedness, custom, and fear,
Get him up and be gone as one shaped awry; he disturbs the order here.

"FOR LIFE I HAD NEVER CARED GREATLY"

For Life I had never cared greatly,
As worth a man's while;
Peradventures unsought,
Peradventures that finished in nought,
Had kept me from youth and through manhood till lately
Unwon by its style.

In earliest years—why I know not—
I viewed it askance;
Conditions of doubt,
Conditions that leaked slowly out,
May haply have bent me to stand and to show not
Much zest for its dance.

With symphonies soft and sweet color
It courted me then,
Till evasions seemed wrong,
Till evasions gave in to its song,
And I warmed, until living aloofly loomed duller
Than life among men.

Anew I found nought to set eyes on,
When, lifting its hand,
It uncloaked a star,
Uncloaked it from fog-damps afar,
And showed its beams burning from pole to horizon
As bright as a brand.

And so, the rough highway forgetting,
I pace hill and dale
Regarding the sky,
Regarding the vision on high,
And thus re-illumed have no humor for letting
My pilgrimage fail.

THE COMING OF THE END

How it came to an end!
The meeting afar from the crowd,
And the love-looks and laughters unpenned,
The parting when much was avowed,
How it came to an end!

It came to an end;
Yes, the outgazing over the stream,
With the sun on each serpentine bend,
Or, later, the luring moon-gleam;
It came to an end.

It came to an end,
The housebuilding, furnishing, planting,
As if there were ages to spend
In welcoming, feasting, and jaunting;
It came to an end.

It came to an end,
That journey of one day a week:
("It always goes on," said a friend,
"Just the same in bright weathers or bleak;")
But it came to an end.

"*How* will come to an end
This orbit so smoothly begun,
Unless some convulsion attend?"
I often said. "What will be done
When it comes to an end?"

Well, it came to an end
Quite silently—stopped without jerk;
Better close no prevision could lend;
Working out as One planned it should work
Ere it came to an end.

THE SELFSAME SONG

A bird sings the selfsame song,
With never a fault in its flow,
That we listened to here those long
Long years ago.

A pleasing marvel is how
A strain of such rapturous rote
Should have gone on thus till now
Unchanged in a note!

—But it's not the selfsame bird.—.
No: perished to dust is he. . . .
As also are those who heard
That song with me.

AN ANCIENT TO ANCIENTS

Where once we danced, where once we sang,
Gentlemen,
The floors are sunken, cobwebs hang,
And cracks creep; worms have fed upon
The doors. Yea, sprightlier times were then
Than now, with harps and tabrets gone,
Gentlemen!

Where once we rowed, where once we sailed,
Gentlemen,
And damsels took the tiller, veiled
Against too strong a stare (God wot
Their fancy, then or anywhen!)
Upon that shore we are clean forgot,
Gentlemen!

We have lost somewhat, afar and near,
Gentlemen,
The thinning of our ranks each year
Affords a hint we are nigh undone,
That we shall not be ever again
The marked of many, loved of one,
Gentlemen.

In dance the polka hit our wish,
Gentlemen,
The paced quadrille, the spry schottische,
"Sir Roger."—And in opera spheres
The "Girl" (the famed "Bohemian"),
And "Trovatore," held the ears,
Gentlemen.

This season's paintings do not please,
Gentlemen,
Like Etty, Mulready, Maclise;
Throbbing romance has waned and wanned;
No wizard wields the witching pen
Of Bulwer, Scott, Dumas, and Sand,
Gentlemen.

The bower we shrined to Tennyson,
Gentlemen,
Is roof-wrecked; damps there drip upon
Sagged seats, the creeper-nails are rust,
The spider is sole denizen;
Even she who voiced those rhymes is dust,
Gentlemen!

We who met sunrise sanguine-souled,
Gentlemen,
Are wearing weary. We are old;
These younger press; we feel our rout
Is imminent to Aïdes' den,—
That evening shades are stretching out,
Gentlemen!

And yet, though ours be failing frames,
Gentlemen,
So were some others' history names,
Who trode their track light-limbed and fast
As these youth, and not alien
From enterprise, to their long last,
Gentlemen.

Sophocles, Plato, Socrates,
Gentlemen,
Pythagoras, Thucydides,
Herodotus, and Homer,—yea,
Clement, Augustin, Origen,
Burnt brightlier towards their setting-day,
Gentlemen.

And ye, red-lipped and smooth-browed; list,
Gentlemen;
Much is there waits you we have missed;
Much lore we leave you worth the knowing,
Much, much has lain outside our ken:
Nay, rush not: time serves: we are going,
Gentlemen.

"WHY DO I?"

Why do I go on doing these things?
Why not cease?
Is it that you are yet in this world of welterings
And unease,
And that, while so, mechanic repetitions please?

When shall I leave off doing these things?—
When I hear
You have dropped your dusty cloak and taken you wondrous wings
To another sphere,
Where no pain is: Then shall I hush this dinning gear.

WAITING BOTH

A star looks down at me,
And says: "Here I and you
Stand, each in our degree:
What do you mean to do,—
Mean to do?"

I say: "For all I know,
Wait, and let Time go by,
Till my change come,"—"Just so."
The star says: "So mean I:—
So mean I."

DEAD "WESSEX," THE DOG, TO THE HOUSEHOLD

Do you think of me at all,
Wistful ones?
Do you think of me at all
As if nigh?

Do you think of me at all
At the creep of evenfall,
Or when the sky-birds call
        As they fly?

Do you look for me at times,
        Wistful ones?
Do you look for me at times
        Strained and still?
Do you look for me at times,
When the hour for walking chimes,
On that grassy path that climbs
        Up the hill?

You may hear a jump or trot,
        Wistful ones,
You may hear a jump or trot—
        Mine, as 'twere—
You may hear a jump or trot
On the stair or path or plot;
But I shall cause it not,
        Be not there.

Should you call as when I knew you,
        Wistful ones,
Should you call as when I knew you,
        Shared your home;
Should you call as when I knew you,
I shall not turn to view you,
I shall not listen to you,
        Shall not come.

ROBERT BRIDGES

Robert Seymour Bridges, fourth son of John Thomas Bridges, of Walmer and St. Nicholas Court, Isle of Thanet, was born at Walmer, on the Kentish coast, on October 23, 1844. As a youth he attended Eton, and then proceeded to Corpus Christi College, Oxford, matriculating there in October, 1863, and receiving his B.A. degree with honors in 1867. For some time after leaving Oxford, he traveled extensively on the Continent, especially in Greece and Italy, and in the East. Upon returning to England he studied medicine, and in 1874 received from Oxford the degrees of Master of Arts and Bachelor of Medicine. He continued his studies at St. Bartholomew's Hospital, London, where he became casualty physician. Later he was assistant physician at the Children's Hospital, Great Ormond Street, and physician at the Great Northern Hospital. He gained a fine reputation in his profession, and was made a Fellow of the Royal College of Physicians. Notwithstanding this success, in 1882 he retired to devote all his time to writing.

He had early cultivated an interest in poetry, and in 1873, even before receiving his medical degree, published a volume of lyrics, *Poems*. This he followed three years later with a sonnet cycle, *The Growth of Love*, and then with two or three other volumes of lyrics. From London he retired to the outskirts of Oxford, beginning there the series of poetic dramas that in quantity constitute the bulk of his poetical work. On September 3, 1884, he married Mary Monica Waterhouse, the eldest daughter of Alfred Waterhouse, an architect of note, and went to live at Yattendon, a village in Berkshire. There in an old manor house, surrounded by a beautiful garden, in which most of his days were lived, he spent many years of what he called "joy in idleness," writing a number of poetic dramas and some of his best lyrics. His books, however, were issued for the most part from private presses, and for a long while few of the general public were aware of his existence.

In addition to his poetry, Bridges has written several critical studies. The best known of these is *Milton's Prosody,* a part of which he wrote as early as 1887, but which he continued to revise until 1921. Another is *John Keats, a Critical Essay* (1895). He has edited two anthologies, *The Spirit of Man* (1916) and *The Chilswell Book of English Poetry* (1924), and has edited, in collaboration with H. Ellis Wooldridge, *The Yattendon Hymnal* (1920). He has also written a number of essays and articles for the Society for Pure English, which he was instrumental in founding in 1913, and has written experimental poems in classical metres. He is among the most learned of living poets, being able to write with facility on art, music, literature, medicine, science, history, and philosophy. He is also a profound student of the classics, and knows well most of the modern European languages.

In 1913, upon the death of Alfred Austin, he was appointed Poet Laureate of England. He has been given the honorary degrees of D. Litt. by Oxford (1912) and Harvard (1924), and LL.D. by St. Andrews (1911) and the University of Michigan (1924). He is Honorary Fellow of his *Alma Mater,* Corpus Christi College. In April, 1924, he made a visit to the United States to deliver a series of lectures at the University of Michigan. He has one son and one daughter, and has lived for some time at Chilswell, Boar's Hill, on the upper Thames, overlooking Oxford.

"THE VERY NAMES OF THINGS BELOVED ARE DEAR"

[*From* THE GROWTH OF LOVE]

The very names of things beloved are dear,
And sounds will gather beauty from their sense,
As many a face through love's long residence
Groweth to fair instead of plain and sere:
But when I say thy name it hath no peer,
And I suppose fortune determined thence
Her dower, that such beauty's excellence
Should have a perfect title for the ear.

Thus may I think the adopting Muses chose
Their sons by name, knowing none would be heard
Or writ so oft in all the world as those,—
Dan Chaucer, mighty Shakespeare, then for third
The classic Milton, and to us arose
Shelley with liquid music in the word.

"O WEARY PILGRIMS, CHANTING OF YOUR WOE"

[*From* THE GROWTH OF LOVE]

O weary pilgrims, chanting of your woe,
That turn your eyes to all the peaks that shine,
Hailing in each the citadel divine
The which ye thought to have entered long ago;
Until at length your feeble steps and slow
Falter upon the threshold of the shrine,
And your hearts overburdened doubt in fine
Whether it be Jerusalem or no:

Disheartened pilgrims, I am one of you;
For, having worshipped many a barren face,
I scarce now greet the goal I journeyed to:
I stand a pagan in the holy place;
Beneath the lamp of truth I am found untrue,
And question with the God that I embrace.

"ALL EARTHLY BEAUTY HATH ONE CAUSE AND PROOF"

[*From* THE GROWTH OF LOVE]

All earthly beauty hath one cause and proof,
To lead the pilgrim soul to beauty above:
Yet lieth the greater bliss so far aloof,
That few there be are weaned from earthly love.
Joy's ladder it is, reaching from home to home,
The best of all the work that all was good;
Whereof 'twas writ the angels aye upclomb,
Down sped, and at the top the Lord God stood.
But I my time abuse, my eyes by day
Centered on thee, by night my heart on fire—
Letting my numbered moments run away—
Nor e'en 'twixt night and day to heaven aspire:
  So true it is that what the eye seeth not
  But slow is loved, and loved is soon forgot.

"THE WORLD COMES NOT TO AN END"

[*From* THE GROWTH OF LOVE]

The world comes not to an end: her city-hives
Swarm with the tokens of a changeless trade,
With rolling wheel, driver and flagging jade,
Rich men and beggars, children, priests, and wives.
New homes on old are set, as lives on lives;
Invention with invention overlaid:
But still or tool or toy or book or blade
Shaped for the hand, that holds and toils and strives.

The men to-day toil as their fathers taught,
With little bettered means; for works depend
On works and overlap, and thought on thought:
And through all change the smiles of hope amend
The weariest face, the same love changed in nought:
In this thing too the world comes not to an end.

ELEGY

The wood is bare: a river-mist is steeping
  The trees that winter's chill of life bereaves:
Only their stiffened boughs break silence, weeping
    Over their fallen leaves;

That lie upon the dank earth brown and rotten,
  Miry and matted in the soaking wet:
Forgotten with the spring, that is forgotten
    By them that can forget.

Yet it was here we walked when ferns were springing,
  And through the mossy bank shot bud and blade:—
Here found in summer, when the birds were singing,
    A green and pleasant shade.

'Twas here we loved in sunnier days and greener;
  And now, in this disconsolate decay,
I come to see her where I most have seen her,
    And touch the happier day.

For on this path, at every turn and corner,
  The fancy of her figure on me falls:
Yet walks she with the slow step of a mourner,
    Nor hears my voice that calls.

So through my heart there winds a track of feeling,
  A path of memory, that is all her own:
Whereto her phantom beauty ever stealing
    Haunts the sad spot alone.

About her steps the trunks are bare, the branches
  Drip heavy tears upon her downcast head;
And bleed from unseen wounds that no sun stanches,
    For the year's sun is dead.

And dead leaves wrap the fruits that summer planted:
  And birds that love the South have taken wing.
The wanderer, loitering o'er the scene enchanted,
    Weeps, and despairs of spring.

"DEAR LADY, WHEN THOU FROWNEST"

Dear lady, when thou frownest,
  And my true love despisest,
And all thy vows disownest
  That sealed my venture wisest;
I think thy pride's displeasure
Neglects a matchless treasure
Exceeding price and measure.

But when again thou smilest,
  And love for love returnest,
And fear with joy beguilest,
  And takest truth in earnest;
Then, though I sheer adore thee,
The sum of my love for thee
Seems poor, scant, and unworthy.

"POOR WITHERED ROSE AND DRY"

Poor withered rose and dry,
  Skeleton of a rose,
Risen to testify
  To love's sad close:

Treasured for love's sweet sake,
  That of joy past
Thou might'st again awake
  Memory at last.

Yet is thy perfume sweet;
Thy petals red
Yet tell of summer heat,
And the gay bed:

Yet, yet recall the glow
Of the gazing sun,
When at thy bush we two
Joined hands in one.

But, rose, thou hast not seen,
Thou hast not wept
The change that passed between,
Whilst thou hast slept.

To me thou seemest yet
The dead dream's thrall:
While I live and forget
Dream, truth and all.

Thou art more fresh than I,
Rose, sweet and red:
Salt on my pale cheeks lie
The tears I shed.

"I WILL NOT LET THEE GO"

I will not let thee go.
Ends all our month-long love in this?
Can it be summed up so,
Quit in a single kiss?
I will not let thee go.

I will not let thee go.
If thy words' breath could scare thy deeds,
As the soft south can blow
And toss the feathered seeds,
Then might I let thee go.

I will not let thee go.
Had not the great sun seen, I might;
Or were he reckoned slow
To bring the false to light,
Then might I let thee go.

I will not let thee go.
The stars that crowd the summer skies
Have watched us so below
With all their million eyes,
I dare not let thee go.

I will not let thee go.
Have we not chid the changeful moon,
Now rising late, and now
Because she set too soon,
And shall I let thee go?

I will not let thee go.
Have not the young flowers been content,
Plucked ere their buds could blow,
To seal our sacrament?
I cannot let thee go.

I will not let thee go.
I hold thee by too many bands:
Thou sayest farewell, and lo!
I have thee by the hands,
And will not let thee go.

TRIOLET

When first we met we did not guess
That Love would prove so hard a master;
Of more than common friendliness
When first we met we did not guess.
Who could foretell this sore distress,
This irretrievable disaster
When first we met?—We did not guess
That Love would prove so hard a master.

TRIOLET

All women born are so perverse
No man need boast their love possessing.
If nought seem better, nothing's worse:
All women born are so perverse.
From Adam's wife, that proved a curse
Though God had made her for a blessing,
All women born are so perverse
No man need boast their love possessing.

A PASSER-BY

Whither, O splendid ship, thy white sails crowding,
Leaning across the bosom of the urgent West,
That fearest nor sea rising, nor sky clouding,
Whither away, fair rover, and what thy quest?
Ah! soon, when Winter has all our vales opprest,
When skies are cold and misty, and hail is hurling,
Wilt thou glide on the blue Pacific, or rest
In a summer haven asleep, thy white sails furling.

I there before thee, in the country that well thou knowest,
Already arrived am inhaling the odorous air:
I watch thee enter unerringly where thou goest,
And anchor queen of the strange shipping there,
Thy sails for awnings spread, thy masts bare:
Nor is aught from the foaming reef to the snow-capped, grandest
Peak, that is over the feathery palms more fair
Than thou, so upright, so stately, and still thou standest.

And yet, O splendid ship, unhailed and nameless,
I know not if, aiming a fancy, I rightly divine
That thou hast a purpose joyful, a courage blameless,
Thy port assured in a happier land than mine.
But for all I have given thee, beauty enough is thine,
As thou, aslant with trim tackle and shrouding,
From the proud nostril curve of a prow's line
In the offing scatterest foam, thy white sails crowding.

LONDON SNOW

When men were all asleep the snow came flying,
In large white flakes falling on the city brown,
Stealthily and perpetually settling and loosely lying,
Hushing the latest traffic of the drowsy town;
Deadening, muffling, stifling its murmurs failing;
Lazily and incessantly floating down and down:
Silently sifting and veiling road, roof and railing;
Hiding difference, making unevenness even,
Into angles and crevices softly drifting and sailing.
All night it fell, and when full inches seven
It lay in the depth of its uncompacted lightness,
The clouds blew off from a high and frosty heaven;
And all woke earlier for the unaccustomed brightness
Of the winter dawning, the strange unheavenly glare:
The eye marvelled—marvelled at the dazzling whiteness;
The ear hearkened to the stillness of the solemn air;
No sound of wheel rumbling nor of foot falling,
And the busy morning cries came thin and spare.
Then boys I heard, as they went to school, calling,
They gathered up the crystal manna to freeze
Their tongues with tasting, their hands with snowballing;
Or rioted in a drift, plunging up to the knees;
Or peering up from under the white-mossed wonder,
"O look at the trees!" they cried, "O look at the trees!"
With lessened load a few carts creak and blunder,
Following along the white deserted way,
A country company long dispersed asunder:
When now already the sun, in pale display
Standing by Paul's high dome, spread forth below
His sparkling beams, and awoke the stir of the day.
For now doors open, and war is waged with the snow;
And trains of somber men, past tale of number,
Tread long brown paths, as toward their toil they go:
But even for them awhile no cares encumber
Their minds diverted; the daily word is unspoken,
The daily thoughts of labor and sorrow slumber
At the sight of the beauty that greets them, for the charm
they have broken.

THE VOICE OF NATURE

I stand on the cliff and watch the veiled sun paling
  A silver field afar in the mournful sea,
The scourge of the surf, and plaintive gulls sailing
  At ease on the gale that smites the shuddering lea:
    Whose smile severe and chaste
  June never hath stirred to vanity, nor age defaced.
In lofty thought strive, O spirit, for ever:
In courage and strength pursue thine own endeavor.

Ah! if it were only for thee, thou restless ocean
  Of waves that follow and roar, the sweep of the tides;
Wer't only for thee, impetuous wind, whose motion
  Precipitate all o'errides, and turns, nor abides:
    For you, sad birds and fair,
  Or only for thee, bleak cliff, erect in the air;
Then well could I read wisdom in every feature,
O well should I understand the voice of Nature.

But far away, I think, in the Thames valley,
  The silent river glides by flowery banks:
And birds sing sweetly in branches that arch an alley
  Of cloistered trees, moss-grown in their ancient ranks:
    Where if a light air stray,
  'Tis laden with hum of bees and scent of may.
Love and peace be thine, O spirit, for ever:
Serve thy sweet desire: despise endeavor.

And if it were only for thee, entrancèd river,
  That scarce dost rock the lily on her airy stem,
Or stir a wave to murmur, or a rush to quiver;
  Wer't but for the woods, and summer asleep in them:
    For you my bowers green,
  My hedges of rose and woodbine, with walks between,
Then well could I read wisdom in every feature,
O well should I understand the voice of Nature.

"THE EVENING DARKENS OVER"

The evening darkens over.
After a day so bright
The windcapt waves discover
That wild will be the night.
There's sound of distant thunder.

The latest sea-birds hover
Along the cliff's sheer height;
As in the memory wander
Last flutterings of delight,
White wings lost on the white.

There's not a ship in sight;
And as the sun goes under
Thick clouds conspire to cover
The moon that should rise yonder.
Thou art alone, fond lover.

"I LOVE ALL BEAUTEOUS THINGS"

I love all beauteous things,
    I seek and adore them;
God hath no better praise,
And man in his hasty days
    Is honored for them.

I too will something make
    And joy in the making;
Although to-morrow it seem
Like the empty words of a dream
    Remembered on waking.

THE WINDMILL

The green corn waving in the dale,
The ripe grass waving on the hill:
I lean across the paddock pale
And gaze upon the giddy mill.

Its hurtling sails a mighty sweep
Cut through the air: with rushing sound
Each strikes in fury down the steep,
Rattles, and whirls in chase around.

Beside his sacks the miller stands
On high within the open door:
A book and pencil in his hands,
His grist and meal he reckoneth o'er.

His tireless merry slave the wind
Is busy with his work to-day:
From whencesoe'er, he comes to grind;
He hath a will and knows the way.

He gives the creaking sails a spin,
The circling millstones faster flee,
The shuddering timbers groan within,
And down the shoot the meal runs free.

The miller giveth him no thanks,
And doth not much his work o'erlook:
He stands beside the sacks, and ranks
The figures in his dusty book.

APRIL, 1885

Wanton with long delay the gay spring leaping cometh;
The blackthorn starreth now his bough on the eve of May:
All day in the sweet box-tree the bee for pleasure hummeth:
The cuckoo sends afloat his note on the air all day.

Now dewy nights again and rain in gentle shower
At root of tree and flower have quenched the winter's drouth:
On high the hot sun smiles, and banks of cloud uptower
In bulging heads that crowd for miles the dazzling south.

A ROBIN

Flame-throated robin on the topmost bough
Of the leafless oak, what singest thou?
Hark! he telleth how—
"Spring is coming now; Spring is coming now.

"Now ruddy are the elm-tops against the blue sky,
The pale larch donneth her jewelry;
Red fir and black fir sigh,
And I am lamenting the year gone by.

"The bushes where I nested are all cut down,
They are felling the tall trees one by one,
And my mate is dead and gone,
In the winter she died and left me lone.

"She lay in the thicket where I fear to go;
For when the March-winds after the snow
The leaves away did blow,
She was not there, and my heart is woe:

"And sad is my song, when I begin to sing,
As I sit in the sunshine this merry spring:
Like a withered leaf I cling
To the white oak-bough, while the wood doth ring.

"Spring is coming now, the sun again is gay;
Each day like a last spring's happy day."—
Thus sang he; then from his spray
He saw me listening and flew away.

NIGHTINGALES

Beautiful must be the mountains whence ye come,
And bright in the fruitful valleys the streams, wherefrom
Ye learn your song:
Where are those starry woods? O might I wander there,
Among the flowers, which in that heavenly air
Bloom the year long!

Nay, barren are those mountains and spent the streams:
Our song is the voice of desire, that haunts our dreams,
A throe of the heart,
Whose pining visions dim, forbidden hopes profound,
No dying cadence nor long sigh can sound,
For all our art.

Alone, aloud in the raptured ear of men
We pour our dark nocturnal secret; and then,
As night is withdrawn
From these sweet-springing meads and bursting boughs of
May,
Dream, while the innumerable choir of day
Welcome the dawn.

"MY DELIGHT AND THY DELIGHT"

My delight and thy delight
Walking, like two angels white,
In the gardens of the night:

My desire and thy desire
Twining to a tongue of fire,
Leaping live, and laughing higher;
Through the everlasting strife
In the mystery of life.

Love, from whom the world begun,
Hath the secret of the sun.

Love can tell, and love alone,
Whence the million stars were strewn,
Why each atom knows its own,
How, in spite of woe and death,
Gay is life, and sweet is breath:

This he taught us, this we knew,
Happy in his science true,
Hand in hand as we stood
Neath the shadows of the wood,
Heart to heart as we lay
In the dawning of the day.

PATER FILIO

Sense with keenest edge unusëd,
  Yet unsteeled by scathing fire;
Lovely feet as yet unbruisëd
  On the ways of dark desire;
Sweetest hope that lookest smiling
O'er the wilderness defiling!

Why such beauty, to be blighted
  By the swarm of foul destruction?
Why such innocence delighted,
  When sin stalks to thy seduction?
All the litanies e'er chaunted
Shall not keep thy faith undaunted.

I have prayed the sainted Morning
  To unclasp her hands to hold thee;
From resignful Eve's adorning
  Stol'n a robe of peace to enfold thee;
With all charms of man's contriving
Armed thee for thy lonely striving.

Me too once unthinking Nature,
  —Whence Love's timeless mockery took me,—
Fashioned so divine a creature,
  Yea, and like a beast forsook me.
I forgave, but tell the measure
Of her crime in thee, my treasure.

SCREAMING TARN

The saddest place that e'er I saw
  Is the deep tarn above the inn
That crowns the mountain-road, whereby
  One southward bound his way must win.

Sunk on the table of the ridge
  From its deep shores is nought to see:
The unresting wind lashes and chills
  Its shivering ripples ceaselessly.

Three sides 'tis banked with stones aslant,
And down the fourth the rushes grow,
And yellow sedge fringing the edge
With lengthened image all arow.

'Tis square and black, and on its face
When noon is still, the mirrored sky
Looks dark and further from the earth
Than when you gaze at it on high.

At mid of night, if one be there,
—So say the people of the hill—
A fearful shriek of death is heard,
One sudden scream both loud and shrill.

And some have seen on stilly nights,
And when the moon was clear and round,
Bubbles which to the surface swam
And burst as if they held the sound.—

'Twas in the days ere hapless Charles
Losing his crown had lost his head,
This tale is told of him who kept
The inn upon the watershed:

He was a lowbred ruined man
Whom lawless times set free from fear:
One evening to his house there rode
A young and gentle cavalier.

With curling hair and linen fair
And jewel-hilted sword he went;
The horse he rode he had ridden far,
And he was with his journey spent.

He asked a lodging for the night,
His valise from his steed unbound,
He let none bear it but himself
And set it by him on the ground.

"Here's gold or jewels," thought the host,
"That's carrying south to find the king."
He chattered many a loyal word,
And scraps of royal airs 'gan sing.

His guest thereat grew more at ease
And o'er his wine he gave a toast,
But little ate, and to his room
Carried his sack behind the host.

"Now rest you well," the host he said,
But of his wish the word fell wide;
Nor did he now forget his son
Who fell in fight by Cromwell's side.

Revenge and poverty have brought
Full gentler heart than his to crime;
And he was one by nature rude,
Born to foul deeds at any time.

With unshod feet at dead of night
In stealth he to the guest-room crept,
Lantern and dagger in his hand,
And stabbed his victim while he slept.

But as he struck a scream there came,
A fearful scream so loud and shrill:
He whelmed the face with pillows o'er,
And leaned till all had long been still.

Then to the face the flame he held
To see there should no life remain:—
When lo! his brutal heart was quelled:
'Twas a fair woman he had slain.

The tan upon her face was paint,
The manly hair was torn away,
Soft was the breast that he had pierced;
Beautiful in her death she lay.

His was no heart to faint at crime,
  Though half he wished the deed undone.
He pulled the valise from the bed
  To find what booty he had won.

He cut the straps, and pushed within
  His murderous fingers to their theft.
A deadly sweat came o'er his brow,
  He had no sense nor meaning left.

He touched not gold, it was not cold,
  It was not hard, it felt like flesh.
He drew out by the curling hair
  A young man's head, and murdered fresh;

A young man's head, cut by the neck.
  But what was dreader still to see,
Her whom he had slain he saw again,
  The twain were like as like can be.

Brother and sister if they were,
  Both in one shroud they now were wound,—
Across his back and down the stair,
  Out of the house without a sound.

He made his way unto the tarn,
  The night was dark and still and dank;
The ripple chuckling 'neath the boat
  Laughed as he drew it to the bank.

Upon the bottom of the boat
  He laid his burden flat and low,
And on them laid the square sandstones
  That round about the margin go.

Stone upon stone he weighed them down,
  Until the boat would hold no more;
The freeboard now was scarce an inch:
  He stripped his clothes and pushed from shore.

All naked to the middle pool
He swam behind in the dark night;
And there he let the water in
And sank his terror out of sight.

He swam ashore, and donned his dress,
And scraped his bloody fingers clean;
Ran home and on his victim's steed
Mounted, and never more was seen.

But to a comrade ere he died
He told his story guessed of none:
So from his lips the crime returned
To haunt the spot where it was done.

MELANCHOLIA

The sickness of desire, that in dark days
Looks on the imagination of despair,
Forgetteth man, and stinteth God his praise;
Nor but in sleep findeth a cure for care.
Incertainty that once gave scope to dream
Of laughing enterprise and glory untold,
Is now a blackness that no stars redeem,
A wall of terror in a night of cold.
Fool! thou that hast impossibly desired
And now impatiently despairest, see
How nought is changed: Joy's wisdom is attired
Splendid for others' eyes if not for thee:
Not love or beauty or youth from earth is fled:
If they delight thee not, 'tis thou art dead.

THE PHILOSOPHER TO HIS MISTRESS

Because thou canst not see,
Because thou canst not know
The black and hopeless woe
That hath encompassed me:

Because, should I confess
The thought of my despair,
My words would wound thee less
Than swords can hurt the air:

Because with thee I seem
As one invited near
To taste the faery cheer
Of spirits in a dream;
Of whom he knoweth nought
Save that they vie to make
All motion, voice and thought
A pleasure for his sake:

Therefore more sweet and strange
Has been the mystery
Of thy long love to me,
That doth not quit, nor change,
Nor tax my solemn heart,
That kisseth in a gloom,
Knowing not who thou art
That givest, nor to whom.

Therefore the tender touch
Is more; more dear the smile:
And thy light words beguile
My wisdom overmuch:
And O with swiftness fly
The fancies of my song
To happy worlds, where I
Still in thy love belong.

VISION

How should I be to Love unjust
Since Love hath been so kind to me?
O how forget thy tender trust
Or slight the bond that set me free?

How should thy spirit's blithe embrace,
    Thy loyalty, have been given in vain,
From the first beckoning of thy grace
    That made a child of me again,
And since hath still my manhood led
    Through scathe and trouble hour by hour,
And in probation perfected
    The explicit fruit of such a flower?

Not ev'n the Apostles, in the days
    They walked with Christ, loved Him so well
As we may now, who ken His praise
    Reading the story that they tell,
Writ by them when their vision grew
    And he, who fled and thrice denied
Christ to His face, was proven true
    And gladly for His memory died:
So strong the Vision, there was none
    O'er whom the Fisher's net was cast,
Ev'n of the fearfullest not one
    Who would have left Him at the last.

So 'tis with me; the time hath cleared
    Not dulled my loving: I can see
Love's passing ecstasies endeared
    In aspects of eternity:
I am like a miser—I can say
    That having hoarded all my gold
I must grow richer every day
    And die possessed of wealth untold.

FORTUNATUS NIMIUM

I have lain in the sun;
I have toiled as I might;
I have thought as I would,
And now it is night.

My bed full of sleep,
My heart of content,
For friends that I met
The way that I went.

I welcome fatigue
While frenzy and care
Like thin summer clouds
Go melting in air.

To dream as I may
And awake when I will
With the song of the birds
And the sun on the hill.

Or death—were it death—
To what should I wake,
Who loved in my home
All life for its sake?

What good have I wrought?
I laugh to have learned
That joy cannot come
Unless it be earned;

For a happier lot
Than God giveth me,
It never hath been,
Nor ever shall be.

"O LOVE, MY MUSE"

O love, my muse, how was't for me
    Among the best to dare,
In thy high courts that bowed the knee
    With sacrifice and prayer?

Their mighty offerings at thy shrine
Shamed me, who nothing bore;
Their suits were mockeries of mine,
I sued for so much more.

Full many I met that crowned with bay
In triumph home returned,
And many a master on the way
Proud of the prize I scorned.

I wished no garland on my head
Nor treasure in my hand;
My gift the longing that me led,
My prayer thy high command,

My love, my muse; and when I spake
Thou mad'st me thine that day,
And more than hundred hearts could take
Gav'st me to bear away.

A. E. HOUSMAN

Alfred Edward Housman was born in Shropshire on March 26, 1859. He was prepared at Bromsgrove School for the university, and then entered St. John's College, Oxford, where he received a thorough classical education. From 1882 to 1892 he was a Higher Division Clerk in the British Patent Office. In 1892 he became Professor of Latin in University College, London, where he remained until 1911. In that year he went to Cambridge University as Professor of Latin, which position he still holds. He became a scholar, publishing numerous articles in the classical journals. His great scholarly work, however, has been to edit Manilius, a first part in 1903, a second in 1912, a third in 1916, and a fourth in 1920. In 1905 he also issued an edition of Juvenal, and in 1926 one of Lucan. His poetical books stand quite apart from his other work, and to all appearances from the outward events of his life. In 1896, at the age of thirty-seven, he published *A Shropshire Lad;* then for twenty-six years he was silent, until 1922, when he issued his only other book of poetry, *Last Poems.*

Housman is unmarried. He is an Honorary Fellow of St. John's College, Oxford, and a Fellow of Trinity College, Cambridge.

"LOVELIEST OF TREES"

Loveliest of trees, the cherry now
Is hung with bloom along the bough,
And stands about the woodland ride,
Wearing white for Eastertide.

Now, of my threescore years and ten,
Twenty will not come again,
And take from seventy springs a score,
It only leaves me fifty more.

And since to look at things in bloom
Fifty springs are little room,
About the woodlands I will go
To see the cherry hung with snow.

REVEILLE

Wake: the silver dusk returning
Up the beach of darkness brims,
And the ship of sunrise burning
Strands upon the eastern rims.

Wake: the vaulted shadow shatters,
Trampled to the floor it spanned,
And the tent of night in tatters
Straws the sky-pavilioned land.

Up, lad, up, 'tis late for lying:
Hear the drums of morning play;
Hark, the empty highways crying
"Who'll beyond the hills away?"

Towns and countries woo together,
Forelands beacon, belfries call;
Never lad that trod on leather
Lived to feast his heart with all.

Up, lad: thews that lie and cumber
Sunlit pallets never thrive;
Morns abed and daylight slumber
Were not meant for man alive.

Clay lies still, but blood's a rover;
Breath's a ware that will not keep.
Up, lad: when the journey's over
There'll be time enough to sleep.

"OH, SEE HOW THICK THE GOLDCUP FLOWERS"

Oh, see how thick the goldcup flowers
Are lying in field and lane,
With dandelions to tell the hours
That never are told again.
Oh, may I squire you round the meads
And pick you posies gay?
—'Twill do no harm to take my arm.
"You may, young man, you may."

Ah, spring was sent for lass and lad,
'Tis now the blood runs gold,
And man and maid had best be glad
Before the world is old.
What flowers to-day may flower to-morrow,
But never as good as new.
—Suppose I wound my arm right round—
" 'Tis true, young man, 'tis true."

Some lads there are, 'tis shame to say,
That only court to thieve,
And once they bear the bloom away
'Tis little enough they leave.
Then keep your heart for men like me
And safe from trustless chaps.
My love is true and all for you.
"Perhaps, young man, perhaps."

Oh, look in my eyes then, can you doubt?
  —Why, 'tis a mile from town.
How green the grass is all about!
  We might as well sit down.
—Ah, life, what is it but a flower?
  Why must true lovers sigh?
Be kind, have pity, my own, my pretty,—
  "Good-bye, young man, good-bye."

"WHEN SMOKE STOOD UP FROM LUDLOW"

When smoke stood up from Ludlow,
    And mist blew off from Teme,
And blithe afield to ploughing
    Against the morning beam
    I strode beside my team,

The blackbird in the coppice
    Looked out to see me stride,
And hearkened as I whistled
    The trampling team beside,
    And fluted and replied:

"Lie down, lie down, young yeoman;
    What use to rise and rise?
Rise man a thousand mornings
    Yet down at last he lies,
    And then the man is wise."

I heard the tune he sang me,
    And spied his yellow bill;
I picked a stone and aimed it
    And threw it with a will:
    Then the bird was still.

Then my soul within me
    Took up the blackbird's strain,
And still beside the horses
    Along the dewy lane
    It sang the song again:

"Lie down, lie down, young yeoman;
The sun moves always west;
The road one treads to labor
Will lead one home to rest,
And that will be the best."

"FAREWELL TO BARN AND STACK AND TREE"

"Farewell to barn and stack and tree,
Farewell to Severn shore.
Terence, look your last at me,
For I come home no more.

"The sun burns on the half-mown hill,
By now the blood is dried;
And Maurice amongst the hay lies still
And my knife is in his side.

"My mother thinks us long away;
'Tis time the field were mown.
She had two sons at rising day,
To-night she'll be alone.

"And here's a bloody hand to shake,
And oh, man, here's good-bye;
We'll sweat no more on scythe and rake,
My bloody hands and I.

"I wish you strength to bring you pride,
And a love to keep you clean,
And I wish you luck, come Lammastide,
At racing on the green.

"Long for me the rick will wait,
And long will wait the fold,
And long will stand the empty plate,
And dinner will be cold."

"ON MOONLIT HEATH AND LONESOME BANK"

On moonlit heath and lonesome bank
The sheep beside me graze;
And yon the gallows used to clank
Fast by the four cross ways.

A careless shepherd once would keep
The flocks by moonlight there,
And high amongst the glimmering sheep
The dead man stood on air.

They hang us now in Shrewsbury jail:
The whistles blow forlorn,
And trains all night groan on the rail
To men that die at morn.

There sleeps in Shrewsbury jail to-night,
Or wakes, as may betide,
A better lad, if things went right,
Than most that sleep outside.

And naked to the hangman's noose
The morning clocks will ring
A neck God made for other use
Than strangling in a string.

And sharp the link of life will snap,
And dead on air will stand
Heels that held up as straight a chap
As treads upon the land.

So here I'll watch the night and wait
To see the morning shine,
When he will hear the stroke of eight
And not the stroke of nine;

And wish my friend as sound a sleep
As lads' I did not know,
That shepherded the moonlit sheep
A hundred years ago.

"WHEN I WAS ONE-AND-TWENTY"

When I was one-and-twenty
  I heard a wise man say,
"Give crowns and pounds and guineas
  But not your heart away;
Give pearls away and rubies
  But keep your fancy free."
But I was one-and-twenty,
  No use to talk to me.

When I was one-and-twenty
  I heard him say again,
"The heart out of the bosom
  Was never given in vain;
'Tis paid with sighs a-plenty
  And sold for endless rue."
And I am two-and-twenty,
  And oh, 'tis true, 'tis true.

TO AN ATHLETE DYING YOUNG

The time you won your town the race
We chaired you through the market-place;
Man and boy stood cheering by,
And home we brought you shoulder-high.

To-day, the road all runners come,
Shoulder-high we bring you home,
And set you at your threshold down,
Townsman of a stiller town.

Smart lad, to slip betimes away
From fields where glory does not stay,
And early though the laurel grows
It withers quicker than the rose.

Eyes the shady night has shut
Cannot see the record cut,
And silence sounds no worse than cheers
After earth has stopped the ears:

Now you will not swell the rout
Of lads that wore their honors out,
Runners whom renown outran
And the name died before the man.

So set, before its echoes fade,
The fleet foot on the sill of shade,
And hold to the low lintel up
The still-defended challenge-cup.

And round that early-laurelled head
Will flock to gaze the strengthless dead,
And find unwithered on its curls
The garland briefer than a girl's.

BREDON HILL

In summertime on Bredon
  The bells they sound so clear;
Round both the shires they ring them
  In steeples far and near,
  A happy noise to hear.

Here of a Sunday morning
  My love and I would lie,
And see the colored counties,
  And hear the larks so high
  About us in the sky.

The bells would ring to call her
  In valleys miles away:
"Come all to church, good people;
  Good people, come and pray."
  But here my love would stay.

And I would turn and answer
Among the springing thyme,
"Oh, peal upon our wedding,
And we will hear the chime,
And come to church in time."

But when the snows at Christmas
On Bredon top were strown,
My love rose up so early
And stole out unbeknown
And went to church alone.

They tolled the one bell only;
Groom there was none to see;
The mourners followed after,
And so to church went she,
And would not wait for me.

The bells they sound on Bredon,
And still the steeples hum.
"Come all to church, good people,"—
Oh, noisy bells, be dumb;
I hear you, I will come.

"IS MY TEAM PLOUGHING?"

"Is my team ploughing,
That I was used to drive
And hear the harness jingle
When I was man alive?"

Ay, the horses trample,
The harness jingles now;
No change though you lie under
The land you used to plough.

"Is football playing
Along the river shore,
With lads to chase the leather,
Now I stand up no more?"

Ay, the ball is flying,
   The lads play heart and soul;
The goal stands up, the keeper
   Stands up to keep the goal.

"Is my girl happy,
   That I thought hard to leave,
And has she tired of weeping
   As she lies down at eve?"

Ay, she lies down lightly,
   She lies not down to weep:
Your girl is well contented.
   Be still, my lad, and sleep.

"Is my friend hearty,
   Now I am thin and pine,
And has he found to sleep in
   A better bed than mine?"

Yes, lad, I lie easy,
   I lie as lads would choose;
I cheer a dead man's sweetheart;
   Never ask me whose.

THE NEW MISTRESS

"Oh, sick I am to see you; will you never let me be?
You may be good for something, but you are not good for
      me.
Oh, go where you are wanted, for you are not wanted here.
And that was all the farewell when I parted from my dear.

"I will go where I am wanted, to a lady born and bred
Who will dress me free for nothing in a uniform of red;
She will not be sick to see me if I only keep it clean:
I will go where I am wanted for a soldier of the Queen.

"I will go where I am wanted, for the sergeant does not
mind;
He may be sick to see me but he treats me very kind:
He gives me beer and breakfast and a ribbon for my cap,
And I never knew a sweetheart spend her money on a chap.

"I will go where I am wanted, where there's room for one or
two,
And the men are none too many for the work there is to do;
Where the standing line wears thinner and the dropping dead
lie thick;
And the enemies of England they shall see me and be sick."

"WHITE IN THE MOON THE LONG ROAD LIES"

White in the moon the long road lies,
The moon stands blank above;
White in the moon the long road lies
That leads me from my love.

Still hangs the hedge without a gust,
Still, still the shadows stay:
My feet upon the moonlit dust
Pursue the ceaseless way.

The world is round, so travellers tell,
And straight though reach the track,
Trudge on, trudge on, 'twill all be well,
The way will guide one back.

But ere the circle homeward hies
Far, far must it remove:
White in the moon the long road lies
That leads me from my love.

"SHOT? SO QUICK, SO CLEAN AN ENDING?"

Shot? so quick, so clean an ending?
Oh, that was right, lad, that was brave:
Yours was not an ill for mending,
'Twas best to take it to the grave.

Oh, you had forethought, you could reason,
And saw your road and where it led,
And early wise and brave in season
Put the pistol to your head.

Oh, soon, and better so than later
After long disgrace and scorn,
You shot dead the household traitor,
The soul that should not have been born.

Right you guessed the rising morrow
And scorned to tread the mire you must:
Dust's your wages, son of sorrow,
But men may come to worse than dust.

Souls undone, undoing others,—
Long time since the tale began.
You would not live to wrong your brothers:
Oh, lad, you died as fits a man.

Now to your grave shall friend and stranger
With ruth and some with envy come:
Undishonored, clear of danger,
Clean of guilt, pass hence and home.

Turn safe to rest, no dreams, no waking;
And here, man, here's the wreath I've made:
'Tis not a gift that's worth the taking,
But wear it and it will not fade.

"THINK NO MORE, LAD"

Think no more, lad; laugh, be jolly:
Why should men make haste to die?
Empty heads and tongues a-talking
Make the rough road easy walking,
And the feather pate of folly
Bears the falling sky.

Oh, 'tis jesting, dancing, drinking
  Spins the heavy world around.
If young hearts were not so clever,
Oh, they would be young for ever:
Think no more; 'tis only thinking
  Lays lads underground.

THE DAY OF BATTLE

"Far I hear the bugle blow
To call me where I would not go,
And the guns begin the song,
'Soldier, fly or stay for long.'

"Comrade, if to turn and fly
Made a soldier never die,
Fly I would, for who would not?
'Tis sure no pleasure to be shot.

"But since the man that runs away
Lives to die another day,
And cowards' funerals, when they come,
Are not wept so well at home,

"Therefore, though the best is bad,
Stand and do the best, my lad;
Stand and fight and see your slain,
And take the bullet in your brain."

"NOW HOLLOW FIRES BURN OUT TO BLACK"

Now hollow fires burn out to black,
  And lights are guttering low:
Square your shoulders, lift your pack,
  And leave your friends and go.

Oh, never fear, man; nought's to dread;
  Look not left nor right:
In all the endless road you tread
  There's nothing but the night.

"TERENCE, THIS IS STUPID STUFF"

"Terence, this is stupid stuff:
You eat your victuals fast enough;
There can't be much amiss, 'tis clear,
To see the rate you drink your beer.
But oh, good Lord, the verse you make,
It gives a chap the belly-ache.
The cow, the old cow, she is dead;
It sleeps well, the hornèd head:
We poor lads, 'tis our turn now
To hear such tunes as killed the cow.
Pretty friendship 'tis to rhyme
Your friends to death before their time
Moping melancholy mad:
Come, pipe a tune to dance to, lad."

Why, if 'tis dancing you would be,
There's brisker pipes than poetry.
Say, for what were hop-yards meant,
Or why was Burton built on Trent?
Oh, many a peer of England brews
Livelier liquor than the Muse,
And malt does more than Milton can
To justify God's ways to man.
Ale, man, ale's the stuff to drink
For fellows whom it hurts to think:
Look into the pewter pot
To see the world as the world's not.
And faith, 'tis pleasant till 'tis past:
The mischief is that 'twill not last.
Oh, I have been to Ludlow fair
And left my necktie God knows where,
And carried half-way home, or near,
Pints and quarts of Ludlow beer:
Then the world seemed none so bad,
And I myself a sterling lad;
And down in lovely muck I've lain,
Happy till I woke again.

Then I saw the morning sky:
Heigho, the tale was all a lie;
The world, it was the old world yet,
I was I, my things were wet,
And nothing now remained to do
But begin the game anew.

Therefore, since the world has still
Much good, but much less good than ill,
And while the sun and moon endure
Luck's a chance, but trouble's sure,
I'd face it as a wise man would,
And train for ill and not for good.
'Tis true, the stuff I bring for sale
Is not so brisk a brew as ale:
Out of a stem that scored the hand
I wrung it in a weary land.
But take it: if the smack is sour,
The better for the embittered hour;
It should do good to heart and head
When your soul is in my soul's stead;
And I will friend you, if I may,
In the dark and cloudy day.

There was a king reigned in the East:
There, when kings will sit to feast,
They get their fill before they think
With poisoned meat and poisoned drink.
He gathered all that springs to birth
From the many-venomed earth;
First a little, thence to more,
He sampled all her killing store;
And easy, smiling, seasoned sound,
Sate the king when healths went round.
They put arsenic in his meat
And stared aghast to watch him eat;
They poured strychnine in his cup
And shook to see him drink it up:

They shook, they stared as white's their shirt:
Them it was their poison hurt.
—I tell the tale that I heard told.
Mithridates, he died old.

"AS I GIRD ON FOR FIGHTING"

As I gird on for fighting
  My sword upon my thigh,
I think on old ill fortunes
  Of better men than I.

Think I, the round world over,
  What golden lads are low
With hurts not mine to mourn for
  And shames I shall not know.

What evil luck soever
  For me remains in store,
'Tis sure much finer fellows
  Have fared much worse before.

So here are things to think on
  That ought to make me brave,
As I strap on for fighting
  My sword that will not save.

"YONDER SEE THE MORNING BLINK"

Yonder see the morning blink:
  The sun is up, and up must I,
To wash and dress and eat and drink
And look at things and talk and think
  And work, and God knows why.

Oh, often have I washed and dressed
  And what's to show for all my pain?
Let me lie abed and rest:
Ten thousand times I've done my best
  And all's to do again.

"NOW DREARY DAWNS THE EASTERN LIGHT"

Now dreary dawns the eastern light,
And fall of eve is drear,
And cold the poor man lies at night
And so goes out the year.

Little is the luck I've had,
And oh, 'tis comfort small
To think that many another lad
Has had no luck at all.

"THE RAIN, IT STREAMS ON STONE AND HILLOCK"

The rain, it streams on stone and hillock,
The boot clings to the clay.
Since all is done that's due and right
Let's home; and now, my lad, good-night,
For I must turn away.

Good-night, my lad, for nought's eternal;
No league of ours, for sure.
To-morrow I shall miss you less,
And ache of heart and heaviness
Are things that time should cure.

Over the hill the highway marches
And what's beyond is wide:
Oh, soon enough will pine to nought
Remembrance and the faithful thought
That sits the grave beside.

The skies, they are not always raining
Nor grey the twelvemonth through;
And I shall meet good days and mirth,
And range the lovely lands of earth
With friends no worse than you.

But oh, my man, the house is fallen
  That none can build again;
My man, how full of joy and woe
Your mother bore you years ago
  To-night to lie in the rain.

"WE'LL TO THE WOODS NO MORE"

We'll to the woods no more,
The laurels all are cut,
The bowers are bare of bay
That once the Muses wore;
The year draws in the day
And soon will evening shut:
The laurels all are cut,
We'll to the woods no more.
Oh, we'll no more, no more
To the leafy woods away,
To the high wild woods of laurel
And the bowers of bay no more.

W. B. YEATS

William Butler Yeats, son of the Irish portrait painter, John Butler Yeats, was born at Sandymount, near Dublin, on June 13, 1865. His father was of Anglo-Irish stock, but his mother's people, the Pollexfens of Sligo, were more purely Irish. The whole immediate family appears to have been talented. His father won recognition as a painter both at home and abroad; his brother, Jack B. Yeats, has been scarcely less successful than the father as an artist; and one of his sisters established the Cuala Industries near Dublin.

During the seventies the elder Yeats moved his family to London, where he had been living in an artists' colony; and there the boy began his education, at the Godolphin School, Hammersmith. In 1880, however, upon the return of the parents to Dublin, William Butler was sent to the Erasmus Smith School. Later he studied for a time at the Metropolitan School of Art. He also read widely on his own account, and was much among the distinguished company that visited his father's house. He met a number of able youths, moreover, among them George W. Russell, became interested in Buddhism and theosophy, passed many days at the country home of his maternal grandfather, a merchant-shipper of Sligo, learning Celtic folklore and observing native customs, and about 1885 began to contribute prose and verse to *The Dublin University Review* and *The Irish Monthly*.

In 1886 appeared his first book, *Mosada,* a dramatic poem. The following year he went with his family again to London, and for some years worked as a journalist.

From 1888 to 1890 he compiled several volumes of folk stories and fairy tales; in 1893 edited, with Edwin J. Ellis, the *Works of William Blake;* occasionally wrote reviews and articles for *The Bookman* and *The National Observer;* and contributed to *The Book of the Rhymers' Club.* He became associated with the "decadent" group of poets, Henley, Dowson, Symons, and in 1894 paid a visit to Verlaine in Paris. Partly because of an acquaintance with John O'Leary and other political leaders, and partly through literary channels, he came to have a deep concern over the literary development of his native country. Before 1890 he had begun to go directly to Celtic sources for inspiration and material; by the end of the nineteenth century he was a recognized leader of the Irish Literary Renaissance.

With the appearance, in 1889, of *The Wanderings of Oisin* his position as a poet was assured; and this volume he followed with *The Countess Kathleen* (1892) and with *Poems* (1895). Henceforth he wrote numerous volumes of poetry, the latest being *The Tower* (1928). From time to time, also, he has published books of prose, of which the most important are *The Celtic Twilight* (1893), *Ideas of Good and Evil* (1903), *Discoveries* (1907), *The Cutting of an Agate* (1912), and the three autobiographical works, *Reveries over Childhood and Youth* (1915), *Four Years* (1921), and *The Trembling of the Veil* (1922), published together in 1927 as *Autobiographies.* In the closing decade of the nineteenth century, he acquired an interest in the drama, and was instrumental, with Lady Gregory and others, in establishing the Irish National Theatre. As early as 1899 his play *The Countess Kathleen* had been produced in Dublic by the Gaelic League; after the establishment of the National Theatre he entered zealously upon the task of supplying it with plays, among them being *Cathleen ni Houlihan, On Baile's*

Strand, The King's Threshold, The Hour-Glass, and *Deirdre.*

Since 1900 Yeats's literary reputation has increased steadily. Several honorary degrees have been conferred upon him, and in 1923 he was awarded the Nobel prize for literature. At one time he was a sympathizer with the Irish independent movement, but since 1922 he has been a senator of the Irish Free State. In 1917 he married Georgie, the eldest daughter of the late W. G. Hyde Lees, of Pickhill Hall, Wrexham, and now has two children, a son and a daughter. He continues to reside in Dublin. He has made several trips to the United States.

THE SONG OF THE FAERIES

[*From* THE LAND OF HEART'S DESIRE]

The wind blows out of the gates of the day,
The wind blows over the lonely of heart,
And the lonely of heart is withered away,
While the faeries dance in a place apart,
Shaking their milk-white feet in a ring,
Tossing their milk-white arms in the air:
For they hear the wind laugh and murmur and sing
Of a land where even the old are fair,
And even the wise are merry of tongue;
But I heard a reed of Coolaney say,
"When the wind has laughed and murmured and sung,
The lonely of heart is withered away!"

THE ROSE OF THE WORLD

Who dreamed that beauty passes like a dream?
For these red lips, with all their mournful pride,
Mournful that no new wonder may betide,
Troy passed away in one high funeral gleam,
And Usna's children died.

We and the laboring world are passing by:
Amid men's souls, that waver and give place,
Like the pale waters in their wintry race,
Under the passing stars, foam of the sky,
Lives on this lonely face.

Bow down, archangels, in your dim abode:
Before you were, or any hearts to beat,
Weary and kind, one lingered by His seat;
He made the world to be a grassy road
Before her wandering feet.

THE LAKE ISLE OF INNISFREE

I will arise and go now, and go to Innisfree,
And a small cabin build there, of clay and wattles made:
Nine bean rows will I have there, a hive for the honey bee,
And live alone in the bee-loud glade.

And I shall have some peace there, for peace comes dropping
slow,
Dropping from the veils of the morning to where the cricket
sings;
There midnight's all a glimmer, and noon a purple glow,
And evening full of the linnet's wings.

I will arise and go now, for always night and day
I hear lake water lapping with low sounds by the shore;
While I stand on the roadway, or on the pavements grey,
I hear it in the deep heart's core.

THE PITY OF LOVE

A pity beyond all telling
Is hid in the heart of love:
The folk who are buying and selling,
The clouds on their journey above,
The cold wet winds ever blowing,
And the shadowy hazel grove
Where mouse-grey waters are flowing,
Threaten the head that I love.

WHEN YOU ARE OLD

When you are old and grey and full of sleep,
And nodding by the fire, take down this book,
And slowly read, and dream of the soft look
Your eyes had once, and of their shadows deep;

How many loved your moments of glad grace,
And loved your beauty with love false or true;
But one man loved the pilgrim soul in you,
And loved the sorrows of your changing face.

And bending down beside the glowing bars
Murmur, a little sadly, how love fled
And paced upon the mountains overhead
And hid his face amid a crowd of stars.

THE LOVER TELLS OF THE ROSE IN HIS HEART

All things uncomely and broken, all things worn out and old,
The cry of a child by the roadway, the creak of a lumbering cart,
The heavy steps of the ploughman, splashing the wintry mould,
Are wronging your image that blossoms a rose in the deeps of my heart.

The wrong of unshapely things is a wrong too great to be told;
I hunger to build them anew and sit on a green knoll apart,
With the earth and the sky and the water, remade, like a casket of gold
For my dreams of your image that blossoms a rose in the deeps of my heart.

THE SONG OF WANDERING ÆNGUS

I went out to the hazel wood,
Because a fire was in my head,
And cut and peeled a hazel wand,
And hooked a berry to a thread;
And when white moths were on the wing,
And moth-like stars were flickering out,
I dropped the berry in a stream
And caught a little silver trout.

When I had laid it on the floor
I went to blow the fire a-flame,
But something rustled on the floor,
And some one called me by my name:
It had become a glimmering girl
With apple blossom in her hair
Who called me by my name and ran
And faded through the brightening air.

Though I am old with wandering
Through hollow lands and hilly lands,
I will find out where she has gone,
And kiss her lips and take her hands;
And walk among long dappled grass,
And pluck till time and times are done
The silver apples of the moon,
The golden apples of the sun.

RED HANRAHAN'S SONG ABOUT IRELAND

The old brown thorn trees break in two high over Cummen
Strand,
Under a bitter black wind that blows from the left hand;
Our courage breaks like an old tree in a black wind and dies,
But we have hidden in our hearts the flame out of the eyes
Of Cathleen, the daughter of Houlihan.

The wind has bundled up the clouds high over Knocknarea,
And thrown the thunder on the stones for all that Maeve
can say.
Angers that are like noisy clouds have set our hearts abeat;
But we have all bent low and low and kissed the quiet feet
Of Cathleen, the daughter of Houlihan.

The yellow pool has overflowed high up on Clooth-na-
Bare,
For the wet winds are blowing out of the clinging air;
Like heavy flooded waters our bodies and our blood:
But purer than a tall candle before the Holy Rood
Is Cathleen, the daughter of Houlihan.

TOM O'ROUGHLEY

"Though logic choppers rule the town,
And every man and maid and boy
Has marked a distant object down,
An aimless joy is a pure joy,"
Or so did Tom O'Roughley say
That saw the surges running by,
"And wisdom is a butterfly
And not a gloomy bird of prey.

"If little planned is little sinned
But little need the grave distress.
What's dying but a second wind?
How but in zig-zag wantonness
Could trumpeter Michael be so brave?"
Or something of that sort he said,
"And if my dearest friend were dead
I'd dance a measure on his grave."

THE WILD SWANS AT COOLE

The trees are in their autumn beauty,
The woodland paths are dry,
Under the October twilight the water
Mirrors a still sky;
Upon the brimming water among the stones
Are nine and fifty swans.

The nineteenth autumn has come upon me
Since I first made my count;
I saw, before I had well finished,
All suddenly mount
And scatter wheeling in great broken rings
Upon their clamorous wings.

I have looked upon those brilliant creatures,
And now my heart is sore.
All's changed since I, hearing at twilight,
The first time on this shore,
The bell-beat of their wings above my head,
Trod with a lighter tread.

Unwearied still, lover by lover,
They paddle in the cold,
Companionable streams or climb the air;
Their hearts have not grown old;
Passion or conquest, wander where they will,
Attend upon them still.

But now they drift on the still water
Mysterious, beautiful;
Among what rushes will they build,
By what lake's edge or pool
Delight men's eyes when I awake some day
To find they have flown away?

THE INDIAN UPON GOD

I passed along the water's edge below the humid trees,
My spirit rocked in evening light, the rushes round my knees,
My spirit rocked in sleep and sighs; and saw the moorfowl pace
All dripping on a grassy slope, and saw them cease to chase
Each other round in circles, and heard the eldest speak:
Who holds the world between His bill and made us strong or weak
Is an undying moorfowl, and He lives beyond the sky.
The rains are from His dripping wing, the moonbeams from His eye.
I passed a little further on and heard a lotus talk:
Who made the world and ruleth it, He hangeth on a stalk,
For I am in His image made, and all this tinkling tide
Is but a sliding drop of rain between His petals wide.

A little way within the gloom a roebuck raised his eyes
Brimful of starlight, and he said: *The Stamper of the Skies,*
He is a gentle roebuck; for how else, I pray, could He
Conceive a thing so sad and soft, a gentle thing like me?
I passed a little further on and heard a peacock say:
Who made the grass and made the worms and made my feathers gay,
He is a monstrous peacock, and He waveth all the night
His languid tail above us, lit with myriad spots of light.

THE MADNESS OF KING GOLL

I sat on cushioned otter skin:
My word was law from Ith to Emen,
And shook at Invar Amargin
The hearts of the world-troubling seamen.
And drove tumult and war away
From girl and boy and man and beast;
The fields grew fatter day by day,
The wild fowl of the air increased;
And every ancient Ollave said,
While he bent down his fading head,
"He drives away the Northern cold."
They will not hush, the leaves a-flutter round me, the beech leaves old.

I sat and mused and drank sweet wine;
A herdsman came from inland valleys,
Crying, the pirates drove his swine
To fill their dark-beaked hollow galleys.
I called my battle-breaking men,
And my loud brazen battle-cars
From rolling vale and rivery glen;
And under the blinking of the stars
Fell on the pirates by the deep,
And hurled them in the gulf of sleep:
These hands won many a torque of gold.
They will not hush, the leaves a-flutter round me, the beech leaves old.

But slowly, as I shouting slew
And trampled in the bubbling mire,
In my most secret spirit grew
A whirling and a wandering fire:
I stood: keen stars above me shone,
Around me shone keen eyes of men:
I laughed aloud and hurried on
By rocky shore and rushy fen;
I laughed because birds fluttered by,
And starlight gleamed, and clouds flew high,
And rushes waved and waters rolled.
They will not hush, the leaves a-flutter round me, the beech leaves old.

And now I wander in the woods
When summer gluts the golden bees,
Or in autumnal solitudes
Arise the leopard-colored trees;
Or when along the wintry strands
The cormorants shiver on their rocks;
I wander on, and wave my hands,
And sing, and shake my heavy locks.
The grey wolf knows me; by one ear
I lead along the woodland deer;
The hares run by me growing bold.
They will not hush, the leaves a-flutter round me, the beech leaves old.

I came upon a little town,
That slumbered in the harvest moon,
And passed a-tiptoe up and down,
Murmuring, to a fitful tune,
How I have followed, night and day,
A tramping of tremendous feet,
And saw where this old tympan lay,
Deserted on a doorway seat,
And bore it to the woods with me;
Of some unhuman misery
Our married voices wildly trolled.
They will not hush, the leaves a-flutter round me, the beech leaves old.

I sang how, when day's toil is done,
Orchil shakes out her long dark hair
That hides away the dying sun
And sheds faint odors through the air:
When my hand passed from wire to wire
It quenched, with sound like falling dew,
The whirling and the wandering fire;
But lift a mournful ulalu,
For the kind wires are torn and still,
And I must wander wood and hill
Through summer's heat and winter's cold.
They will not hush, the leaves a-flutter round me, the beech leaves old.

THE BALLAD OF THE FOXHUNTER

"Now lay me in a cushioned chair
And carry me, you four,
With cushions here and cushions there,
To see the world once more.

"And some one from the stables bring
My Dermot dear and brown,
And lead him gently in a ring,
And gently up and down.

"Now leave the chair upon the grass:
Bring hound and huntsman here,
And I on this strange road will pass,
Filled full of ancient cheer."

His eyelids droop, his head falls low,
His old eyes cloud with dreams;
The sun upon all things that grow
Pours round in sleepy streams.

Brown Dermot treads upon the lawn,
And to the armchair goes,
And now the old man's dreams are gone,
He smooths the long brown nose.

And now moves many a pleasant tongue
Upon his wasted hands,
For leading aged hounds and young
The huntsman near him stands.

"My huntsman, Rody, blow the horn,
And make the hills reply."
The huntsman loosens on the morn
A gay and wandering cry.

A fire is in the old man's eyes,
His fingers move and sway,
And when the wandering music dies
They hear him feebly say,

"My huntsman, Rody, blow the horn,
And make the hills reply."
"I cannot blow upon my horn,
I can but weep and sigh."

The servants round his cushioned place
Are with new sorrow wrung;
And hounds are gazing on his face,
Both aged hounds and young.

One blind hound only lies apart
On the sun-smitten grass;
He holds deep commune with his heart:
The moments pass and pass;

The blind hound with a mournful din
Lifts slow his wintry head;
The servants bear the body in;
The hounds wail for the dead.

CUCHULAIN'S FIGHT WITH THE SEA

A man came slowly from the setting sun,
To Emer, raddling raiment in her dun,
And said, "I am that swineherd, whom you bid
Go dwell upon the cliffs and watch the tide;
But now I have no need to watch it more."

Then Emer cast the web upon the floor,
And raising arms all raddled with the dye,
Parted her lips with a loud sudden cry.

That swineherd stared upon her face and said:
"Not any god alive, nor mortal dead,
Has slain so mighty armies, so great kings,
Nor won the gold that now Cuchulain brings."

"Why do you tremble thus from feet to crown?"

He caught his breath and cast him weeping down
Upon the web-heaped floor, and thus his word:
"With him is one sweet-throated like a bird."

"You dare me to my face," and thereupon
She smote with raddled fist, and where her son
Herded the cattle came with stumbling feet,
And cried with angry voice, "It is not meet
To idle life away with flocks and herds."

"I have long waited, mother, for those words:
But wherefore now?"

"There is a man to die;
You have the heaviest arm under the sky."

"No, somewhere under daylight or the stars
My father stands amid his battle cars."

"But you have grown to be the taller man."

"Yet somewhere under starlight or the sun
My father stands amid his battle cars."

"But he is old and sad with many wars."

"I only ask what way my journey lies.
For He who made you bitter, made you wise."

"The Red Branch gather a great company
Between the game and the horses of the sea.
Go there, and camp upon the forest's rim;
But tell your name and lineage to him
Whose blade compels, and bid them send you one
Who has a like vow from their triple dun."

Among those feasting kings Cuchulain dwelt,
And his young dear one close beside him knelt;
Stared like the Spring upon the ancient skies,
Upon the mournful wonder of his eyes,
And pondered on the glory of his days;
And all around the harp-string told his praise,
And Concobar, the Red Branch king of kings,
With his own fingers touched the brazen strings.

At last Cuchulain spake, "Some man has made
His evening fire amid the leafy shade.
I have often heard him singing to and fro,
I have often heard the sweet sound of his bow,
Seek out what man he is."

One went and came.
"He bade me let all know he gives his name
At the sword point, and bade me bring him one
Who had a like vow from our triple dun."

"I only of the Red Branch hosted now,"
Cuchulain cried, "have made and keep that vow."

After short fighting in the leafy shade,
He spake to the young man, "Is there no maid
Who loves you, no white arms to wrap you round,
Or do you long for the dim sleepy ground,
That you have come and dared me to my face?"

"The dooms of men are in God's hidden place."

"Your head a while seemed like a woman's head
That I loved once."

Again the fighting sped,
But now the war rage in Cuchulain woke,
And through that new blade's guard the old blade broke,
And pierced him.

"Speak before your breath is done."

"Cuchulain I, mighty Cuchulain's son."

"I put you from your pain. I can no more."

While day its burden on to evening bore,
With head bowed on his knees Cuchulain stayed;
Then Concobar sent that sweet-throated maid,
And she, to win him, his grey hair caressed;
In vain her arms, in vain her soft white breast.
Then Concobar, the subtlest of all men,
Ranking his Druids round him ten by ten,
Spake thus, "Cuchulain will dwell there and brood,
For three days more in dreadful quietude,
And then arise, and raving slay us all.
Chaunt in his ear delusions magical,
That he may fight the horses of the sea."
The Druids took them to their mystery,
And chanted for three days.

Cuchulain stirred,
Stared on the horses of the sea, and heard
The cars of battle and his own name cried;
And fought with the invulnerable tide.

EGO DOMINUS TUUS

HIC

On the grey sand beside the shallow stream
Under your old wind-beaten tower, where still
A lamp burns on beside the open book
That Michael Robartes left, you walk in the moon,
And, though you have passed the best of life, still trace,
Enthralled by the unconquerable delusion,
Magical shapes.

ILLE

By the help of an image
I call to my own opposite, summon all
That I have handled least, least looked upon.

HIC

And I would find myself and not an image.

ILLE

That is our modern hope and by its light
We have lit upon the gentle, sensitive mind,
And lost the old nonchalance of the hand;
Whether we have chosen chisel, pen or brush,
We are but critics, or but half create
Timid, entangled, empty and abashed,
Lacking the countenance of our friends.

HIC

And yet
The chief imagination of Christendom,
Dante Alighieri, so utterly found himself
That he has made that hollow face of his
More plain to the mind's eye than any face
But that of Christ.

ILLE

And did he find himself,
Or was the hunger that had made it hollow
A hunger for the apple on the bough
Most out of reach? and is that spectral image
The man that Lapo and that Guido knew?
I think he fashioned from his opposite
An image that might have been a stony face,
Staring upon a bedouin's horse-hair roof
From doored and windowed cliff, or half upturned
Among the coarse grass and the camel dung.
He set his chisel to the hardest stone.
Being mocked by Guido for his lecherous life,
Derided and deriding, driven out
To climb that stair and eat that bitter bread,
He found the unpersuadable justice, he found
The most exalted lady loved by a man.

HIC

Yet surely there are men who have made their art
Out of no tragic war, lovers of life,
Impulsive men that look for happiness
And sing when they have found it.

ILLE

No, not sing,
For those that love the world serve it in action,
Grow rich, popular and full of influence,
And should they paint or write still it is action:
The struggle of the fly in marmalade.
The rhetorician would deceive his neighbors,
The sentimentalist himself; while art
Is but a vision of reality.
What portion in the world can the artist have
Who has awakened from the common dream
But dissipation and despair?

HIC

And yet
No one denies to Keats love of the world;
Remember his deliberate happiness.

ILLE

His art is happy but who knows his mind?
I see a schoolboy when I think of him
With face and nose pressed to a sweet-shop window,
For certainly he sank into his grave
His senses and his heart unsatisfied,
And made—being poor, ailing and ignorant,
Shut out from all the luxury of the world,
The coarse-bred son of a livery stable-keeper—
Luxuriant song.

HIC

Why should you leave the lamp
Burning alone beside an open book,
And trace these characters upon the sands?
A style is found by sedentary toil
And by the imitation of great masters.

ILLE

Because I seek an image, not a book.
Those men that in their writings are most wise
Own nothing but their blind, stupefied hearts.
I call to the mysterious one who yet
Shall walk the wet sands by the edge of the stream
And look most like me, being indeed my double,
And prove of all imaginable things
The most unlike, being my anti-self,
And standing by these characters disclose
All that I seek; and whisper it as though
He were afraid the birds, who cry aloud
Their momentary cries before it is dawn,
Would carry it away to blasphemous men.

A PRAYER FOR MY DAUGHTER

Once more the storm is howling, and half hid
Under this cradle-hood and coverlid
My child sleeps on. There is no obstacle
But Gregory's wood and one bare hill
Whereby the haystack and roof-levelling wind,
Bred on the Atlantic, can be stayed;
And for an hour I have walked and prayed
Because of the great gloom that is in my mind.

I have walked and prayed for this young child an hour
And heard the sea-wind scream upon the tower,
And under the arches of the bridge, and scream
In the elms above the flooded stream;
Imagining in excited reverie
That the future years had come,
Dancing to a frenzied drum,
Out of the murderous innocence of the sea.

May she be granted beauty and yet not
Beauty to make a stranger's eye distraught,
Or hers before a looking-glass, for such,
Being made beautiful overmuch,

Consider beauty a sufficient end,
Lose natural kindness and may be
The heart-revealing intimacy
That chooses right, and never find a friend.

Helen being chosen found life flat and dull
And later had much trouble from a fool,
While that great Queen, that rose out of the spray,
Being fatherless could have her way,
Yet chose a bandy-legged smith for man.
It's certain that fine women eat
A crazy salad with their meat,
Whereby the Horn of Plenty is undone.

In courtesy I'd have her chiefly learned;
Hearts are not had as a gift, but hearts are earned
By those that are not entirely beautiful;
Yet many, that have played the fool
For beauty's very self, has charm made wise,
And many a poor man that has roved,
Loved and thought himself beloved,
From a glad kindness cannot take his eyes.

May she become a flourishing hidden tree
That all her thoughts may like the linnet be,
And have no business but dispensing round
Their magnanimities of sound,
Nor but in merriment begin a chase,
Nor but in merriment a quarrel.
Oh, may she live like some green laurel
Rooted in one dear perpetual place.

My mind, because the minds that I have loved,
The sort of beauty that I have approved,
Prosper but little, has dried up of late,
Yet knows that to be choked with hate
May well be of all evil chances chief.
If there's no hatred in a mind
Assault and battery of the wind
Can never tear the linnet from the leaf.

An intellectual hatred is the worst,
So let her think opinions are accursed.
Have I not seen the loveliest woman born
Out of the mouth of Plenty's horn,
Because of her opinionated mind
Barter that horn and every good
By quiet natures understood
For an old bellows full of angry wind?

Considering that, all hatred driven hence,
The soul recovers radical innocence
And learns at last that it is self-delighting,
Self-appeasing, self-affrighting,
And that its own sweet will is heaven's will;
She can, though every face should scowl
And every windy quarter howl
Or every bellows burst, be happy still.

And may her bride-groom bring her to a house
Where all's accustomed, ceremonious;
For arrogance and hatred are the wares
Peddled in the thoroughfares.
How but in custom and in ceremony
Are innocence and beauty born?
Ceremony's a name for the rich horn,
And custom for the spreading laurel tree.

AMONG SCHOOL CHILDREN

I

I walk through the long schoolroom questioning,
A kind old nun in a white hood replies;
The children learn to cipher and to sing,
To study reading-books and history,
To cut and sew, be neat in everything
In the best modern way—the children's eyes
In momentary wonder stare upon
A sixty year old smiling public man.

II

I dream of a Ledæan body, bent
Above a sinking fire, a tale that she
Told of a harsh reproof, or trivial event
That changed some childish day to tragedy—
Told, and it seemed that our two natures blent
Into a sphere from youthful sympathy,
Or else, to alter Plato's parable,
Into the yolk and white of the one shell.

III

And thinking of that fit of grief or rage
I look upon one child or t'other there
And wonder if she stood so at that age—
For even daughters of the swan can share
Something of every paddler's heritage—
And had that color upon cheek or hair;
And thereupon my heart is driven wild:
She stands before me as a living child.

IV

Her present image floats in to the mind—
Did quattrocento finger fashion it
Hollow of cheek as though it drank the wind
And took a mass of shadows for its meat?
And I though never of Ledæan kind
Had pretty plumage once—enough of that,
Better to smile on all that smile, and show
There is a comfortable kind of old scarecrow.

V

What youthful mother, a shape upon her lap
Honey of generation had betrayed,
And that must sleep, shriek, struggle to escape
As recollection or the drug decide,
Would think her son, did she but see that shape
With sixty or more winters on its head,
A compensation for the pang of his birth,
Or the uncertainty of his setting forth?

VI

Plato thought nature but a spume that plays
Upon a ghostly paradigm of things;
Solider Aristotle played the taws
Upon the bottom of a king of kings;
World-famous golden-thighed Pythagoras
Fingered upon a fiddle stick or strings
What a star sang and careless Muses heard:
Old clothes upon old sticks to scare a bird.

VII

Both nuns and mothers worship images,
But those the candles light are not as those
That animate a mother's reveries,
But keep a marble or a bronze repose.
And yet they too break hearts—O Presences
That passion, piety or affection knows,
And that all heavenly glory symbolize—
O self-born mockers of man's enterprize;

VIII

Labor is blossoming or dancing where
The body is not bruised to pleasure soul,
Nor beauty born out of its own despair,
Nor blear-eyed wisdom out of midnight oil.
O chestnut tree, great rooted blossomer,
Are you the leaf, the blossom or the bole?
O body swayed to music, O brightening glance,
How can we know the dancer from the dance?

THE TOWER

I

What shall I do with this absurdity—
O heart, O troubled heart—this caricature,
Decrepit age that has been tied to me
As to a dog's tail?
Never had I more

Excited, passionate, fantastical
Imagination, nor an ear and eye
That more expected the impossible—
No, not in boyhood when with rod and fly,
Or the humbler worm, I climbed Ben Bulben's back
And had the livelong summer day to spend.
It seems that I must bid the Muse go pack,
Choose Plato and Plotinus for a friend
Until imagination, ear and eye,
Can be content with argument and deal
In abstract things; or be derided by
A sort of battered kettle at the heel.

II

I pace upon the battlements and stare
On the foundations of a house, or where
Tree, like a sooty finger, starts from the earth;
And send imagination forth
Under the day's declining beam, and call
Images and memories
From ruin or from ancient trees,
For I would ask a question of them all.

Beyond that ridge lived Mrs. French, and once
When every silver candlestick or sconce
Lit up the dark mahogany and the wine,
A serving man that could divine
That most respected lady's every wish,
Ran and with the garden shears
Clipped an insolent farmer's ears
And brought them in a little covered dish.

Some few remembered still when I was young,
A peasant girl commended by a song,
Who'd lived somewhere upon that rocky place,
And praised the color of her face,
And had the greater joy in praising her,
Remembering that, if walked she there,
Farmers jostled at the fair
So great a glory did the song confer.

And certain men, being maddened by those rhymes,
Or else by toasting her a score of times,
Rose from the table and declared it right
To test their fancy by their sight;
But they mistook the brightness of the moon
For the prosaic light of day—
Music had driven their wits astray—
And one was drowned in the great bog of Cloone.

Strange, but the man who made the song was blind,
Yet, now I have considered it, I find
That nothing strange; the tragedy began
With Homer that was a blind man,
And Helen has all living hearts betrayed.
O may the moon and sunlight seem
One inextricable beam,
For if I triumph I must make men mad.

And I myself created Hanrahan
And drove him drunk or sober through the dawn
From somewhere in the neighboring cottages.
Caught by an old man's juggleries
He stumbled, tumbled, fumbled to and fro
And had but broken knees for hire
And horrible splendor of desire;
I thought it all out twenty years ago:

Good fellows shuffled cards in an old bawn;
And when that ancient ruffian's turn was on
He so bewitched the cards under his thumb
That all, but the one card, became
A pack of hounds and not a pack of cards,
And that he changed into a hare.
Hanrahan rose in frenzy there
And followed up those baying creatures towards—

O towards I have forgotten what—enough!
I must recall a man that neither love
Nor music nor an enemy's clipped ear
Could, he was so harried, cheer;

A figure that has grown so fabulous
There's not a neighbor left to say
When he finished his dog's day:
An ancient bankrupt master of this house.

Before that ruin came, for centuries,
Rough men-at-arms, cross-gartered to the knees
Or shod in iron, climbed the narrow stairs,
And certain men-at-arms there were
Whose images, in the Great Memory stored,
Come with loud cry and panting breast
To break upon a sleeper's rest
While their great wooden dice beat on the board.

As I would question all, come all who can;
Come old, necessitous, half-mounted man;
And bring beauty's blind rambling celebrant;
The red man the juggler sent
Through God-forsaken meadows; Mrs. French,
Gifted with so fine an ear;
The man drowned in a bog's mire,
When mocking muses chose the country wench.

Did all old men and women, rich and poor,
Who trod upon these rocks or passed this door,
Whether in public or in secret rage
As I do now against old age?
But I have found an answer in those eyes
That are impatient to be gone;
Go therefore; but leave Hanrahan
For I need all his mighty memories.

Old lecher with a love on every wind
Bring up out of that deep considering mind
All that you have discovered in the grave,
For it is certain that you have
Reckoned up every unforeknown, unseeing
Plunge, lured by a softening eye,
Or by a touch or a sigh,
Into the labyrinth of another's being;

Does the imagination dwell the most
Upon a woman won or woman lost?
If on the lost, admit you turned aside
From a great labyrinth out of pride,
Cowardice, some silly over-subtle thought
Or anything called conscience once;
And that if memory recur, the sun's
Under eclipse and the day blotted out.

III

It is time that I wrote my will;
I choose upstanding men,
That climb the streams until
The fountain leap, and at dawn
Drop their cast at the side
Of dripping stone; I declare
They shall inherit my pride,
The pride of people that were
Bound neither to Cause nor to State,
Neither to slaves that were spat on,
Nor to the tyrants that spat,
The people of Burke and of Grattan
That gave, though free to refuse—
Pride, like that of the morn,
When the headlong light is loose,
Or that of the fabulous horn,
Or that of the sudden shower
When all streams are dry,
Or that of the hour
When the swan must fix his eye
Upon a fading gleam,
Float out upon a long
Last reach of glittering stream
And there sing his last song.
And I declare my faith;
I mock Plotinus' thought
And cry in Plato's teeth,
Death and life were not
Till man made up the whole,

Made lock, stock and barrel
Out of his bitter soul,
Aye, sun and moon and star, all,
And further add to that
That, being dead, we rise,
Dream and so create
Translunar Paradise.
I have prepared my peace
With learned Italian things
And the proud stones of Greece,
Poet's imaginings
And memories of love,
Memories of the words of women,
All those things whereof
Man makes a superhuman,
Mirror-resembling dream.

As at the loophole there,
The daws chatter and scream,
And drop twigs layer upon layer.
When they have mounted up,
The mother bird will rest
On their hollow top,
And so warm her wild nest.

I leave both faith and pride
To young upstanding men
Climbing the mountain side,
That under bursting dawn
They may drop a fly;
Being of that metal made
Till it was broken by
This sedentary trade.

Now shall I make my soul
Compelling it to study
In a learned school
Till the wreck of body
Slow decay of blood,
Testy delirium

Or dull decrepitude,
Or what worse evil come—
The death of friends, or death
Of every brilliant eye
That made a catch in the breath—
Seem but the clouds of the sky
When the horizon fades;
Or a bird's sleepy cry
Among the deepening shades.

SAILING TO BYZANTIUM

I

That is no country for old men. The young
In one another's arms, birds in the trees
(Those dying generations) at their song,
The salmon-falls, the mackerel-crowded seas,
Fish, flesh, or fowl, commend all summer long
Whatever is begotten, born, and dies.
Caught in that sensual music, all neglect
Monuments of unaging intellect.

II

An aged man is but a paltry thing,
A tattered coat upon a stick, unless
Soul clap its hands and sing, and louder sing
For every tatter in its mortal dress;
Nor is there singing school but studying
Monuments of its own magnificence;
And therefore I have sailed the seas and come
To the holy city of Byzantium.

III

O sages, standing in God's holy fire
As in the gold mosaic of a wall,
Come from the holy fire, perne in a gyre,
And be the singing masters of my soul.

Consume my heart away, sick with desire
And fastened to a dying animal
It knows not what it is, and gather me
Into the artifice of eternity.

IV

Once out of nature I shall never take
My bodily form from any natural thing,
But such a form as Grecian goldsmiths make
Of hammered gold and gold enamelling
To keep a drowsy emperor awake;
Or set upon a golden bough to sing
To lords and ladies of Byzantium
Of what is past, or passing, or to come.

GEORGE W. RUSSELL ("Æ")[1]

George William Russell, better known by the pseudonym "Æ," was born on April 10, 1867, in the market-town of Lurgan, County Armagh, Ireland. He was the second son of Thomas Ebas Russell, a staunch Ulster man of affairs. As a young lad he was taken to Dublin, where for several years he attended Rathmines School. At sixteen he began the study of painting in the Metropolitan School of Art, Dublin, and while there made the acquaintance of a brilliant fellow-student, W. B. Yeats. The year following he was forced to begin working, and became an accountant at Pim's, a drapery house in the city. During his years as an employee in this establishment he spent his free hours among the hills outside Dublin, or in reading, conversing, and studying, especially the Oriental sacred books. He was much occupied with religious and philosophical speculations, and for a time became leader of a group of young theosophists.

In 1897, upon the recommendation of Yeats, he was invited by Horace Plunkett to become an organizer for the newly formed Irish Agricultural Organization Society. He entered upon the work energetically, and for a number of years devoted himself to establishing co-operative societies, giving instructions to rural communities, studying the economic needs of rural Ireland, and after 1904 to editing the official organ of the Society,

[1] Russell's adoption of "Æ" as a pen name came about as the result of an accident. In his early days, he submitted an article to *The Irish Theosophist*, signing himself "Æon," but so illegibly that the printer was unable to read the last two letters and so omitted them. The substitution proved acceptable to Russell, who used it thereafter.

The Irish Homestead. Of this publication he was editor until 1923, when he took charge of *The Irish Statesman.* He married, resumed his early interest in philosophy, again took up the study of painting, and established a home which has been for many years a resort of writers, thinkers, politicians, and lovers of good conversation. In recent years his reputation has been noteworthy both as a landscape painter and as a poet.

Russell began writing while an accountant at Pim's, publishing both verse and prose in *The Irish Theosophist* and other periodicals. His first volumes, *Homeward, Songs by the Way* (1894) and *The Earth Breath* (1897), were poetry; but later he also wrote much prose, especially philosophical essays and treatises on the economic wants of Ireland. The most important of his prose volumes are *Some Irish Essays* (1906), *Co-operation and Nationality* (1912), *The Rural Community* (1913), *Imaginations and Reveries* (1915), *The National Being* (1916), and *The Interpreters* (1922). In 1907 appeared his *Deirdre,* a prose play previously acted at the Irish National Theatre. His latest book of verse is *Voices of the Stones* (1925).

Practically all of Russell's life has been spent in Ireland. His longest trip to the outside world, in fact, was made in 1928, when he visited America to lecture and read his poems.

AWAKENING

The lights shone down the street
In the long blue close of day:
A boy's heart beat sweet, sweet,
As it flowered in its dreamy clay.

Beyond the dazzling throng
And above the towers of men
The stars made him long, long,
To return to their light again.

They lit the wondrous years
And his heart within was gay;
But a life of tears, tears,
He had won for himself that day.

THE UNKNOWN GOD

Far up the dim twilight fluttered
    Moth-wings of vapor and flame:
The lights danced over the mountains,
    Star after star they came.

The lights grew thicker unheeded,
    For silent and still were we;
Our hearts were drunk with a beauty
    Our eyes could never see.

OVERSOUL

I am Beauty itself among beautiful things.
Bhagavad-Gita.

The East was crowned with snow-cold bloom
And hung with veils of pearly fleece:
They died away into the gloom,
Vistas of peace—and deeper peace.

And earth and air and wave and fire
In awe and breathless silence stood;
For One who passed into their choir
Linked them in mystic brotherhood.

Twilight of amethyst, amid
Thy few strange stars that lit the heights,
Where was the secret spirit hid?
Where was Thy place, O Light of Lights?

The flame of Beauty far in space—
Where rose the fire: in Thee? in Me?
Which bowed the elemental race
To adoration silently?

THE GREAT BREATH

Its edges foamed with amethyst and rose,
Withers once more the old blue flower of day:
There where the ether like a diamond glows
    Its petals fade away.

A shadowy tumult stirs the dusky air;
Sparkle the delicate dews, the distant snows;
The great deep thrills, for through it everywhere
    The breath of Beauty blows.

I saw how all the trembling ages past,
Moulded to her by deep and deeper breath,
Neared to the hour when Beauty breathes her last
    And knows herself in death.

DAWN

Still as the holy of holies breathes the vast,
Within its crystal depths the stars grow dim;
Fire on the altar of the hills at last
    Burns on the shadowy rim.

Moment that holds all moments; white upon
The verge it trembles; then like mists of flowers
Break from the fairy fountain of the dawn
The hues of many hours.

. . . . . .

Thrown downward from that high companionship
Of dreaming inmost heart with inmost heart,
Into the common daily ways I slip
My fire from theirs apart.

THE GIFT

I thought, belovèd, to have brought to you
A gift of quietness and ease and peace,
Cooling your brow as with the mystic dew
Dropping from twilight trees.

Homeward I go not yet; the darkness grows;
Not mine the voice to still with peace divine:
From the first fount the stream of quiet flows
Through other hearts than mine.

Yet of my night I give to you the stars,
And of my sorrow here the sweetest gains,
And out of hell, beyond its iron bars,
My scorn of all its pains.

THE PLACE OF REST

The soul is its own witness and its own refuge.

Unto the deep the deep heart goes,
It lays its sadness nigh the breast:
Only the Mighty Mother knows
The wounds that quiver unconfessed.

It seeks a deeper silence still;
It folds itself around with peace,
Where thoughts alike of good or ill
In quietness unfostered cease.

It feels in the unwounding vast
For comfort for its hopes and fears:
The Mighty Mother bows at last;
She listens to her children's tears.

Where the last anguish deepens—there
The fire of beauty smites through pain:
A glory moves amid despair;
The Mother takes her child again.

THE VIRGIN MOTHER

Who is that goddess to whom men should pray,
But her from whom their hearts have turned away,
Out of whose virgin being they were born,
Whose mother nature they have named with scorn
Calling its holy substance common clay.

Yet from this so despisèd earth was made
The milky whiteness of those queens who swayed
Their generations with a light caress,
And from some image of whose loveliness
The heart built up high heaven when it prayed.

Lover, your heart, the heart on which it lies,
Your eyes that gaze and those alluring eyes,
Your lips, the lips they kiss, alike had birth
Within that dark divinity of earth,
Within that mother being you despise.

Ah, when I think this earth on which I tread
Hath borne these blossoms of the lovely dead,
And makes the living heart I love to beat,
I look with sudden awe beneath my feet
As you with erring reverence overhead.

SACRIFICE

Those delicate wanderers,
The wind, the star, the cloud,
Ever before mine eyes,
As to an altar bowed,
Light and dew-laden airs
Offer in sacrifice.

The offerings arise:
Hazes of rainbow light,
Pure crystal, blue, and gold,
Through dreamland take their flight;
And 'mid the sacrifice
God moveth as of old.

In miracles of fire
He symbols forth his days;
In gleams of crystal light
Reveals what pure pathways
Lead to the soul's desire,
The silence of the height.

THE EARTH

They tell me that the earth is still the same
Although the Red Branch now is but a name,
That yonder peasant lifting up his eyes
Can see the marvel of the morning rise,
The wonder Deirdre gazed on when she came.

I cannot think the hearts that beat so high
Had not a lordlier palace roof of sky,
And that the earth on which the heroes trod
Seemed not to live beneath them like a god
Who loved them and could answer to their cry.

Who said the sun will shine with equal face
Alike upon the noble and the base?
The mighty only to the mighty seems;
The world that loomed through proud and golden dreams
Has dropped behind this world and left no trace.

When that the proud and golden race passed by,
This cold paternal majesty on high,
This unresponsive earth beneath the feet,
Replaced the dear brown breasts that were so sweet,
The face of brooding love within the sky.

How could a beggar wear the kingly crown,
Or those who weakly laid the sceptre down,
Walk 'mid the awful beauty God had made
For those whose hearts were proud and unafraid,
Careless if on His face were smile or frown?

PARTING

As from our dream we died away
Far off I felt the outer things:
Your wind-blown tresses round me play,
Your bosom's gentle murmurings.

And far away our faces met
As on the verge of the vast spheres:
And in the night our cheeks were wet,
I could not say with dew or tears.

O gate by which I entered in!
O face and hair! O lips and eyes!
Through you again the world I win,
How far away from Paradise!

CARROWMORE

It's a lonely road through bogland to the lake at Carrowmore,
And a sleeper there lies dreaming where the water laps the shore;
Though the moth-wings of the twilight in their purples are
unfurled,
Yet his sleep is filled with music by the masters of the world.

There's a hand is white as silver that is fondling with his
hair:
There are glimmering feet of sunshine that are dancing by
him there:
And half-open lips of faery that were dyed a faery red
In their revels where the Hazel Tree its holy clusters shed.

"Come away," the red lips whisper, "all the world is weary
now;
'Tis the twilight of the ages and it's time to quit the plough.
Oh, the very sunlight's weary ere it lightens up the dew,
And its gold is changed and faded before it falls to you.

"Though your colleen's heart be tender, a tenderer heart is
near.
What's the starlight in her glances when the stars are shining
clear?
Who would kiss the fading shadow when the flower-face
glows above?
'Tis the beauty of all Beauty that is calling for your love."

Oh, the great gates of the mountain have opened once again,
And the sound of song and dancing falls upon the ears of
men,
And the Land of Youth lies gleaming, flushed with rainbow
light and mirth,
And the old enchantment lingers in the honey-heart of earth.

REFUGE

Twilight, a timid fawn, went glimmering by,
And Night, the dark-blue hunter, followed fast,
Ceaseless pursuit and flight were in the sky,
But the long chase had ceased for us at last.

We watched together while the driven fawn
Hid in the golden thicket of the day.
We, from whose hearts pursuit and flight were gone,
Knew on the hunter's breast her refuge lay.

THE SILENCE OF LOVE

I could praise you once with beautiful words ere you came
And entered my life with love in a wind of flame.
I could lure with a song from afar my bird to its nest,
But with pinions drooping together silence is best.

In the land of beautiful silence the winds are laid,
And life grows quietly one in the cloudy shade.
I will not waken the passion that sleeps in the heart,
For the winds that blew us together may blow us apart.

Fear not the stillness; for doubt and despair shall cease
With the gentle voices guiding us into peace.
Our dreams will change as they pass through the gates of gold,
And Quiet, the tender shepherd, shall keep the fold.

THE WINDS OF ANGUS

The grey road whereupon we trod became as holy ground:
The eve was all one voice that breathed its message with no
 sound:
And burning multitudes pour through my heart, too bright,
 too blind,
Too swift and hurried in their flight to leave their tale behind.
Twin gates unto that living world, dark honey-colored eyes,
The lifting of whose lashes flushed the face with Paradise,
Beloved, there I saw within their ardent rays unfold
The likeness of enraptured birds that flew from deeps of gold
To deeps of gold within my breast to rest, or there to be
Transfigured in the light, or find a death to life in me.
So love, a burning multitude, a seraph wind that blows
From out the deep of being to the deep of being goes.
And sun and moon and starry fires and earth and air and sea
Are creatures from the deep let loose, who pause in ecstasy,
Or wing their wild and heavenly way until again they find
The ancient deep, and fade therein, enraptured, bright, and
 blind.

INHERITANCE

As flow the rivers to the sea
Adown from rocky hill or plain,
A thousand ages toiled for thee
And gave thee harvest of their gain;
And weary myriads of yore
Dug out for thee earth's buried ore.

The shadowy toilers for thee fought
In chaos of primeval day
Blind battles with they knew not what;
And each before he passed away
Gave clear articulate cries of woe:
Your pain is theirs of long ago.

And all the old heart sweetness sung,
The joyous life of man and maid
In forests when the earth was young,
In rumors round your childhood strayed:
The careless sweetness of your mind
Comes from the buried years behind.

And not alone unto your birth
Their gifts the weeping ages bore,
The old descents of God on earth
Have dowered thee with celestial lore:
So, wise, and filled with sad and gay
You pass unto the further day.

THE TWILIGHT OF EARTH

The wonder of the world is o'er:
    The magic from the sea is gone:
There is no unimagined shore,
    No islet yet to venture on.
The Sacred Hazels' blooms are shed,
The Nuts of Knowledge harvested.

Oh, what is worth this lore of age
    If time shall never bring us back
Our battle with the gods to wage
    Reeling along the starry track.
The battle rapture here goes by
In warring upon things that die.

Let be the tale of him whose love
    Was sighed between white Deirdre's breasts,
It will not lift the heart above
    The sodden clay on which it rests.
Love once had power the gods to bring
All rapt on its wild wandering.

We shiver in the falling dew,
    And seek a shelter from the storm:
When man these elder brothers knew
    He found the mother nature warm,
A hearth fire blazing through it all,
A home without a circling wall.

We dwindle down beneath the skies,
    And from ourselves we pass away:
The paradise of memories
    Grows ever fainter day by day.
The shepherd stars have shrunk within,
The world's great night will soon begin.

Will no one, ere it is too late,
    Ere fades the last memorial gleam,
Recall for us our earlier state?
    For nothing but so vast a dream
That it would scale the steeps of air
Could rouse us from so vast despair.

The power is ours to make or mar
    Our fate as on the earliest morn,
The Darkness and the Radiance are
    Creatures within the spirit born.
Yet, bathed in gloom too long, we might
Forget how we imagined light.

Not yet are fixed the prison bars;
    The hidden light the spirit owns
If blown to flame would dim the stars
    And they who rule them from their thrones:
And the proud sceptred spirits thence
Would bow to pay us reverence.

Oh, while the glory sinks within
    Let us not wait on earth behind,
But follow where it flies, and win
    The glow again, and we may find
Beyond the Gateways of the Day
Dominion and ancestral sway.

AN IRISH FACE

Not her own sorrow only that hath place
Upon yon gentle face.
Too slight have been her childhood's years to gain
The imprint of such pain.
It hid behind her laughing hours, and wrought
Each curve in saddest thought
On brow and lips and eyes. With subtle art
It made that little heart
Through its young joyous beatings to prepare
A quiet shelter there,
Where the immortal sorrows might find a home.
And many there have come;
Bowed in a mournful mist of golden hair
Deirdre hath entered there.
And shrouded in a fall of pitying dew,
Weeping the friend he slew,
The Hound of Ulla lies, with those who shed
Tears for the Wild Geese fled.
And all the lovers on whom fate had warred
Cutting the silver cord
Enter, and softly breath by breath they mould
The young heart to the old,

The old protest, the old pity, whose power
Are gathering to the hour
When their knit silence shall be mightier far
Than leagued empires are.
And dreaming of the sorrow on this face
We grow of lordlier race,
Could shake the rooted rampart of the hills
To shield her from all ills,
And through a deep adoring pity won
Grow what we dream upon.

CONTINUITY

No sign is made while empires pass.
The flowers and stars are still His care,
The constellations hid in grass,
The golden miracles in air.

Life in an instant will be rent
Where death is glittering blind and wild—
The Heavenly Brooding is intent
To that last instant on Its child.

It breathes the glow in brain and heart,
Life is made magical. Until
Body and spirit are apart
The Everlasting works Its will.

In that wild orchid that your feet
In their next falling shall destroy,
Minute and passionate and sweet
The Mighty Master holds His joy.

Though the crushed jewels droop and fade
The Artist's labors will not cease,
And of the ruins shall be made
Some yet more lovely masterpiece.

MUTINY

That blazing galleon the sun,
This dusky coracle I ride,
Both under secret orders sail,
And swim upon the selfsame tide.

The fleet of stars, my boat of soul,
By perilous magic mountains pass,
Or lie where no horizons gleam
Fainting upon a sea of glass.

Come, break the seals and tell us now
Upon what enterprise we roam:
To storm what city of the gods,
Or—sail for the green fields of home!

TIME

At every heart-beat
Through the magic day
A lovely laughing creature
Ran away.
Where have they wandered,
The flock so gay?

I had but looked on them
And away they ran,
The exquisite lips untouched.
As they began
To part, Time swept them
On his caravan.

These new-born beauties
The tyrant took.
Their gaze was on mine
And mine forsook.
I could not stay even
One lovely look.

In what fold are they?
Could I pursue
Through the Everliving
And know anew
All those golden motions
That were you?

Were beauty only
A day the same,
We could know the Maker
And name His name.
We would know the substance
Was holy flame.

Is there an oasis
Where Time stands still,
Where the fugitive beauty
Stays as we will?
Is there an oasis
Where Time stands still?

WHEN

When mine hour is come
Let no teardrop fall
And no darkness hover
Round me where I lie.
Let the vastness call
One who was its lover,
Let me breathe the sky.

Where the lordly light
Walks along the world,
And its silent tread
Leaves the grasses bright,
Leaves the flowers uncurled,
Let me to the dead
Breathe a gay goodnight.

RECONCILIATION

I begin through the grass once again to be bound to the Lord;
  I can see, through a face that has faded, the face full
    of rest
Of the earth, of the mother, my heart with her heart in
    accord,
  As I lie 'mid the cool green tresses that mantle her breast.
I begin with the grass once again to be bound to the Lord.

By the hand of a child I am led to the throne of the King
  For a touch that now fevers me not is forgotten and far,
And His infinite sceptred hands that sway us can bring
  Me in dreams from the laugh of a child to the song
    of a star.
On the laugh of a child I am borne to the joy of the King.

RESURRECTION

Not by me these feet were led
  To the path beside the wave,
Where the naiad lilies shed
  Moonfire o'er a lonely grave.

Let the dragons of the past
  In their caverns sleeping lie.
I am dream-betrayed, and cast
  Into that old agony.

And an anguish of desire
  Burns as in the sunken years,
And the soul sheds drops of fire
  All unquenchable by tears.

I, who sought on high for calm,
  In the Everliving find
All I was in what I am,
  Fierce with gentle intertwined;

Hearts which I had crucified
  With my heart that tortured them:
Penitence, unfallen pride—
  These my thorny diadem!

Thou would'st ease in heaven thy pain,
  Oh, thou fiery, bleeding thing!
All thy wounds will wake again
  At the heaving of a wing.

All thy dead with thee shall rise,
  Dies Irae. If the soul
To the Everliving flies,
  There shall meet it at the goal

Love that Time had overlaid,
  Deaths that we again must die—
Let the dragons we have made
  In their caverns sleeping lie.

PROMISE

Be not so desolate
Because thy dreams have flown
And the hall of the heart is empty
And silent as stone,
As age left by children
Sad and alone.

Those delicate children,
Thy dreams, still endure:
All pure and lovely things
Wend to the Pure.
Sigh not: unto the fold
Their way was sure.

Thy gentlest dreams, thy frailest,
Even those that were
Born and lost in a heart-beat,

Shall meet thee there.
They are become immortal
In shining air.

The unattainable beauty
The thought of which was pain,
That flickered in eyes and on lips
And vanished again:
That fugitive beauty
Thou shalt attain.

The lights innumerable
That led thee on and on,
The Masque of Time ended,
Shall glow into one.
It shall be with thee for ever
Thy travel done.

A MURMUR IN THE GRASS

O pale-lipped blossom
Why do you sigh?
"For the many million
Times I must die
Ere I be as that glory
Up in the sky."

Your sisters with beauty
Are satisfied.
Is it not envy
Dreams of such pride?
"No, there is nothing
To life denied.

"It would be unjust,
Unjust, if we
Could dream of a beauty
We might not be.
Life is becoming
All we see.

"I shall rise from the grass,
I shall fill all the blue,
And I shall be blossom
And fire and dew
In the boundlessness
We travel through."

W. H. DAVIES

William Henry Davies, a son of Welsh parents, was born on April 20, 1871, in Newport, Wales, in a public house, run by his grandfather, a retired sea captain. He attended school a few years, but while still a small boy organized a robber gang among his schoolmates for the purpose of stealing from merchants in the neighborhood, and being caught, was forced to quit school; whereupon his grandfather apprenticed him first to an ironmonger and then to a picture-frame maker. While working at his trade, he read Marlowe, Shakespeare, Byron, Shelley, and other poets, and began to write poetry himself, being encouraged by a young woman of his acquaintance. When she died a little later, however, he gave up the idea of becoming a poet, and determined as soon as he had served his apprenticeship to leave for America. Upon his grandmother's refusal to supply him with funds for his projected trip, he went to Bristol, where he worked for six months until she died, leaving him a small legacy. Securing fifteen pounds of his inheritance, he sailed, at the age of twenty-three, for the United States.

He arrived in New York with ten dollars, and thinking to find work in Chicago, asked the way there of a man he met in a park. This man turned out to be a noted beggar, who invited Davies to join him on a trip west. He accepted and was introduced to the ways of hoboes and beggars. For the next six years he was a professional tramp in the United States, going from coast to coast a number of times, and working occasionally as berry picker in Michigan and as cattleman on freighters between Baltimore and Liverpool. In his thirtieth year, after a short stay in England, he set out for the Klondike gold region, having the naïve idea that gold lay on top of the ground there, and might be had by any one for the picking up. Upon reaching Canada, he was persuaded by a companion to abandon the idea of making the long trip across country aboard a freight train, as had always been his custom in the past, and to steal a ride on a passenger train instead. In boarding the passenger train, however, he slipped under the wheels and had his right foot cut off at the ankle, it later becoming necessary to amputate the leg at the knee. This meant the end of his life as a tramp, and as he lay at the hospital, going over plans for the future, there recurred to him his youthful ambition to write poetry. Forthwith he resolved to return to England and become a poet. The first part of this resolution he put into effect as soon as he was able to travel, but the second part seems to have lain dormant for some months after his arrival at home.

Eventually he drifted to a cheap London lodging house, where he could stay for six pence a day, and began writing, producing a blank verse drama, *The Robber,* a long poem about birds and beasts, a hundred sonnets, and a number of other works; but for none of these could he find a publisher. At last he was forced to take to the road again, this time as a peddler of shoe laces, pins, and other small notions. Having no success at this trade, he finally bargained with a printer to publish for nineteen pounds two hundred and fifty copies of his poems; and these volumes, *The Soul's Destroyer and Other Poems* (1905), he began sending to various persons with the request to buy or return them. One who received a copy was Bernard Shaw; he recognized the merit of the poetry in the book, and with one or two critics of note introduced Davies to the public. From this time his fame as a poet was assured.

Once his reputation was established, Davies began

issuing books in rapid succession, and in a quarter of a century has published more than twenty volumes of poetry and eight books of prose, the best of the latter being *The Autobiography of a Super-Tramp* (1908). He has also made a collection of poetry, *Short Lyrics of the Twentieth Century* (1922), and has done some editing. In 1926 the University of Wales gave him the honorary degree of Doctor of Literature. He is married and lives at Oxted, Surrey.

LEISURE

What is this life if, full of care,
We have no time to stand and stare.

No time to stand beneath the boughs
And stare as long as sheep or cows.

No time to see, when woods we pass,
Where squirrels hide their nuts in grass.

No time to see, in broad daylight,
Streams full of stars, like stars at night.

No time to turn at Beauty's glance,
And watch her feet, how they can dance.

No time to wait till her mouth can
Enrich that smile her eyes began.

A poor life this if, full of care,
We have no time to stand and stare.

THE RAIN

I hear leaves drinking Rain;
    I hear rich leaves on top
Giving the poor beneath
    Drop after drop;
'Tis a sweet noise to hear
These green leaves drinking near.

And when the Sun comes out,
    After this Rain shall stop,
A wondrous Light will fill
    Each dark, round drop;
I hope the Sun shines bright:
'Twill be a lovely sight.

THE EXAMPLE

Here's an example from
A Butterfly;
That on a rough, hard rock
Happy can lie;
Friendless and all alone
On this unsweetened stone.

Now let my bed be hard,
No care take I;
I'll make my joy like this
Small Butterfly;
Whose happy heart has power
To make a stone a flower.

THE SLEEPERS

As I walked down the waterside
This silent morning, wet and dark;
Before the cocks in farmyards crowed,
Before the dogs began to bark;
Before the hour of five was struck
By old Westminster's mighty clock:

As I walked down the waterside
This morning, in the cold damp air,
I saw a hundred women and men
Huddled in rags and sleeping there:
These people have no work, thought I,
And long before their time they die.

That moment, on the waterside,
A lighted car came at a bound;
I looked inside, and saw a score
Of pale and weary men that frowned;
Each man sat in a huddled heap,
Carried to work while fast asleep.

Ten cars rushed down the waterside,
Like lighted coffins in the dark;
With twenty dead men in each car,
That must be brought alive by work:
These people work too hard, thought I,
And long before their time they die.

IN THE COUNTRY

This life is sweetest; in this wood
I hear no children cry for food;
I see no woman, white with care;
No man, with muscles wasting here.

No doubt it is a selfish thing
To fly from human suffering;
No doubt he is a selfish man,
Who shuns poor creatures sad and wan.

But 'tis a wretched life to face
Hunger in almost every place;
Cursed with a hand that's empty, when
The heart is full to help all men.

Can I admire the statue great,
When living men starve at its feet!
Can I admire the park's green tree,
A roof for homeless misery!

When I can see few men in need,
I then have power to help by deed,
Nor lose my cheerfulness in pity—
Which I must do in every city.

For when I am in those great places,
I see ten thousand suffering faces;
Before me stares a wolfish eye,
Behind me creeps a groan or sigh.

CHRIST THE MAN

Lord, I say nothing; I profess
No faith in Thee nor Christ Thy Son:
Yet no man ever heard me mock
A true believing one.

If knowledge is not great enough
To give a man believing power,
Lord, he must wait in Thy great hand
Till revelation's hour.

Meanwhile he'll follow Christ the man,
In that humanity He taught,
Which to the poor and the oppressed,
Gives its best time and thought.

TRULY GREAT

My walls outside must have some flowers,
My walls within must have some books;
A house that's small; a garden large,
And in it leafy nooks.

A little gold that's sure each week;
That comes not from my living kind,
But from a dead man in his grave,
Who cannot change his mind.

A lovely wife, and gentle too;
Contented that no eyes but mine
Can see her many charms, nor voice
To call her beauty fine.

Where she would in that stone cage live,
A self-made prisoner, with me;
While many a wild bird sang around,
On gate, on bush, on tree.

And she sometimes to answer them,
In her far sweeter voice than all;
Till birds, that loved to look on leaves,
Will doat on a stone wall.

With this small house, this garden large,
This little gold, this lovely mate,
With health in body, peace at heart—
Show me a man more great.

JENNY WREN

Her sight is short, she comes quite near;
A foot to me's a mile to her;
And she is known as Jenny Wren,
The smallest bird in England. When
I heard that little bird at first,
Methought her frame would surely burst
With earnest song. Oft had I seen
Her running under leaves so green,
Or in the grass when fresh and wet,
As though her wings she would forget.
And, seeing this, I said to her—
"My pretty runner, you prefer
To be a thing to run unheard
Through leaves and grass, and not a bird!"
'Twas then she burst, to prove me wrong,
Into a sudden storm of song;
So very loud and earnest, I
Feared she would break her heart and die.
"Nay, nay," I laughed, "be you no thing
To run unheard, sweet scold, but sing!
O I could hear your voice near me,
Above the din in that oak tree,
When almost all the twigs on top
Had starlings chattering without stop."

FANCY'S HOME

Tell me, Fancy, sweetest child,
Of thy parents and thy birth;
Had they silk, and had they gold,
And a park to wander forth,
With a castle green and old?

In a cottage I was born,
My kind father was Content,
My dear mother Innocence;
On wild fruits of wonderment
I have nourished ever since.

SHEEP

When I was once in Baltimore,
A man came up to me and cried,
"Come, I have eighteen hundred sheep,
And we will sail on Tuesday's tide.

"If you will sail with me, young man,
I'll pay you fifty shillings down;
These eighteen hundred sheep I take
From Baltimore to Glasgow town."

He paid me fifty shillings down,
I sailed with eighteen hundred sheep;
We soon had cleared the harbor's mouth,
We soon were in the salt sea deep.

The first night we were out at sea
Those sheep were quiet in their mind;
The second night they cried with fear—
They smelt no pastures in the wind.

They sniffed, poor things, for their green fields,
They cried so loud I could not sleep:
For fifty thousand shillings down
I would not sail again with sheep.

THE LITTLE ONES

The little ones are put in bed,
And both are laughing, lying down;
Their father, and their mother too,
Are gone on Christmas-eve to town.

"Old Santa Claus will bring a horse,
Gee up!" cried little Will, with glee;
"If I am good, I'll have a doll
From Santa Claus"—laughed Emily.

The little ones are gone to sleep,
Their father and their mother now
Are coming home, with many more—
They're drunk, and make a merry row.

The little ones on Christmas morn
Jump up, like skylarks from the grass;
And then they stand as still as stones,
And just as cold as stones, alas!

No horse, no doll beside their bed,
No sadder little ones could be;
"We did some wrong," said little Will—
"We must have sinned," sobbed Emily.

THE WAYS OF TIME

As butterflies are but winged flowers,
Half sorry for their change, who fain,
So still and long they lie on leaves,
Would be thought flowers again—

E'en so my thoughts, that should expand,
And grow to higher themes above,
Return like butterflies to lie
On the old things I love.

RAPTURES

Sing for the sun your lyric, lark,
Of twice ten thousand notes;
Sing for the moon, you nightingales,
Whose light shall kiss your throats;
Sing, sparrows, for the soft, warm rain,
To wet your feathers through;
And, when a rainbow's in the sky,
Sing you, cuckoo—"Cuckoo!"

Sing for your five blue eggs, fond thrush,
By many a leaf concealed;
You starlings, wrens, and blackbirds sing
In every wood and field:
While I, who fail to give my love
Long raptures twice as fine,
Will for her beauty breathe this one—
A sigh, that's more divine.

A CHILD'S PET

When I sailed out of Baltimore,
With twice a thousand head of sheep,
They would not eat, they would not drink,
But bleated o'er the deep.

Inside the pens we crawled each day,
To sort the living from the dead;
And when we reached the Mersey's mouth,
Had lost five hundred head.

Yet every night and day one sheep,
That had no fear of man or sea,
Stuck through the bars its pleading face,
And it was stroked by me.

And to the sheep-men standing near,
"You see," I said, "this one tame sheep?
It seems a child has lost her pet,
And cried herself to sleep."

So every time we passed it by,
Sailing to England's slaughter-house,
Eight ragged sheep-men—tramps and thieves—
Would stroke that sheep's black nose.

THE BELL

It is the bell of death I hear,
Which tells me my own time is near,
When I must join those quiet souls
Where nothing lives but worms and moles;
And not come through the grass again,
Like worms and moles, for breath or rain;
Yet let none weep when my life's through,
For I myself have wept for few.

The only things that knew me well
Were children, dogs, and girls that fell;
I bought poor children cakes and sweets,
Dogs heard my voice and danced the streets;
And, gentle to a fallen lass,
I made her weep for what she was.
Good men and women know not me,
Nor love nor hate the mystery.

BIRDS

When our two souls have left this mortal clay,
And, seeking mine, you think that mine is lost—
Look for me first in that Elysian glade
Where Lesbia is, for whom the birds sing most.

What happy hearts those feathered mortals have,
That sing so sweet when they're wet through in spring!
For in that month of May when leaves are young,
Birds dream of song, and in their sleep they sing.

And when the spring has gone and they are dumb,
Is it not fine to watch them at their play:
Is it not fine to see a bird that tries
To stand upon the end of every spray?

See how they tilt their pretty heads aside:
When women make that move they always please.
What cosy homes birds make in leafy walls
That Nature's love has ruined—and the trees.

Oft have I seen in fields the little birds
Go in between a bullock's legs to eat;
But what gives me most joy is when I see
Snow on my doorstep, printed by their feet.

THE CAPTIVE LION

Thou that in fury with thy knotted tail
Hast made this iron floor thy beaten drum;
That now in silence walks thy little space—
Like a sea-captain—careless what may come:

What power has brought your majesty to this,
Who gave those eyes their dull and sleepy look;
Who took their lightning out, and from thy throat
The thunder when the whole wide forest shook?

It was that man who went again, alone,
Into thy forest dark—Lord, he was brave!
That man a fly has killed, whose bones are left
Unburied till an earthquake digs his grave.

WINTER'S BEAUTY

Is it not fine to walk in spring,
When leaves are born, and hear birds sing?
And when they lose their singing powers,
In summer, watch the bees at flowers?
Is it not fine, when summer's past,
To have the leaves, no longer fast,
Biting my heel where'er I go,
Or dancing lightly on my toe?
Now winter's here and rivers freeze;
As I walk out I see the trees,
Wherein the pretty squirrels sleep,
All standing in the snow so deep:
And every twig, however small,
Is blossomed white and beautiful.
Then welcome, winter, with thy power
To make this tree a big white flower;
To make this tree a lovely sight,
With fifty brown arms draped in white,
While thousands of small fingers show
In soft white gloves of purest snow.

STRONG MOMENTS

Sometimes I hear fine ladies sing,
    Sometimes I smoke and drink with men;
Sometimes I play at games of cards—
    Judge me to be no strong man then.

The strongest moment of my life
    Is when I think about the poor;
When, like a spring that rain has fed,
    My pity rises more and more.

The flower that loves the warmth and light
    Has all its mornings bathed in dew;
My heart has moments wet with tears,
    My weakness is they are so few.

MY LOVE COULD WALK

My love could walk in richer hues
Than any bird of paradise,
And no one envy her her dress:
Since in her looks the world would see
A robin's love and friendliness.

And she could be the lily fair,
More richly dressed than all her kind,
And no one envy her her gain:
Since in her looks the world would see
A daisy that was sweet and plain.

Oh, she could sit like any queen
That's nailed by diamonds to a throne,
Her splendor envied by not one:
Since in her looks the world would see
A queen that's more than half a nun.

RAGS AND BONES

This morning, as I wandered forth,
I heard a man cry, "Rags and Bones!"
And little children in the streets
Went home for bottles, bones, and rags,
To barter for his toys and sweets.

And then I thought of grown-up man,
That in our dreams we trust a God
Will think our rags and bones a boon,
And give us His immortal sweets
For these poor lives cast off so soon.

The mind, they say, will gather strength
That broods on what is hard to know:
The fear of unfamiliar things
Is better than their parents' love,
To teach young birds to use their wings.

But riddles are not made for me,
My joy's in beauty, not its cause:
Then give me but the open skies,
And birds that sing in a green wood
That's snow-bound by anemones.

FORGIVENESS

Stung by a spiteful wasp,
I let him go life free:
That proved the difference
In him and me.

For, had I killed my foe,
It had proved me at once
The stronger wasp, and no
More difference.

TELLING FORTUNES

"You'll have a son," the old man said—
"And then a daughter fair to meet
As any summer nights that dance
Upon a thousand silver feet."
"You dear old man, now can you tell
If my fair daughter'll marry well?"
The old man winked his eye and said,
"Well, knowing men for what they are,
She'll break their hearts, because she'll not
Be half as good as she is fair."
The new-made wife was full of pain,
And raised her head and hoped again.
"And will my son be fine and smart
And win a noble lady's heart?"
The old man winked his other eye—
"Well, knowing women as we do,
The kind of man they most prefer,
He'll break their hearts, because he'll be
A fool, a coxcomb, and a cur."

THE OX

Why should I pause, poor beast, to praise
Thy back so red, thy sides so white;
And on thy brow those curls in which
Thy mournful eyes take no delight?

I dare not make fast friends with kine,
Nor sheep, nor fowl that cannot fly;
For they live not for Nature's voice,
Since 'tis man's will when they must die.

So, if I call thee some pet name,
And give thee of my care to-day,
Where wilt thou be to-morrow morn,
When I turn curious eyes thy way?

Nay, I'll not miss what I'll not find,
And I'll find no fond cares for thee;
So take away those great sad eyes
That stare across yon fence at me.

See you that Robin, by himself,
Perched on that leafless apple branch,
His breast like one red apple left—
The last and best of all—by chance?

If I do but give heed to him,
He will come daily to my door;
And 'tis the will of God, not Man,
When Robin Redbreast comes no more.

THE RAINBOW

Rainbows are lovely things:
The bird, that shakes a cold, wet wing,
Chatters with ecstasy,
But has no breath to sing:
No wonder, when the air
Has a double-rainbow there!

Look, there's a rainbow now!
    See how that lovely rainbow throws
Her jewelled arm around
    This world, when the rain goes!
And how I wish the rain
Would come again, and again!

LOVE, LIKE A DROP OF DEW

When I pass down the street and see
    The people smiling so,
It's clear enough that my true love
    Was there awhile ago.

Her lips that, following her two eyes,
    Go smiling here and there,
Seem newly kissed—but 'tis my faith
    That none but I would dare.

Love, like a drop of dew that joins
    Two blades of grass together,
Has made her mine, as I am hers,
    For ever and for ever.

ONE TOKEN

The power was given at birth to me
To stare at a rainbow, bird or tree,
    Longer than any man alive;
And from these trances, when they're gone,
My songs of joy come, one by one.

But what I want I cannot have:
One token from beyond the grave,
    That hour I neither dream nor sleep,
To prove death but a veil to hide
Another life on the other side.

THE RIVALS

Pleasure is not the one I love:
    Her laughter in the market-place
Makes every fool her echo there;
    And from her finger-tips she throws
Wild kisses in the open air.

Give me that little miser, Joy,
    Who hoards at home her quiet charms;
And offers with her two soft lips
    A warmer kiss than any thrown
By Pleasure, from her finger-tips.

THE TWO STARS

Day has her star, as well as Night,
One star is black, the other white.
I saw a white star burn and pant
    And swirl with such a wildness, once—
That I stood still, and almost stared
    Myself into a trance!
The star of Day, both seen and heard,
Is but a little English bird;
The Lark, whose wings beat time to his
    Wild rapture, sings, high overhead;
When silence comes, we almost fear
    That Earth receives its dead.

THE SNOWFLAKE

When we are young and wake from sleep,
    What pillow-fights we share with Life!
We laugh and punch, and never dream
    How Death can end that joyful strife.

We'll not let Time destroy that dream,
But in old age our spirit brave
Shall, like a snowflake in its fall,
Dance while it hovers o'er the grave.

Contented men are still my theme,
Who—though too poor for ivory keys—
Still whistle with their naked lips
Their happy tunes of careless ease.

THE JOY OF LIFE

How sweet is Life, how beautiful,
When lying curled in innocent sleep!
Without one thought that, soon or late,
Death will unbend that graceful curve
And stretch him out, all stiff and straight.

Go, happy Life, and say to Death—
"I gave this man sufficient joy
To last him for a thousand years."
Then ask him why my time's as short
As one whose breath is full of tears.

RALPH HODGSON

Ralph Hodgson was born in Northumberland in 1871. He has lived in America, and has engaged in a number of occupations, chiefly journalistic. He worked as a pressman in Fleet Street, London, became a draughtsman on the pictorial staff of an evening paper, and for a time edited *Fry's Magazine*. His love of the out-of-doors and of animals is intense; and he is one of the leading authorities in England on bull terriers.

Although much of his time and energy has been spent on poetry, he has always regarded the writing of it as an avocation rather than a means of making a living. In 1907 appeared his first book of verse, *The Last Blackbird and Other Lines*. During the next ten years he published several other volumes, all small. In 1913 he went into partnership with Lovat Fraser and Holbrook Jackson in publishing broadsides and chapbooks; and from their press, "The Sign of Flying Fame," was issued *The Bull, The Song of Honor,* and other of Hodgson's own works. In 1924 he accepted an invitation to Sendai University, Japan, as lecturer in English literature. Hodgson is something of a recluse, and has avoided the public discussion and reading of his own poems.

THE LINNET

They say the world's a sham, and life a lease
Of nightmare nothing nicknamed Time, and we
Ghost voyagers in undiscovered seas
Where fact is feign; mirage, reality:

Where all is vain and vanity is all,
And eyes look out and only know they stare
At conjured coasts whose beacons rise and fall
And vanish with the hopes that feigned them there:

Where sea-shell measures urge a phantom dance
Till fancied pleasure drowns imagined pain—
Till Death stares madness out of countenance,
And vanity is all and all is vain.

It may be even as my friends allege.
I'm pressed to prove that life is something more—
And yet a linnet on a hawthorn hedge
Still wants explaining and accounting for.

THE HAMMERS

Noise of hammers once I heard,
Many hammers, busy hammers,
Beating, shaping, night and day,
Shaping, beating dust and clay
To a palace; saw it reared;
Saw the hammers laid away.

And I listened, and I heard
Hammers beating, night and day,
In the palace newly reared,
Beating it to dust and clay:
Other hammers, muffled hammers,
Silent hammers of decay.

THE GIPSY GIRL

"Come, try your skill, kind gentlemen,
A penny for three tries!"
Some threw and lost, some threw and won
A ten-a-penny prize.

She was a tawny gipsy girl,
A girl of twenty years,
I liked her for the lumps of gold
That jingled from her ears;

I liked the flaring yellow scarf
Bound loose about her throat,
I liked her showy purple gown
And flashy velvet coat.

A man came up, too loose of tongue,
And said no good to her;
She did not blush as Saxons do,
Or turn upon the cur;

She fawned and whined, "Sweet gentleman,
A penny for three tries!"
—But oh, the den of wild things in
The darkness of her eyes!

TIME, YOU OLD GIPSY MAN

Time, you old gipsy man,
   Will you not stay,
Put up your caravan
   Just for one day?

All things I'll give you
Will you be my guest,
Bells for your jennet
Of silver the best,

Goldsmiths shall beat you
A great golden ring,
Peacocks shall bow to you,
Little boys sing.
Oh, and sweet girls will
Festoon you with may,
Time, you old gipsy,
Why hasten away?

Last week in Babylon,
Last night in Rome,
Morning, and in the crush
Under Paul's dome;
Under Paul's dial
You tighten your rein—
Only a moment,
And off once again;
Off to some city
Now blind in the womb,
Off to another
Ere that's in the tomb.

Time, you old gipsy man,
  Will you not stay,
Put up your caravan
  Just for one day?

EVE

Eve, with her basket, was
Deep in the bells and grass,
Wading in bells and grass
Up to her knees,
Picking a dish of sweet
Berries and plums to eat,
Down in the bells and grass
Under the trees.

Mute as a mouse in a
Corner the cobra lay,
Curled round a bough of the
Cinnamon tall. . . .
Now to get even and
Humble proud heaven and
Now was the moment or
Never at all.

"Eva!" Each syllable
Light as a flower fell;
"Eva!" he whispered the
Wondering maid;
Soft as a bubble sung
Out of a linnet's lung,
Soft and most silverly
"Eva!" he said.

Picture that orchard sprite,
Eve, with her body white,
Supple and smooth to her
Slim finger tips,
Wondering, listening,
Listening, wondering,
Eve with a berry
Half-way to her lips.

Oh, had our simple Eve
Seen through the make-believe!
Had she but known the
Pretender he was!
Out of the boughs he came,
Whispering still her name,
Tumbling in twenty rings
Into the grass.

Here was the strangest pair
In the world anywhere,
Eve in the bells and grass
Kneeling, and he

Telling his story low. . . .
Singing birds saw them go
Down the dark path to
The Blasphemous Tree.

Oh, what a clatter when
Titmouse and Jenny Wren
Saw him successful and
Taking his leave!
How the birds rated him,
How they all hated him!
How they all pitied
Poor motherless Eve!

Picture her crying
Outside in the lane,
Eve, with no dish of sweet
Berries and plums to eat,
Haunting the gate of the
Orchard in vain. . . .
Picture the lewd delight
Under the hill to-night—
"Eva!" the toast goes round,
"Eva!" again.

THE SONG OF HONOR

I climbed a hill as light fell short,
And rooks came home in scramble sort,
And filled the trees and flapped and fought
And sang themselves to sleep;
An owl from nowhere with no sound
Swung by and soon was nowhere found,
I heard him calling half-way round,
Holloing loud and deep;
A pair of stars, faint pins of light,
Then many a star, sailed into sight,
And all the stars, the flower of night,
Were round me at a leap;

To tell how still the valleys lay
I heard a watchdog miles away,
And bells of distant sheep.
I heard no more of bird or bell,
The mastiff in a slumber fell,
I stared into the sky,
As wondering men have always done
Since beauty and the stars were one,
Though none so hard as I.

It seemed, so still the valleys were,
As if the whole world knelt at prayer,
Save me and me alone;
So pure and wide that silence was
I feared to bend a blade of grass,
And there I stood like stone.

There, sharp and sudden, there I heard—
Ah! some wild lovesick singing bird
Woke singing in the trees?
The nightingale and babble-wren
Were in the English greenwood then,
And you heard one of these?
The babble-wren and nightingale
Sang in the Abyssinian vale
That season of the year!
Yet, true enough, I heard them plain,
I heard them both again, again,
As sharp and sweet and clear
As if the Abyssinian tree
Had thrust a bough across the sea,
Had thrust a bough across to me
With music for my ear!

I heard them both, and oh! I heard
The song of every singing bird
That sings beneath the sky,
And with the song of lark and wren
The song of mountains, moths and men
And seas and rainbows vie!

I heard the universal choir,
The Sons of Light exalt their Sire
With universal song,
Earth's lowliest and loudest notes,
Her million times ten million throats
Exalt Him loud and long,
And lips and lungs and tongues of Grace
From every part and every place
Within the shining of His face,
The universal throng.

I heard the hymn of being sound
From every well of honor found
In human sense and soul:
The song of poets when they write
The testament of Beauty sprite
Upon a flying scroll,
The song of painters when they take
A burning brush for Beauty's sake
And limn her features whole—

The song of men divinely wise
Who look and see in starry skies
Not stars so much as robins' eyes,
And when these pale away
Hear flocks of shiny pleiades
Among the plums and apple trees
Sing in the summer day—

The song of all both high and low
To some blest vision true,
The song of beggars when they throw
The crust of pity all men owe
To hungry sparrows in the snow,
Old beggars hungry too—
The song of kings of kingdoms when
They rise above their fortune Men,
And crown themselves anew—

The song of courage, heart and will
And gladness in a fight,
Of men who face a hopeless hill
With sparkling and delight,
The bells and bells of song that ring
Round banners of a cause or king
From armies bleeding white—

The song of sailors every one
When monstrous tide and tempest run
At ships like bulls at red,
When stately ships are twirled and spun
Like whipping tops and help there's none
And mighty ships ten thousand ton
Go down like lumps of lead—

And song of fighters stern as they
At odds with fortune night and day,
Crammed up in cities grim and grey
As thick as bees in hives,
Hosannas of a lowly throng
Who sing unconscious of their song,
Whose lips are in their lives—

And song of some at holy war
With spells and ghouls more dread by far
Than deadly seas and cities are
Or hordes of quarrelling kings—
The song of fighters great and small,
The song of pretty fighters all
And high heroic things—

The song of lovers—who knows how
Twitched up from place and time
Upon a sigh, a blush, a vow,
A curve or hue of cheek or brow,
Borne up and off from here and now
Into the void sublime!

And crying loves and passions still
In every key from soft to shrill
And numbers never done,
Dog-loyalties to faith and friend,
And loves like Ruth's of old no end,
And intermission none—

And burst on burst for beauty and
For numbers not behind,
From men whose love of motherland
Is like a dog's for one dear hand,
Sole, selfless, boundless, blind—
And song of some with hearts beside
For men and sorrows far and wide,
Who watch the world with pity and pride
And warm to all mankind—

And endless joyous music rise
From children at their play,
And endless soaring lullabies
From happy, happy mothers' eyes,
And answering crows and baby-cries,
How many who shall say!
And many a song as wondrous well
With pangs and sweets intolerable
From lonely hearths too grey to tell,
God knows how utter grey!
And song from many a house of care
When pain has forced a footing there,
And there's a Darkness on the stair
Will not be turned away—

And song—that song whose singers come
With old kind tales of pity from
The Great Compassion's lips,
That make the bells of Heaven to peal
Round pillows frosty with the feel
Of Death's cold finger tips—

The song of men all sorts and kinds,
As many tempers, moods and minds
As leaves are on a tree,
As many faiths and castes and creeds,
As many human bloods and breeds
As in the world may be;

The song of each and all who gaze
On Beauty in her naked blaze,
Or see her dimly in a haze,
Or get her light in fitful rays
And tiniest needles even,
The song of all not wholly dark,
Not wholly sunk in stupor stark
Too deep for groping Heaven—

And alleluias sweet and clear
And wild with beauty men mishear,
From choirs of song as near and dear
To Paradise as they,
The everlasting pipe and flute
Of wind and sea and bird and brute,
And lips deaf men imagine mute
In wood and stone and clay,

The music of a lion strong
That shakes a hill a whole night long,
A hill as loud as he,
The twitter of a mouse among
Melodious greenery,
The ruby's and the rainbow's song,
The nightingale's—all three,
The song of life that wells and flows
From every leopard, lark and rose
And everything that gleams or goes
Lack-lustre in the sea

I heard it all, each, every note
Of every lung and tongue and throat,
Ay, every rhythm and rhyme

Of everything that lives and loves
And upward, ever upward moves
From lowly to sublime!
Earth's multitudinous Sons of Light,
I heard them lift their lyric might
With each and every chanting sprite
That lit the sky that wondrous night
As far as eye could climb!

I heard it all, I heard the whole
Harmonious hymn of being roll
Up through the chapel of my soul
And at the altar die,
And in the awful quiet then
Myself I heard, Amen, Amen,
Amen I heard me cry!
I heard it all and then although
I caught my flying senses, Oh,
A dizzy man was I!
I stood and stared; the sky was lit,
The sky was stars all over it,
I stood, I knew not why,
Without a wish, without a will,
I stood upon that silent hill
And stared into the sky until
My eyes were blind with stars, and still
I stared into the sky.

THE MYSTERY

He came and took me by the hand
  Up to a red rose tree,
He kept His meaning to Himself
  But gave a rose to me.

I did not pray Him to lay bare
  The mystery to me,
Enough the rose was Heaven to smell,
  And His own face to see.

STUPIDITY STREET

I saw with open eyes
Singing birds sweet
Sold in the shops
For the people to eat,
Sold in the shops of
Stupidity Street.

I saw in vision
The worm in the wheat,
And in the shops nothing
For people to eat;
Nothing for sale in
Stupidity Street.

THE BULL

See an old unhappy bull,
Sick in soul and body both,
Slouching in the undergrowth
Of the forest beautiful,
Banished from the herd he led,
Bulls and cows a thousand head.

Cranes and gaudy parrots go
Up and down the burning sky;
Tree-top cats purr drowsily
In the dim-day green below;
And troops of monkeys, nutting, some,
All disputing, go and come;

And things abominable sit
Picking offal buck or swine,
On the mess and over it
Burnished flies and beetles shine,
And spiders big as bladders lie
Under hemlocks ten foot high;

And a dotted serpent curled
Round and round and round a tree,
Yellowing its greenery,
Keeps a watch on all the world,
All the world and this old bull
In the forest beautiful.

Bravely by his fall he came:
One he led, a bull of blood
Newly come to lustihood,
Fought and put his prince to sname,
Snuffed and pawed the prostrate head
Tameless even while it bled.

There they left him, every one,
Left him there without a lick,
Left him for the birds to pick,
Left him there for carrion,
Vilely from their bosom cast
Wisdom, worth and love at last.

When the lion left his lair
And roared his beauty through the hills,
And the vultures pecked their quills
And flew into the middle air,
Then this prince no more to reign
Came to life and lived again.

He snuffed the herd in far retreat,
He saw the blood upon the ground,
And snuffed the burning airs around
Still with beevish odors sweet,
While the blood ran down his head
And his mouth ran slaver red.

Pity him, this fallen chief,
All his splendor, all his strength,
All his body's breadth and length
Dwindled down with shame and grief,
Half the bull he was before,
Bones and leather, nothing more.

See him standing dewlap-deep
In the rushes at the lake,
Surly, stupid, half asleep,
Waiting for his heart to break
And the birds to join the flies
Feasting at his bloodshot eyes;

Standing with his head hung down
In a stupor, dreaming things:
Green savannas, jungles brown,
Battlefields and bellowings,
Bulls undone and lions dead
And vultures flapping overhead.

Dreaming things: of days he spent
With his mother gaunt and lean
In the valley warm and green,
Full of baby wonderment,
Blinking out of silly eyes
At a hundred mysteries;

Dreaming over once again
How he wandered with a throng
Of bulls and cows a thousand strong,
Wandered on from plain to plain,
Up the hill and down the dale,
Always at his mother's tail;

How he lagged behind the herd,
Lagged and tottered, weak of limb,
And she turned and ran to him
Blaring at the loathly bird
Stationed always in the skies,
Waiting for the flesh that dies.

Dreaming maybe of a day
When her drained and drying paps
Turned him to the sweets and saps,
Richer fountains by the way,
And she left the bull she bore
And he looked to her no more;

And his little frame grew stout,
And his little legs grew strong,
And the way was not so long;
And his little horns came out,
And he played at butting trees
And boulder-stones and tortoises,

Joined a game of knobby skulls
With the youngsters of his year,
All the other little bulls,
Learning both to bruise and bear,
Learning how to stand a shock
Like a little bull of rock.

Dreaming of a day less dim,
Dreaming of a time less far,
When the faint but certain star
Of destiny burned clear for him,
And a fierce and wild unrest
Broke the quiet of his breast,

And the gristles of his youth
Hardened in his comely pow,
And he came to fighting growth,
Beat his bull and won his cow,
And flew his tail and trampled off
Past the tallest, vain enough,

And curved about in splendor full
And curved again and snuffed the airs
As who should say, Come out who dares!
And all beheld a bull, a Bull,
And knew that here was surely one
That backed for no bull, fearing none,

And the leader of the herd
Looked and saw, and beat the ground,
And shook the forest with his sound,
Bellowed at the loathly bird
Stationed always in the skies,
Waiting for the flesh that dies.

Dreaming, this old bull forlorn,
Surely dreaming of the hour
When he came to sultan power,
And they owned him master-horn,
Chiefest bull of all among
Bulls and cows a thousand strong;

And in all the tramping herd
Not a bull that barred his way,
Not a cow that said him nay,
Not a bull or cow that erred
In the furnace of his look
Dared a second, worse rebuke;

Not in all the forest wide,
Jungle, thicket, pasture, fen,
Not another dared him then,
Dared him and again defied;
Not a sovereign buck or boar
Came a second time for more;

Not a serpent that survived
Once the terrors of his hoof
Risked a second time reproof,
Came a second time and lived,
Not a serpent in its skin
Came again for discipline;

Not a leopard bright as flame,
Flashing fingerhooks of steel,
That a wooden tree might feel,
Met his fury once and came
For a second reprimand,
Not a leopard in the land;

Not a lion of them all,
Not a lion of the hills,
Hero of a thousand kills,
Dared a second fight and fall,
Dared that ram terrific twice,
Paid a second time the price.

Pity him, this dupe of dream,
Leader of the herd again
Only in his daft old brain,
Once again the bull supreme
And bull enough to bear the part
Only in his tameless heart.

Pity him that he must wake;
Even now the swarm of flies
Blackening his bloodshot eyes
Bursts and blusters round the lake,
Scattered from the feast half-fed,
By great shadows overhead;

And the dreamer turns away
From his visionary herds
And his splendid yesterday,
Turns to meet the loathly birds
Flocking round him from the skies,
Waiting for the flesh that dies.

THE BELLS OF HEAVEN

'Twould ring the bells of Heaven
The wildest peal for years,
If Parson lost his senses
And people came to theirs,
And he and they together
Knelt down with angry prayers
For tamed and shabby tigers
And dancing dogs and bears,
And wretched, blind pit ponies,
And little hunted hares.

THE SWALLOW

The morning that my baby came
They found a baby swallow dead,
And saw a something, hard to name,
Flit moth-like over baby's bed.

My joy, my flower, my baby dear
Sleeps on my bosom well, but Oh!
If in the autumn of the year
When swallows gather round and go—

THE HOUSE ACROSS THE WAY

The leaves looked in at the window
Of the house across the way,
At a man that had sinned like you and me
And all poor human clay.

He muttered: "In a gambol
I took my soul astray,
But to-morrow I'll drag it back from danger,
In the morning, come what may;
For no man knows what season
He shall go his ghostly way."
And his face fell down upon the table,
And where it fell it lay.

And the wind blew under the carpet,
And it said, or it seemed to say:
"Truly, all men must go a-ghosting
And no man knows his day."
And the leaves stared in at the window
Like the people at a play.

THE NIGHT

Fond muse surrender, weary as thou art,
To sleep at last; a meadow's breadth from thee,
In yon dim copse and still, a sister heart
Hath respite from its old sweet agony.

The wall of night is up; around, across,
Above nor sound nor sense of day remains;
Comes only now the fitful drive and toss
Of moths upon the yellow window-panes.

AFTER

"How fared you when you mortal were?
  What did you see on my peopled star?"
"Oh, well enough," I answered her,
  "It went for me where mortals are!

"I saw blue flowers and the merlin's flight
  And the rime on the wintry tree,
Blue doves I saw and summer light
  On the wings of the cinnamon bee."

WALTER DE LA MARE

Walter John de la Mare was born April 25, 1873, in Charlton, a village on the coast of Kent. His father, James Edward Delamare, was a church-warden, and a brother of the Rev. Abraham Delamare, rector of St. Thomas's, Woolwich; the family was of Huguenot descent, and had emigrated to England in 1730. His mother was Lucy Sophia, a daughter of Dr. Colin Arrot Browning, naval surgeon at Woolwich Dockyard, and a distant relative of Robert Browning.

At an early age Walter entered St. Paul's Cathedral Choir School, where he remained until Easter, 1890. There his talents were such that for a number of years he ranked in scholarship among the first three or four of his class, and during his last three terms was at the top. Shortly before leaving, he conceived the idea of a school magazine, and in September, 1889, with some of his classmates he founded *The Choristers' Journal.*

Upon reaching the age of seventeen, he left school, and accepting a clerkship, labored for eighteen years in the offices of the Anglo-American Oil Company. His duties there were not so arduous, however, as to prevent him from prosecuting his literary efforts outside, and in 1895 *The Sketch* carried a short story by him entitled *Kismet*. In the following year, through the kindly efforts of his brother-in-law, Roger Ingpen, then connected with *The Cornhill,* he gained access to that magazine, in which his next stories appeared. Meanwhile he was devoting part of his time to writing poetry, and in 1901 *Songs of Childhood,* a collection of his verse, appeared as his first published volume. Next came *Henry*

Brocken (1904), a novel, followed by *Poems* (1906), a further book of verse. For all of his work up to the publication of *Henry Brocken* he used the pseudonym Walter Ramal (which he made by spelling part of his name backwards).

Through the recommendation of Sir Henry Newbolt, the Asquith Government made him a grant from the Privy Purse of £100 a year, and in 1908 de la Mare felt able to resign from his clerkship in the statistics department of the Anglo-American Oil Company, and to occupy himself only with literary pursuits. For a while, however, he found it necessary to supplement his pension by reviewing books for such periodicals as *The Saturday Westminster, The Bookman,* and *The London Times Literary Supplement;* but in time he was able to escape even this sort of work, and for a number of years he has given his whole attention to his creative writing, with the result that he is one of the most prolific of contemporary men of letters. As early as 1910 he won recognition by receiving the Edmond de Polignac prize for his novel *The Return.* Subsequently he has written *Memoirs of a Midget* (1921), *The Riddle, and Other Stories* (1923), and other prose works, and has edited a volume of children's verse, *Come Hither! An Anthology for the Young of all Ages* (1923). To-day he is well established as a novelist, short story writer, and author of children's books. It is as a lyric poet, however, that he is best known, and it is probably upon his work as a poet that his reputation in the future will chiefly rest.

He married Constance Elfrida Ingpen, and has four children. He lives at Hill House, Taplow, Buckinghamshire.

OLD SUSAN

When Susan's work was done, she would sit,
With one fat guttering candle lit,
And window opened wide to win
The sweet night air to enter in.
There, with a thumb to keep her place,
She would read, with stern and wrinkled face,
Her mild eyes gliding very slow
Across the letters to and fro,
While wagged the guttering candle flame
In the wind that through the window came.
And sometimes in the silence she
Would mumble a sentence audibly,
Or shake her head as if to say,
"You silly souls, to act this way!"
And never a sound from night I would hear,
Unless some far-off cock crowed clear;
Or her old shuffling thumb should turn
Another page; and rapt and stern,
Through her great glasses bent on me,
She would glance into reality;
And shake her round old silvery head,
With—"You!—I thought you was in bed!"—
Only to tilt her book again,
And rooted in Romance remain.

MISS LOO

When thin-strewn memory I look through,
I see most clearly poor Miss Loo,
Her tabby cat, her cage of birds,
Her nose, her hair, her muffled words,

And how she would open her green eyes,
As if in some immense surprise,
Whenever as we sat at tea
She made some small remark to me.

'Tis always drowsy summer when
From out the past she comes again;
The westering sunshine in a pool
Floats in her parlor still and cool;
While the slim bird its lean wires shakes,
As into piercing song it breaks;
Till Peter's pale-green eyes ajar
Dream, wake; wake, dream, in one brief bar.
And I am sitting, dull and shy,
And she with gaze of vacancy,

And large hands folded on the tray,
Musing the afternoon away;
Her satin bosom heaving slow
With sighs that softly ebb and flow;
And her plain face in such dismay,
It seems unkind to look her way:
Until all cheerful back will come
Her gentle gleaming spirit home:
And one would think that poor Miss Loo
Asked nothing else, if she had you.

THE VEIL

I think and think; yet still I fail—
Why does this lady wear a veil?
Why thus elect to mask her face
Beneath that dainty web of lace?
The tip of a small nose I see,
And two red lips, set curiously
Like twin-born cherries on one stem,
And yet she has netted even them.
Her eyes, it's plain, survey with ease
Whatever to glance upon they please.
Yet, whether hazel, grey, or blue,

Or that even lovelier lilac hue,
I cannot guess: why—why deny
Such beauty to the passer-by?
Out of a bush a nightingale
May expound his song; beneath that veil
A happy mouth no doubt can make
English sound sweeter for its sake.
But then, why muffle in, like this,
What every blossomy wind would kiss?
Why in that little night disguise
A daybreak face, those starry eyes?

SILVER

Slowly, silently, now the moon
Walks the night in her silver shoon;
This way, and that, she peers, and sees
Silver fruit upon silver trees;
One by one the casements catch
Her beams beneath the silvery thatch;
Couched in his kennel, like a log,
With paws of silver sleeps the dog;
From their shadowy cote the white breasts peep
Of doves in a silver-feathered sleep;
A harvest mouse goes scampering by,
With silver claws, and silver eye;
And moveless fish in the water gleam,
By silver reeds in a silver stream.

THE LISTENERS

"Is there anybody there?" said the Traveller,
  Knocking on the moonlit door;
And his horse in the silence champed the grasses
  Of the forest's ferny floor:
And a bird flew up out of the turret,
  Above the Traveller's head:
And he smote upon the door again a second time;
  "Is there anybody there?" he said.

But no one descended to the Traveller;
  No head from the leaf-fringed sill
Leaned over and looked into his grey eyes,
  Where he stood perplexed and still.
But only a host of phantom listeners
  That dwelt in the lone house then
Stood listening in the quiet of the moonlight
  To that voice from the world of men:
Stood thronging the faint moonbeams on the dark stair,
  That goes down to the empty hall,
Hearkening in an air stirred and shaken
  By the lonely Traveller's call.
And he felt in his heart their strangeness,
  Their stillness answering his cry,
While his horse moved, cropping the dark turf,
  'Neath the starred and leafy sky;
For he suddenly smote on the door, even
  Louder, and lifted his head:—
"Tell them I came, and no one answered,
  That I kept my word," he said.
Never the least stir made the listeners,
  Though every word he spake
Fell echoing through the shadowiness of the still house
  From the one man left awake:
Ay, they heard his foot upon the stirrup,
  And the sound of iron on stone,
And how the silence surged softly backward,
  When the plunging hoofs were gone.

SAM'S THREE WISHES: *or* LIFE'S LITTLE WHIRLIGIG

"I'm thinking and thinking," said old Sam Shore,
" 'Twere somebody *knocking* I heard at the door."

From the clock popped the cuckoo and cuckooed out eight,
As there in his chair he wondering sate . . .
"There's no one I knows on would come so late,

A-clicking the latch of an empty house
With nobbut inside 'un but me and a mouse. . . .
Maybe a-waking in sleep I be,
And 'twere out of a dream came that tapping to me."
At length he cautiously rose, and went,
And with thumb upon latch awhile listening bent,
Then slowly drew open the door. And behold!
There stood a Fairy!—all green and gold,
Mantled up warm against dark and cold,
And smiling up into his candle shine,
Lips like wax, and cheeks like wine,
As saucy and winsome a thing to see
As are linden buds on a linden tree.

Stock-still in the doorway stood simple Sam,
A-ducking his head, with "Good-e'en to 'ee, Ma'am."

Dame Fairy she nods, and cries clear and sweet,
" 'Tis a *very* good-e'en, sir, when such folks meet.
I know thee, Sam; though thou wist not of me,
And I'm come in late gloaming to speak with thee;
Though my eyes do dazzle at glint of your rush,
All under this pretty green fuchsia bush."

Sam ducked once more, smiling simple and slow.
Like the warbling of birds her words did flow,
And she laughed, very merry, to see how true
Shone the old man's kindness his courtesy through.
And she nodded her head, and the stars on high
Sparkled down on her smallness from out of the sky.

"A friend is a friend, Sam, and wonderful pleasant,
And I'm come for old sake's sake to bring thee a present.
Three wishes, three wishes are thine, Sam Shore,
Just three wishes—and wish no more,
All for because, ruby-ripe to see,
The pixy-pears burn in yon hawthorn tree,
And your old milch cow, wheresoever she goes
Never crops over the fairy-knowes.
Ay, Sam, thou art old and thy house is lone,
But there's Potencies round thee, and here is one!"

Poor Sam, he stared: and the stars o'erhead
A shimmering light on the elm-tops shed.
Like rilling of water her voice rang sweet,
And the night-wind sighed at the sound of it.
He frowned—glanced back at the empty grate,
And shook very slowly his grey old pate:
"Three wishes, my dear! Why, I scarcely knows
Which be my crany and which my toes!
But I thank 'ee, Ma'am, kindly, and this I'd say,
That the night of your passing is Michaelmas Day;
And if it were company come on a sudden,
Why, I'd ax for a fat goose to fry in the oven!"

And lo, and forsooth! as the words he was uttering,
A rich puff of air set his candle a-guttering,
And there rose in the kitchen a sizzling and sputtering,
With a crackling of sparks and of flames a great fluttering,
And—of which here could not be two opinions—
A smoking-hot savor of sage and onions.
Beam, wall and flagstones the kitchen was lit,
Every dark corner and cranny of it
With the blaze from the hearthstone. Copper and brass
Winked back the winking of platter and glass.
And a wonderful squeaking of mice went up
At the smell of a Michaelmas supper to sup—
Unctuous odors that wreathed and swirled
Where'er frisked a whisker or mouse-tail twirled,
While out of the chimney up into the night
That ne'er-to-be-snuffed-too-much smoke took flight.

"That's one," says the Fairy, finger on thumb,
"So now, Mister Sam, there's but two to come!"
She leaned her head sidelong; she lifted her chin,
With a twinkling of eye from the radiance within.
Poor Sam stood astounded; he says, says he,
"I *wish* my old Mother was back with me,
For if there was one thing she couldn't refuse
'Twas a sweet thick slice from the breast of a goose."
But his cheek grew stiff and his eyes stared bright,

For there, on her stick, pushing out of the night,
Tap-tapping along, herself and no other,
Came who but the shape of his dear old Mother!
Straight into the kitchen she hastened and went,
Her breath coming quick as if all but spent.
"Why, Sam," says she, "the bird be turning,
For my nose tells I that the skin's a-burning!"
And down at the oven the ghost of her sat
And basted the goose with the boiling fat.

"Oho," cries the Fairy, sweet and small,
"Another wish gone will leave nothing at all."
And Sam sighs, "Bless 'ee, Ma'am, keep the other,
There's nowt that I want now I have my Mother."
But the Fairy laughs softly, and says, says she,
"There's one wish left, Sam, I promised 'ee three.
Hasten your wits, the hour creeps on,
There's calling afield and I'm soon to be gone.
Soon as haps midnight the cocks will crow
And me to the gathering and feasting must go."

Sam gazed at his Mother—withered and wan,
The rose in her cheek, her bright hair, gone,
And her poor old back bent double with years—
And he scarce could speak for the salt, salt tears.
"Well, well," he says, "I'm unspeakable glad:
But—it bain't quite the same as when I was a lad.
There's joy and there's joy, Ma'am, but to tell 'ee the truth
There's none can compare with the joy of one's youth.
And if it was possible, how could I choose
But be back in boy's breeches to eat the goose;
And all the old things—and my Mother the most,
To shine again real as my own gatepost.
What wouldn't I give, too, to see again wag
The dumpity tail of my old dog, Shag!
Your kindness, Ma'am, but all wishing was vain
Unless us can both be young again."
A shrill, faint laughter from nowhere came . . .
Empty the dark in the candle-flame. . . .

And there stood our Sam, about four foot high,
Snub nose, shock hair, and round blue eye.
Breeches and braces and coat of him too,
Shirt on his back, and each clodhopping shoe
Had shrunk to a nicety—button and hem
To fit the small Sammie tucked up into them.

There was his Mother, too; smooth, clear cheek,
Lips as sooth as a blackbird's beak,
Pretty arched eyebrows, the daintiest nose—
While the smoke of the baking deliciously rose.

"Come, Sammie," she cries, "your old Mammikin's joy,
Climb up on your stool, supper's ready, my boy.
Bring in the candle, and shut out the night;
There's goose, baked taties and cabbage to bite.
Why, bless the wee lamb, he's all shiver and shake,
And you'd think from the look of him scarcely awake!
If 'ee glour wi' those eyes, Sam, so dark and round,
The elves will away with 'ee, I'll be bound!"
So Sam and his Mother by wishes three
Were made just as happy as happy can be.
And there—with a bumpity tail to wag—
Sat laughing, with tongue out, their old dog, Shag.
To clatter of platter, bones, giblets and juice,
Between them they ate up the whole of the goose.

But time is a river for ever in flow,
The weeks went by as the weeks must go.
Soon fifty-two to a year did grow.
The long years passed, one after another,
Making older and older our Sam and his Mother;
And, alas and alack, with nine of them gone,
Poor Shag lay asleep again under a stone.
And a sorrowful dread would sometimes creep
Into Sam's dreams, as he lay asleep,
That his Mother was lost, and away he'd fare,
Calling her, calling her, everywhere,
In dark, in rain, by roads unknown,

Under echoing hills, and alone, alone.
What bliss in the morning to wake and see
The sun shining green in the linden tree,
And out of that dream's dark shadowiness
To slip in on his Mother and give her a kiss,
Then go whistling off in the dew to hear
The thrushes all mocking him, sweet and clear.

Still, moon after moon from heaven above
Shone on Mother and son, and made light of love.
Her roses faded, her pretty brown hair
Had sorrowful grey in it everywhere.
And at last she died, and was laid to rest,
Her tired hands crossed on her shrunken breast.
And Sam, now lonely, lived on and on
Till most of his workaday life seemed gone.

Yet spring came again with its green and blue,
And presently summer's wild roses too.
Pinks, Sweet William, and sops-in-wine,
Blackberry, lavender, eglantine.
And when these had blossomed and gone their way,
'Twas apples, and daisies and Michaelmas Day—
Yes, spider-webs, dew, and haws in the may,
And seraphs singing in Michaelmas Day.

Sam worked all morning and *couldn't* get rest
For a kind of a feeling of grief in his breast.
And yet, not grief, but something more
Like the thought that what happens has happened before.
He fed the chickens, he fed the sow,
On a three-legged stool sate down to the cow,
With a pail 'twixt his legs in the green in the meadow,
Under the elm trees' lengthening shadow;
And woke at last with a smile and a sigh
To find he had milked his poor Jingo dry.

As dusk set in, even the birds did seem
To be calling and calling from out of a dream.
He chopped up kindling, shut up his shed,
In a bucket of well-water soused his head

To freshen his eyes up a little and make
The drowsy old wits of him wider awake.
As neat as a womanless creature is able
He swept up his hearthstone and laid the table.
And then o'er his platter and mug, if you please,
Sate gloomily gooming at loaf and cheese—
Gooming and gooming as if the mere sight
Of his victuals could satisfy appetite!
And the longer and longer he looked at them
The slimmer slimmed upward his candle flame,
Blue in the air. And when squeaked a mouse
'Twas loud as a trump in the hush of the house.
Then, sudden, a soft little wind puffed by,
'Twixt the thick-thatched roof and the star-sown sky;
And died. And then
That deep, dead, wonderful silence again.

Then—soft as a rattle a-counting her seeds
In the midst of a tangle of withered-up weeds—
Came a faint, faint knocking, a rustle like silk,
And a breath at the keyhole as soft as milk—
Still as the flit of a moth. And then . . .
That infinitesimal knocking again.

Sam lifted his chin from his fists. He listened.
His wandering eyes in the candle glistened,
Then slowly, slowly, rolled round by degrees—
And there sat a mouse on the top of his cheese.
He stared at this Midget, and it at him,
Over the edge of his mug's round rim,
And—as if it were Christian—he says, "Did 'ee hear
A faint little tap-tap-tap-tapping, my dear?
You was at supper and me in a maze;
'Tis dark for a caller in these lone days;
There's nowt in the larder. We're both of us old.
And all of my loved ones sleep under the mould,
And yet—and yet—as I've told 'ee before . . ."

But if Sam's story you'd read to the end,
Turn back to page 1, and press onward, dear friend;

Yes, if you would stave the last note of this song,
Turn back to page primus, and warble along!
For all sober records of life (come to write 'em),
Are bound to continue—well—ad infinitum!

THE TRUANTS

Ere my heart beats too coldly and faintly
To remember sad things, yet be gay,
I would sing a brief song of the world's little children
Magic hath stolen away.

The primroses scattered by April,
The stars of the wide Milky Way,
Cannot outnumber the hosts of the children
Magic hath stolen away.

The buttercup green of the meadows,
The snow of the blossoming may,
Lovelier are not than the legions of children
Magic hath stolen away.

The waves tossing surf in the moonbeam,
The albatross lone on the spray,
Alone know the tears wept in vain for the children
Magic hath stolen away.

In vain: for at hush of the evening
When the stars twinkle into the grey,
Seems to echo the far-away calling of children
Magic hath stolen away.

THE SONG OF SHADOWS

Sweep thy faint strings, Musician,
With thy long lean hand;
Downward the starry tapers burn,
Sinks soft the waning sand;

The old hound whimpers couched in sleep,
The embers smolder low;
Across the walls the shadows
Come, and go.

Sweep softly thy strings, Musician,
The minutes mount to hours;
Frost on the windless casement weaves
A labyrinth of flowers;
Ghosts linger in the darkening air,
Hearken at the open door;
Music hath called them, dreaming,
Home once more.

JOHN MASEFIELD

John Masefield was born on June 1, 1878, in Ledbury, Herefordshire. His parents died while he was a child, and he and the other Masefield children were reared by an aunt, who lived in Ledbury. Here he attended school for a few years, learning to like Scott and Macaulay, and writing poetry in imitation of Macaulay's *Lays of Ancient Rome*. He preferred tramping the countryside to studying, however, and as a curb to his tendency to wander was indentured at the age of fourteen to the captain of the *Conway*, a merchant ship. For the next three years he served before the mast, visiting many countries, and learning thoroughly the ways of the sea and of seamen. Wishing for a literary career, but failing as a sailor to find time for reading and writing, he quit the service, and in April, 1895, turned up in New York, with five dollars in his pocket. He found a tiny room in Greenwich Village, and for a while earned his living at a number of rough jobs—at work in a bakery, at a livery stable, as assistant to the barkeeper in a saloon at the Columbia Hotel, and then for two years in a carpet factory in Yonkers. While working in the latter place he lived at 8 Maple Street. It was his custom on each Friday, which was pay-day at the factory, to buy a book of poetry at East's Book Shop, and to read it during the week-end. One day in 1896 he took home a volume of Chaucer, and on a Sunday afternoon read *The Parlement of Foules;* this gave him such delight that he began to read with "passion and system," to use his own terms. Next he read Keats, Shelley, Milton, and Shakespeare, each of whom in turn he imitated with poems of his own. In 1897 he returned to England, settled near London, and began his career as a writer.

In 1902 he published his first volume, *Salt Water Ballads.* This brought him to the notice of literary men. He met Synge, and spent a summer in Devonshire with William Butler Yeats, who encouraged him to continue his writing. Except for the reissue of some of his "Salt Water Ballads," his next books were prose, *A Mainsail Haul* (1905), a collection of sea tales; and *Sea Life in Nelson's Time* (1905). He followed these with two novels, *Captain Margaret* (1908) and *Multitude and Solitude* (1909), and several stories of adventure. Meantime he had begun to experiment in the drama, and next published *The Tragedy of Nan* (1909) and *The Tragedy of Pompey the Great* (1910), besides several one-act plays. His first great success, however, came in 1911 with the publication in *The English Review* of *The Everlasting Mercy,* his first long narrative poem. After this he wrote in rapid succession several other long narrative poems, *The Widow in the Bye Street* (1912), *Dauber* (1913), and *The Daffodil Fields* (1913); and in recent years has added to this list *Reynard the Fox* (1919), *Right Royal* (1920), *King Cole* (1921), and two or three others less successful. Interspersed among these are several volumes of lyrics, a number of other plays, some prose works dealing with the war—*Gallipoli* (1916) and *The Old Front Line* (1917) among others—and further novels and stories.

During the World War, Masefield served with the Red Cross in France and on the Gallipoli peninsula, and was appointed by General Haig historian of the Somme. He came to America in 1916, fresh from his experiences in the Dardanelles, and traveled as far as the Pacific coast, lecturing and reading his poetry, and in 1918 lectured in this country on the war.

In 1912 the Academic Committee of the Royal Society of Literature awarded him the Edmond de Polignac prize for poetry, and in November, 1913, elected him a member of the Academic Committee. He has been given the D.Litt. degree by Oxford (1922), and the LL.D. degree by St. Andrews (1922). In 1903 he married Constance de la Cherois-Crommelin, whose father was from Cushendun, County Antrim, Ireland. He has one son and one daughter, and lives at Boar's Hill, near Oxford.

A CONSECRATION

Not of the princes and prelates with periwigged charioteers
Riding triumphantly laurelled to lap the fat of the years,—
Rather the scorned—the rejected—the men hemmed in with the spears;

The men of the tattered battalion which fights till it dies,
Dazed with the dust of the battle, the din and the cries,
The men with the broken heads and the blood running into their eyes.

Not the be-medalled Commander, beloved of the throne,
Riding cock-horse to parade when the bugles are blown,
But the lads who carried the koppie and cannot be known.

Not the ruler for me, but the ranker, the tramp of the road,
The slave with the sack on his shoulders pricked on with the goad,
The man with too weighty a burden, too weary a load.

The sailor, the stoker of steamers, the man with the clout,
The chantyman bent at the halliards putting a tune to the shout,
The drowsy man at the wheel and the tired lookout.

Others may sing of the wine and the wealth and the mirth,
The portly presence of potentates goodly in girth;—
Mine be the dirt and the dross, the dust and scum of the earth!

THEIRS be the music, the color, the glory, the gold;
Mine be a handful of ashes, a mouthful of mold.
Of the maimed, of the halt and the blind in the rain and the cold—
Of these shall my songs be fashioned, my tales be told.

SEA-FEVER

I must go down to the seas again, to the lonely sea and the sky,
And all I ask is a tall ship and a star to steer her by,
And the wheel's kick and the wind's song and the white sail's shaking,
And a grey mist on the sea's face and a grey dawn breaking.

I must go down to the seas again, for the call of the running tide
Is a wild call and a clear call that may not be denied;
And all I ask is a windy day with the white clouds flying,
And the flung spray and the blown spume, and the sea-gulls crying.

I must go down to the seas again to the vagrant gypsy life,
To the gull's way and the whale's way where the wind's like a whetted knife;
And all I ask is a merry yarn from a laughing fellow-rover,
And quiet sleep and a sweet dream when the long trick's over.

THE WEST WIND

It's a warm wind, the west wind, full of birds' cries;
I never hear the west wind but tears are in my eyes.
For it comes from the west lands, the old brown hills,
And April's in the west wind, and daffodils.

It's a fine land, the west land, for hearts as tired as mine;
Apple orchards blossom there, and the air's like wine.
There is cool green grass there, where men may lie at rest,
And the thrushes are in song there, fluting from the nest.

"Will you not come home, brother? you have been long away,
It's April, and blossom time, and white is the spray;
And bright is the sun, brother, and warm is the rain,—
Will you not come home, brother, home to us again?

"The young corn is green, brother, where the rabbits run,
It's blue sky, and white clouds, and warm rain and sun.
It's song to a man's soul, brother, fire to a man's brain,
To hear the wild bees and see the merry spring again.

"Larks are singing in the west, brother, above the green
wheat,
So will you not come home, brother, and rest your tired feet?
I've a balm for bruised hearts, brother, sleep for aching eyes,"
Says the warm wind, the west wind, full of birds' cries.

It's the white road westwards is the road I must tread
To the green grass, the cool grass, and rest for heart and head,
To the violets and the brown brooks and the thrushes' song,
In the fine land, the west land, the land where I belong.

"ALL YE THAT PASS BY"

On the long dusty ribbon of the long city street,
The pageant of life is passing me on multitudinous feet,
With a word here of the hills, and a song there of the sea,
And—the great movement changes—the pageant passes me.

Faces—passionate faces—of men I may not know,
They haunt me, burn me to the heart, as I turn aside to go:
The king's face and the cur's face, and the face of the stuffed
swine,
They are passing, they are passing, their eyes look into mine.

I never can tire of the music of the noise of many feet,
The thrill of the blood pulsing, the tick of the heart's beat,
Of the men many as sands, of the squadrons ranked and
massed
Who are passing, changing always, and never have changed
or passed.

BIOGRAPHY

When I am buried, all my thoughts and acts
Will be reduced to lists of dates and facts,
And long before this wandering flesh is rotten
The dates which made me will be all forgotten;
And none will know the gleam there used to be
About the feast days freshly kept by me,
But men will call the golden hour of bliss
"About this time," or "shortly after this."

Men do not heed the rungs by which men climb
Those glittering steps, those milestones upon Time,
Those tombstones of dead selves, those hours of birth,
Those moments of the soul in years of earth;
They mark the height achieved, the main result,
The power of freedom in the perished cult,
The power of boredom in the dead man's deeds,
Not the bright moments of the sprinkled seeds.

By many waters and on many ways
I have known golden instants and bright days;
The day on which, beneath an arching sail,
I saw the Cordilleras and gave hail;
The summer day on which in heart's delight
I saw the Swansea Mumbles bursting white,
The glittering day when all the waves wore flags
And the ship *Wanderer* came with sails in rags;
That curlew-calling time in Irish dusk
When life became more splendid than its husk,

When the rent chapel on the brae at Slains
Shone with a doorway opening beyond brains;
The dawn when, with a brace-block's creaking cry,
Out of the mist a little barque slipped by,
Spilling the mist with changing gleams of red,
Then gone, with one raised hand and one turned head;
The howling evening when the spindrift's mists
Broke to display the four Evangelists,

Snow-capped, divinely granite, lashed by breakers,
Wind-beaten bones of long since buried acres;
The night alone near water when I heard
All the sea's spirit spoken by a bird;
The English dusk when I beheld once more
(With eyes so changed) the ship, the citied shore,
The lines of masts, the streets so cheerly trod
(In happier seasons) and gave thanks to God.
All had their beauty, their bright moments' gift,
Their something caught from Time, the ever-swift.

All of those gleams were golden; but life's hands
Have given more constant gifts in changing lands,
And when I count those gifts, I think them such
As no man's bounty could have bettered much:
The gift of country life, near hills and woods
Where happy waters sing in solitudes,
The gift of being near ships, of seeing each day
A city of ships with great ships under weigh,
The great street paved with water, filled with shipping,
And all the world's flags flying and seagulls dipping.

Yet when I am dust my penman may not know
Those water-trampling ships which made me glow,
But think my wonder mad and fail to find
Their glory, even dimly, from my mind,
And yet they made me:

not alone the ships
But men hard-palmed from tallying-on to whips,
The two close friends of nearly twenty years,
Sea-followers both, sea-wrestlers and sea-peers,
Whose feet with mine wore many a bolt-head bright
Treading the decks beneath the riding light.
Yet death will make that warmth of friendship cold
And who'll know what one said and what one told
Our hearts' communion and the broken spells
When the loud call blew at the strike of bells?
No one, I know, yet let me be believed:
A soul entirely known is life achieved.

Years blank with hardship never speak a word
Live in the soul to make the being stirred,
Towns can be prisons where the spirit dulls
Away from mates and ocean-wandering hulls,
Away from all bright water and great hills
And sheep-walks where the curlews cry their fills,
Away in towns, where eyes have nought to see
But dead museums and miles of misery
And floating life unrooted from man's need
And miles of fish-hooks baited to catch greed
And life made wretched out of human ken
And miles of shopping women served by men.
So, if the penman sums my London days,
Let him but say that there were holy ways,
Dull Bloomsbury streets of dull brick mansions old,
With stinking doors where women stood to scold,
And drunken waits at Christmas with their horn
Droning the news, in snow, that Christ was born;
And windy gas lamps and the wet roads shining
And that old carol of the midnight whining,
And that old room (above the noisy slum)
Where there was wine and fire and talk with some
Under strange pictures of the wakened soul
To whom this earth was but a burnt-out coal.

O Time, bring back those midnights and those friends,
Those glittering moments that a spirit lends
That all may be imagined from the flash,
The cloud-hid god-game through the lightning gash,
Those hours of stricken sparks from which men took
Light to send out to men in song or book.
Those friends who heard St. Pancras' bells strike two
Yet stayed until the barber's cockerel crew,
Talking of noble styles, the Frenchman's best,
The thought beyond great poets not expressed,
The glory of mood where human frailty failed,
The forts of human light not yet assailed,
Till the dim room had mind and seemed to brood,
Binding our wills to mental brotherhood,

Till we become a college, and each night
Was discipline and manhood and delight,
Till our farewells and winding down the stairs
At each grey dawn had meaning that Time spares
That we, so linked, should roam the whole world round,
Teaching the ways our brooding minds had found,
Making that room our Chapter, our one mind
Where all that this world soiled should be refined.

Often at night I tread those streets again
And see the alley glimmering in the rain,
Yet now I miss that sight of earlier tramps,
A house with shadows of plane-boughs under lamps,
The secret house where once a beggar stood
Trembling and blind to show his woe for food.
And now I miss that friend who used to walk
Home to my lodgings with me, deep in talk,
Wearing the last of night out in still streets
Trodden by us and policemen on their beats
And cats, but else deserted; now I miss
That lively mind and guttural laugh of his
And that strange way he had of making gleam,
Like something real, the art we used to dream.
London has been my prison; but my books
Hills and great waters, laboring men and brooks,
Ships and deep friendships and remembered days
Which even now set all my mind ablaze
As that June day when, in the red bricks' chinks,
I saw the old Roman ruins white with pinks
And felt the hillside haunted even then
By not dead memory of the Roman men;
And felt the hillside thronged by souls unseen
Who knew the interest in me and were keen
That man alive should understand man dead
So many centuries since the blood was shed;
And quickened with strange hush because this comer
Sensed a strange soul alive behind the summer:
That other day on Ercall when the stones
Were sunbleached white, like long unburied bones,

While the bees droned and all the air was sweet
From honey buried underneath my feet,
Honey of purple heather and white clover
Sealed in its gummy bags till summer's over:
Then other days by water, by bright sea,
Clear as clean glass, and my bright friend with me,
The cove clean bottomed where we saw the brown
Red spotted plaice go skimming six feet down,
And saw the long fronds waving, white with shells,
Waving, unfolding, drooping, to the swells:
That sadder day when we beheld the great
And terrible beauty of a Lammas spate
Roaring white-mouthed in all the great cliff's gaps
Headlong, tree-tumbling fury of collapse,
While drenching clouds drove by, and every sense
Was water roaring or rushing or in offence,
And mountain sheep stood huddled, and blown gaps gleamed
Where torn white hair of torrents shook and streamed:
That sadder day when we beheld again
A spate going down in sunshine after rain,
When the blue reach of water leaping bright
Was one long ripple and clatter, flecked with white:
And that far day, that never blotted page,
When youth was bright like flowers about old age,
Fair generations bringing thanks for life
To that old kindly man and trembling wife
After their sixty years: Time never made
A better beauty since the Earth was laid
Than that thanksgiving given to grey hair
For the great gift of life which brought them there.

Days of endeavor have been good: the days
Racing in cutters for the comrades' praise;
The day they led my cutter at the turn,
Yet could not keep the lead and dropped astern;
The moment in the spurt when both boats' oars
Dipped in each other's wash and throats grew hoarse
And teeth ground into teeth and both strokes quickened,

Lashing the sea, and gasps came, and hearts sickened,
And coxswains damned us, dancing, banking stroke,
To put our weights on, though our hearts were broke,
And both boats seemed to stick and sea seemed glue,
The tide a mill race we were struggling through,
And every quick recover gave us squints
Of them still there, and oar tossed water-glints;
And cheering came, our friends, our foemen cheering,
A long, wild, rallying murmur on the hearing—
"Port Fore!" and "Starboard Fore!" "Port Fore." "Port
Fore!"
"Up with her, Starboard," and at that each oar
Lightened, though arms were bursting, and eyes shut,
And the oak stretchers grunted in the strut,
And the curse quickened from the cox, our bows
Crashed, and drove talking water, we made vows,
Chastity vows and temperance; in our pain
We numbered things we'd never eat again
If we could only win; then came the yell,
"Starboard," "Port Fore," and then a beaten bell
Rung as for fire to cheer us. "Now." Oars bent;
Soul took the looms now body's bolt was spent,
"Damn it, come on now," "On now," "On now," "Star-
board."
"Port Fore." "Up with her, Port"; each cutter harbored
Ten eye-shut painsick strugglers, "Heave, oh, heave,"
Catcalls waked echoes like a shrieking sheave.
"Heave," and I saw a back, then two. "Port Fore."
"Starboard." "Come on." I saw the midship oar
And knew we had done them. "Port Fore." "Starboard."
"Now."
I saw bright water spurting at their bow,
Their cox' full face an instant. They were done.
The watcher's cheering almost drowned the gun.
We had hardly strength to toss our oars; our cry
Cheering the losing cutter was a sigh.

Other bright days of action have seemed great:
Wild days in a pampero off the Plate;

Good swimming days, at Hog Back or the Coves
Which the young gannet and the corbie loves;
Surf-swimming between rollers, catching breath
Between the advancing grave and breaking death,
Then shooting up into the sunbright smooth
To watch the advancing roller bare her tooth,
And days of labor also, loading, hauling;
Long days at winch or capstan, heaving, pawling;
The days with oxen, dragging stone from blasting,
And dusty days in mills, and hot days masting;
Trucking on dust-dry deckings smooth like ice,
And hunts in mighty wool-racks after mice;
Mornings with buckwheat when the fields did blanch
With White Leghorns come from the chicken ranch;
Days near the spring upon the sunburnt hill,
Plying the maul or gripping tight the drill;
Delights of work most real, delights that change
The headache life of towns to rapture strange
Not known by townsmen, nor imagined; health
That puts new glory upon mental wealth
And makes the poor man rich.
But that ends, too,
Health with its thoughts of life; and that bright view,
That sunny landscape from life's peak, that glory,
And all a glad man's comments on life's story
And thoughts of marvellous towns and living men
And what pens tell and all beyond the pen
End, and are summed in words so truly dead
They raise no image of the heart and head,
The life, the man alive, the friend we knew,
The mind ours argued with or listened to,
None but are dead, and all life's keenness, all,
Is dead as print before the funeral,
Even deader after, when the dates are sought,
And cold minds disagree with what we thought.
This many pictured world of many passions
Wears out the nations as a woman fashions,
And what life is is much to very few,
Men being so strange, so mad, and what men do

So good to watch or share; but when men count
Those hours of life that were a bursting fount,
Sparkling the dusty heart with living springs,
There seems a world, beyond our earthly things,
Gated by golden moments, each bright time
Opening to show the city white like lime,
High towered and many peopled. This made sure,
Work that obscures those moments seems impure,
Making our not-returning time of breath
Dull with the ritual and records of death,
That frost of fact by which our wisdom gives
Correctly stated death to all that lives.

Best trust the happy moments. What they gave
Makes man less fearful of the certain grave,
And gives his work compassion and new eyes.
The days that make us happy make us wise.

SPANISH WATERS

Spanish waters, Spanish waters, you are ringing in my ears,
Like a slow sweet piece of music from the grey forgotten years;
Telling tales, and beating tunes, and bringing weary thoughts to me
Of the sandy beach at Muertos, where I would that I could be.

There's a surf breaks on Los Muertos, and it never stops to roar,
And it's there we came to anchor, and it's there we went ashore,
Where the blue lagoon is silent amid snags of rotting trees,
Dropping like the clothes of corpses cast up by the seas.

We anchored at Los Muertos when the dripping sun was red,
We left her half-a-mile to sea, to west of Nigger Head;
And before the mist was on the Cay, before the day was done,
We were all ashore on Muertos with the gold that we had won.

We bore it through the marshes in a half-score battered chests,
Sinking, in the sucking quagmires, to the sunburn on our breasts,
Heaving over tree-trunks, gasping, damning at the flies and heat,
Longing for a long drink, out of silver, in the ship's cool lazareet.

The moon came white and ghostly as we laid the treasure down,
There was gear there'd make a beggarman as rich as Lima Town,
Copper charms and silver trinkets from the chests of Spanish crews,
Gold doubloons and double moydores, louis d'ors and portagues,

Clumsy yellow-metal earrings from the Indians of Brazil,
Uncut emeralds out of Rio, bezoar stones from Guayaquil;
Silver, in the crude and fashioned, pots of old Arica bronze,
Jewels from the bones of Incas desecrated by the Dons.

We smoothed the place with mattocks, and we took and blazed the tree,
Which marks yon where the gear is hid that none will ever see,
And we laid aboard the ship again, and south away we steers,
Through the loud surf of Los Muertos which is beating in my ears.

I'm the last alive that knows it. All the rest have gone their ways,
Killed, or died, or come to anchor in the old Mulatas Cays,
And I go singing, fiddling, old and starved and in despair,
And I know where all that gold is hid, if I were only there.

It's not the way to end it all. I'm old, and nearly blind,
And an old man's past's a strange thing, for it never leaves his mind.

And I see in dreams, awhiles, the beach, the sun's disc dipping red,
And the tall ship, under topsails, swaying in past Nigger Head.

I'd be glad to step ashore there. Glad to take a pick and go
To the lone blazed coco-palm tree in the place no others know,
And lift the gold and silver that has moldered there for years
By the loud surf of Los Muertos which is beating in my ears.

CARGOES

Quinquireme of Nineveh from distant Ophir,
Rowing home to haven in sunny Palestine,
With a cargo of ivory,
And apes and peacocks,
Sandalwood, cedarwood, and sweet white wine.

Stately Spanish galleon coming from the Isthmus,
Dipping through the Tropics by the palm-green shores,
With a cargo of diamonds,
Emeralds, amethysts,
Topazes, and cinnamon, and gold moidores.

Dirty British coaster with a salt-caked smoke stack,
Butting through the Channel in the mad March days,
With a cargo of Tyne coal,
Road-rails, pig-lead,
Firewood, iron-ware, and cheap tin trays.

LONDON TOWN

Oh, London Town's a fine town, and London sights are rare,
And London ale is right ale, and brisk's the London air,
And busily goes the world there, but crafty grows the mind,
And London Town of all towns I'm glad to leave behind.

Then hey for croft and hop-yard, and hill, and field, and
pond,
With Bredon Hill before me and Malvern Hill beyond.
The hawthorn white i' the hedgerow, and all the spring's
attire
In the comely land of Teme and Lugg, and Clent, and Clee,
and Wyre.

Oh, London girls are brave girls, in silk and cloth o' gold,
And London shops are rare shops where gallant things are
sold,
And bonnily clinks the gold there, but drowsily blinks the
eye,
And London Town of all towns I'm glad to hurry by.

Then hey for covert and woodland, and ash and elm and
oak,
Tewkesbury inns, and Malvern roofs, and Worcester chimney
smoke,
The apple trees in the orchard, the cattle in the byre,
And all the land from Ludlow town to Bredon church's
spire.

Oh, London tunes are new tunes, and London books are
wise,
And London plays are rare plays, and fine to country
eyes,
But wretchedly fare the most there and merrily fare the
few,
And London Town of all towns I'm glad to hurry through.

So hey for the road, the west road, by mill and forge and
fold,
Scent of the fern and song of the lark by brook, and field,
and wold,
To the comely folk at the hearth-stone and the talk beside
the fire,
In the hearty land, where I was bred, my land of heart's
desire.

C. L. M.

In the dark womb where I began
My mother's life made me a man.
Through all the months of human birth
Her beauty fed my common earth.
I cannot see, nor breathe, nor stir,
But through the death of some of her.

Down in the darkness of the grave
She cannot see the life she gave.
For all her love, she cannot tell
Whether I use it ill or well,
Nor knock at dusty doors to find
Her beauty dusty in the mind.

If the grave's gates could be undone,
She would not know her little son,
I am so grown. If we should meet
She would pass by me in the street,
Unless my soul's face let her see
My sense of what she did for me.

What have I done to keep in mind
My debt to her and womankind?
What woman's happier life repays
Her for those months of wretched days?
For all my mouthless body leeched
Ere Birth's releasing hell was reached?

What have I done, or tried, or said
In thanks to that dear woman dead?
Men triumph over women still,
Men trample women's rights at will,
And man's lust roves the world untamed.

* * * * * *

O grave, keep shut lest I be shamed.

"IF I COULD COME AGAIN TO THAT DEAR PLACE"

If I could come again to that dear place
Where once I came, where Beauty lived and moved,
Where, by the sea, I saw her face to face,
That soul alive by which the world has loved;
If, as I stood at gaze among the leaves,
She would appear again, as once before,
While the red herdsman gathered up his sheaves
And brimming waters trembled up the shore;
If, as I gazed, her Beauty that was dumb,
In that old time, before I learned to speak,
Would lean to me and revelation come,
Words to the lips and color to the cheek,
  Joy with its searing-iron would burn me wise,
  I should know all; all powers, all mysteries.

"THERE, ON THE DARKENED DEATHBED, DIES THE BRAIN"

There, on the darkened deathbed, dies the brain
That flared three several times in seventy years;
It cannot lift the silly hand again,
Nor speak, nor sing; it neither sees nor hears.
And muffled mourners put it in the ground
And then go home, and in the earth it lies,
Too dark for vision and too deep for sound,
The million cells that made a good man wise.
Yet for a few short years an influence stirs
A sense or wraith or essence of him dead,
Which makes insensate things its ministers
To those beloved, his spirit's daily bread;
  Then that, too, fades; in book or deed a spark
  Lingers, then that, too, fades; then all is dark.

"I NEVER SEE THE RED ROSE CROWN THE YEAR"

I never see the red rose crown the year,
Nor feel the young grass underneath my tread,
Without the thought, "This living beauty here
Is earth's remembrance of a beauty dead.
Surely where all this glory is displayed
Love has been quick, like fire, to high ends,
Here, in this grass, an altar has been made
For some white joy, some sacrifice of friends;
Here, where I stand, some leap of human brains
Has touched immortal things and left its trace,
The earth is happy here, the gleam remains;
Beauty is here, the spirit of the place,
    I touch the faith which nothing can destroy,
    The earth, the living church of ancient joy."

"THERE IS NO GOD, AS I WAS TAUGHT IN YOUTH"

There is no God, as I was taught in youth,
Though each, according to his stature, builds
Some covered shrine for what he thinks the truth,
Which day by day his reddest heart-blood gilds.
There is no God; but death, the clasping sea,
In which we move like fish, deep over deep
Made of men's souls that bodies have set free,
Floods to a Justice though it seems asleep.
There is no God, but still, behind the veil,
The hurt thing works, out of its agony.
Still, like a touching of a brimming Grail,
Return the pennies given to passers-by.
    There is no God, but we, who breathe the air,
    Are God ourselves and touch God everywhere.

THE LEMMINGS

Once in a hundred years the Lemmings come
Westward, in search of food, over the snow,
Westward, until the salt sea drowns them dumb,
Westward, till all are drowned, those Lemmings go.
Once, it is thought, there was a westward land,
(Now drowned) where there was food for those starved
things,
And memory of the place has burnt its brand
In the little brains of all the Lemming Kings.
Perhaps, long since, there was a land beyond
Westward from death, some city, some calm place,
Where one could taste God's quiet and be fond
With the little beauty of a human face;
But now the land is drowned, yet still we press
Westward, in search, to death, to nothingness.

ON GROWING OLD

Be with me, Beauty, for the fire is dying;
My dog and I are old, too old for roving;
Man, whose young passion sets the spindrift flying,
Is soon too lame to march, too cold for loving.
I take the book and gather to the fire,
Turning old yellow leaves; minute by minute,
The clock ticks to my heart; a withered wire
Moves a thin ghost of music in the spinet.
I cannot sail your seas, I cannot wander
Your cornland, nor your hill-land nor your valleys,
Ever again, nor share the battle yonder
Where the young knight the broken squadron rallies.
Only stay quiet while my mind remembers
The beauty of fire from the beauty of embers.

Beauty, have pity, for the strong have power,
The rich their wealth, the beautiful their grace,
Summer of man its sunlight and its flower,
Spring time of man all April in a face.

Only, as in the jostling in the Strand,
Where the mob thrusts or loiters or is loud
The beggar with the saucer in his hand
Asks only a penny from the passing crowd,
So, from this glittering world with all its fashion,
Its fire and play of men, its stir, its march,
Let me have wisdom, Beauty, wisdom and passion,
Bread to the soul, rain where the summers parch.
  Give me but these, and though the darkness close
  Even the night will blossom as the rose.

THE COUNTRYMEN

[*From* REYNARD THE FOX]

Ock Gurney and old Pete were there,
Riding their bonny cobs and swearing.
Ock's wife had giv'n them both a fairing,
A horse-rosette, red, white, and blue.
Their cheeks were brown as any brew,
And every comer to the meet
Said "Hello, Ock" or "Morning, Pete;
Be you a going to a wedding?"
"Why, noa," they said, "we'm going a bedding;
Now ben't us, uncle, ben't us, Ock?"
Pete Gurney was a lusty cock
Turned sixty-three, but bright and hale,
A dairy-farmer in the vale,
Much like a robin in the face,
Much character in little space,
With little eyes like burning coal.
His mouth was like a slit or hole
In leather that was seamed and lined.
He had the russet-apple mind
That betters as the weather worsen.
He was a manly English person,
Kind to the core, brave, merry, true;
One grief he had, a grief still new,

That former Parson joined with Squire
In putting down the Playing Quire,
In church, and putting organ in.
"Ah, boys, that was a pious din
That Quire was; a pious praise
The noise was that we used to raise;
I and my serpent, George with his'n,
On Easter Day in He is Risen,
Or blessed Christmas in Venite;
And how the trombone came in mighty,
In Alleluias from the heart—
Pious, for each man played his part,
Not like 'tis now." Thus he, still sore
For changes forty years before,
When all (that could) in time and tune,
Blew trumpets to the newë moon.
He was a bachelor, from choice.
He and his nephew farmed the Boyce,
Prime pasture land for thirty cows.
Ock's wife, Selina Jane, kept house,
And jolly were the three together.

Ock had a face like summer weather,
A broad red sun, split by a smile.
He mopped his forehead all the while,
And said "By damn," and "Ben't us, Unk?"
His eyes were close and deeply sunk.
He cursed his hunter like a lover,
"Now blast your soul, my dear, give over.
Woa, now, my pretty, damn your eyes."
Like Pete he was a middle size,
Dean-oak-like, stuggy, strong in shoulder,
He stood a wrestle like a boulder,
He had a back for pitching hay.
His singing voice was like a bay.
In talk he had a sideways spit,
Each minute, to refresh his wit.
He cracked Brazil nuts with his teeth.
He challenged Cobbett of the Heath

(Weight-lifting champion) once, but lost.
Hunting was what he loved the most,
Next to his wife and Uncle Pete.
With beer to drink and cheese to eat,
And rain in May to fill the grasses,
This life was not a dream that passes
To Ock, but like the summer flower.

From DAUBER

(SECTION VI)

All through the windless night the clipper rolled
In a great swell with oily gradual heaves
Which rolled her down until her time-bells tolled,
Clang, and the weltering water moaned like beeves.
The thundering rattle of slatting shook the sheaves,
Startles of water made the swing ports gush,
The sea was moaning and sighing and saying "Hush!"

It was all black and starless. Peering down
Into the water, trying to pierce the gloom,
One saw a dim, smooth, oily glitter of brown
Heaving and dying away and leaving room
For yet another. Like the march of doom
Came those great powers of marching silences;
Then fog came down, dead-cold, and hid the seas.

They set the Dauber to the foghorn. There
He stood upon the poop, making to sound
Out of the pump the sailor's nasal blare,
Listening lest ice should make the note resound.
She bayed there like a solitary hound
Lost in a covert; all the watch she bayed.
The fog, come closelier down, no answer made.

Denser it grew, until the ship was lost.
The elemental hid her; she was merged
In mufflings of dark death, like a man's ghost,
New to the change of death, yet thither urged.

Then from the hidden waters something surged—
Mournful, despairing, great, greater than speech,
A noise like one slow wave on a still beach.

Mournful, and then again mournful, and still
Out of the night that mighty voice arose;
The Dauber at his foghorn felt the thrill.
Who rode that desolate sea? What forms were those?
Mournful, from things defeated, in the throes
Of memory of some conquered hunting-ground,
Out of the night of death arose the sound.

"Whales!" said the Mate. They stayed there all night long
Answering the horn. Out of the night they spoke,
Defeated creatures who had suffered wrong,
But were still noble underneath the stroke.
They filled the darkness when the Dauber woke;
The men came peering to the rail to hear,
And the sea sighed, and the fog rose up sheer.

A wall of nothing at the world's last edge,
Where no life came except defeated life.
The Dauber felt shut in within a hedge,
Behind which form was hidden and thought was rife,
And that a blinding flash, a thrust, a knife
Would sweep the hedge away and make all plain,
Brilliant beyond all words, blinding the brain.

So the night passed, but then no morning broke—
Only a something showed that night was dead.
A sea-bird, cackling like a devil, spoke,
And the fog drew away and hung like lead.
Like mighty cliffs it shaped, sullen and red;
Like glowering gods at watch it did appear,
And sometimes drew away, and then drew near.

Like islands, and like chasms, and like hell,
But always mighty and red, gloomy and ruddy,
Shutting the visible sea in like a well;
Slow heaving in vast ripples, blank and muddy,

Where the sun should have risen it streaked bloody.
The day was still-born; all the sea-fowl scattering
Splashed the still water, mewing, hovering, clattering.

Then Polar snow came down little and light,
Till all the sky was hidden by the small,
Most multitudinous drift of dirty white
Tumbling and wavering down and covering all—
Covering the sky, the sea, the clipper tall,
Furring the ropes with white, casing the mast,
Coming on no known air, but blowing past.

And all the air seemed full of gradual moan,
As though in those cloud-chasms the horns were blowing
The mort for gods cast out and overthrown,
Or for the eyeless sun plucked out and going.
Slow the low gradual moan came in the snowing;
The Dauber felt the prelude had begun.
The snowstorm fluttered by; he saw the sun

Show and pass by, gleam from one towering prison
Into another, vaster and more grim,
Which in dull crags of darkness had arisen
To muffle-to a final door on him.
The gods upon the dull crags lowered dim,
The pigeons chattered, quarrelling in the track.
In the south-west the dimness dulled to black.

Then came the cry of "Call all hands on deck!"
The Dauber knew its meaning; it was come:
Cape Horn, that tramples beauty into wreck,
And crumples steel and smites the strong man dumb.
Down clattered flying kites and staysails: some
Sang out in quick, high calls: the fair-leads skirled,
And from the south-west came the end of the world.

"Caught in her ball-dress," said the Bosun, hauling;
"Lee-ay, lee-ay!" quick, high, come the men's call;
It was all wallop of sails and startled calling.
"Let fly!" "Let go!" "Clew up!" and "Let go all!"

"Now up and make them fast!" "Here, give us a haul!"
"Now up and stow them! Quick! By God! we're done!"
The blackness crunched all memory of the sun.

"Up!" said the Mate. "Mizen top-gallants. Hurry!"
The Dauber ran, the others ran, the sails
Slatted and shook; out of the black a flurry
Whirled in fine lines, tattering the edge to trails.
Painting and art and England were old tales
Told in some other life to that pale man,
Who struggled with white fear and gulped and ran.

He struck a ringbolt in his haste and fell—
Rose, sick with pain, half-lamed in his left knee;
He reached the shrouds where clambering men pell-mell
Hustled each other up and cursed him; he
Hurried aloft with them: then from the sea
Came a cold, sudden breath that made the hair
Stiff on the neck, as though Death whispered there.

A man below him punched him in the side.
"Get up, you Dauber, or let me get past."
He saw the belly of the skysail skied,
Gulped, and clutched tight, and tried to go more fast.
Sometimes he missed his ratline and was grassed,
Scraped his shin raw against the rigid line;
The clamberers reached the futtock-shrouds' incline.

Cursing they came; one, kicking out behind,
Kicked Dauber in the mouth, and one below
Punched at his calves; the futtock-shrouds inclined;
It was a perilous path for one to go.
"Up, Dauber, up!" A curse followed a blow.
He reached the top and gasped, then on, then on.
And one voice yelled "Let go!" and one "All gone!"

Fierce clamberers, some in oilskins, some in rags,
Hustling and hurrying up, up the steep stairs.
Before the windless sails were blown to flags,
And whirled like dirty birds athwart great airs,

Ten men in all, to get this mast of theirs
Snugged to the gale in time. "Up! Damn you, run!"
The mizen topmast head was safely won.

"Lay out!" the Bosun yelled. The Dauber laid
Out on the yard, gripping the yard and feeling
Sick at the mighty space of air displayed
Below his feet, where mewing birds were wheeling.
A giddy fear was on him; he was reeling.
He bit his lip half through, clutching the jack.
A cold sweat glued the shirt upon his back.

The yard was shaking, for a brace was loose.
He felt that he would fall; he clutched, he bent,
Clammy with natural terror to the shoes
While idiotic promptings came and went.
Snow fluttered on a wind-flaw and was spent;
He saw the water darken. Someone yelled,
"Frap it; don't stay to furl! Hold on!" He held.

Darkness came down—half darkness—in a whirl;
The sky went out, the waters disappeared.
He felt a shocking pressure of blowing hurl
The ship upon her side. The darkness speared
At her with wind; she staggered, she careered,
Then down she lay. The Dauber felt her go;
He saw his yard tilt downwards. Then the snow

Whirled all about—dense, multitudinous, cold—
Mixed with the wind's one devilish thrust and shriek,
Which whiffled out men's tears, deafened, took hold,
Flattening the flying drift against the cheek.
The yards buckled and bent, man could not speak.
The ship lay on her broadside; the wind's sound
Had devilish malice at having got her downed.

* * * * * *

How long the gale had blown he could not tell,
Only the world had changed, his life had died.
A moment now was everlasting hell.
Nature, an onslaught from the weather side,

A withering rush of death, a frost that cried,
Shrieked, till he withered at the heart; a hail
Plastered his oilskins with an icy mail.

"Cut!" yelled his mate. He looked—the sail was gone,
Blown into rags in the first furious squall;
The tatters drummed the devil's tattoo. On
The buckling yard a block thumped like a mall.
The ship lay—the sea smote her, the wind's bawl
Came, "loo, loo, loo!" The devil cried his hounds
On to the poor spent stag strayed in his bounds.

"Cut! Ease her!" yelled his mate; the Dauber heard,
His mate wormed up the tilted yard and slashed,
A rag of canvas skimmed like a darting bird.
The snow whirled, the ship bowed to it, the gear lashed,
The sea-tops were cut off and flung down smashed;
Tatters of shouts were flung, the rags of yells—
And clang, clang, clang, below beat the two bells.

"O God!" the Dauber moaned. A roaring rang,
Blasting the royals like a cannonade;
The backstays parted with a crackling clang,
The upper spars were snapped like twigs decayed—
Snapped at their heels, their jagged splinters splayed,
Like white and ghastly hairs erect with fear.
The Mate yelled, "Gone, by God, and pitched them clear!"

"Up!" yelled the Bosun; "up and clear the wreck!"
The Dauber followed where he led: below
He caught one giddy glimpsing of the deck
Filled with white water, as though heaped with snow.
He saw the streamers of the rigging blow
Straight out like pennons from the splintered mast,
Then, all sense dimmed, all was an icy blast,

Roaring from nether hell and filled with ice,
Roaring and crashing on the jerking stage,
An utter bridle given to utter vice,
Limitless power mad with endless rage

Withering the soul; a minute seemed an age.
He clutched and hacked at ropes, at rags of sail,
Thinking that comfort was a fairy-tale

Told long ago—long, long ago—long since
Heard of in other lives—imagined, dreamed—
There where the basest beggar was a prince
To him in torment where the tempest screamed.
Comfort and warmth and ease no longer seemed
Things that a man could know: soul, body, brain,
Knew nothing but the wind, the cold, the pain.

"Leave that!" the Bosun shouted; "Crojick save!"
The splitting crojick, not yet gone to rags,
Thundered below, beating till something gave,
Bellying between its buntlines into bags.
Some birds were blown past, shrieking: dark, like shags,
Their backs seemed, looking down. "Leu, leu!" they cried.
The ship lay, the seas thumped her; she had died.

They reached the crojick yard, which buckled, buckled
Like a thin whalebone to the topsail's strain.
They laid upon the yard and heaved and knuckled,
Pounding the sail, which jangled and leapt again.
It was quite hard with ice, its rope like chain,
Its strength like seven devils; it shook the mast.
They cursed and toiled and froze: a long time passed.

Two hours passed, then a dim lightening came.
Those frozen ones upon the yard could see
The mainsail and the foresail still the same,
Still battling with the hands and blowing free,
Rags tattered where the staysails used to be.
The lower topsails stood; the ship's lee deck
Seethed with four feet of water filled with wreck.

An hour more went by; the Dauber lost
All sense of hands and feet, all sense of all
But of a wind that cut him to the ghost,
And of a frozen fold he had to haul,

Of heavens that fell and never ceased to fall,
And ran in smoky snatches along the sea,
Leaping from crest to wave-crest, yelling. He

Lost sense of time; no bells went, but he felt
Ages go over him. At last, at last
They frapped the cringled crojick's icy pelt;
In frozen bulge and bunt they made it fast.
Then, scarcely live, they laid in to the mast.
The Captain's speaking trumpet gave a blare,
"Make fast the topsail, Mister, while you're there."

Some seamen cursed, but up they had to go—
Up to the topsail yard to spend an hour
Stowing a topsail in a blinding snow,
Which made the strongest man among them cower.
More men came up, the fresh hands gave them power,
They stowed the sail; then with a rattle of chain
One half the crojick burst its bonds again.

* * * * * *

They stowed the sail, frapping it round with rope,
Leaving no surface for the wind, no fold,
Then down the weather shrouds, half dead, they grope;
That struggle with the sail had made them old.
They wondered if the crojick furl would hold.
"Lucky," said one, "it didn't spring the spar."
"Lucky!" the Bosun said, "Lucky! We are!"

She came within two shakes of turning top
Or stripping all her shroud-screws, that first quiff.
"Now fish those wash-deck buckets out of the slop.
Here's Dauber says he doesn't like Cape Stiff.
This isn't wind, man, this is only a whiff.
Hold on, all hands, hold on!" a sea, half seen,
Paused, mounted, burst, and filled the main-deck green.

The Dauber felt a mountain of water fall.
It covered him deep, deep, he felt it fill,
Over his head, the deck, the fife-rails, all,
Quieting the ship; she trembled and lay still.

Then with a rush and shatter and clanging shrill
Over she went; he saw the water cream
Over the bitts; he saw the half-deck stream.

Then in the rush he swirled, over she went;
Her lee-rail dipped, he struck, and something gave;
His legs went through a port as the roll spent;
She paused, then rolled, and back the water drave.
He drifted with it as a part of the wave,
Drowning, half-stunned, exhausted, partly frozen,
He struck the booby hatchway; then the Bosun

Leaped, seeing his chance, before the next sea burst,
And caught him as he drifted, seized him, held,
Up-ended him against the bitts, and cursed.
"This ain't the George's Swimming Baths," he yelled;
"Keep on your feet!" Another grey-back felled
The two together, and the Bose, half-blind,
Spat: "One's a joke," he cursed, "but two's unkind."

"Now, damn it, Dauber!" said the Mate. "Look out,
Or you'll be over the side!" The water freed;
Each clanging freeing-port became a spout.
The men cleared up the decks as there was need.
The Dauber's head was cut, he felt it bleed
Into his oilskins as he clutched and coiled.
Water and sky were devil's brews which boiled,

Boiled, shrieked, and glowered; but the ship was saved.
Snugged safely down, though fourteen sails were split.
Out of the dark a fiercer fury raved.
The grey-backs died and mounted, each crest lit
With a white toppling gleam that hissed from it
And slid, or leaped, or ran with whirls of cloud,
Mad with inhuman life that shrieked aloud.

The watch was called; Dauber might go below.
"Splice the main brace!" the Mate called. All laid aft
To get a gulp of momentary glow
As some reward for having saved the craft.

The steward ladled mugs, from which each quaff'd
Whisky, with water, sugar, and lime-juice, hot,
A quarter of a pint each made the tot.

Beside the lamp-room door the steward stood
Ladling it out, and each man came in turn,
Tipped his sou'-wester, drank it, grunted "Good!"
And shambled forward, letting it slowly burn:
When all were gone the Dauber lagged astern,
Torn by his frozen body's lust for heat,
The liquor's pleasant smell, so warm, so sweet,

And by a promise long since made at home
Never to taste strong liquor. Now he knew
The worth of liquor; now he wanted some.
His frozen body urged him to the brew;
Yet it seemed wrong, an evil thing to do
To break that promise. "Dauber," said the Mate,
"Drink, and turn in, man; why the hell d'ye wait?"

"Please, sir, I'm temperance." "Temperance are you, hey?
That's all the more for me! So you're for slops?
I thought you'd had enough slops for to-day.
Go to your bunk and ease her when she drops.
And—damme, steward! you brew with too much hops!
Stir up the sugar, man!—and tell your girl
How kind the Mate was teaching you to furl."

Then the Mate drank the remnants, six men's share,
And ramped into his cabin, where he stripped
And danced unclad, and was uproarious there.
In waltzes with the cabin cat he tripped,
Singing in tenor clear that he was pipped—
That "he who strove the tempest to disarm,
Must never first embrail the lee yard-arm,"

And that his name was Ginger. Dauber crept
Back to the round-house, gripping by the rail.
The wind howled by; the passionate water leapt;
The night was all one roaring with the gale.

Then at the door he stopped, uttering a wail;
His hands were perished numb and blue as veins,
He could not turn the knob for both the Spains.

A hand came shuffling aft, dodging the seas,
Singing "her nut-brown hair" between his teeth;
Taking the ocean's tumult at his ease
Even when the wash about his thighs did seethe.
His soul was happy in its happy sheath;
"What, Dauber, won't it open? Fingers cold?
You'll talk of this time, Dauber, when you're old."

He flung the door half open, and a sea
Washed them both in, over the splashboard, down;
"You silly, salt miscarriage!" sputtered he.
"Dauber, pull out the plug before we drown!
That's spoiled my laces and my velvet gown.
Where is the plug?" Groping in pitch dark water,
He sang between his teeth "The Farmer's Daughter."

It was pitch dark within there; at each roll
The chests slid to the slant; the water rushed,
Making full many a clanging tin pan bowl
Into the black below-bunks as it gushed.
The dog-tired men slept through it; they were hushed.
The water drained, and then with matches damp
The man struck heads off till he lit the lamp.

"Thank you," the Dauber said; the seaman grinned.
"This is your first foul weather?" "Yes." "I thought
Up on the yard you hadn't seen much wind.
Them's rotten sea-boots, Dauber, that you brought.
Now I must cut on deck before I'm caught."
He went; the lamp-flame smoked; he slammed the door;
A film of water loitered across the floor.

The Dauber watched it come and watched it go;
He had had revelation of the lies
Cloaking the truth men never choose to know;
He could bear witness now and cleanse their eyes.

He had beheld in suffering; he was wise;
This was the sea, this searcher of the soul—
This never-dying shriek fresh from the Pole.

He shook with cold; his hands could not undo
His oilskin buttons, so he shook and sat,
Watching his dirty fingers, dirty blue,
Hearing without the hammering tackle slat;
Within, the drops from dripping clothes went pat,
Running in little patters, gentle, sweet,
And "Ai, ai!" went the wind, and the seas beat.

His bunk was sopping wet; he clambered in,
None of his clothes were dry: his fear recurred.
Cramps bunched the muscles underneath his skin.
The great ship rolled until the lamp was blurred.
He took his Bible and tried to read a word;
Trembled at going aloft again, and then
Resolved to fight it out and show it to men.

Faces recurred, fierce memories of the yard,
The frozen sail, the savage eyes, the jests,
The oaths of one great seaman, syphilis-scarred,
The tug of leeches jammed beneath their chests,
The buntlines bellying bunts out into breasts,
The deck so desolate-grey, the sky so wild.
He fell asleep, and slept like a young child.

But not for long; the cold awoke him soon,
The hot-ache and the skin-cracks and the cramp,
The seas thundering without, the gale's wild tune,
The sopping misery of the blankets damp.
A speaking-trumpet roared; a sea-boot's stamp
Clogged at the door. A man entered to shout:
"All hands on deck! Arouse here! Tumble out!"

The caller raised the lamp; his oilskins clicked
As the thin ice upon them cracked and fell.
"Rouse out!" he said. "This lamp is frozen wick'd.
Rouse out!" His accent deepened to a yell.

"We're among ice; it's blowing up like hell.
We're going to hand both topsails. Time, I guess,
We're sheeted up. Rouse out! Don't stay to dress!"

"Is it cold on deck?" said Dauber. "Is it cold?
We're sheeted up, I tell you, inches thick!
The fo'c'sle's like a wedding-cake, I'm told.
Now tumble out, my sons; on deck here, quick!
Rouse out, away, and come and climb the stick.
I'm going to call the half-deck. Bosun! Hey!
Both topsails coming in. Heave out! Away!"

He went; the Dauber tumbled from his bunk,
Clutching the side. He heard the wind go past,
Making the great ship wallow as if drunk.
There was a shocking tumult up the mast.
"This is the end," he muttered, "come at last!
I've got to go aloft, facing this cold.
I can't. I can't. I'll never keep my hold.

"I cannot face the topsail yard again.
I never guessed what misery it would be."
The cramps and hot-ache made him sick with pain.
The ship stopped suddenly from a devilish sea,
Then, with a triumph of wash, a rush of glee,
The door burst in, and in the water rolled,
Filling the lower bunks, black, creaming, cold.

The lamp sucked out. "Wash!" went the water back,
Then in again, flooding; the Bosun swore.
"You useless thing! You Dauber! You lee slack!
Get out, you heekapoota! Shut the door!
You coo-ilyaira, what are you waiting for?
Out of my way, you thing—you useless thing!"
He slammed the door indignant, clanging the ring.

And then he lit the lamp, drowned to the waist;
"Here's a fine house! Get at the scupper-holes"—
He bent against it as the water raced—
"And pull them out to leeward when she rolls.

They say some kinds of landsmen don't have souls.
I well believe. A Port Mahon baboon
Would make more soul then you got with a spoon."

Down in the icy water Dauber groped
To find the plug; the racing water sluiced
Over his head and shoulders as she sloped.
Without, judged by the sound, all hell was loosed.
He felt cold Death about him tightly noosed.
That Death was better than the misery there
Iced on the quaking foothold high in air.

And then the thought came: "I'm a failure. All
My life has been a failure. They were right.
It will not matter if I go and fall;
I should be free then from this hell's delight.
I'll never paint. Best let it end to-night.
I'll slip over the side. I've tried and failed."
So in the ice-cold in the night he quailed.

Death would be better, death, than this long hell
Of mockery and surrender and dismay—
This long defeat of doing nothing well,
Playing the part too high for him to play.
"O Death! who hides the sorry thing away,
Take me; I've failed. I cannot play these cards."
There came a thundering from the topsail yards.

And then he bit his lips, clenching his mind,
And staggered out to muster, beating back
The coward frozen self of him that whined.
Come what cards might he meant to play the pack.
"Ai!" screamed the wind; the topsail sheet went clack;
Ice filled the air with spikes; the grey-backs burst.
"Here's Dauber," said the Mate, "on deck the first.

"Why, holy sailor, Dauber, you're a man!
I took you for a soldier. Up now, come!"
Up on the yards already they began
That battle with the gale which strikes men dumb.

The leaping topsail thundered like a drum.
The frozen snow beat in the face like shots.
The wind spun whipping wave-crests into clots.

So up upon the topsail yard again,
In the great tempest's fiercest hour, began
Probation to the Dauber's soul, of pain
Which crowds a century's torment in a span.
For the next month the ocean taught this man,
And he, in that month's torment, while she wested,
Was never warm nor dry, nor full nor rested;

But still it blew, or, if it lulled, it rose
Within the hour and blew again; and still
The water as it burst aboard her froze.
The wind blew off an ice-field, raw and chill,
Daunting man's body, tampering with his will;
But after thirty days a ghostly sun
Gave sickly promise that the storms were done.

W. W. GIBSON

Wilfrid Wilson Gibson was born on October 2, 1878, in the ancient town of Hexham, Northumberland, where he lived until 1912. As a boy he attended private schools, and travelled occasionally. He early evinced an interest in poetry, and has been fortunate in being able to devote to it, almost without interruption, the best years of his life. His first important appearance in print was in *The Spectator* of September 4, 1897, which contains his poem *Blind*. In 1902 appeared his little volume *Urlyn the Harper and Other Song;* in the same year a second volume, *The Queen's Vigil and Other Song;* and in 1903 *The Golden Helm and Other Verse*. Since then he has continued steadily the writing of poetry, publishing more than twenty books.

In 1912 Gibson removed to London, but in the following year, after marrying, he went to reside in the country again, this time in the west of England. When the War began he volunteered for service, but was rejected four times. Later he accepted an invitation to visit the United States, and from January to July, 1917, gave readings of his poems in towns and cities over the country, making Chicago his headquarters for three months of that time. Returning to England, he once more offered himself to the military authorities, and in October, 1917, was accepted and assigned to the Army Service Corps. In this branch of the service he remained as a private until January, 1919. At present he lives in Hertfordshire.

"ALL LIFE MOVING TO ONE MEASURE"

All life moving to one measure—
Daily bread, daily bread—
Bread of life, and bread of labor,
Bread of bitterness and sorrow,
Hand-to-mouth, and no to-morrow,
Dearth for housemate, death for neighbor . . .

"Yet, when all the babes are fed,
Love, are there not crumbs to treasure?"

THE SCAR

Persons:

ABEL FORSTER, *a shepherd.*
MARGARET FORSTER, *his wife.*

Scene: *The Scar, a shepherd's cottage on the fells.* ABEL FORSTER *is seated with his back to the open door, gazing with unseeing eyes into a smoldering peat-fire, the dull glow from which is the only light in the room. The pendulum of the hanging-clock is silent and motionless, and the choral voice of the moorland-burn and the intermittent hunting-cry of the owl are the only sounds that break the frosty silence of the night. Presently, a step is heard on the threshold, and* MARGARET FORSTER *enters, wrapped in a shawl which covers the bundle she is carrying in her arms. As she sinks wearily into a chair by the door,* ABEL *looks up at her, uncertainly; then fixes his eyes again on the fire, from which he does not raise them while speaking.*

ABEL. So, you are back!
MARGARET. Yes, I am back.
ABEL. I knew,
Sooner or later, you would come again.
I have expected you these many nights,
But thought to see you sooner, lass.

MARGARET. And yet,
You could not know: I did not know myself;
And even at the door I almost turned.

ABEL. Yet, you are here.

MARGARET. Yes, I am here to-night;
But where the dawn shall find me I don't know.

ABEL. You would not go again! Lass, do you think
My door shall ever stand ajar for you
To come and go when it may please your whim?

MARGARET. No; if I go again, I don't come back.

ABEL. You shall not go.

MARGARET. Ah! have you not learned aught
From the long months that taught so much to me?

ABEL. Ay, lass, I have learned something. Do not leave me.
You, too, have learned, you say; and have come home.
Why go again into the world to starve
While there is food and shelter for you here?
But you will bide. We shall forget the past.
Let us forgive each other. . . .

MARGARET. I don't come
To crave forgiveness—nor would I forget.

ABEL. Why have you come then? Were you hunger-driven?
O lass, I hoped . . .

MARGARET. No, I don't come to beg;
Nor would I starve while I have hands to work.
I lacked nor food nor shelter since I left.

ABEL. Then, why have you returned?

MARGARET. I have come back
Because I am the mother of your son.

(She rises from her seat and throws back her shawl, revealing a baby at her breast.)

ABEL (*looking up*). My son! Ah, Margaret! Now I understand.
To think I didn't know!

MARGARET. The boy was born
A month ago.

ABEL. Your babe has brought you home.
You will not go again. You have come back
Because you could not quite forget!
MARGARET. I've come
Because the babe is yours. I would not keep
Your own from you; nor would I rob the child
Of home and father.
ABEL. Had you no other thought?
Had you forgotten in so brief a while
How we had loved, lass?
MARGARET. We knew naught of love.
ABEL. Did we not know love when we wedded?
MARGARET. No!
It was not love, but passion wedded us;
And passion parted us as easily.
ABEL. Ay, passion parted us. Yet, surely, love
Brings us again together. We were young
And hasty, maybe, when we wed; but, lass,
I have awaited these seven weary months
For your return; and with the sheep by day,
Or brooding every night beside the hearth,
I have thought long on many things. The months
Have brought me wisdom; and I love. I knew
You would return; for you, too, have found love.
MARGARET. Is this your wisdom? Little have you learned.
You are as hasty as the day we wed!
I, too, have brooded long on many things.
Maybe, my wisdom is no more than yours,
But only time will tell. Who knows! I've lived
And labored in the city these long months;
And though I found friends even there, and folk
Were good to me; and, when the boy was born,
A neighbor tended me—yet, to my heart,
The city was a solitude; I lived
Alone in all that teeming throng of folk.
Yet, I was not afraid to be alone;
Nor, in my loneliness, did I regret
That we had parted; for the solitude

Revealed so much that else I had not learned
Of my own heart to me. But, when, at length
I knew another life within me stirred,
My thoughts turned homewards to the hills; it seemed
So pitiful that a baby should be born
Amid that stifling squalor. As I watched
The little children, starved and pinched and white,
Already old in evil ere their time,
Who swarmed in those foul alleys, and who played
In every gutter of the reeking courts,
I vowed no child of mine should draw its breath
In that dark city, by our waywardness
Robbed of the air and sun, ay, and the hills,
And the wide playground of the windy heath:
And yet, I lingered till the boy was born.
But, as he nestled at my breast, he drew
The angry pride from me; and as I looked
Upon him I remembered you. He brought
Me understanding; and his wide, blue eyes
Told me that he was yours; and, while he slept,
I often lay awake and thought of you;
And wondered what life held for this wee babe.
And sometimes in the night . . .

ABEL. Have you, too, known
The long night-watches? Since you went away,
Each morning, as I left the lonely house,
My heart said: surely she will come to-day;
And when each evening I returned from work,
I looked to meet you on the threshold; yet,
By night alone within the silent house
I longed for you the sorest. Through lone hours
My heart has listened for your step, until
I trembled at the noises of the night.
I am no craven, yet the moor-owl's shriek
At midnight, or the barking of a fox,
Or even the drumming of the snipe ere dawn
Has set me quaking. Ay, night long, for you
The door was left ajar. And, hour by hour,
I've listened to the singing of the burn

Until I had each tinkling note by heart.
Though I have lived my life among the hills,
I never listened to a stream before.
Yet, little comfort all its melody
Could bring my heart; but now that you are back
It seems to sing you welcome to your home.
You have come home. You could not quite forget.
MARGARET. I have forgotten naught; and naught I rue:
Yet, when the weakness left me, I arose
To bring your babe to you.
ABEL. Naught but the babe?
MARGARET. Lad, shut the door; for I am cold; and fetch
Some peats to mend the fire; it's almost out.
You need a woman's hand to tend you, lad.
See, you have let the clock run down!
ABEL. My heart
Kept bitter count of all those lonely hours.
Margaret, your wisdom is no less than mine;
And mine is love, lass.
MARGARET. Only time will tell.

ON THE ROAD

Persons:

REUBEN APPLEBY.
JESSIE APPLEBY, *his wife.*
PETER NIXON, *a stonebreaker.*

REUBEN APPLEBY *and his wife sit under a hedge by the highway.* REUBEN *is eating bread and cheese, while* JESSIE *is feeding her baby with milk out of a bottle.*

REUBEN. "Married!" he says,
And looks at me quite sharply—
"A boy like you!"
And civilly I answered:
"Not such a boy, sir;
I am nineteen, past."
"Nineteen!" says he, and laughs;
"And you a husband, with a wife to keep—

A wife and family, I suppose."
"We have a baby, sir."
"A baby! and you're just a child yourself!
What right have you to marry,
And bring into the world
A tribe of helpless children
To starve, and beg, and steal?"
With that he took his children by the hand,
And walked away.
I could have flung his money after him,
But I had labored for it
And was hungry,
And knew that you were famished;
And the boy must have his milk.
What right!—
I could have flung . . .
JESSIE. Then, you had flung away
Your baby's life!
REUBEN. Ay, lass, that stopt me,
And the thought of you;
And so, I took the sixpence,
And bought the bread and cheese and milk.
JESSIE. You brought it just in time.
He'd cried himself to sleep;
But in my arms he lay so still and white,
That I was frightened.
REUBEN. You were famished, lass.
JESSIE. Yes; I was done.
I scarce could hold him,
Though he's light—
So thin and light.
But, when I laid him down, he cried so,
I could not bear . . .
REUBEN. Well, he looks happy now.
He's drinking like a fish.
The milk will make him fat again.
But you eat nothing, Jessie.
JESSIE. I cannot eat.
REUBEN. You cannot?

JESSIE. Not just now.
REUBEN. Jessie, you must;
You'll die of hunger.
JESSIE. I'm not hungry now;
But only weary.
After, perhaps . . .
REUBEN. What right had I to marry!
What right had he—
He, with his wife and children,
To speak to me like that?
I could have flung . . .
JESSIE. Nay, lad; don't vex yourself
With thought of such as he.
How can it matter what he said to you,
Now that it's over,
And the boy is fed?
REUBEN. His money bought the milk—
Ay, and the bread and cheese.
JESSIE. And do they not taste sweet?
You seem to relish them.
REUBEN. They're well enough.
But, would not any food taste sweet,
After starvation?
And I'd worked for it.
JESSIE. How could it be his money,
If you'd earned it?
REUBEN. True, lass.
Still, you eat nothing.
JESSIE. I cannot eat.
REUBEN. It's ill work tramping all the livelong day,
With naught but hunger in the belly,
As we did yesterday;
And then, at night,
To shelter 'neath a stack;
And lie, and think—
Too cold and tired to sleep—
To lie, and think,
And wonder if to-morrow
Would bring us bite and sup;

Envying the very beasts that they could feed
Upon the hay that bedded us.
And still, 'twas good to rest
From tramping the hard road.
But, you were plucky, lass;
And trudged so bravely.

JESSIE. Yet I could have dropped,
Had I not hoped to get him milk ere night.

REUBEN. Poor babe!
He cried all day.
My sleeve was wet with tears.

JESSIE. 'Twas a hard road, and long.

REUBEN. The road is hard and long the poor must travel.

JESSIE. Ay, and the end?

REUBEN. The end?
Where the end lies, who knows?

(*A pause.*)

Wife, he spake truly;
I'd no right to marry—
No right to wed, and bring into the world . . .

JESSIE. What's that you say?
You're wearied of me, husband?

REUBEN. Nay, wife, you know . . .
Still, he spake truly.
I never thought of it like this before;
I never should have thought of it at all,
Had he not spoken;
I'd not wits enough.
But now, I see;
I had no right to marry,
And bring into the world
A baby . . .

JESSIE. Don't you love your son?

REUBEN. Love him!
I wouldn't see him starve.
I had no right . . .
Yet, when we married,
Things looked so different, Jessie.

I earned my weekly wage,
Enough to live on,
And to keep a wife on;
And we were happy in our home,
Together, weren't we, wife?
  JESSIE. Ay, we were happy, Reuben.
  REUBEN. And then, the baby came,
And we were happier still;
For, how could we foresee
Bad times would follow,
And work be slack;
And all the mills be stopt;
And we be bundled out of house and home,
With naught to do
But take the road,
And look for work elsewhere?
It's a long looking . . .
Nay, but he spake truly . . .
I had no right . . .
  JESSIE. Nay, Reuben, you talk foolishness;
Your head is light with fasting.
An empty belly makes an empty head.
Leave idle talking to the rich;
A poor man can't afford it.
And I've no patience with such folly.
  REUBEN. Nay, it's not folly, lass,
But truth, the bitter truth.
Is it not true, we're on the road,
I, and my starving wife and babe?
  JESSIE. Nay, husband; see!
He's drunk the milk;
And sleeps so sweetly:
  REUBEN. But you're ill.
  JESSIE. Ill?
Nay, I'm well enough.
  REUBEN. Yet you're too ill to eat.
  JESSIE. Nay, I was only tired.
But I'll eat now, lad,

If you've left me aught!
See how it goes!
REUBEN. I had no right . . .
JESSIE. Not if you did not love me!
REUBEN. You know . . .
JESSIE. How can I tell?
You talk so strangely;
And say that you'd no right to wed me . . .
Why did you wed me, then?
REUBEN. Because I couldn't help . . .
I could not do without you.
I did not think . . .
How could I think, when I was mad for you?
JESSIE. And yet you had no right?
REUBEN. Right! What thought I of right?
I only thought of you, lass.
Nay, but I did not think . . .
I only felt,
And knew I needs must have you.
JESSIE. You loved me . . .
Then, was love not right enough?
Why talk of right?
Or, have you wearied of us—
Your wife and son?
Poor babe!
He doesn't love us any longer.
REUBEN. Nay, wife, you know . . .

(PETER NIXON, *an elderly man, gaunt and bent with labor, comes slowly down the road, with his stone-breaker's hammer on his shoulder. He glances at* REUBEN *and* JESSIE, *in passing; hesitates, then turns, and comes towards them.*)

PETER. Fine morning, mate and mistress!
Might you be looking for a job, my lad?
Well . . . there's a heap of stones to break, down yonder.
I was just on my way . . .
But I am old:
And, maybe, a bit idle;

And you look young,
And not afraid of work,
Or I'm an ill judge of a workman's hands.
And when the job's done, lad,
There'll be a shilling.
And there's worse work than breaking stones for bread.
And I'll just have a nap,
While you are busy,
And, maybe, sleep away the afternoon,
Like the old, idle rascal that I am.
Nay, but there's naught to thank me for.
I'm old;
And I've no wife and children,
And so, don't need the shilling.
But you are young;
And you must work for it,
While I sit by and watch you
And keep you at it.
I like to watch folk working,
For I am old and idle.
Perhaps I'll sleep a bit, with one eye open;
And when you think I'm nodding,
I'll come down on you like a load of metal.
Don't fear!
I'll make you earn it;
You'll have to sweat,
Before that shilling's yours;
Unless you're proud—
Too proud to work . . .
Nay?
Well, the heap's down yonder—
There, at the turning.
Ah, the bonnie babe!
We had no children, mistress.
And what can any old man do with shillings,
With no one but himself to spend them on—
An idle, good-for-nothing, lone old man?

(*He leads them to the turning of the road.*)

HOLIDAY

Persons:

EVA SPARK, *a widow.*
NELLY SPARK, } *her daughters.*
POLLY SPARK, }
DANIEL WEBB, *a navvy.*

Scene: *A room in tenements: evening.* NELLY SPARK *lies unconscious on the bed with her eyes open and her hands moving in a regular succession of mechanical motions. Her mother sits by the bed sewing.* POLLY SPARK *stands near the window looking out into the dingy court.*

EVA. Her hands are never quiet.
POLLY. She's tending the machine;
And slipping in the brush-backs
As we do all day long.
Day after day, and every day,
Year in, year out, year in, year out,
Save Sunday and the holiday . . .
To think to-day's a holiday—
And what a holiday for her!
EVA. She cannot rest a moment.
Her hands are working, working . . .
It must be weary work, at best;
But now . . .
POLLY. And yet we do it,
Year in, year out, year in, year out,
Until it drives us dizzy,
And we, maybe, slip in a hand as she did—
Six holes it drills—
And then they call it carelessness!
EVA. Ay! that began the trouble—
Her poor hand!
It gives me quite a turn to think of it.
She's never been herself since.
It's hard she cannot rest.
POLLY. To think to-day's a holiday!
And last year she was dancing . . .

EVA. She's ever been a dancer,
From a baby:
Ay! even as a child-in-arms,
I could not keep her quiet,
If she but heard an organ;
And though 'twas half a street away,
'Twould take me all my time to hold her
From tumbling off my lap.
'Twas in her blood;
I danced before I married—
Though afterwards, God knows,
I'd little list for dancing—
And, in my day,
While I'd the heart for it,
I danced among the best.
When first your father saw me,
I was dancing.

POLLY. Last year, she danced the live-long day;
She danced us all out easily,
Although the sun was blazing;
And we were fit to drop.
She would have danced herself to death;
But, some one stopped the music—
I think 'twas Daniel—
Even he was done,
Though he's not beaten easily.

EVA. He'd scarcely go to-day.
He said, he could not go without her.
I told him that 'twas worse than useless
For him to sit here, watching her.
I think he only went, at last,
Because he could not bear to see her hands.
It's bad enough for me . . .
I could not have him, too . . .
I cannot help but watch . . .
Her poor, poor hands!
They're never still a moment.
All night, I watched them working.

POLLY. And, last year, she was dancing—

Was dancing in the sun!
And there was none could dance with her—
Not one!
I never knew where she could pick the steps up:
There seemed to be no end to them,
As though she made them up as she went on.
They came to her, I fancy,
As trudging comes to us.
EVA. Ay! she'd a dancing heart.
POLLY. You scarcely saw her feet move,
Because they went so quickly:
It dazzled me to watch them.
And, as she danced so madly,
She waved a branch of hawthorn
That Daniel plucked for her.
EVA. That night when she came home
Her arms were full of blossom.
The room was white for days:
She'd scarcely left a pot or pan
For me to cook a meal in:
And, yet, I dared not toss it out.
The scent was nigh too much for me:
A hawthorn grew beside the door at home;
And, in the drenching rain,
It used to smell so fresh and sweet.
'Twill be there still . . . but I . . .
And she was born about the blossom-time;
For I remember how I lay,
And dreamt that I could smell the hawthorn,
Though we had left the country then,
And I was far from any blowing thing.
And I can smell it now,
Though I've not seen a growing thorn for years.
POLLY. The smell of hawthorn, and the heat,
Together, turned me faint.
She did not seem to mind it,
But danced till I was dizzy—
Quite dizzy, watching her:
And, when I called to stop her,

She only laughed, and answered:
That she could dance for ever—
For ever in the sunshine,
Until she dropt down dead.
Then Daniel stopped the music,
Suddenly . . .
Her feet stopt with it:
And, she nearly tumbled:
But, Daniel caught her in his arms:
And she was dazed and quiet:
And scarcely spoke a word,
Till we were home in bed,
And I had blown the light out.
I did not take much notice at the time:
For I was half-asleep:
Yet, I remember every word,
As though she said them over, lying there:
"At least, I've danced a day away!
To-morrow, we'll be working—
To-morrow, and to-morrow,
Till we're dead.
And yet, to-day,
The job was nearly done:
If they'd not stopt the music,
I might have finished, dancing!"
   EVA. Her hands are never quiet:
They're always working, working . . .
They move so quickly,
I can scarcely follow . . .
   POLLY. She always worked like that:
Indeed, the only wonder is
She'd never slipt her hand before.
She worked as madly as she danced:
And she danced madly.
   EVA. Ay . . . she'll dance no more.
Poor Daniel, I'd no heart to tell him,
That there . . . that there's no hope for her.
He never asked me what the doctor said:
I think he knew, somehow.

He'd scarcely go:
But, he . . . he could not bear to see . . .
I cannot bear to watch them;
Yet, cannot keep my eyes off:
They're always working, working—
Poor broken hands!
And, once, they'd beat to music, on my breast,
When she was but a baby in my lap.
Would God, that time had never passed . . .

POLLY. To think they'll all be dancing.
While she . . . she's lying . . .

EVA. Daniel went, poor lad;
But, he was loth to go;
And there'll be little dancing,
For him, to-day,
And many days to come.
He'll not stay late:
I looked for him, ere now.

POLLY. Ay! we are only "hands."
And, in the end . . .
I wonder if I'll lie like that, one day,
With useless fingers working . . .
God spare me!
But I think there's little chance.
I never worked, or danced, as she did.
She danced, and danced . . .

EVA. I smell the hawthorn now, as strongly
As we could smell it, after rain . . .

POLLY. There's some one on the stairs:
I think it's Dan.

(*The door opens, gently; and* DANIEL WEBB *enters, quietly, carrying a branch of hawthorn.*)

DANIEL. How's Nelly, now?
I've brought some bloom for her.
I thought she might . . .
Last year, she liked the hawthorn:
A year to-day, she danced beneath the blossom . . .

I could not stay,
And see them jigging . . .
And yet I cannot bear to watch . . .

EVA (*turning suddenly*). Her hands have stopt!
She's quiet now . . .
Ah, God!
She's getting up!
She'll fall . . .

(*They all rush towards* NELLY, *as she rises from the bed; but, something in her eyes stays them half-way; and they stand, spellbound, watching her, as she steps to the floor; and moves towards* DANIEL, *stretching out her hand for the hawthorn, which he gives to her without a word. Holding the branch over her head, she begins to dance slowly; her feet gradually moving more rapidly.*)

NELLY. Faster . . . faster . . . fast . . .
Who's stopt the music?

(*She pauses; stands a moment, dazed; then drops to the floor in a heap.*)

EVA (*running towards her*). Ah, God!
She's done!
She does not breathe . . .

(*They bend over her; and* DANIEL *picks up the dropt branch.*)

DANIEL. It's fallen, now—
The bloom . . .
I thought she might . . .
Last year . . .
And now!
I brought the bloom . . .

EVA. Her hands stopt working,
When she smelt it.
It set her dancing . . . dancing to her death.

DANIEL. Oh, Christ!
What have I done!
Nelly!
I brought the bloom . . .
POLLY. She's had her wish.

THE FLUTE

"Good-night!" he sang out cheerily:
"Good-night!" and yet again: "Good-night!"

And I was gay that night to be
Once more in my clean countryside,
Among the windy hills and wide.
Six days of city slush and mud,
Of hooting horn, and spattering wheel,
Made me rejoice again to feel
The tingling frost that fires the blood,
And sets life burning keen and bright;
And down the ringing road to stride
The eager swinging stride that braces
The straining thews from hip to heel:
To breathe again the wind that sweeps
Across the grassy, Northern steeps,
From crystal deeps and starry spaces.

And I was glad again to hear
The old man's greeting of good cheer:
For every night for many a year
At that same corner we had met,
Summer and Winter, dry and wet:
And though I never once had heard
The old man speak another word,
His cheery greeting at the bend
Seemed like the welcome of a friend.

But, as we neared to-night, somehow,
I felt that he would stop and speak—
Though he went by: and when I turned,

I saw him standing in the road,
And looking back, with hand to brow,
As if to shade old eyes, grown weak
Awaiting the long sleep they'd earned:
Though, as again towards him I strode,
A friendly light within them burned.
And then, as I drew nigh, he spoke
With shaking head, and voice that broke:
"I've missed you these last nights," he said:
"And I have not so many now
That I can miss friends easily . . .
Ay: friends grow scarce, as you grow old:
And roads are rough: and winds are cold:
And when you feel you're losing hold,
Life does not go too merrily."
And then he stood with nodding head,
And spoke no more. And so I told
How I had been, six days and nights,
Exiled from pleasant sounds and sights.
And now, as though my voice had stirred
His heart to speech, he told right out,
With quickening eye and quavering word,
The things I care to hear about,
The little things that make up life:
How he'd been lonesome, since his wife
Had died, some thirty year ago:
And how he trudged three mile or so
To reach the farmstead where he worked,
And three mile back to his own door . . .
For he dwelt outby on the moor:
And every day the distance irked
More sorely still his poor, old bones;
And all the road seemed strewn with stones
To trip you up, when you were old—
When you were old, and friends were few:
How, since the farmstead had been sold,
The master and the men were new,
All save himself; and they were young;
And Mistress had a raspy tongue:

So, often, he would hardly speak
A friendly word from week to week
With any soul. Old friends had died,
Or else had quit the countryside:
And since his wife was taken, he
Had lived alone, this thirty year:
And there were few who cared to hear
An old man's jabber . . . and too long
He'd kept me, standing in the cold,
With his long tongue, and such a song
About himself! And I would be . . .

I put my arm through his; and turned
To go upon his way with him:
And once again that warm light burned
In those old eyes, so weak and dim:
While, with thin, piping voice, he told
How much it meant to him each night
To change a kindly word with me:
To think that he'd at least one friend
Who'd maybe miss him, in the end.

Then, as we walked, he said no more:
And, silent, in the starry light,
Across the wide, sweet-smelling bent,
Between the grass and stars we went
In quiet, friendly company:
And, all the way, we only heard
A chirrup where some partridge stirred,
And ran before us through the grass,
To hide his head till we should pass.

At length we reached the cottage-door:
But when I stopped, and turned to go,
His words came falteringly and slow:
If I would step inside, and rest,
I'd be right welcome: not a guest
Had crossed his threshold, thirty year . . .
He'd naught but bread and cheese and beer
To offer me . . . but, I'd know best . . .

He spoke with hand upon the latch;
And when I answered, opened wide
The cottage-door, and stepped inside;
And, as I followed, struck a match,
And lit a tallow-dip: and stirred
The banked-up peats into a glow:
And then with shuffling step and slow
He moved about: and soon had set
Two mugs of beer, and bread and cheese:
And while we made a meal off these,
The old man never spoke a word;
But, brooding in the ingle-seat,
With eyes upon the kindling peat,
He seemed a while to quite forget
He was not sitting by himself
To-night, like any other night;
When, as in the dim candle-light
I glanced around me, with surprise
I saw upon the rafter-shelf
A flute, nigh hidden in the shade.

And when I asked him if he played,
The light came back into his eyes:
Ay, ay, he sometimes piped a bit,
But not so often since she died.
And then, as though old memories lit
His poor, old heart, and made it glad,
He told how he, when quite a lad,
Had taught himself: and they would play
On penny whistles all the day—
He and the miller's son, beside
The millpool, chirping all they knew,
Till they could whistle clean and true:
And how, when old enough to earn,
They both saved up to buy a flute;
And they had played it, turn for turn:
But Jake was dead, this long while back . . .
Ah! if I'd only heard him toot,
I'd know what music meant. Ay, ay . . .

He'd play me something, bye-and-bye;
Though he was nought to Jake . . . and now
His breath was scant, and fingering slack . . .
He used to play to her at night
The melodies that she liked best,
While she worked on: she'd never rest
By daylight, or by candle-light . . .
And then, with hand upon his brow,
He brooded, quiet in his chair,
With eyes upon the red peat-glare;
Until, at length, he roused himself,
And reached the flute down from the shelf;
And, carrying it outside the door,
I saw him take a can, and pour
Fresh water through the instrument,
To make it sweet of tone, he said.
Then in his seat, so old and bent,
With kindling eyes and swaying head,
He played the airs he used to play
To please his wife, before she died.
And as I watched his body sway
In time and tune, from side to side—
So happy, just to play, and please
With old familiar melodies—
His eyes grew brighter and more bright,
As though they saw some well-loved sight:
And, following his happy gaze,
I turned, and saw, without amaze,
A woman standing, young and fair,
With hazel eyes, and thick, brown hair
Brushed smoothly backward from the brow,
Beside the table that but now,
Save for the empty mugs, was bare.
Upon it she had spread a sheet,
And stood there, ironing a shirt,
Her husband's, as he played to her
Her favorite tunes, so old and sweet.
I watched her move with soundless stir;
Then stand with listening eyes, and hold

The iron near her glowing cheek,
Lest it, too hot, should do some hurt,
And she, so careful not to burn
The well-darned shirt, so worn and old.
Then, something seemed to make me turn
To look on the old man again:
And, as I looked, the playing stopped;
And now I saw that he had dropped
Into his brooding mood once more,
With eyes again grown dull and weak.
He seemed the oldest of old men
Who grope through life with sight worn dim:
And, even as I looked at him,
Too full of tender awe to speak,
I knew once more the board was bare,
With no young woman standing there
With hazel eyes and thick, brown hair.

And so, at last, I rose, and took
His hand: and as he clasped mine tight,
I saw again that friendly look
Fill his old weary eyes with light,
And wish me, without words, good-night.
And in my heart, that look glowed bright
Till I reached home across the moor.

And, at the corner of the lane,
Next night, I hear the old voice cry
In greeting, as I struggled by,
Head-down against the wind and rain.
And so each night, until one day,
His master chanced across my way:
But, when I spoke of him, he said:
Did I not know the man was dead,
And had been dead a week or so?
One morn he'd not turned up to work,
And never having known him shirk,
And hearing that he lived alone,
He thought it best himself to go

And see what ailed: and coming there,
He found the old man in his chair,
Stone-dead beside the cold hearthstone.
It must be full a week, or more . . .
Ay, just two weeks, come Saturday,
He'd found him; but he must have died
O'ernight—(the night I heard him play!)
And they had found, dropt by his side,
A broken flute upon the floor.

Yet, every night, his greeting still
At that same corner of the hill,
Summer and Winter, wet or dry,
'Neath cloud, or moon, or cold starlight,
Is waiting there to welcome me:
And ever as I hurry by,
The old voice sings out cheerily:
"Good-night!" and yet again, "Good-night!"

THE WHISPERERS

As beneath the moon I walked,
Dog-at-heel my shadow stalked,
Keeping ghostly company:
And as we went gallantly
Down the fell-road, dusty-white,
Round us in the windy night
Bracken, rushes, bent and heather
Whispered ceaselessly together:
"Would he ever journey more,
Ever stride so carelessly,
If he knew what lies before,
And could see what we can see?"

As I listened, cold with dread,
Every hair upon my head
Strained to hear them talk of me,
Whispering, whispering ceaselessly:

"Folly's fool the man must be,
Surely, since, though where he goes
He knows not, his shadow knows:
And his secret shadow never
Utters warning words, or ever
Seeks to save him from his fate,
Reckless, blindfold, and unknown,
Till death tells him all, too late,
And his shadow walks alone."

SIGHT

By the lamplit stall I loitered, feasting my eyes
On colors ripe and rich for the heart's desire—
Tomatoes, redder than Krakatoa's fire,
Oranges like old sunsets over Tyre,
And apples golden-green as the glades of Paradise.

And as I lingered, lost in divine delight,
My heart thanked God for the goodly gift of sight
And all youth's lively senses keen and quick . . .
When suddenly, behind me in the night,
I heard the tapping of a blind man's stick.

BEFORE ACTION

I sit beside the brazier's glow,
And, drowsing in the heat,
I dream of daffodils that blow
And lambs that frisk and bleat—

Black lambs that frolic in the snow
Among the daffodils,
In a far orchard that I know
Beneath the Malvern hills.

Next year the daffodils will blow,
And lambs will frisk and bleat;
But I'll not feel the brazier's glow,
Nor any cold or heat.

THE QUESTION

I wonder if the old cow died or not.
Gey bad she was the night I left, and sick.
Dick reckoned she would mend. He knows a lot—
At least he fancies so himself, does Dick.

Dick knows a lot. But maybe I did wrong
To leave the cow to him, and come away.
Over and over like a silly song
These words keep bumming in my head all day.

And all I think of, as I face the foe
And take my lucky chance of being shot,
Is this—that if I'm hit, I'll never know
Till Doomsday if the old cow died or not.

THE RETURN

He went, and he was gay to go;
And I smiled on him as he went.
My son—'twas well he couldn't know
My darkest dread, nor what it meant—

Just what it meant to smile and smile
And let my son go cheerily—
My son . . . and wondering all the while
What stranger would come back to me.

RAINING

The night I left, my father said:
"You'll go and do some stupid thing.
You've no more sense in that fat head
Than Silly Billy Witterling.

"Not sense to come in when it rains—
Not sense enough for that, you've got.
You'll get a bullet through your brains,
Before you know, as like as not."

And now I'm lying in the trench
And shells and bullets through the night
Are raining in a steady drench,
I'm thinking the old man was right.

COMRADES

As I was marching in Flanders
A ghost kept step with me—
Kept step with me and chuckled
And muttered ceaselessly:

"Once I too marched in Flanders,
The very spit of you,
And just a hundred years since,
To fall at Waterloo.

"They buried me in Flanders
Upon the field of blood,
And long I've lain forgotten
Deep in the Flemish mud.

"But now you march in Flanders,
The very spit of me;
To the ending of the day's march
I'll bear you company."

THE LARK

A lull in the racket and brattle,
And a lark soars into the light—
And its song seems the voice of the light
Quelling the voices of night
And the shattering fury of battle.

But again the fury of battle
Breaks out, and he drops from the height—
Dead as a stone from the height—
Drops dead, and the voice of the light
Is drowned in the shattering brattle.

BACK

They ask me where I've been,
And what I've done and seen.
But what can I reply
Who know it wasn't I,
But someone just like me,
Who went across the sea
And with my head and hands
Killed men in foreign lands . .
Though I must bear the blame
Because he bore my name.

THE JOKE

He'd even have his joke
While we were sitting tight,
And so he needs must poke
His silly head in sight
To whisper some new jest
Chortling, but as he spoke
A rifle cracked. . . .
And now God knows when I shall hear the rest!

THE MESSAGES

"I cannot quite remember. . . . There were five
Dropt dead beside me in the trench—and three
Whispered their dying messages to me. . . ."

Back from the trenches, more dead than alive,
Stone-deaf and dazed, and with a broken knee,
He hobbled slowly, muttering vacantly:

"I cannot quite remember. . . . There were five
Dropt dead beside me in the trench, and three
Whispered their dying messages to me. . . .

"Their friends are waiting, wondering how they thrive—
Waiting a word in silence patiently. . . .
But what they said, or who their friends may be

"I cannot quite remember. . . . There were five
Dropt dead beside me in the trench,—and three
Whispered their dying messages to me. . . ."

PETER PROUDFOOT

He cleaned out middens for his daily bread:
War took him overseas and on a bed
Of lilies-of-the-valley dropt him, dead.

THE CONSCRIPT

Indifferent, flippant, earnest, but all bored,
The doctors sit in the glare of electric light
Watching the endless stream of naked white
Bodies of men for whom their hasty award
Means life or death maybe or the living death
Of mangled limbs, blind eyes or a darkened brain:
And the chairman as his monocle falls again
Pronounces each doom with easy indifferent breath.

Then suddenly I shudder as I see
A young man move before them wearily,
Cadaverous as one already dead:
But still they stare untroubled as he stands
With arms outstretched and drooping thorn-crowned head,
The nail-marks glowing in his feet and hands.

REVEILLE

Still bathed in its moonlight slumber, the little white house
by the cedar
Stands silent against the red dawn;
And nothing I know of who sleeps there, to the travail of
day yet unwakened,
Behind the blue curtains undrawn:

But I dream as we march down the roadway, ringing loud
and rime-white in the moonlight,
Of a little dark house on a hill
Wherein when the battle is over, to the rapture of day yet
unwakened,
We shall slumber as soundless and still.

LAMENT

We who are left, how shall we look again
Happily on the sun, or feel the rain,
Without remembering how they who went
Ungrudgingly, and spent
Their all for us, loved, too, the sun and rain?

A bird among the rain-wet lilac sings—
But we, how shall we turn to little things
And listen to the birds and winds and streams
Made holy by their dreams,
Nor feel the heart-break in the heart of things?

RUPERT BROOKE

II

Once in my garret—you being far away
Tramping the hills and breathing upland air,
Or so I fancied—brooding in my chair,
I watched the London sunshine feeble and grey

Dapple my desk, too tired to labor more,
When, looking up, I saw you standing there —
Although I'd caught no footstep on the stair,—
Like sudden April at my open door.

Though now beyond earth's farthest hills you fare,
Song-crowned, immortal, sometimes it seems to me
That, if I listen very quietly,
Perhaps I'll hear a light foot on the stair
And see you, standing with your angel air,
Fresh from the uplands of eternity.

ON BROADWAY

Daffodils dancing by moonlight in English meadows,
Moon-pale daffodils under the April moon—
Here in the throng and clangor and hustle of Broadway,
Broadway brawling and loud in the glare of the noon,
Comes to me now as a half-remembered tune
The silence and wonder of daffodils dancing by moonlight,
Dreamily dancing in dew-sprinkled moonshiny meadows,
Ghostly daffodils under a ghostly moon.

"SO LONG HAD I TRAVELLED THE LONELY ROAD"

So long had I travelled the lonely road,
Though, now and again, a wayfaring friend
Walked shoulder to shoulder, and lightened the load,
I often would think to myself as I strode,
No comrade will journey with you to the end.

And it seemed to me, as the days went past,
And I gossiped with cronies, or brooded alone,
By wayside fires, that my fortune was cast
To sojourn by other men's hearths to the last,
And never to come to my own hearthstone.

The lonely road no longer I roam.
We met, and were one in the heart's desire.
Together we came through the wintry gloam
To the little old house by the cross-ways, home;
And crossed the threshold, and kindled the fire.

TENANTS

Suddenly, out of dark and leafy ways,
We came upon the little house asleep
In cold blind stillness, shadowless and deep,
In the white magic of the full moon-blaze:
Strangers without the gate, we stood agaze,
Fearful to break that quiet, and to creep
Into the house that had been ours to keep
Through a long year of happy nights and days.

So unfamiliar in the white moon-gleam,
So old and ghostly like a house of dream
It seemed, that over us there stole the dread
That even as we watched it, side by side,
The ghosts of lovers, who had lived and died
Within its walls, were sleeping in our bed.

SEA-CHANGE

Wind-flicked and ruddy her young body glowed
In sunny shallows, splashing them to spray:
But when on rippled silver sand she lay,
And over her the little green waves flowed,
Coldly translucent and moon-colored showed
Her frail young beauty, as if rapt away
From all the light and laughter of the day
To some twilit, forlorn sea-god's abode.

Again into the sun with happy cry
She leapt alive and sparkling from the sea,
Sprinkling white spray against the hot blue sky,

A laughing girl . . . and yet, I see her lie
Under a deeper tide eternally
In cold moon-colored immortality.

GIRL'S SONG

I saw three black pigs riding
In a blue and yellow cart—
Three black pigs riding to the fair
Behind the old grey dappled mare—
But it wasn't black pigs riding
In a gay and gaudy cart
That sent me into hiding
With a flutter in my heart.

I heard the cart returning,
The jolting, jingling cart—
Returning empty from the fair
Behind the old jog-trotting mare—
But it wasn't the returning
Of a clattering, empty cart
That sent the hot blood burning
And throbbing through my heart.

WILLIAM AND AGNES PRINGLE

You've locked the doors and snecked the windows tight?

I've locked up as I've locked up every night
Since father crept that last time painfully
Upstairs and left the locking-up to me—
Since for the last time father went to bed
To rise no more. To think that he's been dead
Just twenty years—ay, to the very hour!
The clock was striking in the Abbey tower
When he sat up. "Are all the windows fast?"
He whispered, then dropped back and breathed his last.
To think I'd nigh forgotten!

Ay, to-day,
Your thoughts have all been turned a different way.

True, lass: and yet it's queer I should forget.

Queer, that a bridegroom's thoughts should not be set
On death?

Nay, queer I didn't choose instead
A different day in all the year to wed.

Ay—but you've not forgotten to secure
The doors and windows: so you may feel sure
While such important things you think of still
Your mind's not getting over-flighty, Will.
But you must never let a harebrained wife
Divert you from the habits of a life.
Yet, here's just one thing, Will, that puzzles me:
What is it you lock out so carefully
That you've locked out each night these twenty years,
And your old father with his anxious fears
Locked out before you, and his father, too,
As likely as not, before him? Why should you
Secure yourself against the harmless night?

I never looked upon it in that light—
But it's the custom . . .

What is it that you dread
Will come upon you as you lie in bed,
If you should leave a window or a door
Unfastened?

Well, I hardly know, I'm sure!

No bolt or bar has ever locked out death:
So your old father might have spared his breath.
Or is it, rather, something you lock in
Each night, lest thieves . . .

There's naught for thieves to win;
Though I had left the doors and windows wide
These many years . . .

But then, you'd no young bride.
And now, I wonder if you know aright
Or realise what you lock in to-night?

THE PAISLEY SHAWL

What were his dreams who wove this colored shawl—
The grey, hard-bitten weaver, gaunt and dour,
Out of whose grizzled memory, even as a flower
Out of bleak Winter at young April's call
In the old tradition of flowers breaks into bloom,
Blossomed the ancient intricate design
Of softly-glowing hues and exquisite line—
What were his dreams, crouched at his cottage loom?

What were her dreams, the laughing April lass
Who first, in the flowering of young delight,
With parted lips and eager tilted head
And shining eyes, about her shoulders white
Drew the soft fabric of kindling green and red,
Standing before the candle-lighted glass?

THE PUFFIN

He stooped down suddenly and thrust his hand
Into a tunnel in the shallow sand
Beneath a campion-clump, and brought to light
A brooding puffin with black wings clasped tight
To her white breast: but twisting round her sleek,
Pied, darting head, her scarlet razor-beak
She snapped in anger, cutting his finger clean
To the very bone; and on the clump of green
Among the campion blossoms white as foam

He dropped the bird and watched her scurry home;
And laughed, while from the wounded finger dripped
Blood redder even than the beak that ripped
The flesh so cruelly, and, chuckling, said:
"Well, anyway, the blood still runs as red
In my old veins as when I saw it spill
The first time that I felt a puffin's bill
Long years since: and it seems as though I had
As little sense as when I was a lad
To let myself be caught so easily
And that brave bird make such a fool of me
Who thought myself as wise as Solomon.
Yet it is better to feel a fool's blood run
Still quick and lively in the veins and be
A living fool beside the April sea
Than lie like Solomon in his unknown grave,
A pinch of dry dust that no wit could save."

THE MUGGER'S SONG

Driving up the Mallerstang,
The mugger cracked his whip and sang—
And all his crocks went rattle, rattle—

"The road runs fair and smooth and even
From Appleby to Kirkby Stephen—
And womenfolk are kittle cattle.

"And Kirkby Stephen's fair to see,
And inns are good in Appleby"—
And all his crocks went rattle, rattle.

"But what care I for Kirkby Stephen,
Or whether roads are rough or even—
And womenfolk are kittle cattle?

"And what care I for Appleby,
Since Bess of the Blue Bell jilted me?"—
And all his crocks went rattle, rattle.

"And wed to-day in Kirkby Stephen,
A sweep whose legs are odd and even?—
And womenfolk are kittle cattle."

THE EMPTY PURSE

One song leads on to another,
One friend to another friend,
So I'll travel along
With a friend and a song—
I'll travel along
Ten thousand strong—
To the end.

But if all songs should fail me,
And friend fail after friend,
I'll still have you,
O tried and true—
I'll still have you,
And a stone in my shoe,
To the end.

CURLEW CALLING

Curlew calling down the slack,
When grey rains are falling,
From the bitter town and black,
Curlew, I am coming back,
Curlew calling!

Hawk a-hover on the wind,
Look for me, your lover,
Come from barren ways and blind,
Where men seek but never find,—
Hawk a-hover!

Grey snipe drumming in the gloam,
I am coming, coming,
Never from my kind to roam.
Grey snipe, I am coming home,
Grey snipe drumming.

LUCK

What bring you, sailor, home from the sea—
Coffers of gold and of ivory?

When first I went to sea as a lad
A new jack-knife was all I had:

And I've sailed for fifty years and three
To the coasts of gold and of ivory:

And now at the end of a lucky life,
Well, still I've got my old jack-knife.

I HEARD A SAILOR . . .

I heard a sailor talking,
As he tossed upon his bed
In hot uneasy slumber,
And this is what he said:

Why does she shake her head at me
Until her ear-rings tinkle,
Though all the while her merry smile
Keeps her blue eyes atwinkle?

Why does she slyly glance at me
As she pours out the wine,
Then pucker up her pretty lips
And hold them up to mine?

Why does she suddenly draw back
And o'er my shoulder stare?
Why does that silly parrot screech?
Why does the gas-jet flare?

And who's the lad that's running round
Upon the heaving floor
With a knife betwixt his shoulder-blades—
And cannot find the door?

Why does the scarlet parrot screech?
Why does the gas flare red?
Why do her tinkling ear-rings dance
A horn-pipe in my head?

IN COURSE OF TIME

The sarsen-stone
Door-post of temple, altar-throne
Of some old god, or monument
Erected by a warrior-host
To mark the fallen chieftain's tomb,
In course of time has come
To serve the old black sow for scratching-post.

A lad's light word,
Breathed low and scarcely heard
Or heeded in the babblement
And blare of other tongues, has time
Remembered, and the souls of men
Again and yet again
Take fire at that dead lad's undying rhyme.

HAROLD MONRO

Harold Edward Monro, poet, editor, publisher, and bookseller, was born in Brussels in 1879. He was educated at the grammar school, Radley, and at Caius College, Cambridge, from which he received the B.A. degree in 1901. He published his first book, *Poems* (1906), at the age of twenty-seven, although his interest in poetry had begun much earlier. In 1912 he established in London the Poetry Bookshop, which became a meeting place of the younger poets in the city. Of these younger poets Monro was a leader, his quarterly, *Poetry and Drama,* doing much to forward the interests of the newer movements, as did likewise a later periodical, *The Chapbook,* begun in 1919 and continued until December, 1921. Monro has published a number of volumes of poetry, the best being *Children of Love* (1914), *Strange Meetings* (1917), and *Real Property* (1922). He also has one book of criticism, *Some Contemporary Poets (1920)* (1920).

During the World War Monro was in the army, but afterwards he returned to London, to the Poetry Bookshop, which he still maintains. He is married and has one son.

CHILDREN OF LOVE

The holy boy
Went from his mother out in the cool of the day
Over the sun-parched fields
And in among the olives shining green and shining grey.

There was no sound,
No smallest voice of any shivering stream.
Poor sinless little boy,
He desired to play, and to sing; he could only sigh and dream.

Suddenly came
Running along to him naked, with curly hair,
That rogue of the lovely world,
That other beautiful child whom the virgin Venus bare.

The holy boy
Gazed with those sad blue eyes that all men know.
Impudent Cupid stood
Panting, holding an arrow and pointing his bow.

(Will you not play?
Jesus, run to him, run to him, swift for our joy.
Is he not holy, like you?
Are you afraid of his arrows, O beautiful dreaming boy?)

And now they stand
Watching one another with timid gaze;
Youth has met youth in the wood,
But holiness will not change its melancholy ways.

Cupid at last
Draws his bow and softly lets fly a dart.
Smile for a moment, sad world!—
It has grazed the white skin and drawn blood from the sorrowful heart.

Now, for delight,
Cupid tosses his locks and goes wantonly near;
But the child that was born to the cross
Has let fall on his cheek, for the sadness of life, a compassionate tear.

Marvellous dream!
Cupid has offered his arrows for Jesus to try;
He has offered his bow for the game.
But Jesus went weeping away, and left him there wondering why.

THE REBELLIOUS VINE

One day, the vine
That clomb on God's own house
Cried, "I will not *grow*,"
And, "I will *not* grow,"
And, "I *will* not grow,"
And, "*I* will not grow."
So God leaned out his head,
And said:
"You need not." Then the vine
Fluttered its leaves, and cried to all the winds:
"Oh, have I not permission from the Lord?
And may I not begin to cease to grow?"
But that wise God had pondered on the vine
Before he made it.
And, all the while it labored *not* to grow,
It grew; it grew;
And all the time God knew.

LONDON INTERIOR

Autumn is in the air,
The children are playing everywhere.

One dare not open this old door too wide;
It is so dark inside.
The hall smells of dust;

A narrow squirt of sunlight enters high,
Cold, yellow.
The floor creaks, and I hear a sigh,
Rise in the gloom and die.

Through the hall, far away,
I just can see
The dingy garden with its wall and tree.
A yellow cat is sitting on the wall
Blinking toward the leaves that fall.
And now I hear a woman call
Some child from play.

Then all is still. Time must go
Ticking slow, glooming slow.

The evening will turn grey.
It is sad in London after two.
All, all the afternoon
What can old men, old women do?

It is sad in London when the gloom
Thickens, like wool,
In the corners of the room;
The sky is shot with steel,
Shot with blue.

The bells ring the slow time;
The chairs creak, the hours climb;
The sunlight lays a streak upon the floor.

SUBURB

Dull and hard the low wind creaks
Among the rustling pampas plumes.
Drearily the year consumes
Its fifty-two insipid weeks.

Most of the grey-green meadow land
Was sold in parsimonious lots;
The dingy houses stand
Pressed by some stout contractor's hand
Tightly together in their plots.

Through builded banks the sullen river
Gropes, where its houses crouch and shiver.
Over the bridge the tyrant train
Shrieks, and emerges on the plain.

In all the better gardens you may pass,
(Product of many careful Saturdays),
Large red geraniums and tall pampas grass
Adorn the plots and mark the gravelled ways.

Sometimes in the background may be seen
A private summer-house in white or green.
Here on warm nights the daughter brings
Her vacillating clerk,
To talk of small exciting things
And touch his fingers through the dark.

He, in the uncomfortable breach
Between her trilling laughters,
Promises, in halting speech,
Hopeless immense Hereafters.

She trembles like the pampas plumes.
Her strained lips haggle. He assumes
The serious quest . . .

Now as the train is whistling past
He takes her in his arms at last.

It's done. She blushes at his side
Across the lawn—a bride, a bride.

* * * * * *

The stout contractor will design,
The lazy laborers will prepare,
Another villa on the line;
In the little garden-square
Pampas grass will rustle there.

MILK FOR THE CAT

When the tea is brought at five o'clock,
And all the neat curtains are drawn with care,
The little black cat with bright green eyes
Is suddenly purring there.

At first she pretends, having nothing to do,
She has come in merely to blink by the grate,
But, though tea may be late or the milk may be sour,
She is never late.

And presently her agate eyes
Take a soft large milky haze,
And her independent casual glance
Becomes a stiff hard gaze.

Then she stamps her claws or lifts her ears
Or twists her tail and begins to stir,
Till suddenly all her lithe body becomes
One breathing, trembling purr.

The children eat and wriggle and laugh;
The two old ladies stroke their silk:
But the cat is grown small and thin with desire,
Transformed to a creeping lust for milk.

The white saucer like some full moon descends
At last from the clouds of the table above;
She sighs and dreams and thrills and glows,
Transfigured with love.

She nestles over the shining rim,
Buries her chin in the creamy sea;
Her tail hangs loose; each drowsy paw
Is doubled under each bending knee.

A long dim ecstasy holds her life;
Her world is an infinite shapeless white,
Till her tongue has curled the last holy drop,
Then she sinks back into the night,

Draws and dips her body to heap
Her sleepy nerves in the great arm-chair,
Lies defeated and buried deep
Three or four hours unconscious there.

STRANGE MEETINGS

I

If suddenly a clod of earth should rise,
And walk about, and breathe, and speak, and love,
How one would tremble, and in what surprise
Gasp: "Can *you* move?"

I see men walking, and I always feel:
"Earth! How have you done this? What can you be?"
I can't learn how to know men, or conceal
How strange they are to me.

* * * * * *

III

Rising toward the surface, we are men
A moment, till we dive again, and then
We take our ease of breathing: we are sent
Unconscious to our former element,
There being perfect, living without pain
Till we emerge like men, and meet again.

* * * * * *

EVERY THING

Since man has been articulate,
Mechanical, improvidently wise
(Servant of Fate),
He has not understood the little cries
And foreign conversations of the small
Delightful creatures that have followed him
Not far behind;
Has failed to hear the sympathetic call
Of Crockery and Cutlery, those kind
Reposeful Teraphim
Of his domestic happiness; the Stool
He sat on, or the Door he entered through:
He has not thanked them, overbearing fool!
What is he coming to?

But you should listen to the talk of these.
Honest they are, and patient they have kept,
Served him without his *Thank-you* or his *Please* . . .
I often heard
The gentle Bed, a sigh between each word,
Murmuring, before I slept.
The Candle, as I blew it, cried aloud,
Then bowed,
And in a smoky argument
Into the darkness went.
The Kettle puffed a tentacle of breath:—
"Pooh! I have boiled his water, I don't know
Why; and he always says I boil too slow.
He never calls me 'Sukie dear,' and oh,
I wonder why I squander my desire
Sitting submissive on his kitchen fire."

Now the old Copper Basin suddenly
Rattled and tumbled from the shelf,
Bumping and crying: "I can fall by myself;
Without a woman's hand

To patronize and coax and flatter me,
I understand
The lean and poise of gravitable land."
It gave a raucous and tumultuous shout,
Twisted itself convulsively about,
Rested upon the floor, and, while I stare,
It stares and grins at me.
The old impetuous Gas above my head
Begins irascibly to flare and fret,
Wheezing into its epileptic jet,
Reminding me I ought to go to bed.

The Rafters creak; an Empty-Cupboard door
Swings open; now a wild Plank of the floor
Breaks from its joist, and leaps behind my foot.
Down from the chimney half a pound of Soot
Tumbles, and lies, and shakes itself again.
The Putty cracks against the window-pane.
A piece of Paper in the basket shoves
Another piece, and toward the bottom moves.
My independent Pencil, while I write,
Breaks at the point: the ruminating Clock
Stirs all its body and begins to rock,
Warning the waiting presence of the Night,
Strikes the dead hour, and tumbles to the plain
Ticking of ordinary work again.

You do well to remind me, and I praise
Your strangely individual foreign ways.
You call me from myself to recognize
Companionship in your unselfish eyes.
I want your dear acquaintances, although
I pass you arrogantly over, throw
Your lovely sounds, and squander them along
My busy days. I'll do you no more wrong.
Purr for me, Sukie, like a faithful cat.
You, my well trampled Boots, and you, my Hat,
Remain my friends: I feel, though I don't speak,
Your touch grow kindlier from week to week.

It well becomes our mutual happiness
To go toward the same end more or less.
There is not much dissimilarity,
Not much to choose, I know it well, in fine,
Between the purposes of you and me,
And your eventual Rubbish Heap, and mine.

SOLITUDE

When you have tidied all things for the night,
And while your thoughts are fading to their sleep,
You'll pause a moment in the late firelight,
Too sorrowful to weep.

The large and gentle furniture has stood
In sympathetic silence all the day
With that old kindness of domestic wood;
Nevertheless the haunted room will say:
"Some one must be away."

The little dog rolls over half awake,
Stretches his paws, yawns, looking up at you,
Wags his tail very slightly for your sake,
That you may feel he is unhappy too.

A distant engine whistles, or the floor
Creaks, or the wandering night-wind bangs a door.

Silence is scattered like a broken glass.
The minutes prick their ears and run about,
Then one by one subside again and pass
Sedately in, monotonously out.

You bend your head and wipe away a tear.
Solitude walks one heavy step more near.

GRAVITY

II

While people meet in reverent groups
And sing to their domestic God,
You, all that time, dear tyrant (How I laugh!)
Could, without effort, place your hand among them,
And sprinkle them.

But all your ways are carefully ordered,
For you have never questioned duty.
We watch your everlasting combinations;
We call them fate; we turn them to our pleasure,
And when they most delight us, call them beauty.

REAL PROPERTY

Tell me about that harvest field.
Oh! Fifty acres of living bread.
The color has painted itself in my heart.
The form is patterned in my head.

So now I take it everywhere;
See it whenever I look round;
Hear it growing through every sound,
Know exactly the sound it makes—
Remembering, as one must all day,
Under the pavement the live earth aches.

Trees are at the farther end,
Limes all full of the mumbling bee:
So there must be a harvest field
Whenever one thinks of a linden tree.

A hedge is about it, very tall,
Hazy and cool, and breathing sweet.
Round paradise is such a wall
And all the day, in such a way,
In paradise the wild birds call.

You only need to close your eyes
And go within your secret mind,
And you'll be into paradise:
I've learnt quite easily to find
Some linden trees and drowsy bees,
A tall sweet hedge with the corn behind.

I will not have that harvest mown:
I'll keep the corn and leave the bread.
I've bought that field; it's now my own:
I've fifty acres in my head.
I take it as a dream to bed.
I carry it about all day. . . .

Sometimes when I have found a friend
I give a blade of corn away.

THE NIGHTINGALE NEAR THE HOUSE

Here is the soundless cypress on the lawn:
It listens, listens. Taller trees beyond
Listen. The moon at the unruffled pond
        Stares. And you sing, you sing.

That star-enchanted song falls through the air
From lawn to lawn down terraces of sound,
Darts in white arrows on the shadowed ground;
        While all the night you sing.

My dreams are flowers to which you are a bee,
As all night long I listen, and my brain
Receives your song, then loses it again
        In moonlight on the lawn.

Now is your voice a marble high and white,
Then like a mist on fields of paradise;
Now is a raging fire, then is like ice,
        Then breaks, and it is dawn.

MIDNIGHT LAMENTATION

When you and I go down
Breathless and cold,
Our faces both worn back
To earthly mold,
How lonely we shall be!
What shall we do,
You without me,
I without you?

I cannot bear the thought
You, first, may die,
Nor of how you will weep,
Should I.
We are too much alone;
What can we do
To make our bodies one:
You, me; I, you?

We are most nearly born
Of one same kind;
We have the same delight,
The same true mind.
Must we then part, we part;
Is there no way
To keep a beating heart,
And light of day?

I could now rise and run
Through street on street
To where you are breathing—you,
That we might meet,
And that your living voice
Might sound above
Fear, and we two rejoice
Within our love,

How frail the body is,
And we are made
As only in decay
To lean and fade.
I think too much of death;
There is a gloom
When I can't hear your breath
Calm in some room.

Oh, but how suddenly
Either may droop;
Countenance be so white,
Body stoop.
Then there may be a place
Where fading flowers
Drop on a lifeless face
Through weeping hours.

Is then nothing safe?
Can we not find
Some everlasting life
In our one mind?
I feel it like disgrace
Only to understand
Your spirit through your word,
Or by your hand.

I cannot find a way
Through love and through;
I cannot reach beyond
Body, to you.
When you or I must go
Down evermore,
There'll be no more to say
—But a locked door.

HOLY MATRIMONY

I

It was a fatal trick to play upon him.
With lusty life all pointing to one aim,
And his whole body watchful:
She at the moment came.

Could he resist? Could she? That one blue glance
Was not her own: oh, a far stronger power
Than hers shone at him through her
And fixed their mating hour.

II

Words, hardly needed, then were spoken,
All having only one intent.
They walked like children staring downward,
With body toward body bent.

Now all the others mumble darkly,
Wonder and enviously stare.
There is a glowing in the household:
Desire will dwell a moment here.

But older eyes gleam coldly on them;
Stiffer bodies step between.
Now while the preparations start
They must be cleanly kept apart:
So has the custom always been.

"You cannot kneel before the altar
Until we've trimmed the lamp for you.
Meanwhile you may a little woo;
We've much to do:
We'll bake and sew and watch you sidelong,
And make your wedding bed for you."

III

But he and she
They hear, they stare,
And they are asking:
Who are we?

They cling and cry:
What have we done?
Through us what ceremonial
Is begun?

The dark doors close
Upon the sky.
They shall be locked within
Till they do die.

IV

O prison church! O warder-priest!
Now they who used to walk the wind of freedom
Are living in your gloomy house of stone;
And they and it are growing older;
She is becoming every day less fair.
The more together, they are more alone:
They pile the fire and yet the hearth is colder.

THE EARTH FOR SALE

I

How perilous life will become on earth
When the great breed of man has covered all.
The world, that was too large, will be too small.
Deserts and mountains will have been explored,
Valleys swarmed through; and our prolific breed,
Exceeding death ten million times by birth,
Will halt (bewildered, bored),
And then may droop and dwindle like an autumn weed.

How shall we meet that moment when we know
There is no room to grow;
We, conscious, and with lonely startled eyes
Glaring upon ourselves, and with no Lord
To pray to: judged, without appeal,
What shall we feel?
He, being withdrawn, no supplicating cries
Will call Him back. He'll speak no further word.

Can special vision be required to see
What few pale centuries will take us there,
Where, at the barrier of the future, we
Shall stand condemned, in serried ranks, and stare
At Nothing—fearing Something may appear?
The Earth is covered with large auction boards,
And all her lands are reckoned up for sale.
The spaces that are now called virgin soil
Will soon be bought, and covered with great breed
Of human seed;
And, when the driven hordes
Cry "Food!"—but find no more for any toil,
Fear, fear will strike all eyes and faces pale.
Then no one more will speak,
But, rising from a murmur to a wail,
One voice, for all, will, like a Siren, shriek.

II

Is there no pledge to make at once with Earth
While yet we have not murdered all her trees;
Before it is too late for oath or pledge;
While yet man may be happy in his birth—
Before we have to fall upon our knees,
Clinging for safety to her farthest edge?
It is not very noble that we kill
Her lions and tigers, all. Is that our reign?—
Then let us build ourselves on earth again.
What is the human will?

Is it so clearly better than the ant's?
And is our life more holy than the plants'?
They do fulfil their purpose every year,
And bring no pain, nor fear.

III

Woe to that miserable last mankind;
And, when I think of that, I have a dread
I may awake on earth, again, to find
Myself, among it, living, oh, not dead.

IV

I had been thinking of that final Earth.
Then I remembered she herself would lick
Her own lithe body clean, and from her girth
Wipe any vermin that might cling too thick.

Damned! Damned! Apparent conqueror to-day—
Oh, evanescent sway!
O drunken lust!
O swarming dust!

Man makes himself believe he has a claim
To plant bright flags on every hill he swarms;
But in the end, and in his own wild name,
And for the better prospect of his fame,
Whether it be a person or a race,
Earth, with a smiling face,
Will hold and smother him in her large arms.

ALFRED NOYES

Alfred Noyes, the eldest son of Alfred and Amelia Adams Rowley Noyes, was born on September 16, 1880, in Staffordshire. He was educated at Exeter College, Oxford, and rowed on his college crew. He began when but a boy to write verse, at college showed a fine taste for literature, and in 1902 published his first volume, *The Loom of Years,* following it the same year with another volume, *Poems.* During the next twenty-five years he issued books of poetry at the rate of one a year, besides various other writings.

In 1913 he made his first visit to the United States, coming to give a series of lectures at the Lowell Institute, Boston, on "The Sea in English Poetry." He was received cordially in this country, being given an honorary D.Litt. degree by Yale in 1913, and elected by Princeton University, Professor of Modern English Literature on the Murray Foundation. He remained at Princeton until 1923, when he resigned to return to England. During these years he made a number of lecture trips across the United States, speaking in favor of the older forms of poetry, and reading his own work.

Because of defective eyesight he was unable to enter the army during the World War, but was attached temporarily to the Foreign Office of the British Government in 1916. In recognition of his work while in this service, he was appointed in 1918 a Commander of the Order of the British Empire.

He has edited a number of volumes, among them *The Magic Casement, an Anthology of Fairy Poetry* (1909), *A Poet's Anthology of Poems* (1911), and *A Book of*

Princeton Verse (1916); and has written a book of criticism, *Some Aspects of Modern Poetry* (1924), in which he attacks many of the new forms of verse, and defends the superiority of the older poetry. He is the author of a life of William Morris in the English Men of Letters Series (1908), of a book of short stories, *Walking Shadows* (1917), and of a novel, *The Hidden Player* (1924). In addition he has been a frequent contributor to such periodicals as *Blackwood's Magazine, The Cornhill Magazine, The Fortnightly Review,* and *The Atlantic Monthly.*

He has been twice married, the first time in 1907 to Garnett Daniels, the youngest daughter of Colonel Byron G. Daniels, of the United States Army. She died in France on October 8, 1926, and on September 27, 1927, he married Mrs. Mary Weld-Blundell, the widow of Richard Weld-Blundell, and a daughter of Captain J. G. Mayne. He now lives in England, but makes frequent lecture tours in America.

THE BARREL-ORGAN

There's a barrel-organ carolling across a golden street
  In the City as the sun sinks low;
And the music's not immortal; but the world has made it sweet
  And fulfilled it with the sunset glow;
And it pulses through the pleasures of the City and the pain
  That surround the singing organ like a large eternal light;
And they've given it a glory and a part to play again
  In the Symphony that rules the day and night.

And now it's marching onward through the realms of old romance,
  And trolling out a fond familiar tune,
And now it's roaring cannon down to fight the King of France,
  And now it's prattling softly to the moon,
And all around the organ there's a sea without a shore
  Of human joys and wonders and regrets;
To remember and to recompense the music evermore
  For what the cold machinery forgets. . . .

Yes; as the music changes,
  Like a prismatic glass,
It takes the light and ranges
  Through all the moods that pass;
Dissects the common carnival
  Of passions and regrets,
And gives the world a glimpse of all
  The colors it forgets.

And there *La Traviata* sighs
  Another sadder song;
And there *Il Trovatore* cries
  A tale of deeper wrong;

And bolder knights to battle go
With sword and shield and lance,
Than ever here on earth below
Have whirled into—*a dance!*—

Go down to Kew in lilac-time, in lilac-time, in lilac-time;
Go down to Kew in lilac-time (it isn't far from London!),
And you shall wander hand in hand with love in summer's wonderland;
Go down to Kew in lilac-time (it isn't far from London!).

The cherry-trees are seas of bloom and soft perfume and sweet perfume,
The cherry-trees are seas of bloom (and oh, so near to London!),
And there they say, when dawn is high and all the world's a blaze of sky
The cuckoo, though he's very shy, will sing a song for London.

The Dorian nightingale is rare, and yet they say you'll hear him there
At Kew, at Kew in lilac-time (and oh, so near to London!),
The linnet and the throstle, too, and after dark the long halloo
And golden-eyed *tu-whit, tu-whoo* of owls that ogle London.

For Noah hardly knew a bird of any kind that isn't heard
At Kew, at Kew in lilac-time (and oh, so near to London!),
And when the rose begins to pout and all the chestnut spires are out
You'll hear the rest without a doubt, all chorussing for London:—

Come down to Kew in lilac-time, in lilac-time, in lilac-time;
Come down to Kew in lilac-time (it isn't far from London!),

And you shall wander hand in hand with love in summer's wonderland;
Come down to Kew in lilac-time (it isn't far from London!).

And then the troubadour begins to thrill the golden street,
In the City as the sun sinks low;
And in all the gaudy busses there are scores of weary feet
Marking time, sweet time, with a dull mechanic beat,
And a thousand hearts are plunging to a love they'll never meet,
Through the meadows of the sunset, through the poppies and the wheat,
In the land where the dead dreams go.

Verdi, Verdi, when you wrote *Il Trovatore* did you dream
Of the City when the sun sinks low,
Of the organ and the monkey and the many-colored stream
On the Piccadilly pavement, of the myriad eyes that seem
To be litten for a moment with a wild Italian gleam
As *A che la morte* parodies the world's eternal theme
And pulses with the sunset-glow?

There's a thief, perhaps, that listens with a face of frozen stone
In the City as the sun sinks low;
There's a portly man of business with a balance of his own,
There's a clerk and there's a butcher of a soft reposeful tone.
And they're all of them returning to the heavens they have known:
They are crammed and jammed in busses and—they're each of them alone
In the land where the dead dreams go.

There's a very modish woman and her smile is very bland
In the City as the sun sinks low;
And her hansom jingles onward, but her little jewelled hand
Is clenched a little tighter and she cannot understand
What she wants or why she wanders to that undiscovered land,

For the parties there are not at all the sort of thing she planned,
In the land where the dead dreams go.

There's a rowing man that listens and his heart is crying out
In the City as the sun sinks low;
For the barge, the eight, the Isis, and the coach's whoop and shout,
For the minute-gun, the counting, and the long dishevelled rout,
For the howl along the tow-path and a fate that's still in doubt,
For a roughened oar to handle and a race to think about
In the land where the dead dreams go.

There's a laborer that listens to the voices of the dead
In the City as the sun sinks low;
And his hand begins to tremble and his face to smolder red
As he sees a loafer watching him and—there he turns his head
And stares into the sunset where his April love is fled,
For he hears her softly singing and his lonely soul is led
Through the land where the dead dreams go.

There's an old and haggard demi-rep, it's ringing in her ears,
In the City as the sun sinks low;
With the wild and empty sorrow of the love that blights and sears,
Oh, and if she hurries onward, then be sure, be sure she hears,
Hears and bears the bitter burden of the unforgotten years,
And her laugh's a little harsher and her eyes are brimmed with tears
For the land where the dead dreams go.

There's a barrel-organ carolling across a golden street
In the City as the sun sinks low;
Though the music's only Verdi there's a world to make it sweet
Just as yonder yellow sunset where the earth and heaven meet
Mellows all the sooty City! Hark, a hundred thousand feet
Are marching on to glory through the poppies and the wheat
In the land where the dead dreams go.

So it's Jeremiah, Jeremiah,
What have you to say
When you meet the garland girl
Tripping on their way?

All around my gala hat
I wear a wreath of roses
(A long and lonely year it is
I've waited for the May!).
If any one should ask you,
The reason why I wear it is—
My own love, my true love,
Is coming home to-day.

And it's buy a bunch of violets for the lady
(It's lilac-time in London; it's lilac-time in London!),
Buy a bunch of violets for the lady
While the sky burns blue above:

On the other side the street you'll find it shady
(It's lilac-time in London; it's lilac-time in London!),
But buy a bunch of violets for the lady,
And tell her she's your own true love.

There's a barrel-organ carolling across a golden street
In the City as the sun sinks glittering and slow;
And the music's not immortal; but the world has made it sweet
And enriched it with the harmonies that make a song complete
In the deeper heavens of music where the night and morning meet,
As it dies into the sunset-glow;
And it pulses through the pleasures of the City and the pain
That surround the singing organ like a large eternal light,
And they've given it a glory and a part to play again
In the Symphony that rules the day and night.

And there, as the music changes,
The song runs round again.
Once more it turns and ranges
Through all its joy and pain,

Dissects the common carnival
Of passions and regrets;
And the wheeling world remembers all
The wheeling song forgets.

Once more *La Traviata* sighs
Another sadder song:
Once more *Il Trovatore* cries
A tale of deeper wrong;
Once more the knights to battle go
With sword and shield and lance
Till once, once more, the shattered foe
Has whirled into—*a dance!*

Come down to Kew in lilac-time, in lilac-time, in lilac-time;
Come down to Kew in lilac-time (it isn't far from London!),
And you shall wander hand in hand with love in summer's wonderland;
Come down to Kew in lilac-time (it isn't far from London!).

FORTY SINGING SEAMEN

"In our lands be Beeres and Lyons of dyvers colours as ye redd, grene, black, and white. And in our land be also unicornes and these Unicornes slee many Lyons. . . . Also there dare no man make a lye in our lande, for if he dyde he sholde incontynent be sleyn."

Mediaeval Epistle, of Pope Prester John.

I

Across the seas of Wonderland to Mogadore we plodded,
Forty singing seamen in an old black barque,
And we landed in the twilight where a Polyphemus nodded
With his battered moon-eye winking red and yellow through the dark!
For his eye was growing mellow,
Rich and ripe and red and yellow,

As was time, since old Ulysses made him bellow in the dark!
CHO.—Since Ulysses bunged his eye up with a pine-torch in the dark!

II

Were they mountains in the gloaming or the giant's ugly shoulders
Just beneath the rolling eyeball, with its bleared and vinous glow,
Red and yellow o'er the purple of the pines among the boulders
And the shaggy horror brooding on the sullen slopes below,
Were they pines among the boulders
Or the hair upon his shoulders?
We were only simple seamen, so of course we didn't know.
CHO.—We were simple singing seamen, so of course we couldn't know.

III

But we crossed a plain of poppies, and we came upon a fountain
Not of water, but of jewels, like a spray of leaping fire;
And behind it, in an emerald glade, beneath a golden mountain
There stood a crystal palace, for a sailor to admire;
For a troop of ghosts came round us,
Which with leaves of bay they crowned us,
Then with grog they well nigh drowned us, to the depth of our desire!
CHO.—And 'twas very friendly of them, as a sailor can admire!

IV

There was music all about us, we were growing quite forgetful
We were only singing seamen from the dirt of London-town,

Though the nectar that we swallowed seemed to vanish half regretful
As if we wasn't good enough to take such vittles down,
When we saw a sudden figure,
Tall and black as any nigger,
Like the devil—only bigger—drawing near us with a frown!
CHO.—Like the devil—but much bigger—and he wore a golden crown!

V

And "What's all this?" he growls at us! With dignity we chaunted,
"Forty singing seamen, sir, as won't be put upon!"
"What? Englishmen?" he cries, "Well, if ye don't mind being haunted,
Faith you're welcome to my palace; I'm the famous Prester John!
Will ye walk into my palace?
I don't bear 'ee any malice!
One and all ye shall be welcome in the halls of Prester John!"
CHO.—So we walked into the palace and the halls of Prester John!

VI

Now the door was one great diamond and the hall a hollow ruby—
Big as Beachy Head, my lads, nay bigger by a half!
And I sees the mate wi' mouth agape, a-staring like a booby,
And the skipper close behind him, with his tongue out like a calf!
Now the way to take it rightly
Was to walk along politely
Just as if you didn't notice—so I couldn't help but laugh!
CHO.—For they both forgot their manners and the crew was bound to laugh!

VII

But he took us through his palace and, my lads, as I'm a
sinner,
We walked into an opal like a sunset-colored cloud—
"My dining-room," he says, and, quick as light we saw a
dinner
Spread before us by the fingers of a hidden fairy crowd;
And the skipper, swaying gently
After dinner, murmurs faintly,
"I looks to-wards you, Prester John, you've done us very
proud!"
CHO.—And we drank his health with honors, for he *done*
us *very* proud!

VIII

Then he walks us to his garden where we sees a feathered
demon
Very splendid and important on a sort of spicy tree!
"That's the Phœnix," whispers Prester, "which all eddicated
seamen
Knows the only one existent, and *he's* waiting for to flee!
When his hundred years expire
Then he'll set hisself a-fire
And another from his ashes rise most beautiful to see!"
CHO.—With wings of rose and emerald most beautiful to see!

IX

Then he says, "In younder forest there's a little silver river,
And whosoever drinks of it, his youth shall never die!
The centuries go by, but Prester John endures for ever
With his music in the mountains and his magic on the sky!
While *your* hearts are growing colder,
While your world is growing older,
There's a magic in the distance, where the sea-line meets
the sky."
CHO.—It shall call to singing seamen till the fount o' song
is dry!

X

So we thought we'd up and seek it, but that forest fair defied us,—
First a crimson leopard laughs at us most horrible to see,
Then a sea-green lion came and sniffed and licked his chops and eyed us,
While a red and yellow unicorn was dancing round a tree!
We was trying to look thinner,
Which was hard, because our dinner
Must ha' made us very tempting to a cat o' high degree!
CHO.—Must ha' made us very tempting to the whole menarjeree!

XI

So we scuttled from that forest and across the poppy meadows
Where the awful shaggy horror brooded o'er us in the dark!
And we pushes out from shore again a-jumping at our shadows,
And pulls away most joyful to the old black barque!
And home again we plodded
While the Polyphemus nodded
With his battered moon-eye winking red and yellow through the dark.
CHO.—Oh, the moon above the mountains, red and yellow through the dark!

XII

Across the seas of Wonderland to London-town we blundered,
Forty singing seamen as was puzzled for to know
If the visions that we saw was caused by—here again we pondered—
A tipple in a vision forty thousand years ago.
Could the grog we *dreamt* we swallowed
Make us *dream* of all that followed?
We were only simple seamen, so of course we didn't know!
CHO.—We were simple singing seamen, so of course we could not know!

THE HIGHWAYMAN

PART ONE

I

The wind was a torrent of darkness among the gusty trees,
The moon was a ghostly galleon tossed upon cloudy seas,
The road was a ribbon of moonlight over the purple moor,
And the highwayman came riding—
Riding—riding—
The highwayman came riding, up to the old inn door.

II

He'd a French cocked-hat on his forehead, a bunch of lace at his chin,
A coat of the claret velvet, and breeches of brown doe-skin;
They fitted with never a wrinkle: his boots were up to the thigh!
And he rode with a jewelled twinkle,
His pistol butts a-twinkle,
His rapier hilt a-twinkle, under the jewelled sky.

III

Over the cobbles he clattered and clashed in the dark inn-yard,
And he tapped with his whip on the shutters, but all was locked and barred;
He whistled a tune to the window, and who should be waiting there
But the landlord's black-eyed daughter,
Bess, the landlord's daughter,
Plaiting a dark red love-knot into her long black hair.

IV

And dark in the dark old inn-yard a stable-wicket creaked
Where Tim the ostler listened; his face was white and peaked;
His eyes were hollows of madness, his hair like moldy hay,
But he loved the landlord's daughter,
The landlord's red-lipped daughter;
Dumb as a dog he listened, and he heard the robber say—

V

"One kiss, my bonny sweetheart, I'm after a prize to-night,
But I shall be back with the yellow gold before the morning
light;
Yet, if they press me sharply, and harry me through the day,
Then look for me by moonlight,
Watch for me by moonlight,
I'll come to thee by moonlight, though hell should bar the
way."

VI

He rose upright in the stirrups; he scarce could reach her
hand,
But she loosened her hair i' the casement! His face burnt like
a brand
As the black cascade of perfume came tumbling over his
breast;
And he kissed its waves in the moonlight,
(Oh, sweet black waves in the moonlight!)
Then he tugged at his rein in the moonlight, and galloped
away to the West.

PART TWO

I

He did not come in the dawning; he did not come at noon;
And out o' the tawny sunset, before the rise o' the moon,
When the road was a gipsy's ribbon, looping the purple moor,
A red-coat troop came marching—
Marching—marching—
King George's men came marching, up to the old inn-door.

II

They said no word to the landlord, they drank his ale instead,
But they gagged his daughter and bound her to the foot of
her narrow bed;
Two of them knelt at her casement, with muskets at their
side!

There was death at every window;
And hell at one dark window;
For Bess could see, through her casement, the road that *he* would ride.

III

They had tied her up to attention, with many a sniggering jest;
They had bound a musket beside her, with the barrel beneath her breast!
"Now keep good watch!" and they kissed her.
She heard the dead man say—
Look for me by moonlight;
Watch for me by moonlight;
I'll come to thee by moonlight, though hell should bar the way!

IV

She twisted her hands behind her; but all the knots held good!
She writhed her hands till her fingers were wet with sweat or blood!
They stretched and strained in the darkness, and the hours crawled by like years,
Till, now, on the stroke of midnight,
Cold, on the stroke of midnight,
The tip of one finger touched it! The trigger at least was hers!

V

The tip of one finger touched it; she strove no more for the rest!
Up, she stood up to attention, with the barrel beneath her breast,
She would not risk their hearing; she would not strive again;
For the road lay bare in the moonlight;
Blank and bare in the moonlight;
And the blood of her veins in the moonlight throbbed to her love's refrain.

VI

Tlot-tlot; tlot-tlot! Had they heard it? The horse-hoofs ringing clear;
Tlot-tlot, tlot-tlot, in the distance? Were they deaf that they did not hear?
Down the ribbon of moonlight, over the brow of the hill,
The highwayman came riding,
Riding, riding!
The red-coats looked to their priming! She stood up, straight and still!

VII

Tlot-tlot, in the frosty silence! *Tlot-tlot,* in the echoing night!
Nearer he came and nearer! Her face was like a light!
Her eyes grew wide for a moment; she drew one last deep breath,
Then her finger moved in the moonlight,
Her musket shattered the moonlight,
Shattered her breast in the moonlight and warned him—with her death.

VIII

He turned; he spurred to the West; he did not know who stood
Bowed, with her head o'er the musket, drenched with her own red blood!
Not till the dawn he heard it, his face grew grey to hear
How Bess, the landlord's daughter,
The landlord's black-eyed daughter,
Had watched for her love in the moonlight, and died in the darkness there.

IX

Back, he spurred like a madman, shrieking a curse to the sky,
With the white road smoking behind him and his rapier brandished high!
Blood-red were his spurs i' the golden noon; wine-red was his velvet coat,

When they shot him down on the highway,
Down like a dog on the highway,
And he lay in his blood on the highway, with the bunch of lace at his throat.

* * * * * *

X

And still of a winter's night, they say, when the wind is in the trees,
When the moon is a ghostly galleon tossed upon cloudy seas,
When the road is a ribbon of moonlight over the purple moor,
A highwayman comes riding—
Riding—riding—
A highwayman comes riding, up to the old inn-door.

XI

Over the cobbles he clatters and clangs in the dark inn-yard;
He taps with his whip on the shutters, but all is locked and barred;
He whistles a tune to the window, and who should be waiting there
But the landlord's black-eyed daughter,
Bess, the landlord's daughter,
Plaiting a dark red love-knot into her long black hair.

SONG

[*From* DRAKE]

Now the purple night is past,
Now the moon more faintly glows,
Dawn has through thy casement cast
Roses on thy breast, a rose;
Now the kisses are all done,
Now the world awakes anew,
Now the charmèd hour is gone,
Let not love go, too.

When old winter, creeping nigh,
  Sprinkles raven hair with white,
Dims the brightly glancing eye,
  Laughs away the dancing light,
Roses may forget their sun,
  Lilies may forget their dew,
Beauties perish, one by one,
  Let not love go, too.

Palaces and towers of pride
  Crumble year by year away;
Creeds like robes are laid aside,
  Even our very tombs decay!
When the all-conquering moth and rust
  Gnaw the goodly garment through,
When the dust returns to dust,
  Let not love go, too.

Kingdoms melt away like snow,
  Gods are spent like wasting flames,
Hardly the new peoples know
  Their divine thrice-worshipped names!
At the last great hour of all,
  When thou makest all things new,
Father, hear Thy children call,
  Let not love go, too.

THOMAS DEKKER'S SONG

[*From* TALES OF THE MERMAID TAVERN]

I

Seven wise men on an old black settle,
  Seven wise men of the Mermaid Inn,
Ringing blades of the one right metal,
  What is the best that a blade can win?
Bread and cheese, and a few small kisses?
  Ha! ha! ha! Would you take them—you?
—Ay, if Dame Venus would add to her blisses
  A roaring fire and a friend or two!

CHORUS: Up now, answer me, tell me true!—
—Ay, if the hussy would add to her blisses
A roaring fire and a friend or two!

II

What will you say when the world is dying?
What, when the last wild midnight falls
Dark, too dark for the bat to be flying
Round the ruins of old St. Paul's?
What will be last of the lights to perish?
What but the little red ring we knew,
Lighting the hands and the hearts that cherish
A fire, a fire, and a friend or two!

CHORUS: Up now, answer me, tell me true!
What will be last of the stars to perish?
—The fire that lighteth a friend or two!

III

Up now, answer me, on your mettle,
Wisest man of the Mermaid Inn,
Soberest man on the old black settle,
Out with the truth! It was never a sin.—
Well, if God saved me alone of the seven,
Telling me *you* must be damned, or *you*,
"This," I would say, "This is hell, not heaven!
Give me the fire and a friend or two!"

CHORUS: Steel was never so ringing true:
"God," we would say, "this is hell, not heaven!
Give us the fire, and a friend or two!"

THE SILVER CROOK

I was mistuk, once, for the Poape of Roame . . .
The drawled fantastic words came floating down
Behind me, five long years ago, when last
I left the old shepherd, Bramble, by his fold.

Bramble was fond, you'll judge, of his own tales,
And cast a gorgeous fly for the unwary:
But I was late, and could not listen then,
Despite his eager leer.
Yet, many a night,
And many a league from home, out of a dream
Of white chalk coats, and roofs of Horsham stone,
Colored like russet apples, there would come
Music of sheep-bells, baaing of black-nosed lambs,
Barking of two wise dogs, crushed scents of thyme,
A silver crook, bright as the morning star,
Above the naked downs.
Then—Bramble's voice,
I was mistuk, once, for the Poape of Roame,
Would almost wake me, wondering what he meant.
Now, five years later, while the larks went up
Over the dew-ponds in a wild-winged glory,
And all the Sussex downs, from weald to sea,
Were patched like one wide crazy quilt, in squares
Of yellow and crimson, clover and mustard-flower,
Edged with white chalk, I found him once again.
He leaned upon his crook, unbudged by war,
Unchanged, and leering eagerly as of old.
How should I paint old Bramble—the shrewd face,
Brown as the wrinkled loam, the bright brown eyes,
The patriarchal beard, the moleskin cap,
The boots that looked like tree-stumps, the loose cloak
Tanned by all weathers,—every inch of him
A growth of Sussex soil. His back was bent
Like wind-blown hawthorn, turning from the sea,
With roots that strike the deeper.
Well content
With all his world, and boastful as a child,
In splendid innocence of the worldling's way,
Whose murderous ego skulks behind a hedge
Of modest privet,—no, I cannot paint him.
Better to let him talk, and paint himself.

"Marnin'," he said; and swept away five years.
Then, with complete dominion over time,
Waiving all prelude, he picked up the thread
We dropped that day, and cast his bait again:—
I was mistuk, once, for the Poape of Roame.—
"Tell me," I said. "Explain. I've dreamed of it."—
"I rackon you doan't believe it. Drunken Dick,
'Ull tell you 'tis as true's I'm stannin' here.
It happened along of this old silver crook.
I call it silver 'cos it shines so far.
My wife can see it over at Ovingdean
When I'm on Telscombe Tye. They doan't mek crooks
Like this in Sussex now. They've lost the way
To shape 'em. That's what they French papists knowed
Over at Arundel. They tried to buy
My crook, to carry in church. But I woan't sell 'en.
I've heerd there's magic in a crook like this.—
White magic. Well, I rackon it did save Dick
More ways than one, that night, from the old Black Ram.
I've med a song about it. There was once
A Lunnon poet, down here for his health,
Asked me to sing it to 'un, an' I did.
It med him laff, too. 'Sing it again,' he says,
'But go slow, this time.' 'No, I woan't,' I says
(I knowed what *he* was trying). 'No,' I says,
'I woan't go slow. You'll ketch 'un if I do.'
You see, he meks a tedious mort of money
From these here ballad books, an' I wer'n't goin'
To let these Lunnon chuckle-heads suck my brains.
I med it to thet ancient tune you liked,
The Brown Girl. 'Member it?"

Bramble cleared his throat,
Spat at a bee, leaned forward on his crook,
Fixed his brown eyes upon a distant spire,
Solemnly swelled his lungs, once, twice, and thrice;
Then, like an old brown thrush, began to sing:—

"The Devil turns round when he hears the sound
Of bells in a Sussex foald.

One crack, I rackon, from this good crook
  Would make old Scratch leave hoald.
They can't shape crooks to-day like mine,
  For the liddle folk helped 'em then.
I've heerd some say as they've see'd 'en shine
  From Ditchling to Fairlight Glen.

"I loaned 'em a loanst o' my crook one day
  To carry in Arundel.
They'd buy 'en to show in their church, they say;
  But goald woan't mek me sell.
I never should find a crook so slick,
  So silver in the sun;
And, if you talk to Drunken Dick,
  He'll tell you what it's done.

"You'll find him spannelling round the Plough;
  And, Lord! when Dick was young,
He'd drink enough to draown a cow,
  And roughen a tiger's tongue.
He'd drink Black Ram till his noäse turned blue,
  And the liddle black mice turned white.
You ask 'en what my crook can do,
  An' what he see'd that night.

"He says, as through the fern he ran
  ('Twas Pharisees' fern, say I),
A wild potatur, as big as a man,
  Arose and winked its eye.
He says it took his arm that night,
  And waggled its big brown head,
Then sang: '*This world will never go right*
  Till Drunken Dick be dead.'

"He shooked it off and, rambling round,
  Among the goalden gorse,
He heers a kin' of sneering sound
  Pro-ciddin' from a horse,
Which reared upright, then said out loud
  (While Dick said, 'I'll be danged!')

'His parents will be tedious proud
When Drunken Dick is hanged!'

"I rackon 'twould take a barrel of ale,
Betwix' my dinner and tea,
To mek me see the very nex' thing
That Drunken Dick did see;
For first he thought 'twas elephants walked
Behind him on the Tye,
And then he saw fower ricks of straw
That heaved against the sky.

"He saw 'em lift. He saw 'em shift.
He saw gurt beards arise,
He saw 'em slowly lumbering down
A hundred times his size;
And, as he ran, he heer'd 'em say,
Whenever his head he turned,
'This world will never be bright and gay
Till Drunken Dick be burned.'

"And then as Dick escaped again
And squirmed the churchyard through,
The cock that crowns the weather-vane
Cried *'How d'ye doodle doo?'*
'Why, how d'ye doodle do?' says Dick,
'I know why *you* go round.'
'There'll be no luck,' that rooster shruck,
'Till Drunken Dick be drowned!'

"And then, as Dick dodged round they barns,
And med for the white chalk coast,
He meets Himself, with the two black horns,
And eyes 'twud mek you roast.
'Walcome! walcome!' old Blackamoor cried,
' 'Tis muttonless day in hell,
So I think I'll have your kidneys, fried,
And a bit of your liver as well.'

"Then Dick he loosed a tarr'ble shout,
    And the Devil stopped dead to look;
And the sheep-bells rang, and the moon came out,
    And it shone on my silver crook.
'I rackon,' says Dick, 'if you're oald Nick,
    You'd batter be scramblin' home;
For *those* be the ringers of Arundel,
    And *that* is the Poape of Roame.' "

JAMES STEPHENS

James Stephens, the son of poor Irish parents, was born in Dublin in February, 1882. He received but little formal education, and at an early age began making his own living. He married, became the father of several children, learned typing, and supported his family by working at a small salary in a solicitor's office. Some of his contributions to an Irish periodical attracted the attention of George W. Russell, who visited him and encouraged him to become a man of letters. In 1909 he published *Insurrections* and *The Lonely God and Other Poems,* books of verse which received favorable comment. Next appeared *The Hill of Vision* (1912), *The Charwoman's Daughter* (1912), and *The Crock of Gold* (1912), the latter two being works of prose fiction. After 1912 his ability as a prose writer was so widely announced that for the time being readers almost forgot his poetry. He celebrated the success of his fiction by taking his family to Paris for a vacation, the immediate literary result of which was a book of stories, *Here Are Ladies* (1913). He has continued since to write both prose and poetry.

After gaining a literary reputation Stephens was appointed Assistant to the Director of the National Gallery of Ireland, a position allowing him much leisure. He lives in Dublin, but makes occasional journeys to Paris and elsewhere. In 1925 he came to the United States, where he proved to be a highly successful reader of his own poems.

THE SNARE

I hear a sudden cry of pain!
There is a rabbit in a snare:
Now I hear the cry again,
But I cannot tell from where.

But I cannot tell from where
He is calling out for aid!
Crying on the frightened air,
Making everything afraid!

Making everything afraid!
Wrinkling up his little face!
As he cries again for aid;
—And I cannot find the place!

And I cannot find the place
Where his paw is in the snare!
Little One! Oh, Little One!
I am searching everywhere!

LITTLE THINGS

Little things, that run, and quail,
And die, in silence and despair!

Little things, that fight, and fail,
And fall, on sea, and earth, and air!

All trapped and frightened little things,
The mouse, the coney, hear our prayer!

As we forgive those done to us,
—The lamb, the linnet, and the hare—

Forgive us all our trespasses,
Little creatures, everywhere!

CHILL OF THE EVE

A long green swell
Slopes soft to the sea;
And a far-off bell
Swings sweet to me;
As the grey
Chill day
Slips away
From the lea.

Spread cold and far,
Without one glow
From a mild pale star,
Is the sky's steel bow;
And the grey
Chill day
Slips away
Below.

Yon green tree grieves
To the air around;
And the whispering leaves
Have a lonely sound;
As the grey
Chill day
Slips away
From the ground.

And dark, more dark,
The shades settle down;
Far off is a spark
From the lamp-lit town;
And the grey
Chill day
Slips away
With a frown.

THE SHELL

I

And then I pressed the shell
Close to my ear,
And listened well.

And straightway, like a bell,
Came low and clear
The slow, sad murmur of far distant seas,

Whipped by an icy breeze
Upon a shore
Wind-swept and desolate.

It was a sunless strand that never bore
The footprint of a man,
Nor felt the weight

Since time began
Of any human quality or stir,
Save what the dreary winds and wave incur.

II

And in the hush of waters was the sound
Of pebbles, rolling round;
For ever rolling, with a hollow sound:

And bubbling sea-weeds, as the waters go,
Swish to and fro
Their long cold tentacles of slimy grey;

There was no day;
Nor ever came a night
Setting the stars alight

To wonder at the moon:
Was twilight only, and the frightened croon,
Smitten to whimpers, of the dreary wind

And waves that journeyed blind . . .
And then I loosed my ear.—Oh, it was sweet
To hear a cart go jolting down the street!

DEIRDRE

Do not let any woman read this verse!
It is for men, and after them their sons,
And their son's sons!

The time comes when our hearts sink utterly;
When we remember Deirdre, and her tale,
And that her lips are dust.

Once she did tread the earth: men took her hand;
They looked into her eyes and said their say,
And she replied to them.

More than two thousand years it is since she
Was beautiful: she trod the waving grass;
She saw the clouds.

Two thousand years! The grass is still the same;
The clouds as lovely as they were that time
When Deirdre was alive.

But there has been again no woman born
Who was so beautiful; not one so beautiful
Of all the women born.

Let all men go apart and mourn together!
No man can ever love her! Not a man
Can dream to be her lover!

No man can bend before her! No man say—
What could one say to her? There are no words
That one could say to her!

Now she is but a story that is told
Beside the fire! No man can ever be
The friend of that poor queen!

SHAME

I was ashamed! I dared not lift my eyes!
I could not bear to look upon the skies!
What I had done! sure, everybody knew!
From everywhere hands pointed where I stood,
And scornful eyes were piercing through and through
The moody armor of my hardihood!

I heard their voices too, each word an asp
That buzz'd and stung me sudden as a flame!
And all the world was jolting on my name!
And now and then there came a wicked rasp
Of laughter, jarring me to deeper shame!

And then I looked, and there was no one nigh!
No eyes that stabbed like swords or glinted sly!
No laughter creaking on the silent air!
—And then I saw that I was all alone
Facing my soul! And next I was aware
That this mad mockery was all my own!

ETCHED IN FROST

The corn is down,
The stooks are gone,
The fields are brown,
And the early dawn
Grows slowly behind
Where the mountains frown,
And a thin white sun
Is shivering down.

There isn't a leaf,
Nor anything green,
To aid belief
That summer has been;

And the puffed-up red-breast
(Ball o' Grief)
Hops at the window
For relief.

The cows are in byre,
The sheep in fold;
The mare and the sire
Are safe from cold;
The hens are sheltered,
In wood and wire,
And the sheep-dog snoozes
Before the fire.

The farmer can grin,
And rub his hands,
For his crops are in
From the resting lands;
And his wheat is stored
In the oaken bin,
And his buxom wife
Makes merry within.

BARBARIANS

I pause beside the stream, and hear
The waters talking on the way;
If I had a proper ear
I could tell you what they say!

Yon lovely tree against the sky,
Which the sun first rests upon,
Has a message for my eye;
If I had a proper one!

On the golden heath a wind,
Whispered to me as I stood;
If I had a proper mind
I could answer, so I could!

I am deaf and dumb and blind!
No reply can I invent
When a stream, a tree, a wind,
Asks am I intelligent!

THE GOAT PATHS

The crooked paths go every way
  Upon the hill—they wind about
  Through the heather, in and out
Of the quiet sunniness.
And there the goats, day after day,
  Stray in sunny quietness,
Cropping here and cropping there,
  As they pause and turn and pass,
Now a bit of heather spray,
  Now a mouthful of the grass.

In the deeper sunniness,
  In the place where nothing stirs,
Quietly in quietness,
  In the quiet of the furze,
For a time they come and lie
Staring on the roving sky.

If you approach they run away,
  They leap and stare, away they bound,
  With a sudden angry sound,
To the sunny quietude;
  Crouching down where nothing stirs
  In the silence of the furze,
Couching down again to brood
In the sunny solitude.

If I were as wise as they
  I would stray apart and brood,
I would beat a hidden way
Through the quiet heather spray

To a sunny solitude;
And should you come I'd run away,
I would make an angry sound,
I would stare and turn and bound
To the deeper quietude,
To the place where nothing stirs
In the silence of the furze.

In that airy quietness
I would think as long as they;
Through the quiet sunniness
I would stray away to brood
By a hidden beaten way
In a sunny solitude.

I would think until I found
Something I can never find,
Something lying on the ground,
In the bottom of my mind.

THE WASTE PLACES

I

As a naked man I go
Through the desert sore afraid,
Holding up my head, although
I am as frightened as a maid.

The couching lion there I saw
From barren rocks lift up his eye,
He parts the cactus with his paw,
He stares at me as I go by.

He would follow on my trace
If he knew I was afraid,
If he knew my hardy face
Hides the terrors of a maid.

In the night he rises, and
He stretches forth, he snuffs the air,
He roars and leaps along the sand,
He creeps and watches everywhere.

His burning eyes, his eyes of bale,
Through the darkness I can see;
He lashes fiercely with his tail,
He would love to spring at me.

I am the lion in his lair,
I am the fear that frightens me,
I am the desert of despair,
And the nights of agony.

Night or day, whate'er befall,
I must walk that desert land,
Until I can dare to call
The lion out to lick my hand.

II

As a naked man I tread
The gloomy forests, ring on ring,
Where the sun that's overhead
Cannot see what's happening.

There I go: the deepest shade,
The deepest silence pressing me,
And my heart is more afraid
Than a maiden's heart would be.

Every day I have to run
Underneath the demon tree,
Where the ancient wrong is done,
While I shrink in agony.

There the demon held a maid
In his arms, and as she, daft,
Screamed again in fear he laid
His lips upon her lips and laughed.

And she beckoned me to run,
And she called for help to me.
And the ancient wrong was done
Which is done eternally.

I am the maiden and the fear,
I am the sunless shade, the strife,
I the demon lips, the sneer
Showing under every life.

I must tread that gloomy way
Until I shall dare to run
And bear the demon with his prey
From the forest to the sun.

A WOMAN IS A BRANCHY TREE

A woman is a branchy tree
And man a singing wind;
And from her branches carelessly
He takes what he can find:

Then wind and man go far away,
While winter comes with loneliness;
With cold, and rain, and slow decay,
On woman and on tree till they

Droop to the earth again, and be
A withered woman, a withered tree;
While wind and man woo in the glade
Another tree, another maid.

WHY TOMAS CAM WAS GRUMPY

If I were rich what would I do?
I'd leave the horse just ready to shoe;
I'd leave the pail beside the cow;
I'd leave the furrow beneath the plough;

I'd leave the ducks, tho' they should quack,
"Our eggs will be stolen before you're back";
I'd buy a diamond brooch, a ring,
A chain of gold that I would fling
Around her neck. . . . Ah, what an itch,
If I were rich!

What would I do if I were wise?
I would not debate about the skies;
Nor would I try a book to write;
Or find the wrong in the tangled right;
I would not debate with learned men
Of how, and what, and why, and when;
—I'd train my tongue to a linnet's song,
I'd learn the words that couldn't go wrong—
And then I'd say . . . And win the prize,
If I were wise!

But I'm not that nor t'other, I bow
My back to the work that's waiting now:
I'll shoe the horse that's standing ready;
I'll milk the cow if she'll be steady;
I'll follow the plough that turns the loam;
I'll watch the ducks don't lay from home:
—And I'll curse, and curse, and curse again
Till the devil joins in with his big amen;
And none but he and I will wot
When the heart within me starts to rot;
To fester and churn its ugly brew
. . . Where's my spade! I've work to do!

WHAT TOMAS SAID IN A PUB

I saw God! Do you doubt it?
Do you dare to doubt it?
I saw the Almighty Man! His hand
Was resting on a mountain! And
He looked upon the World, and all about it:
I saw Him plainer than you see me now
—You mustn't doubt it!

He was not satisfied;
His look was all dissatisfied!
His beard swung on a wind, far out of sight
Behind the world's curve! And there was light
Most fearful from His forehead! And he sighed
—That star went always wrong, and from the start
I was dissatisfied!—

He lifted up His hand!
I say He heaved a dreadful hand
Over the spinning earth! Then I said,—Stay,
You must not strike it, God! I'm in the way!
And I will never move from where I stand!—
He said,—Dear child, I feared that you were dead,—
. . . And stayed His hand!

WHAT THE DEVIL SAID

It was night time! God, the Father Good,
Weary of praises, on a sudden stood
From His great Throne, and leaned upon the sky:
For He had heard a sound; a little cry,
Thin as a whisper, climbing up the Steep.

And so He looked to where the Earth, asleep,
Rocked with the moon: He saw the whirling sea
Swing round the world in surgent energy,
Tangling the moonlight in its netted foam;
And, nearer, saw the white and fretted dome
Of the ice-capped pole spin back again a ray
To whistling stars, bright as a wizard's day.

But these He passed, with eyes intently wide,
Till, closer still, the mountains He espied
Squatting tremendous on the broad-backed Earth,
Each nursing twenty rivers at a birth!
And then, minutely, sought He for the cry
That had climbed the slant of space so hugely high.

He found it in a ditch outside a town:
A tattered hungry woman, crouching down
By a dead babe—So there was nought to do,
For what is done is done! And sad He drew
Back to His Heaven of ivory and gold:
And, as He sat, all suddenly there rolled,
From where the woman wept upon the sod,
Satan's deep voice—*O thou unhappy God!*

BESSIE BOBTAIL

As down the road she wambled slow,
She had not got a place to go:
She had not got a place to fall
And rest herself—no place at all!
She stumped along, and wagged her pate;
And said a thing was desperate.

Her face was screwed and wrinkled tight
Just like a nut—and, left and right,
On either side, she wagged her head
And said a thing; and what she said
Was desperate as any word
That ever yet a person heard.

I walked behind her for a while,
And watched the people nudge and smile:
But ever, as she went, she said,
As left and right she swung her head,
—*O God He knows: And, God He knows!*
And, surely God Almighty knows!

THE TWINS

Good and bad are in my heart,
But I cannot tell to you
—For they never are apart—
Which is better of the two.

I am this! I am the other!
And the devil is my brother!
But my father He is God!
And my mother is the Sod!
I am safe enough, you see,
Owing to my pedigree.

So I shelter love and hate
Like twin brothers in a nest;
Lest I find, when it's too late,
That the other was the best.

OPTIMIST

I

All ye that labor! Every broken man
Bending beneath his load! Each tired heart
That cannot quit its burden! All the clan
Black-browed and fierce, who feel the smart

Of fortune's lances, wayward, uncontrolled!
All ye who writhe in silence 'neath the sin
That no man knows about! And ye that sold
The freedom of your souls if ye might win

A little ease from strife, and hate the thing
That bought it! Ye that droop, trembling with pain,
And hunger-haunted, lacking everything
That dignifies existence, and are fain

To lay ye down and die! Hear the behest
—All ye that labor, come to Me, and rest—

II

Let ye be still, ye tortured ones! Nor strive
Where striving's futile! Ye can ne'er attain
To lay your burdens down! All things alive
Must bear the woes of life, and if the pain

Be more than ye can bear, then ye can die!
That is the law! And bootless 'tis to seek
In the deeps of space; beyond the high
Pearl-tincted clouds; out where the moon doth peak

Her silver horns; for all that vastness bows
To Tyrant Toil, and weeps to find
Somewhere an aid. Be ye patient! Rouse
Your shoulders to the load to ye assigned,

And dree your weird! Be sure ye shall not moan
Stretched in the narrow bed, beneath the stone!

III

Lo, we are mocked with fancies! And we stretch
Our unavailing arms to anywhere
Where help is none. The north wind will not fetch
An answer to our cries! Nor on the air,

Fanned by the south wind's fan, is friend or aid!
What then is left, but this—that we be brave,
And steadfast in our places! Not afraid
However fell our lot! And we will lave

Us deep in human waters, till the mind
Grows wise and kindly, and we haply steal
A paradise from Nature. Naught can bind
Man closer unto man than that he feel

The trouble of his comrade! So we grope
Through courage, truth, and kindness, back to Hope.

HATE

My enemy came nigh;
And I
Stared fiercely in his face:
My lips went writhing back in a grimace,
And stern I watched him from a narrowed eye:

Then, as I turned away,
My enemy,
That bitter-heart, and savage, said to me:

—Some day, when this is past;
When all the arrows that we have are cast;
We may ask one another why we hate?
And fail to find a story to relate:
It may seem to us, then, a mystery
That we could hate each other—
Thus said he; and did not turn away;
Waiting to hear what I might have to say!

But I fled quickly: fearing, if I stayed,
I might have kissed him, as I would a maid.

ON A LONELY SPRAY

Under a lonely sky a lonely tree
Is beautiful! All that is loneliness
Is beautiful! A feather, lost at sea;
A staring owl; a moth; a yellow tress
Of seaweed on a rock, is beautiful!

The night-lit moon, wide-wandering in sky!
A blue-bright spark, where ne'er a cloud is up!
A wing, where no wing is, it is so high!
A bee in winter! and a buttercup,
Late blown! are lonely, and are beautiful!

She, whom you saw but once, and saw no more!
That he, who startled you, and went away!
The eye that watched you from a cottage door!
The first leaf, and the last! The break of day!
The mouse, the cuckoo, and the cloud, are beautiful!

For all that is, is lonely! All that may
Will be as lonely as is that you see!
The lonely heart sings on a lonely spray!
The lonely soul swings lonely in the sea;
And all that loneliness is beautiful!

All: all alone: and all without a part
Is beautiful! for beauty is all where!
Where is an eye, is beauty! Where an heart,
Is beauty, brooding out, on empty air,
All that is lonely, and is beautiful!

SIEGFRIED SASSOON

Siegfried Lorraine Sassoon, the son of a well-to-do country gentleman of Anglo-Jewish stock, was born on September 8, 1886. His mother, an Englishwoman, formerly a Miss Thornycroft, was the sister of Sir William H. Thornycroft, the sculptor. As a boy he attended the grammar school, Marlborough, going from there to Clare College, Cambridge, where he matriculated in 1905. He enjoyed the out-of-doors, was fond of music, excelled in field sports, became a master of fox-hounds, and devoted much time to the study of poetry. His favorite poets, Shelley, Masefield, and Hardy, he read assiduously, and from time to time issued privately small volumes of verse of his own; between 1911 and 1916 seven such volumes appeared. Upon the outbreak of the World War he enlisted and went to the front; before hostilities ceased he had reached the rank of captain in the Royal Welsh Fusiliers. He served once in Palestine, three times in France, and won the Military Cross for valor in rescuing the wounded. Amid the turmoil of the battle-front he continued his interest in poetry, although eventually he began using it as a means of denouncing war, which had become horrible to him.

Sassoon's first important book, *The Old Huntsman and Other Poems,* was published in 1917, and his second, *Counter-Attack and Other Poems,* in 1918. After the War he was, for a time, a journalist in London, but he continued his work as a poet. In 1920 he visited America, where he read his poems to many audiences.

THE OLD HUNTSMAN

I've never ceased to curse the day I signed
A seven years' bargain for the Golden Fleece.
'Twas a bad deal all round; and dear enough
It cost me, what with my daft management,
And the mean folk as owed and never paid me,
And backing losers; and the local bucks
Egging me on with whiskies while I bragged
The man I was when huntsman to the Squire.

I'd have been prosperous if I'd took a farm
Of seventy acres, drove my gig and haggled
At Monday markets; now I've squandered all
My savings; nigh three hundred pound I got
As testimonial when I'd grown too stiff
And slow to press a beaten fox.
The Fleece!
'Twas the damned Fleece that wore my Emily out,
The wife of thirty years who served me well;
(Not like this beldam clattering in the kitchen,
That never trims a lamp nor sweeps the floor,
And brings me greasy soup in a foul crock.)

Blast the old harridan! What's fetched her now,
Leaving me in the dark, and short of fire?
And where's my pipe? 'Tis lucky I've a turn
For thinking, and remembering all that's past.
And now's my hour, before I hobble to bed,
To set the works a-wheezing, wind the clock
That keeps the time of life with feeble tick
Behind my bleared old face that stares and wonders.

. . . . .

It's queer how, in the dark, comes back to mind
Some morning of September. We've been digging
In a steep, sandy warren, riddled with holes,

And I've just pulled the terrier out and left
A sharp-nosed cub-face blinking there and snapping
Then in a moment seen him mobbed and torn
To strips in the baying hurly of the pack.
I picture it so clear: the dusty sunshine
On bracken, and the men with spades, that wipe
Red faces: one tilts up a mug of ale.
And, having stooped to clean my gory hands,
I whistle the jostling beauties out o' the wood.

I'm but a daft old fool! I often wish
The Squire were back again—ah, he was a man!
They don't breed men like him these days; he'd come
For sure, and sit and talk and suck his briar
Till the old wife brings up a dish of tea.

Ay, those were days, when I was serving Squire!
I never knowed such sport as '85,
The winter afore the one that snowed us silly.

. . . . .

Once in a way the parson will drop in
And read a bit o' the Bible, if I'm bad,—
Pray the Good Lord to make my spirit whole
In faith: he leaves some 'baccy on the shelf,
And wonders I don't keep a dog to cheer me,
Because he knows I'm mortal fond of dogs!

I ask you, what's a gent like that to me,
As wouldn't know Elijah if I saw him,
Nor have the wit to keep him on the talk?
'Tis kind of parson to be troubling still
With such as me; but he's a town-bred chap,
Full of his college notions and Christmas hymns.

Religion beats me. I'm amazed at folk
Drinking the gospels in and never scratching
Their heads for questions. When I was a lad
I learned a bit from mother, and never thought
To educate myself for prayers and psalms.

But now I'm old and bald and serious-minded,
With days to sit and ponder. I'd no chance
When young and gay to get the hang of all
This Hell and Heaven: and when the clergy hoick
And holloa from their pulpits, I'm asleep,
However hard I listen; and when they pray
It seems we're all like children sucking sweets
In school, and wondering whether master sees.

I used to dream of Hell when I was first
Promoted to a huntsman's job, and scent
Was rotten, and all the foxes disappeared,
And hounds were short of blood; and officers
From barracks over-rode 'em all day long
On weedy, whistling nags that knocked a hole
In every fence; good sportsmen to a man
And brigadiers by now, but dreadful hard
On a young huntsman keen to show some sport.

Ay, Hell was thick with captains, and I rode
The lumbering brute that's beat in half a mile,
And blunders into every blind old ditch.
Hell was the coldest scenting land I've known,
And both my whips were always lost, and hounds
Would never get their heads down; and a man
On a great yawing chestnut trying to cast 'em
While I was in a corner pounded by
The ugliest hog-backed stile you've clapped your eyes on.
There was an iron-spiked fence round all the coverts,
And civil-spoken keepers I couldn't trust,
And the main earth unstopp'd. The fox I found
Was always a three-legged 'un from a bag
Who reeked of aniseed and wouldn't run.
The farmers were all ploughing their old pasture
And bellowing at me when I rode their beans
To cast for beaten fox, or galloped on
With hounds to a lucky view. I'd lost my voice
Although I shouted fit to burst my guts,
And couldn't blow my horn.

And when I woke,
Emily snored, and barn-cocks started crowing,
And morn was at the window; and I was glad
To be alive because I heard the cry
Of hounds like church-bells chiming on a Sunday,—
Ay, that's the song I'd wish to hear in Heaven!
The cry of hounds was Heaven for me: I know
Parson would call me crazed and wrong to say it,
But where's the use of life and being glad
If God's not in your gladness?

I've no brains
For book-learned studies; but I've heard men say
There's much in print that clergy have to wink at:
Though many I've met were jolly chaps, and rode
To hounds, and walked me puppies; and could pick
Good legs and loins and necks and shoulders, ay,
And feet,—'twas necks and feet I looked at first.

Some hounds I've known were wise as half your saints,
And better hunters. That old dog of the Duke's,
Harlequin; what a dog he was to draw!
And what a note he had, and what a nose
When foxes ran down wind and scent was catchy!
And that light lemon bitch of the Squire's, old Dorcas,—
She were a marvellous hunter, were old Dorcas!
Ay, oft I've thought: "If there were hounds in Heaven,
With God as Master, taking no subscription;
And all His blessèd country farmed by tenants;
And a straight-necked old fox in every gorse!"
But when I came to work it out, I found
There'd be too many huntsmen wanting places,—
Though some I've known might get a job with Nick!

. . . . .

I've come to think of God as something like
The figure of a man the old Duke was
When I was turning hounds to Nimrod King,
Before his Grace was took so bad with gout,

And had to quit the saddle. Tall and spare,
Clean-shaved and grey, with shrewd, kind eyes, that twinkled,
And easy walk; who, when he gave good words,
Gave them whole-hearted; and would never blame
Without just cause. Lord God might be like that,
Sitting alone in a great room of books
Some evening after hunting.

Now I'm tired
With hearkening to the tick-tack on the shelf;
And pondering makes me doubtful.

Riding home
On a moonless night of cloud that feels like frost
Though stars are hidden (hold your feet up, horse!),
And thinking what a task I had to draw
A pack with all those lame 'uns, and the lot
Wanting a rest from all this open weather,—
That's what I'm doing now.

And likely, too,
The frost'll be a long 'un, and the night
One sleep. The parsons say we'll wake to find
A country blinding-white with dazzle of snow.

The naked stars make men feel lonely,—wheeling
And glinting on the puddles in the road.
And then you listen to the wind, and wonder
If folk are quite such bucks as they appear
When dressed by London tailors, looking down
Their boots at covert side, and thinking big.

. . . . .

This world's a funny place to live in. Soon
I'll need to change my country; but I know
'Tis little enough I've understood my life,
And a power of sights I've missed, and foreign marvels.
I used to feel it, riding on spring days
In meadows pied with sun and chasing clouds,

And half forget how I was there to catch
The foxes; lose the angry, eager feeling
A huntsman ought to have, that's out for blood,
And means his hounds to get it!

Now I know
It's God that speaks to us when we're bewitched,
Smelling the hay in June and smiling quiet;
Or when there's been a spell of summer drought,
Lying awake and listening to the rain.

. . . . .

I'd like to be the simpleton I was
In the old days when I was whipping-in
To a little harrier-pack in Worcestershire,
And loved a dairymaid, but never knew it
Until she'd wed another. So I've loved
My life; and when the good years are gone down,
Discover what I've lost.

I never broke
Out of my blundering self into the world,
But let it all go past me, like a man
Half-asleep in a land that's full of wars.

What a grand thing 'twould be if I could go
Back to the kennels now and take my hounds
For summer exercise; be riding out
With forty couple when the quiet skies
Are streaked with sunrise, and the silly birds
Grown hoarse with singing; cobwebs on the furze
Up on the hill, and all the country strange,
With no one stirring; and the horses fresh,
Sniffing the air I'll never breathe again.

. . . . .

You've brought the lamp then, Martha? I've no mind
For newspaper to-night, nor bread and cheese.
Give me the candle, and I'll get to bed.

MORNING GLORY

In this meadow starred with spring
Shepherds kneel before their king.
Mary throned, with dreaming eyes,
Gowned in blue like rain-washed skies,
Lifts her tiny son that he
May behold their courtesy.
And green-smocked children, awed and good,
Bring him blossoms from the wood.

Clear the sunlit steeples chime
Mary's coronation-time.
Loud the happy children quire
To the golden-windowed morn;
While the lord of their desire
Sleeps below the crimson thorn.

A WORKING PARTY

Three hours ago he blundered up the trench,
Sliding and poising, groping with his boots;
Sometimes he tripped and lurched against the walls
With hands that pawed the sodden bags of chalk.
He couldn't see the man who walked in front;
Only he heard the drum and rattle of feet
Stepping along the trench-boards,—often splashing
Wretchedly where the sludge was ankle-deep.

Voices would grunt, "Keep to your right,—make way!"
When squeezing past the men from the front-line:
White faces peered, puffing a point of red;
Candles and braziers glinted through the chinks
And curtain-flaps of dug-outs; then the gloom
Swallowed his sense of sight; he stooped and swore
Because a sagging wire had caught his neck.
A flare went up; the shining whiteness spread

And flickered upward, showing nimble rats,
And mounds of glimmering sand-bags, bleached with rain;
Then the slow, silver moment died in dark.
The wind came posting by with chilly gusts
And buffeting at corners, piping thin
And dreary through the crannies; rifle-shots
Would split and crack and sing along the night,
And shells came calmly through the drizzling air
To burst with hollow bang below the hill.

Three hours ago he stumbled up the trench;
Now he will never walk that road again:
He must be carried back, a jolting lump
Beyond all need of tenderness and care;
A nine-stone corpse with nothing more to do.

He was a young man with a meagre wife
And two pale children in a Midland town;
He showed the photograph to all his mates;
And they considered him a decent chap
Who did his work and hadn't much to say,
And always laughed at other people's jokes
Because he hadn't any of his own.

That night when he was busy at his job
Of piling bags along the parapet,
He thought how slow time went, stamping his feet,
And blowing on his fingers, pinched with cold.
He thought of getting back by half-past twelve,
And tot of rum to send him warm to sleep
In draughty dug-out frowsty with the fumes
Of coke, and full of snoring, weary men.

He pushed another bag along the top,
Craning his body outward; then a flare
Gave one white glimpse of No Man's Land and wire;
And as he dropped his head the instant split
His startled life with lead, and all went out.

"THEY"

The Bishop tells us: "When the boys come back
They will not be the same; for they'll have fought
In a just cause: they lead the last attack
On Anti-Christ; their comrade's blood has bought
New right to breed an honorable race.
They have challenged Death and dared him face to face."

"We're none of us the same!" the boys reply.
"For George lost both his legs; and Bill's stone blind;
Poor Jim's shot through the lungs and like to die;
And Bert's gone syphilitic: you'll not find
A chap who's served that hasn't found *some* change."
And the Bishop said: "The ways of God are strange!"

THE HERO

"Jack fell as he'd have wished," the Mother said,
And folded up the letter that she'd read.
"The Colonel writes so nicely." Something broke
In the tired voice that quavered to a choke.
She half looked up. "We mothers are so proud
Of our dead soldiers." Then her face was bowed.

Quietly the Brother Officer went out.
He'd told the poor old dear some gallant lies
That she would nourish all her days, no doubt.
For while he coughed and mumbled, her weak eyes
Had shone with gentle triumph, brimmed with joy,
Because he'd been so brave, her glorious boy.

He thought how "Jack," cold-footed, useless swine,
Had panicked down the trench that night the mine
Went up at Wicked Corner; how he'd tried
To get sent home; and how, at last, he died,
Blown to small bits. And no one seemed to care
Except that lonely woman with white hair.

PRELUDE: THE TROOPS

Dim, gradual thinning of the shapeless gloom
Shudders to drizzling daybreak that reveals
Disconsolate men who stamp their sodden boots
And turn dulled, sunken faces to the sky
Haggard and hopeless. They, who have beaten down
The stale despair of night, must now renew
Their desolation in the truce of dawn,
Murdering the livid hours that grope for peace.

Yet these, who cling to life with stubborn hands,
Can grin through storms of death and find a gap
In the clawed, cruel tangles of his defence.
They march from safety, and the bird-sung joy
Of grass-green thickets, to the land where all
Is ruin, and nothing blossoms but the sky
That hastens over them where they endure
Sad, smoking, flat horizons, reeking woods,
And foundered trench-lines volleying doom for doom.

O my brave brown companions, when your souls
Flock silently away, and the eyeless dead
Shame the wild beast of battle on the ridge,
Death will stand grieving in that field of war
Since your unvanquished hardihood is spent.
And through some mooned Valhalla there will pass
Battalions and battalions, scarred from hell;
The unreturning army that was youth;
The legions who have suffered and are dust.

DREAMERS

Soldiers are citizens of death's grey land,
  Drawing no dividend from time's to-morrows.
In the great hour of destiny they stand,
  Each with his feuds, and jealousies, and sorrows.

Soldiers are sworn to action; they must win
Some flaming, fatal climax with their lives.
Soldiers are dreamers; when the guns begin
They think of firelit homes, clean beds, and wives.

I see them in foul dug-outs, gnawed by rats,
And in the ruined trenches, lashed with rain,
Dreaming of things they did with balls and bats,
And mocked by hopeless longing to regain
Bank-holidays, and picture shows, and spats,
And going to the office in the train.

PICTURE-SHOW

And still they come and go: and this is all I know—
That from the gloom I watch an endless picture-show,
Where wild or listless faces flicker on their way,
With glad or grievous hearts I'll never understand
Because Time spins so fast, and they've no time to stay
Beyond the moment's gesture of a lifted hand.

And still, between the shadow and the blinding flame,
The brave despair of men flings onward, ever the same
As in those doom-lit years that wait them, and have been . . .
And life is just the picture dancing on a screen.

MEMORY

When I was young my heart and head were light,
And I was gay and feckless as a colt
Out in the fields, with morning in the may,
Wind on the grass, wings in the orchard bloom.
O thrilling sweet, my joy, when life was free,
And all the paths led on from hawthorn-time
Across the carolling meadows into June.

But now my heart is heavy-laden. I sit
Burning my dreams away beside the fire:
For death has made me wise and bitter and strong;
And I am rich in all that I have lost.
O starshine on the fields of long-ago,
Bring me the darkness and the nightingale;
Dim wealds of vanished summer, peace of home,
And silence; and the faces of my friends.

ON READING THE WAR DIARY OF A DEFUNCT AMBASSADOR

So that's your Diary—that's your private mind
Translated into shirt-sleeved History. That
Is what diplomacy has left behind
For after-ages to peruse, and find
What passed beneath your elegant silk-hat.

You were a fine old gentleman; compact
Of shrewdness, charm, refinement and finesse.
Impeccable in breeding, taste and dress,
No diplomatic quality you lacked—
No tittle of ambassadorial tact.

I can imagine you among "the guns,"
Urbanely peppering partridge, grouse, or pheasant—
Guest of those infinitely privileged ones
Whose lives are padded, petrified, and pleasant.
I visualize you feeding off gold plate
And gossiping on grave affairs of State.

Now you're defunct; your gossip's gravely printed;
The world discovers where you lunched and dined
On such and such a day; and what was hinted
By ministers and generals far behind
The all-important conflict, carnage-tinted.

The world can read the rumors that you gleaned
From various Fronts; the well-known Names you met;
Each conference you attended and convened;

And (at appropriate moments) what you ate.
Thus (if the world's acute) it can derive
Your self, exact, uncensored and alive.

The world will find no pity in your pages;
No exercise of spirit worthy of mention;
Only a public-funeral grief-convention;
And all the circumspection of the ages.
But I, for one, am grateful, overjoyed,
And unindignant that your punctual pen
Should have been so constructively employed
In manifesting to unprivileged men
The visionless officialized fatuity
That once kept Europe safe for Perpetuity.

AN OLD-WORLD EFFECT

While blue-eyed children, goggle-faced and giggling,
Stare, swollen-cheeked (bad-mannered little wretches),
Two Nature-loving ladies dip their brushes,
Glance up, gaze down; with touches broad or niggling,
Remain absorbed in half-completed sketches
Where embryonic apple-blossom flushes
Round a decrepit cottage whence they catch
The ultimate rusticity of thatch.

You ask me why these artists have selected
An unhygienic dwelling as their theme . . .
"Have they no palate for the unexpected,—
No easel for a Cubist housing-scheme?"

A sapless unprolific Past they paint,
Who ramble through the guide-book toward the Quaint.
Meanwhile a blackbird pipes from the vicinity
His free fantasia against virginity.

ROBERT GRAVES

Robert Ranke Graves, son of Amalie Graves and Alfred Perceval Graves, the Irish school inspector and author, was born in London on July 26, 1895. He was educated at Charterhouse and St. John's College, Oxford. During the World War he went to France, and served, with Siegfried Sassoon, in the Royal Welsh Fusiliers, rising to the rank of captain before fighting ceased. Although he had begun the writing of verse while at Charterhouse, it was not until reaching the battle fields that he began producing poetry in earnest. In France he became conspicuous among the group of young English war poets, which included Brooke, Sassoon, and Nichols. In 1916 appeared *Over the Brazier*, in 1917 the more distinctive *Fairies and Fusiliers*, and subsequently a number of other volumes. Since 1920 Graves has shown a scholarly interest in poetry and poetical phenomena, and has made several critical contributions to the subject—*On English Poetry* (1922), *The Meaning of Dreams* (1924), *Poetic Unreason* (1925), *Contemporary Techniques of Poetry* (1925), and *The English Ballad* (1927).

In 1918 he married Nancy Nicholson, and they have four children, two sons and two daughters. In 1926 he was appointed Professor of English at the Egyptian University, which position he still holds.

BABYLON

The child alone a poet is:
Spring and Fairyland are his.
Truth and Reason show but dim,
And all's poetry with him.
Rhyme and music flow in plenty
For the lad of one-and-twenty,
But Spring for him is no more now
Than daisies to a munching cow;
Just a cheery pleasant season,
Daisy buds to live at ease on.
He's forgotten how he smiled
And shrieked at snowdrops when a child,
Or wept one evening secretly
For April's glorious misery.
Wisdom made him old and wary
Banishing the Lords of Faery.
Wisdom made a breach and battered
Babylon to bits: she scattered
To the hedges and ditches
All our nursery gnomes and witches.
Lob and Puck, poor frantic elves,
Drag their treasures from the shelves.
Jack the Giant-killer's gone,
Mother Goose and Oberon,
Bluebeard and King Solomon.
Robin, and Red Riding Hood
Take together to the wood,
And Sir Galahad lies hid
In a cave with Captain Kidd.
None of all the magic hosts,
None remain but a few ghosts
Of timorous heart, to linger on
Weeping for lost Babylon.

THE CATERPILLAR

Under this loop of honeysuckle,
A creeping, colored caterpillar,
I gnaw the fresh green hawthorn spray,
I nibble it leaf by leaf away.

Down beneath grow dandelions,
Daisies, old-man's-looking-glasses;
Rooks flap croaking across the lane.
I eat and swallow and eat again.

Here come raindrops helter-skelter;
I munch and nibble unregarding:
Hawthorn leaves are juicy and firm.
I'll mind my business: I'm a good worm.

When I'm old, tired, melancholy,
I'll build a leaf-green mausoleum
Close by, here on this lovely spray,
And die and dream the ages away.

Some say worms win resurrection,
With white wings beating flitter-flutter,
But wings or a sound sleep, why should I care?
Either way I'll miss my share.

Under this loop of honeysuckle,
A hungry, hairy caterpillar,
I crawl on my high and swinging seat,
And eat, eat, eat—as one ought to eat.

MARIGOLDS

With a fork drive Nature out,
  She will ever yet return;
Hedge the flowerbed all about,
  Pull or stab or cut or burn,
  She will ever yet return.

Look: the constant marigold
  Springs again from hidden roots.
Baffled gardener, you behold
  New beginnings and new shoots
  Spring again from hidden roots.
  Pull or stab or cut or burn,
  They will ever yet return.

Gardener, cursing at the weed,
  Ere you curse it further, say:
Who but you planted the seed
  In my fertile heart, one day?
  Ere you curse me further, say!
  New beginnings and new shoots
  Spring again from hidden roots.
  Pull or stab or cut or burn,
  Love must ever yet return.

WHEN I'M KILLED

When I'm killed, don't think of me
Buried there in Cambrin Wood,
Nor as in Zion think of me
With the Intolerable Good.
And there's one thing that I know well,
I'm damned if I'll be damned to Hell!

So when I'm killed, don't wait for me,
Walking the dim corridor;
In Heaven or Hell, don't wait for me,
Or you must wait for evermore.
You'll find me buried, living-dead
In these verses that you've read.

So when I'm killed, don't mourn for me,
Shot, poor lad, so bold and young,
Killed and gone—don't mourn for me.
On your lips my life is hung:
O friends and lovers, you can save
Your playfellow from the grave.

ESCAPE

August 6, 1916.—Officer previously reported died of wounds, now reported wounded: Graves, Captain R., Royal Welsh Fusiliers.

. . . But I *was* dead, an hour or more.
I woke when I'd already passed the door
That Cerberus guards, and half-way down the road
To Lethe, as an old Greek signpost showed.
Above me, on my stretcher swinging by,
I saw new stars in the subterrene sky:
A Cross, a Rose in bloom, a Cage with bars,
And a barbed Arrow feathered in fine stars.
I felt the vapors of forgetfulness
Float in my nostrils. Oh, may Heaven bless
Dear Lady Proserpine, who saw me wake,
And, stooping over me, for Henna's sake
Cleared my poor buzzing head and sent me back
Breathless, with leaping heart along the track.
After me roared and clattered angry hosts
Of demons, heroes, and policeman-ghosts.
"Life! life! I can't be dead! I won't be dead!
Damned if I'll die for anyone!" I said. . . .
Cerberus stands and grins above me now,
Wearing three heads—lion, and lynx, and sow.
"Quick, a revolver! But my Webley's gone,
Stolen! . . . No bombs . . . no knife. . . . The crowd swarms on,
Bellows, hurls stones. . . . Not even a honeyed sop . . .
Nothing. . . . Good Cerberus! . . . Good dog! . . . but stop!
Stay! . . . A great luminous thought. . . I do believe
There's still some morphia that I bought on leave."
Then swiftly Cerberus' wide mouths I cram
With army biscuit smeared with ration jam;

And sleep lurks in the luscious plum and apple.
He crunches, swallows, stiffens, seems to grapple
With the all-powerful poppy . . . then a snore,

A crash; the beast blocks up the corridor
With monstrous hairy carcase, red and dun—
Too late! for I've sped through.
O life! O Sun!

CORPORAL STARE

Back from the line one night in June,
I gave a dinner at Bethune—
Seven courses, the most gorgeous meal
Money could buy or batman steal.
Five hungry lads welcomed the fish
With shouts that nearly cracked the dish;
Asparagus came with tender tops,
Strawberries in cream, and mutton chops.
Said Jenkins, as my hand he shook,
"They'll put this in the history book."
We bawled Church anthems *in choro*
Of Bethlehem and Hermon snow,
With drinking songs, a jolly sound
To help the good red Pommard round.
Stories and laughter interspersed,
We drowned a long La Bassée thirst—
Trenches in June make throats damned dry.
Then through the window suddenly,
Badge, stripes and medals all complete,
We saw him swagger up the street,
Just like a live man—Corporal Stare!
Stare! Killed last May at Festubert.
Caught on patrol near the Boche wire,
Torn horribly by machine-gun fire!
He paused, saluted smartly, grinned,
Then passed away like a puff of wind,
Leaving us blank astonishment.
The song broke, up we started, leant
Out of the window—nothing there,
Not the least shadow of Corporal Stare,
Only a quiver of smoke that showed
A fag-end dropped on the silent road.

HATE NOT, FEAR NOT

Kill if you must, but never hate:
Man is but grass and hate is blight,
The sun will scorch you soon or late,
Die wholesome then, since you must fight.

Hate is a fear, and fear is rot
That cankers root and fruit alike;
Fight cleanly then, hate not, fear not,
Strike with no madness when you strike.

Fever and fear distract the world,
But calm be you though madmen shout;
Through blazing fires of battle hurled,
Hate not, strike, fear not, stare Death out!

IN THE WILDERNESS

Christ of His gentleness
Thirsting and hungering,
Walked in the wilderness;
Soft words of grace He spoke
Unto lost desert-folk
That listened wondering.
He heard the bitterns call
From ruined palace-wall,
Answered them brotherly.
He held communion
With the she-pelican
Of lonely piety.
Basilisk, cockatrice,
Flocked to his homilies,
With mail of dread device,
With monstrous barbéd slings,
With eager dragon-eyes;
Great rats on leather wings
And poor blind broken things,

Foul in their miseries.
And ever with Him went,
Of all His wanderings
Comrade, with ragged coat,
Gaunt ribs—poor innocent—
Bleeding foot, burning throat,
The guileless old scapegoat;
For forty nights and days
Followed in Jesus' ways,
Sure guard behind Him kept,
Tears like a lover wept.

THE THREE DRINKERS

Blacksmith Green had three strong sons,
With bread and beef did fill 'em,
Now John and Ned are perished and dead,
But plenty remains of William.

John Green was a whiskey drinker,
The Land of Cakes supplied him,
Till at last his soul flew out by the hole
That the fierce drink burned inside him.

Ned Green was a water drinker,
And, Lord, how Ned would fuddle!
He rotted away his mortal clay
Like an old boot thrown in a puddle.

Will Green was a wise young drinker,
Shrank from whiskey or water,
But he made good cheer with headstrong beer,
And married an alderman's daughter.

THE BOY OUT OF CHURCH

As Jesus and his followers
Upon a Sabbath morn
Were walking by a wheat field
They plucked the ears of corn.

They plucked it, they rubbed it,
  They blew the husks away,
Which grieved the pious Pharisees
  Upon the Sabbath day.

And Jesus said, "A riddle
  Answer if you can,
Was man made for the Sabbath
  Or Sabbath made for man?"

I do not love the Sabbath,
  The soapsuds and the starch,
The troops of solemn people
  Who to Salvation march.

I take my book, I take my stick
  On the Sabbath day,
In woody nooks and valleys
  I hide myself away,

To ponder there in quiet
  God's Universal Plan,
Resolved that church and Sabbath
  Were never made for man.

BRITTLE BONES

Though I am an old man
  With my bones very brittle,
Though I am a poor old man
  Worth very little,
Yet I suck at my long pipe
  At peace in the sun,
I do not fret nor much regret
  That my work is done.

If I were a young man
  With my bones full of marrow,
Oh, if I were a bold young man
  Straight as an arrow,

And if I had the same years
To live once again,
I would not change their simple range
Of laughter and pain.

If I were a young man
And young was my Lily,
A smart girl, a bold young man,
Both of us silly,
And though from time before I knew
She'd stab me with pain,
Though well I knew she'd not be true,
I'd love her again.

If I were a young man
With a brisk, healthy body,
Oh, if I were a bold young man
With love of rum toddy,
Though I knew that I was spiting
My old age with pain,
My happy lip would touch and sip
Again and again.

If I were a young man
With my bones full of marrow,
Oh, if I were a bold young man
Straight as an arrow,
I'd store up no virtue
For Heaven's distant plain,
I'd live at ease as I did please
And sin once again.

THE PIER-GLASS

To T. E. Lawrence, who helped me with it.

Lost manor where I walk continually
A ghost, while yet in woman's flesh and blood:
Up your broad stairs mounting with outspread fingers
And gliding steadfast down your corridors

I come by nightly custom to this room,
And even on sultry afternoons I come
Drawn by a thread of time-sunk memory.

Empty, unless for a huge bed of state
Shrouded with rusty curtains drooped awry
(A puppet theatre where malignant fancy
Peoples the wings with fear). At my right hand
A ravelled bell-pull hangs in readiness
To summon me from attic glooms above
Service of elder ghosts; here at my left
A sullen pier-glass cracked from side to side
Scorns to present the face as do new mirrors
With a lying flush, but shows it melancholy
And pale, as faces grow that look in mirrors.

Is here no life, nothing but the thin shadow
And blank foreboding, never a wainscote rat
Rasping a crust? Or at the window pane
No fly, no bluebottle, no starveling spider?
The windows frame a prospect of cold skies
Half-merged with sea, as at the first creation,
Abstract, confusing welter. Face about,
Peer rather in the glass once more, take note
Of self, the grey lips and long hair dishevelled,
Sleep-staring eyes. Ah, mirror, for Christ's love
Give me one token that there still abides
Remote, beyond this island mystery
So be it only this side Hope, somewhere,
In streams, on sun-warm mountain pasturage,
True life, natural breath; not this phantasma.

A rumor, scarcely yet to be reckoned sound,
But a pulse quicker or slower, then I know
My plea is granted; death prevails not yet.
For bees have swarmed behind in a close place
Pent up between this glass and the outer wall.
The combs are founded, the queen rules her court,
Bee-serjeants posted at the entrance chink

Are sampling each returning honey-cargo
With scrutinizing mouth and commentary,
Slow approbation, quick dissatisfaction.

Disquieting rhythm, that leads me home at last
From labyrinthine wandering. This new mood
Of judgment orders me my present duty,
To face again a problem strongly solved
In life gone by, but now again proposed
Out of due time for fresh deliberation.
Did not my answer please the Master's ear?
Yet, I'll stay obstinate. How went the question,
A paltry question set on the elements
Of love and the wronged lover's obligation;
Kill or forgive? Still does the bed ooze blood?
Let it drip down till every floor-plank rot!
Yet shall I answer, challenging the judgment:—
"Kill, strike the blow again, spite what shall come."
"Kill, strike, again, again," the bees in chorus hum.

DISTANT SMOKE

Seth and the sons of Seth who followed him
Halted in silence: labor, then, was vain.
Fast at the zenith, blazoned in his splendor,
Hung the fierce Sun, wherefore these travelling folk
Stood centered each in his own disc of shade.
The term proposed was ended; now to enjoy
The moment's melancholy; their tears fell shining.

Yesterday early at the dreadful hour,
When life ebbs lowest, when the strand of being
Is slowly bared until discovered show
Weed-mantelled hulks that foundered years ago
At autumn anchorage, then father Adam
Summoned in haste his elder generations
To his death-tent, and gasping spoke to them,
Forthwith defining an immediate journey

Beyond the eastern ridge, in quest for one
Whom he named Cain, brother to Seth, true uncle
To these young spearmen; they should lead him here
For a last benediction at his hands.
First-born yet outlawed! Scarcely they believed
In this strange word of "Cain," in this new man,
Man, yet outside the tents; but Adam swore
And gave them a fair sign of recognition.
There was a brand, he said, a firm red pillar
Parting Cain's brows, and Cain had mighty hands,
Sprouting luxurious hair, red, like his beard.
Moreover Adam said that by huge strength
Himself could stay this ebb of early morning,
Yet three days longer, three days, though no more—
This for the stern desire and long disquietude
That was his love for Cain, whom God had cursed.
Then would he kiss all fatherly and so die—
Kneeling, with eyes abased, they made him promise,
Swore, at the midpoint of their second day,
If unsped in the search of whom he named,
They would come hasting home to Adam's tent.
They touched his bony fingers; forth they went.

Now Seth, shielding his eyes, sees mistily
Breaking the horizon thirty miles away
(A full day's journey) what but a wisp, a feather,
A thin line, half a nothing—distant smoke!
Blown smoke, a signal from that utmost ridge
Of desolation—the camp fire of Cain.
He to restrain his twelve impetuous sons
(He knows the razor-edge of their young spirit)
Dissembles seeing, turns his steps about,
Bids them come follow, but they little heeding,
Scarce noting his commands, fasten their eyes
On smoke, so forfeit Adam's benediction,
Striding forward into the wilderness
With eager thighs, forgetful of their oath,
Adventurous for this monster, a new man,
Their own kin—how accursed?—they haste for wonder.

SULLEN MOODS

Love, do not count your labor lost
  Though I turn sullen, grim, retired
Even at your side; my thought is crossed
  With fancies by old longings fired.

And when I answer you, some days
  Vaguely and wildly, do not fear
That my love walks forbidden ways,
  Breaking the ties that hold it here.

If I speak gruffly, this mood is
  Mere indignation at my own
Shortcomings, plagues, uncertainties;
  I forget the gentler tone.

You, now that you have come to be
  My one beginning, prime and end,
I count at last as wholly me,
  Lover no longer nor yet friend.

Friendship is flattery, though close hid;
  Must I then flatter my own mind?
And must (which laws of shame forbid)
  Blind love of you make self-love blind?

Do not repay me my own coin,
  The sharp rebuke, the frown, the groan;
Remind me, rather, to disjoin
  Your emanation from my own.

Help me to see you as before
  When overwhelmed and dead, almost,
I stumbled on that secret door
  Which saves the live man from the ghost.

Be once again the distant light,
  Promise of glory, not yet known
In full perfection—wasted quite
  When on my imperfection thrown.

OLD WIVES' TALES

Were the tales they told absurd,
  Random tags for a child's ear?
Soon I mocked at all I heard,
  Though with cause indeed for fear.

Of the mermaids' doleful game
  In deep water I heard tell,
Of lofty dragons blowing flame,
  Of the hornèd fiend of Hell.

Now I have met the mermaid kin
  And find them bound by natural laws,
They have neither tail nor fin,
  But are the deadlier for that cause.

Dragons have no darting tongues,
  Teeth saw-edged nor rattling scales,
No fire issues from their lungs,
  Poison has not slimed their tails.

But they are creatures of dark air,
  Unsubstantial tossing forms,
Thunderclaps of man's despair
  In mid whirl of mental storms.

And there's a true and only fiend
  Worse than prophets prophesy,
Whose full powers to hurt are screened
  Lest the race of man should die.

Ever in vain may courage plot
  The dragon's death with shield and sword,
Or love abjure the mermaid grot,
  Or faith be fixed in one blest word.

Mermaids will not be denied
  Of our last enduring shame,
The dragon flaunts his unpierced hide,
  The fiend makes laughter with God's Name.

A FORCED MUSIC

Of Love he sang, full-hearted one.
But when the song was done
The King demanded more,
Ay, and commanded more.
The boy found nothing for encore,
Words, melodies, none:
Ashamed the song's glad rise and plaintive fall
Had so charmed King and Queen and all.

He sang the same verse once again,
But urging less Love's pain,
With altered time and key
He showed variety,
Seemed to refresh the harmony
Of his only strain,
So still the glad rise and the plaintive fall
Could charm the King, the Queen, and all.

He of his song then wearying ceased,
But was not yet released;
The Queen's request was *More,*
And her behest was *More.*
He played of random notes some score,
He found his rhymes at least—
Then suddenly let his twangling harp down fall
And fled in tears from King and Queen and all.

TO ANY SAINT

You turn the unsmitten other cheek,
 In silence welcoming God's grace,
Disdaining, though they scourge, to speak,
 Smiling forgiveness face to face.

You plunge your arms in tyrant flame,
 From ravening beasts you do not fly,
Calling aloud on one sweet Name,
 Hosannah-singing till you die.

So angered by your undefeat,
   Revenge through Christ they meditate,
Disciples at the bishop's feet
   They learn this newer sort of hate,

This unresisting meek assault
   On furious foe or stubborn friend,
This virtue purged of every fault
   By furtherance of the martyr's end,

This baffling stroke of naked pride,
   When satires fail and curses fail
To pierce the justice's tough hide,
   To abash the cynics of the jail.

Oh, not less violent, not less keen
   And barbèd more than murder's blade!
"The brook," you sigh, "that washes clean,
   The flower of love that will not fade!"

PART TWO

THE AMERICAN POETS

EDWIN ARLINGTON ROBINSON

Edwin Arlington Robinson was born in the village of Head Tide, Maine, December 22, 1869. His parents were Edward and Mary E. Palmer Robinson. The trade of Edward Robinson in Head Tide was that of grain merchant, but when his son was scarcely a year old he accepted an offer to go to the larger town of Gardiner, Maine, as director of a bank; and in Gardiner, the "Tilbury Town" of the poems, the boy grew up. He attended the local high school, visited frequently at the home of Laura E. Richards and listened to her stories, and in his spare time secluded himself in his father's barn and wrote poetry. In 1891 he entered Harvard University, where he studied for two years, before the ill-health of his father and the straitened circumstances of the family forced him to withdraw and turn his hand to earning a living.

In 1896 Robinson published privately his first book of poetry, *The Torrent and the Night Before,* which carried the notice, "This book is dedicated to any man, woman, or critic who will cut the edges of it. I have done the top." The volume was commented upon favorably in *The Bookman* (February, 1897), but one sentence, ". . . the world is not beautiful to him, but a prison-house," stirred Robinson to this reply, which is worth preserving as his view of life at that time:

> I am sorry to learn that I have painted myself in such lugubrious colors. The world is not a "prison-house," but a kind of spiritual kindergarten, where millions of bewildered infants are trying to spell God with the wrong blocks.—[*The Bookman,* March, 1897.]

In the years that followed this publication, Robinson lived in Boston and New York, devoting himself to the double task of earning a living and writing poetry. In New York he worked for a time as inspector of construction on the new subways, living during this time in cheap boarding houses in Yonkers and later in West Twenty-Third Street, New York City. In 1905, however, President Roosevelt, who had become interested in his poetry, offered him a consulship in Mexico, and upon Robinson's refusal to leave New York, secured for him a position in the New York Custom House. There Robinson worked until 1909, when he resigned to devote himself solely to writing. In 1911 he discovered the MacDowell Colony, at Peterborough, New Hampshire; and finding its atmosphere congenial, has since spent most of his summers and written much of his poetry there. In the winters he lives in New York, where he occupies himself chiefly in reading and in attending the theatre. He is unmarried, and maintains no permanent establishment.

Robinson is a member of the National Institute of Arts and Letters, and of the International P. E. N. Club. In 1922 Yale University conferred upon him the honorary degree of Doctor of Literature; and in 1921 and again in 1925 he won the Pulitzer prize for poetry.

FLAMMONDE

The man Flammonde, from God knows where,
With firm address and foreign air,
With news of nations in his talk
And something royal in his walk,
With glint of iron in his eyes,
But never doubt, nor yet surprise,
Appeared, and stayed, and held his head
As one by kings accredited.

Erect, with his alert repose
About him, and about his clothes,
He pictured all tradition hears
Of what we owe to fifty years.
His cleansing heritage of taste
Paraded neither want nor waste;
And what he needed for his fee
To live, he borrowed graciously.

He never told us what he was,
Or what mischance, or other cause,
Had banished him from better days
To play the Prince of Castaways.
Meanwhile he played surpassing well
A part, for most, unplayable;
In fine, one pauses, half afraid
To say for certain that he played.

For that, one may as well forego
Conviction as to yes or no;
Nor can I say just how intense
Would then have been the difference
To several, who, having striven
In vain to get what he was given,
Would see the stranger taken on
By friends not easy to be won.

Moreover, many a malcontent
He soothed and found munificent;
His courtesy beguiled and foiled
Suspicion that his years were soiled;
His mien distinguished any crowd,
His credit strengthened when he bowed;
And women, young and old, were fond
Of looking at the man Flammonde.

There was a woman in our town
On whom the fashion was to frown;
But while our talk renewed the tinge
Of a long-faded scarlet fringe,
The man Flammonde saw none of that,
And what he saw we wondered at—
That none of us, in her distress,
Could hide or find our littleness.

There was a boy that all agreed
Had shut within him the rare seed
Of learning. We could understand,
But none of us could lift a hand.
The man Flammonde appraised the youth,
And told a few of us the truth;
And thereby, for a little gold,
A flowered future was unrolled.

There were two citizens who fought
For years and years, and over nought;
They made life awkward for their friends,
And shortened their own dividends.
The man Flammonde said what was wrong
Should be made right; nor was it long
Before they were again in line,
And had each other in to dine.

And these I mention are but four
Of many out of many more.
So much for them. But what of him—
So firm in every look and limb?

What small satanic sort of kink
Was in his brain? What broken link
Withheld him from the destinies
That came so near to being his?

What was he, when we came to sift
His meaning, and to note the drift
Of incommunicable ways
That make us ponder while we praise?
Why was it that his charm revealed
Somehow the surface of a shield?
What was it that we never caught?
What was he, and what was he not?

How much it was of him we met
We cannot ever know; nor yet
Shall all he gave us quite atone
For what was his, and his alone;
Nor need we now, since he knew best,
Nourish an ethical unrest:
Rarely at once will nature give
The power to be Flammonde and live.

We cannot know how much we learn
From those who never will return,
Until a flash of unforeseen
Remembrance falls on what has been.
We've each a darkening hill to climb;
And this is why, from time to time
In Tilbury Town, we look beyond
Horizons for the man Flammonde.

JOHN GORHAM

"Tell me what you're doing over here, John Gorham,
Sighing hard and seeming to be sorry when you're not;
Make me laugh or let me go now, for long faces in the moon-
light
Are a sign for me to say again a word that you forgot."—

"I'm over here to tell you what the moon already
May have said or maybe shouted ever since a year ago;
I'm over here to tell you what you are, Jane Wayland,
And to make you rather sorry, I should say, for being so."—

"Tell me what you're saying to me now, John Gorham,
Or you'll never see as much of me as ribbons any more;
I'll vanish in as many ways as I have toes and fingers,
And you'll not follow far for one where flocks have been before."—

"I'm sorry now you never saw the flocks, Jane Wayland,
But you're the one to make of them as many as you need.
And then about the vanishing. It's I who mean to vanish;
And when I'm here no longer you'll be done with me indeed."—

"That's a way to tell me what I am, John Gorham!
How am I to know myself until I make you smile?
Try to look as if the moon were making faces at you,
And a little more as if you meant to stay a little while."—

"You are what it is that over rose-blown gardens
Make a pretty flütter for a season in the sun;
You are what it is that with a mouse, Jane Wayland,
Catches him and lets him go and eats him up for fun."—

"Sure I never took you for a mouse, John Gorham;
All you say is easy, but so far from being true
That I wish you wouldn't ever be again the one to think so;
For it isn't cats and butterflies that I would be to you."—

"All your little animals are in one picture—
One I've had before me since a year ago to-night;
And the picture where they live will be of you, Jane Wayland,
Till you find a way to kill them or to keep them out of sight."—

"Won't you ever see me as I am, John Gorham,
Leaving out the foolishness and all I never meant?
Somewhere in me there's a woman, if you know the way to find her.
Will you like me any better if I prove it and repent?"—

"I doubt if I shall ever have the time, Jane Wayland;
And I dare say all this moonlight lying round us might as well
Fall for nothing on the shards of broken urns that are forgotten,
As on two that have no longer much of anything to tell."

THE UNFORGIVEN

When he, who is the unforgiven,
Beheld her first, he found her fair:
No promise ever dreamt in heaven
Could then have lured him anywhere
That would have been away from there;
And all his wits had lightly striven,
Foiled with her voice, and eyes, and hair.

There's nothing in the saints and sages
To meet the shafts her glances had,
Or such as hers have had for ages
To blind a man till he be glad,
And humble him till he be mad.
The story would have many pages,
And would be neither good nor bad.

And, having followed, you would find him
Where properly the play begins;
But look for no red light behind him—
No fumes of many-colored sins,
Fanned high by screaming violins.
God knows what good it was to blind him,
Or whether man or woman wins.

And by the same eternal token,
Who knows just how it will all end?—
This drama of hard words unspoken,
This fireside farce, without a friend
Or enemy to comprehend
What augurs when two lives are broken,
And fear finds nothing left to mend.

He stares in vain for what awaits him,
And sees in Love a coin to toss;
He smiles, and her cold hush berates him
Beneath his hard half of the cross;
They wonder why it ever was;
And she, the unforgiving, hates him
More for her lack than for her loss.

He feeds with pride his indecision,
And shrinks from what will not occur,
Bequeathing with infirm derision
His ashes to the days that were,
Before she made him prisoner;
And labors to retrieve the vision
That he must once have had of her.

He waits, and there awaits an ending,
And he knows neither what nor when;
But no magicians are attending
To make him see as he saw then,
And he will never find again
The face that once had been the rending
Of all his purpose among men.

He blames her not, nor does he chide her,
And she has nothing new to say;
If he were Bluebeard he could hide her,
But that's not written in the play,
And there will be no change to-day;
Although, to the serene outsider,
There still would seem to be a way.

BEWICK FINZER

Time was when his half million drew
  The breath of six per cent;
But soon the worm of what-was-not
  Fed hard on his content;
And something crumbled in his brain
  When his half million went.

Time passed, and filled along with his
  The place of many more;
Time came, and hardly one of us
  Had credence to restore,
From what appeared one day, the man
  Whom we had known before.

The broken voice, the withered neck,
  The coat worn out with care,
The cleanliness of indigence,
  The brilliance of despair,
The fond imponderable dreams
  Of affluence,—all were there.

Poor Finzer, with his dreams and schemes,
  Fares hard now in the race,
With heart and eye that have a task
  When he looks in the face
Of one who might so easily
  Have been in Finzer's place.

He comes unfailing for the loan
  We give and then forget;
He comes, and probably for years
  Will he be coming yet,—
Familiar as an old mistake,
  And futile as regret.

THE HOUSE ON THE HILL

They are all gone away,
  The House is shut and still,
There is nothing more to say.

Through broken walls and gray
  The winds blow bleak and shrill:
They are all gone away.

Nor is there one to-day
  To speak them good or ill:
There is nothing more to say.

Why is it then we stray
  Around the sunken sill?
They are all gone away,

And our poor fancy-play
  For them is wasted skill:
There is nothing more to say.

There is ruin and decay
  In the House on the Hill:
They are all gone away,
There is nothing more to say.

RICHARD CORY

Whenever Richard Cory went down town,
We people on the pavement looked at him:
He was a gentleman from sole to crown,
Clean favored, and imperially slim.

And he was always quietly arrayed,
And he was always human when he talked;
But still he fluttered pulses when he said,
"Good-morning," and he glittered when he walked.

And he was rich—yes, richer than a king—
And admirably schooled in every grace:
In fine, we thought that he was everything
To make us wish that we were in his place.

So on we worked, and waited for the light,
And went without the meat, and cursed the bread;
And Richard Cory, one calm summer night,
Went home and put a bullet through his head.

ISAAC AND ARCHIBALD

Isaac and Archibald were two old men.
I knew them, and I may have laughed at them
A little; but I must have honored them
For they were old, and they were good to me.

I do not think of either of them now,
Without remembering, infallibly,
A journey that I made one afternoon
With Isaac to find out what Archibald
Was doing with his oats. It was high time
Those oats were cut, said Isaac; and he feared
That Archibald—well, he could never feel
Quite sure of Archibald. Accordingly
The good old man invited me—that is,
Permitted me—to go along with him;
And I, with a small boy's adhesiveness
To competent old age, got up and went.
I do not know that I cared overmuch
For Archibald's or anybody's oats,
But Archibald was quite another thing,
And Isaac yet another; and the world
Was wide, and there was gladness everywhere.
We walked together down the River Road
With all the warmth and wonder of the land
Around us, and the wayside flash of leaves,—
And Isaac said the day was glorious;

But somewhere at the end of the first mile
I found that I was figuring to find
How long those ancient legs of his would keep
The pace that he had set for them. The sun
Was hot, and I was ready to sweat blood;
But Isaac, for aught I could make of him,
Was cool to his hat-band. So I said then,
With a dry gasp of affable despair,
Something about the scorching days we have
In August without knowing it sometimes;
But Isaac said the day was like a dream,
And praised the Lord, and talked about the breeze.
I made a fair confession of the breeze,
And crowded casually on his thought
The nearness of a profitable nook
That I could see. First I was half inclined
To caution him that he was growing old,
But something that was not compassion soon
Made plain the folly of all subterfuge.
Isaac was old, but not so old as that.

So I proposed, without an overture,
That we be seated in the shade a while,
And Isaac made no murmur. Soon the talk
Was turned on Archibald, and I began
To feel some premonitions of a kind
That only childhood knows; for the old man
Had looked at me and clutched me with his eye,
And asked if I had ever noticed things.
I told him that I could not think of them,
And I knew then, by the frown that left his face
Unsatisfied, that I had injured him.
"My good young friend," he said, "you cannot feel
What I have seen so long. You have the eyes—
Oh, yes—but you have not the other things:
The sight within that never will deceive,
You do not know—you have no right to know;
The twilight warning of experience,
The singular idea of loneliness,—

These are not yours. But they have long been mine,
And they have shown me now for seven years
That Archibald is changing. It is not
So much that he should come to his last hand,
And leave the game, and go the old way down;
But I have known him in and out so long,
And I have seen so much of good in him
That other men have shared and have not seen,
And I have gone so far through thick and thin,
Through cold and fire with him, that now it brings
To this old heart of mine an ache that you
Have not yet lived enough to know about.
But even unto you, and your boy's faith,
Your freedom, and your untried confidence,
A time will come to find out what it means
To know that you are losing what was yours,
To know that you are being left behind;
And then the long contempt of innocence—
God bless you, boy!—don't think the worse of it
Because an old man chatters in the shade—
Will all be like a story you have read
In childhood and remembered for the pictures.
And when the best friend of your life goes down,
When first you know in him the slackening
That comes, and coming always tells the end,—
Now in a common word that would have passed
Uncaught from any other lips than his,
Now in some trivial act of every day,
Done as he might have done it all along
But for a twinging little difference
That nips you like a squirrel's teeth—oh, yes,
Then you will understand it well enough.
But oftener it comes in other ways;
It comes without your knowing when it comes;
You know that he is changing, and you know
That he is going—just as I know now
That Archibald is going, and that I
Am staying. . . . Look at me, my boy,
And when the time shall come for you to see

That I must follow after him, try then
To think of me, to bring me back again,
Just as I was to-day. Think of the place
Where we are sitting now, and think of me—
Think of old Isaac as you knew him then,
When you set out with him in August once
To see old Archibald."—The words come back
Almost as Isaac must have uttered them,
And there comes with them a dry memory
Of something in my throat that would not move.

If you had asked me then to tell just why
I made so much of Isaac and the things
He said, I should have gone far for an answer;
For I knew it was not sorrow that I felt,
Whatever I may have wished it, or tried then
To make myself believe. My mouth was full
Of words, and they would have been comforting
To Isaac, spite of my twelve years, I think;
But there was not in me the willingness
To speak them out. Therefore I watched the ground;
And I was wondering what made the Lord
Create a thing so nervous as an ant,
When Isaac, with commendable unrest,
Ordained that we should take the road again—
For it was yet three miles to Archibald's,
And one to the first pump. I felt relieved
All over when the old man told me that;
I felt that he had stilled a fear of mine
That those extremities of heat and cold
Which he had long gone through with Archibald
Had made the man impervious to both;
But Isaac had a desert somewhere in him,
And at the pump he thanked God for all things
That He had put on earth for men to drink,
And he drank well,—so well that I proposed
That we go slowly lest I learn too soon
The bitterness of being left behind,
And all those other things. That was a joke

To Isaac, and it pleased him very much;
And that pleased me—for I was twelve years old.

At the end of an hour's walking after that
The cottage of old Archibald appeared.
Little and white and high on a smooth round hill
It stood, with hackmatacks and apple-trees
Before it, and a big barn-roof beyond;
And over the place—trees, house, fields and all—
Hovered an air of still simplicity
And a fragrance of old summers—the old style
That lives the while it passes. I dare say
That I was lightly conscious of all this
When Isaac, of a sudden, stopped himself,
And for the long first quarter of a minute
Gazed with incredulous eyes, forgetful quite
Of breezes and of me and of all else
Under the scorching sun but a smooth-cut field,
Faint yellow in the distance. I was young,
But there were a few things that I could see,
And this was one of them.—"Well, well!" said he;
And "Archibald will be surprised, I think,"
Said I. But all my childhood subtlety
Was lost on Isaac, for he strode along
Like something out of Homer—powerful
And awful on the wayside, so I thought.
Also I thought how good it was to be
So near the end of my short-legged endeavor
To keep the pace with Isaac for five miles.

Hardly had we turned in from the main road
When Archibald, with one hand on his back
And the other clutching his huge-headed cane,
Came limping down to meet us.—"Well! well! well!"
Said he; and then he looked at my red face,
All streaked with dust and sweat, and shook my hand,
And said it must have been a right smart walk
That we had had that day from Tilbury Town.—
"Magnificent," said Isaac; and he told

About the beautiful west wind there was
Which cooled and clarified the atmosphere.
"You must have made it with your legs, I guess,"
Said Archibald; and Isaac humored him
With one of those infrequent smiles of his
Which he kept in reserve, apparently,
For Archibald alone. "But why," said he,
"Should Providence have cider in the world
If not for such an afternoon as this?"
And Archibald, with a soft light in his eyes,
Replied that if he chose to go down cellar,
There he would find eight barrels—one of which
Was newly tapped, he said, and to his taste
An honor to the fruit. Isaac approved
Most heartily of that, and guided us
Forthwith, as if his venerable feet
Were measuring the turf in his own door-yard,
Straight to the open rollway. Down we went,
Out of the fiery sunshine to the gloom,
Grateful and half sepulchral, where we found
The barrels, like eight potent sentinels,
Close ranged along the wall. From one of them
A bright pine spile stuck out alluringly,
And on the black flat stone, just under it,
Glimmered a late-spilled proof that Archibald
Had spoken from unfeigned experience.
There was a fluted antique water-glass
Close by, and in it, prisoned, or at rest,
There was a cricket, of the brown soft sort
That feeds on darkness. Isaac turned him out,
And touched him with his thumb to make him jump,
And then composedly pulled out the plug
With such a practised hand that scarce a drop
Did even touch his fingers. Then he drank
And smacked his lips with a slow patronage
And looked along the line of barrels there
With a pride that may have been forgetfulness
That they were Archibald's and not his own.
"I never twist a spigot nowadays,"

He said, and raised the glass up to the light,
"But I thank God for orchards." And that glass
Was filled repeatedly for the same hand
Before I thought it worth while to discern
Again that I was young, and that old age,
With all his woes, had some advantages.

"Now, Archibald," said Isaac, when we stood
Outside again, "I have it in my mind
That I shall take a sort of little walk—
To stretch my legs and see what you are doing.
You stay and rest your back and tell the boy
A story: Tell him all about the time
In Stafford's cabin forty years ago,
When four of us were snowed up for ten days
With only one dried haddock. Tell him all
About it, and be wary of your back.
Now I will go along."—I looked up then
At Archibald, and as I looked I saw
Just how his nostrils widened once or twice
And then grew narrow. I can hear to-day
The way the old man chuckled to himself—
Not wholesomely, not wholly to convince
Another of his mirth,—as I can hear
The lonely sigh that followed.—But at length
He said: "The orchard now's the place for us;
We may find something like an apple there,
And we shall have the shade, at any rate."
So there we went and there we laid ourselves
Where the sun could not reach us; and I champed
A dozen of worm-blighted astrakhans
While Archibald said nothing—merely told
The tale of Stafford's cabin, which was good,
Though "master chilly"—after his own phrase—
Even for a day like that. But other thoughts
Were moving in his mind, imperative,
And writhing to be spoken: I could see
The glimmer of them in a glance or two,
Cautious, or else unconscious, that he gave

Over his shoulder: . . . "Stafford and the rest—
But that's an old song now, and Archibald
And Isaac are old men. Remember, boy,
That we are old. Whatever we have gained,
Or lost, or thrown away, we are old men.
You look before you and we look behind,
And we are playing life out in the shadow—
But that's not all of it. The sunshine lights
A good road yet before us if we look,
And we are doing that when least we know it;
For both of us are children of the sun,
Like you, and like the weed there at your feet.
The shadow calls us, and it frightens us—
We think; but there's a light behind the stars,
And we old fellows who have dared to live,
We see it—and we see the other things,
The other things . . . Yes, I have seen it come
These eight years, and these ten years, and I know
Now that it cannot be for very long
That Isaac will be Isaac. You have seen—
Young as you are, you must have seen the strange
Uncomfortable habit of the man?
He'll take my nerves and tie them in a knot
Sometimes, and that's not Isaac. I know that—
And I know what it is: I get it here
A little, in my knees, and Isaac—here."
The old man shook his head regretfully
And laid his knuckles three times on his forehead.
"That's what it is: Isaac is not quite right.
You see it, but you don't know what it means:
The thousand little differences—no,
You do not know them, and it's well you don't;
You'll know them soon enough—God bless you, boy!—
You'll know them, but not all of them—not all.
So think of them as little as you can:
There's nothing in them for you, or for me—
But I am old and I must think of them;
I'm in the shadow, but I don't forget
The light, my boy,—the light behind the stars.

Remember that: remember that I said it;
And when the time that you think far away
Shall come for you to say it—say it, boy;
Let there be no confusion or distrust
In you, no snarling of a life half lived,
Nor any cursing over broken things
That your complaint has been the ruin of.
Live to see clearly and the light will come
To you, and as you need it.—But there, there,
I'm going it again, as Isaac says,
And I'll stop now before you go to sleep.—
Only be sure that you growl cautiously,
And always where the shadow may not reach you."

Never shall I forget, long as I live,
The quaint thin crack in Archibald's voice,
The lonely twinkle in his little eyes,
Or the way it made me feel to be with him.
I know I lay and looked for a long time
Down through the orchard and across the road,
Across the river and the sun-scorched hills
That ceased in a blue forest, where the world
Ceased with it. Now and then my fancy caught
A flying glimpse of a good life beyond—
Something of ships and sunlight, streets and singing,
Troy falling, and the ages coming back,
And ages coming forward: Archibald
And Isaac were good fellows in old clothes,
And Agamemnon was a friend of mine;
Ulysses coming home again to shoot
With bows and feathered arrows made another,
And all was as it should be. I was young.

So I lay dreaming of what things I would,
Calm and incorrigibly satisfied
With apples and romance and ignorance,
And the still smoke from Archibald's clay pipe.
There was a stillness over everything,
As if the spirit of heat had laid its hand
Upon the world and hushed it; and I felt

Within the mightiness of the white sun
That smote the land around us and wrought out
A fragrance from the trees, a vital warmth
And fullness for the time that was to come,
And a glory for the world beyond the forest.
The present and the future and the past,
Isaac and Archibald, the burning bush,
The Trojans and the walls of Jericho,
Were beautifully fused; and all went well
Till Archibald began to fret for Isaac
And said it was a master day for sunstroke.
That was enough to make a mummy smile,
I thought; and I remained hilarious,
In face of all precedence and respect,
Till Isaac (who had come to us unheard)
Found he had no tobacco, looked at me
Peculiarly, and asked of Archibald
What ailed the boy to make him chirrup so.
From that he told us what a blessed world
The Lord had given us.—"But, Archibald,"
He added, with a sweet severity
That made me think of peach-skins and goose-flesh,
"I'm half afraid you cut those oats of yours
A day or two before they were well set."
"They were set well enough," said Archibald,—
And I remarked the process of his nose
Before the words came out. "But never mind
Your neighbor's oats: you stay here in the shade
And rest yourself while I go find the cards.
We'll have a little game of seven-up
And let the boy keep count."—"We'll have the game,
Assuredly," said Isaac; "and I think
That I will have a drop of cider, also."

They marched away together towards the house
And left me to my childish ruminations
Upon the ways of men. I followed them
Down cellar with my fancy, and then left them
For a fairer vision of all things at once

That was anon to be destroyed again
By the sound of voices and of heavy feet—
One of the sounds of life that I remember,
Though I forget so many that rang first
As if they were thrown down to me from Sinai.

So I remember, even to this day,
Just how they sounded, how they placed themselves,
And how the game went on while I made marks
And crossed them out, and meanwhile made some Trojans.
Likewise I made Ulysses, after Isaac,
And a little after Flaxman. Archibald
Was injured when he found himself left out,
But he had no heroics, and I said so:
I told him that his white beard was too long
And too straight down to be like things in Homer.
"Quite so," said Isaac.—"Low," said Archibald;
And he threw down a deuce with a deep grin
That showed his yellow teeth and made me happy.
So they played on till a bell rang from the door,
And Archibald said, "Supper."—After that
The old men smoked while I sat watching them
And wondered with all comfort what might come
To me, and what might never come to me;
And when the time came for the long walk home
With Isaac in the twilight, I could see
The forest and the sunset and the sky-line,
No matter where it was that I was looking:
The flame beyond the boundary, the music,
The foam and the white ships, and two old men
Were things that would not leave me.—And that night
There came to me a dream—a shining one,
With two old angels in it. They had wings,
And they were sitting where a silver light
Suffused them, face to face. The wings of one
Began to palpitate as I approached,
But I was yet unseen when a dry voice
Cried thinly, with unpatronizing triumph,
"I've got you, Isaac; high, low, jack, and the game."

Isaac and Archibald have gone their way
To the silence of the loved and well-forgotten.
I knew them, and I may have laughed at them;
But there's a laughing that has honor in it,
And I have no regret for light words now.
Rather I think sometimes they may have made
Their sport of me,—but they would not do that,
They were too old for that. They were old men,
And I may laugh at them because I knew them.

PARTNERSHIP

Yes, you have it; I can see.
Beautiful? . . . Dear, look at me!
Look and let my shame confess
Triumph after weariness.
Beautiful? Ah, yes.

Lift it where the beams are bright;
Hold it where the western light,
Shining in above my bed,
Throws a glory on your head.
Now it is all said.

All there was for me to say
From the first until to-day.
Long denied and long deferred,
Now I say it in one word—
Now; and you have heard.

Life would have its way with us,
And I've called it glorious:
For I know the glory now
And I read it on your brow.
You have shown me how.

I can feel your cheeks all wet,
But your eyes will not forget:
In the frown you cannot hide
I can read where faith and pride
Are not satisfied.

But the word was, two should live:
Two should suffer—and forgive:
By the steep and weary way,
For the glory of the clay,
Two should have their day.

We have toiled and we have wept
For the gift the gods have kept:
Clashing and unreconciled
When we might as well have smiled,
We have played the child.

But the clashing is all past,
And the gift is yours at last.
Lift it—hold it high again! . . .
Did I doubt you now and then?
Well, we are not men.

Never mind; we know the way,—
And I do not need to stay.
Let us have it well confessed:
You to triumph, I to rest.
That will be the best.

THE FIELD OF GLORY

War shook the land where Levi dwelt,
And fired the dismal wrath he felt,
That such a doom was ever wrought
As his, to toil while others fought;
To toil, to dream—and still to dream,
With one day barren as another;
To consummate, as it would seem,
The dry despair of his old mother.

Far off one afternoon began
The sound of man destroying man;
And Levi, sick with nameless rage,
Condemned again his heritage,

And sighed for scars that might have come,
And would, if once he could have sundered
Those harsh, inhering claims of home
That held him while he cursed and wondered.

Another day, and then there came,
Rough, bloody, ribald, hungry, lame,
But yet themselves, to Levi's door,
Two remnants of the day before.
They laughed at him and what he sought;
They jeered him, and his painful acre;
But Levi knew that they had fought,
And left their manners to their Maker.

That night, for the grim widow's ears,
With hopes that hid themselves in fears,
He told of arms, and fiery deeds,
Whereat one leaps the while he reads,
And said he'd be no more a clown,
While others drew the breath of battle.—
The mother looked him up and down,
And laughed—a scant laugh with a rattle.

She told him what she found to tell,
And Levi listened, and heard well
Some admonitions of a voice
That left him no cause to rejoice.—
He sought a friend, and found the stars,
And prayed aloud that they should aid him;
But they said not a word of wars,
Or of a reason why God made him.

And who's of this or that estate
We do not wholly calculate,
When baffling shades that shift and cling
Are not without their glimmering;
When even Levi, tired of faith,
Beloved of none, forgot by many,
Dismissed as an inferior wraith,
Reborn may be as great as any.

THE TOWN DOWN THE RIVER

I

Said the Watcher by the Way
To the young and the unladen,
To the boy and to the maiden,
"God be with you both to-day.
First your song came ringing,
Now you come, you two,—
Knowing naught of what you do,
Or of what your dreams are bringing.

"O you children who go singing
To the Town down the River,
Where the millions cringe and shiver,
Tell me what you know to-day;
Tell me how far you are going,
Tell me how you find your way.
O you children who go dreaming,
Tell me what you dream to-day."

"He is old and we have heard him,"
Said the boy then to the maiden;
"He is old and heavy laden
With a load we throw away.
Care may come to find us,
Age may lay us low;
Still, we seek the light we know,
And the dead we leave behind us.

"Did he think that he would blind us
Into such a small believing
As to live without achieving,
When the lights have led so far?
Let him watch or let him wither,—
Shall he tell us where we are?
We know best who go together,
Downward, onward, and so far."

II

Said the Watcher by the Way
To the fiery folk that hastened,
To the loud and the unchastened,
"You are strong, I see, to-day.
Strength and hope may lead you
To the journey's end,—
Each to be the other's friend
If the Town should fail to need you.

"And are ravens there to feed you
In the Town down the River,
Where the gift appalls the giver
And youth hardens day by day?
O you brave and you unshaken,
Are you truly on your way?
And are sirens in the River,
That you come so far to-day?"

"You are old, and we have listened,"
Said the voice of one who halted;
"You are sage and self-exalted,
But your way is not our way.
You that cannot aid us
Give us words to eat.
Be assured that they are sweet,
And that we are as God made us.

"Not in vain have you delayed us,
Though the River still be calling
Through the twilight that is falling,
And the Town be still so far.
By the whirlwind of your wisdom
Leagues are lifted as leaves are;
But a king without a kingdom
Fails us, who have come so far."

III

Said the Watcher by the Way
To the slower folk who stumbled,
To the weak and the world-humbled,
"Tell me how you fare to-day.
Some with ardor shaken,
All with honor scarred,
Do you falter, finding hard
The far chance that you have taken?

"Or, do you at length awaken
To an antic retribution,
Goading to a new confusion
The drugged hopes of yesterday?
O you poor mad men that hobble,
Will you not return, or stay?
Do you trust, you broken people,
To a dawn without the day?"

"You speak well of what you know not,"
Muttered one; and then a second:
"You have begged and you have beckoned,
But you see us on our way.
Who are you to scold us,
Knowing what we know?
Jeremiah, long ago,
Said as much as you have told us.

"As we are, then, you behold us:
Derelicts of all conditions,
Poets, rogues, and sick physicians,
Plodding forward from afar;
Forward now into the darkness
Where the men before us are;
Forward, onward, out of grayness,
To the light that shone so far."

IV

Said the Watcher by the Way
To some aged ones who lingered,
To the shrunken, the claw-fingered,
"So you come for me to-day."—
"Yes, to give you warning;
You are old," one said;
"You have old hairs on your head,
Fit for laurel, not for scorning.

"From the first of early morning
We have toiled along to find you;
We, as others, have maligned you,
But we need your scorn to-day.
By the light that we saw shining,
Let us not be lured alway;
Let us hear no River calling
When to-morrow is to-day."

"But your lanterns are unlighted
And the Town is far before you:
Let us hasten, I implore you,"
Said the Watcher by the Way.
"Long have I waited,
Longer have I known
That the Town would have its own,
And the call be for the fated.

"In the name of all created,
Let us hear no more, my brothers;
Are we older than all others?
Are the planets in our way?"—
"Hark," said one; "I hear the River,
Calling always, night and day."—
"Forward, then! The lights are shining,"
Said the Watcher by the Way.

MINIVER CHEEVY

Miniver Cheevy, child of scorn,
Grew lean while he assailed the seasons;
He wept that he was ever born,
And he had reasons.

Miniver loved the days of old
When swords were bright and steeds were prancing;
The vision of a warrior bold
Would set him dancing.

Miniver sighed for what was not,
And dreamed, and rested from his labors;
He dreamed of Thebes and Camelot,
And Priam's neighbors.

Miniver mourned the ripe renown
That made so many a name so fragrant;
He mourned Romance, now on the town,
And Art, a vagrant.

Miniver loved the Medici,
Albeit he had never seen one;
He would have sinned incessantly
Could he have been one.

Miniver cursed the commonplace
And eyed a khaki suit with loathing;
He missed the mediæval grace
Of iron clothing.

Miniver scorned the gold he sought,
But sore annoyed was he without it;
Miniver thought, and thought, and thought,
And thought about it.

Miniver Cheevy, born too late,
Scratched his head and kept on thinking;
Miniver coughed, and called it fate,
And kept on drinking.

NEIGHBORS

As often as we thought of her,
We thought of a gray life
That made a quaint economist
Of a wolf-haunted wife;
We made the best of all she bore
That was not ours to bear,
And honored her for wearing things
That were not things to wear.

There was a distance in her look
That made us look again;
And if she smiled, we might believe
That we had looked in vain.
Rarely she came inside our doors,
And had not long to stay;
And when she left, it seemed somehow
That she was far away.

At last, when we had all forgot
That all is here to change,
A shadow on the commonplace
Was for a moment strange.
Yet there was nothing for surprise,
Nor much that need be told:
Love, with his gift of pain, had given
More than one heart could hold.

THE MILL

The miller's wife had waited long,
The tea was cold, the fire was dead;
And there might yet be nothing wrong
In how he went and what he said:
"There are no millers any more,"
Was all that she had heard him say;
And he had lingered at the door
So long that it seemed yesterday.

Sick with a fear that had no form
She knew that she was there at last;
And in the mill there was a warm
And mealy fragrance of the past.
What else there was would only seem
To say again what he had meant;
And what was hanging from a beam
Would not have heeded where she went.

And if she thought it followed her,
She may have reasoned in the dark
That one way of the few there were
Would hide her and would leave no mark:
Black water, smooth above the weir
Like starry velvet in the night,
Though ruffled once, would soon appear
The same as ever to the sight.

LONDON BRIDGE

"Do I hear them? Yes, I hear the children singing—and what of it?
Have you come with eyes afire to find me now and ask me that?
If I were not their father and if you were not their mother,
We might believe they made a noise. . . . What are you—driving at!"

"Well, be glad that you can hear them, and be glad they are so near us,—
For I have heard the stars of heaven, and they were nearer still.
All within an hour it is that I have heard them calling,
And though I pray for them to cease, I know they never will;
For their music on my heart, though you may freeze it, will fall always,
Like summer snow that never melts upon a mountain-top.

Do you hear them? Do you hear them overhead—the children—singing?
Do you hear the children singing? . . . God, will you make them stop!"

"And what now in His holy name have you to do with mountains?
We're back to town again, my dear, and we've a dance to-night.
Frozen hearts and falling music? Snow and stars, and—what the devil!
Say it over to me slowly, and be sure you have it right."

"God knows if I be right or wrong in saying what I tell you,
Or if I know the meaning any more of what I say.
All I know is, it will kill me if I try to keep it hidden—
Well, I met him. . . . Yes, I met him, and I talked with him—to-day."

"You met him? Did you meet the ghost of someone you had poisoned,
Long ago, before I knew you for the woman that you are?
Take a chair; and don't begin your stories always in the middle.
Was he man, or was he demon? Anyhow, you've gone too far
To go back, and I'm your servant. I'm the lord, but you're the master.
Now go on with what you know, for I'm excited."

"Do you mean—
Do you mean to make me try to think that you know less than I do?"

"I know that you foreshadow the beginning of a scene.
Pray be careful, and as accurate as if the doors of heaven
Were to swing or to stay bolted from now on for evermore."

"Do you conceive, with all your smooth contempt of every feeling,
Of hiding what you know and what you must have known before?

Is it worth a woman's torture to stand here and have you
smiling,
With only your poor fetish of possession on your side?
No thing but one is wholly sure, and that's not one to scare
me;
When I meet it I may say to God at last that I have tried.
And yet, for all I know, or all I dare believe, my trials
Henceforward will be more for you to bear than are your
own;
And you must give me keys of yours to rooms I have not
entered.
Do you see me on your threshold all my life, and there alone?
Will you tell me where you see me in your fancy—when it
leads you
Far enough beyond the moment for a glance at the abyss?"

"Will you tell me what intrinsic and amazing sort of non-
sense
You are crowding on the patience of the man who gives you
—this?
Look around you and be sorry you're not living in an attic,
With a civet and a fish-net, and with you to pay the rent.
I say words that you can spell without the use of all your
letters;
And I grant, if you insist, that I've a guess at what you
meant."

"Have I told you, then, for nothing, that I met him? Are
you trying
To be merry while you try to make me hate you?"

"Think again,
My dear, before you tell me, in a language unbecoming
To a lady, what you plan to tell me next. If I complain,
If I seem an atom peevish at the preference you mention—
Or imply, to be precise—you may believe, or you may not,
That I'm a trifle more aware of what he wants than you are.
But I shouldn't throw that at you. Make believe that I forgot.

Make believe that he's a genius, if you like,—but in the meantime
Don't go back to rocking-horses. There, there, there, now."

"Make believe!
When you see me standing helpless on a plank above a whirlpool,
Do I drown, or do I hear you when you say it? Make believe?
How much more am I to say or do for you before I tell you
That I met him! What's to follow now may be for you to choose.
Do you hear me? Won't you listen? It's an easy thing to listen. . . ."

"And it's easy to be crazy when there's everything to lose."

"If at last you have a notion that I mean what I am saying,
Do I seem to tell you nothing when I tell you I shall try?
If you save me, and I lose him—I don't know—it won't much matter.
I dare say that I've lied enough, but now I do not lie."

"Do you fancy me the one man who has waited and said nothing
While a wife has dragged an old infatuation from a tomb?
Give the thing a little air and it will vanish into ashes.
There you are—piff! presto!"

"When I came into this room,
It seemed as if I saw the place, and you there at your table,
As you are now at this moment, for the last time in my life;
And I told myself before I came to find you, 'I shall tell him,
If I can, what I have learned of him since I became his wife.'
And if you say, as I've no doubt you will before I finish,
That you have tried unceasingly, with all your might and main,
To teach me, knowing more than I of what it was I needed,
Don't think, with all you may have thought, that you have tried in vain;

For you have taught me more than hides in all the shelves
of knowledge
Of how little you found that's in me and was in me all along.
I believed, if I intruded nothing on you that I cared for,
I'd be half as much as horses,—and it seems that I was
wrong;—
I believed there was enough of earth in me, with all my
nonsense
Over things that made you sleepy, to keep something still
awake;
But you taught me soon to read my book, and God knows
I have read it—
Ages longer than an angel would have read it for your sake.
I have said that you must open other doors than I have
entered,
But I wondered while I said it if I might not be obscure.
Is there anything in all your pedigrees and inventories
With a value more elusive than a dollar's? Are you sure
That if I starve another year for you I shall be stronger
To endure another like it—and another—till I'm dead?"

"Has your tame cat sold a picture?—or more likely had a
windfall?
Or for God's sake, what's broke loose? Have you a bee-hive
in your head?
A little more of this from you will not be easy hearing—
Do you know that? Understand it, if you do; for if you
won't . . .
What the devil are you saying! Make believe you never said it,
And I'll say I never heard it. . . . Oh, you. . . . If you. . . ."

"If I don't?"

"There are men who say there's reason hidden somewhere in
a woman,
But I doubt if God himself remembers where the key was
hung."

"He may not; for they say that even God himself is growing.
I wonder if He makes believe that He is growing young;
I wonder if He makes believe that women who are giving

All they have in holy loathing to a stranger all their lives
Are the wise ones who build houses in the Bible. . . ."

"Stop—you devil!"

". . . Or that souls are any whiter when their bodies are called wives.
If a dollar's worth of gold will hoop the walls of hell together,
Why need heaven be such a ruin of a place that never was?
And if at last I lied my starving soul away to nothing,
Are you sure you might not miss it? Have you come to such a pass
That you would have me longer in your arms if you discovered
That I made you into someone else. . . . Oh! . . . Well, there are worse ways.
But why aim it at my feet—unless you fear you may be sorry. . . .
There are many days ahead of you."

"I do not see those days."

"I can see them. Granted even I am wrong, there are the children.
And are they to praise their father for his insight if we die?
Do you hear them? Do you hear them overhead—the children—singing?
Do you hear them? Do you hear the children?"

"Damn the children!"

"Why?
What have *they* done? . . . Well, then,—do it. . . . Do it now, and have it over."

"Oh, you devil! . . . Oh, you . . ."

"No, I'm not a devil, I'm a prophet—
One who sees the end already of so much that one end more
Would have now the small importance of one other small illusion,

Which in turn would have a welcome where the rest have
gone before.
But if I were you, my fancy would look on a little farther
For the glimpse of a release that may be somewhere still in
sight.
Futhermore, you must remember those two hundred invitations
For the dancing after dinner. We shall have to shine to-night.
We shall dance, and be as happy as a pair of merry spectres,
On the grave of all the lies that we shall never have to tell;
We shall dance among the ruins of the tomb of our endurance,
And I have not a doubt that we shall do it very well.
There!—I'm glad you've put it back; for I don't like it.
Shut the drawer now.
No—no—don't cancel anything. I'll dance until I drop.
I can't walk yet, but I'm going to. . . . Go away somewhere, and leave me. . . .
Oh, you children! Oh, you children! . . . God, will they
never stop!"

DISCOVERY

We told of him as one who should have soared
And seen for us the devastating light
Whereof there is not either day or night,
And shared with us the glamor of the Word
That fell once upon Amos to record
For men at ease in Zion, when the sight
Of ills obscured aggrieved him and the might
Of Hamath was a warning of the Lord.

Assured somehow that he would make us wise,
Our pleasure was to wait; and our surprise
Was hard when we confessed the dry return
Of his regret. For we were still to learn
That earth has not a school where we may go
For wisdom, or for more than we may know.

FIRELIGHT

Ten years together without yet a cloud,
They seek each other's eyes at intervals
Of gratefulness to firelight and four walls
For love's obliteration of the crowd.
Serenely and perennially endowed
And bowered as few may be, their joy recalls
No snake, no sword; and over them there falls
The blessing of what neither says aloud.

Wiser for silence, they were not so glad
Were she to read the graven tale of lines
On the wan face of one somewhere alone;
Nor were they more content could he have had
Her thoughts a moment since of one who shines
Apart, and would be hers if he had known.

MR. FLOOD'S PARTY

Old Eben Flood, climbing alone one night
Over the hill between the town below
And the forsaken upland hermitage
That held as much as he should ever know
On earth again of home, paused warily.
The road was his with not a native near;
And Eben, having leisure, said aloud,
For no man else in Tilbury Town to hear:

"Well, Mr. Flood, we have the harvest moon
Again, and we may not have many more;
The bird is on the wing, the poet says,
And you and I have said it here before.
Drink to the bird." He raised up to the light
The jug that he had gone so far to fill,
And answered huskily: "Well, Mr. Flood,
Since you propose it, I believe I will."

Alone, as if enduring to the end
A valiant armor of scarred hopes outworn,
He stood there in the middle of the road
Like Roland's ghost winding a silent horn.
Below him, in the town among the trees,
Where friends of other days had honored him,
A phantom salutation of the dead
Rang thinly till old Eben's eyes were dim.

Then, as a mother lays her sleeping child
Down tenderly, fearing it may awake,
He set the jug down slowly at his feet
With trembling care, knowing that most things break;
And only when assured that on firm earth
It stood, as the uncertain lives of men
Assuredly did not, he paced away,
And with his hand extended paused again:

"Well, Mr. Flood, we have not met like this
In a long time; and many a change has come
To both of us, I fear, since last it was
We had a drop together. Welcome home!"
Convivially returning with himself,
Again he raised the jug up to the light;
And with an acquiescent quaver said:
"Well, Mr. Flood, if you insist, I might.

"Only a very little, Mr. Flood—
For auld lang syne. No more, sir; that will do."
So, for the time, apparently it did,
And Eben evidently thought so too;
For soon amid the silver loneliness
Of night he lifted up his voice and sang,
Secure, with only two moons listening,
Until the whole harmonious landscape rang—

"For auld lang syne." The weary throat gave out,
The last word wavered; and the song being done,
He raised again the jug regretfully
And shook his head, and was again alone.

There was not much that was ahead of him,
And there was nothing in the town below—
Where strangers would have shut the many doors
That many friends had opened long ago.

KARMA

Christmas was in the air and all was well
With him, but for a few confusing flaws
In divers of God's images. Because
A friend of his would neither buy nor sell,
Was he to answer for the axe that fell?
He pondered; and the reason for it was,
Partly, a slowly freezing Santa Claus
Upon the corner, with his beard and bell.

Acknowledging an improvident surprise,
He magnified a fancy that he wished
The friend whom he had wrecked were here again.
Not sure of that, he found a compromise;
And from the fulness of his heart he fished
A dime for Jesus who had died for men.

WHY HE WAS THERE

Much as he left it when he went from us
Here was the room again where he had been
So long that something of him should be seen,
Or felt—and so it was. Incredulous,
I turned about, loath to be greeted thus,
And there he was in his old chair, serene
As ever, and as laconic and as lean
As when he lived, and as cadaverous.

Calm as he was of old when we were young,
He sat there gazing at the pallid flame
Before him. "And how far will this go on?"
I thought. He felt the failure of my tongue,
And smiled: "I was not here until you came;
And I shall not be here when you are gone."

AMY LOWELL

Amy Lowell, a daughter of Augustus Lowell and his wife, Katherine Bigelow Lawrence, was born on February 9, 1874, in Brookline, Massachusetts. Her father traced his descent from Percival Lowell, a merchant of Bristol, who came to New England in 1637. In the family were many persons of importance: among others, Francis Cabot Lowell, who founded the city of Lowell in 1822; John Lowell, founder of the Lowell Institute of Boston; and James Russell Lowell, diplomat and man of letters, who was a cousin of Amy Lowell's grandfather. Of her own family, one brother, Abbott Lawrence Lowell, is president of Harvard University; another brother, Percival Lowell, established the Lowell Observatory at Harvard and at Flagstaff, Arizona; and a sister, Mrs. J. T. Bowlker, was founder and president of the Women's Municipal League in Boston. Her mother's family was also noted, Miss Lowell's grandfather, Abbott Lawrence, being at one time Minister to the Court of St. James's.

As a child, Amy Lowell had the advantage of wealth and of the care of a mother who was an accomplished musician and linguist. At the age of eight she was taken on a tour of virtually all the countries of Europe. She attended private schools, where she studied hard; her recreations were tennis and horseback riding. After the completion of her education, and the death of her mother in 1895, she traveled extensively, spending the winter of 1897-98 on the Nile, the next on a ranch in California, and the summer of 1899 in Europe. Upon the death of her father in 1900, however, she purchased Sevenels, the family place in Brookline, and for a while devoted herself to educational and library work in the interests of her native town.

At the age of thirteen she began to write verse, but it was not until 1902 that she decided to make the writing of poetry her main work. With that decision she began an apprenticeship, lasting eight years, that consisted of reading the masters, studying the technique of poetry, and practicing the art of writing. Her first published poem appeared in *The Atlantic Monthly* for August, 1910. Two years later she issued her first volume, *A Dome of Many-Colored Glass.* Thereafter she worked diligently, publishing a number of volumes of poetry, several books of criticism, many critical articles, and a monumental life of John Keats, as well as lecturing on contemporary poetry.

In the early years of her apprenticeship, she spent her time between her home in Brookline and her summer place in Dublin, New Hampshire; but she passed the summer of 1905 in Europe, and during the winter and spring of 1908 was in Greece and Turkey. In 1913 she visited England, and became associated with the Imagists. From that time she identified herself actively with the group who sought to further interest in the newer forms of poetry, and did much to popularize the newer movements.

She was Phi Beta Kappa poet at Tufts College in 1918, and at Columbia University in 1920. In the latter year Baylor University conferred upon her the degree of Doctor of Literature. She lectured at the Brooklyn Institute of Arts and Sciences during 1917-18, at Yale University on the Francis Bergen Foundation in 1921, and at Brown University in the same year on the Marshall Woods Lectureship. In 1923 she received the Levinson prize, offered by *Poetry: A Magazine of Verse;*

and in 1926 her posthumous volume, *What's O'Clock?*, was awarded the Pulitzer prize for poetry.

She died on May 12, 1925. The body was cremated, and the ashes buried in the family plot in Mt. Auburn Cemetery, Cambridge.

A GIFT

See! I give myself to you, Beloved!
My words are little jars
For you to take and put upon a shelf.
Their shapes are quaint and beautiful,
And they have many pleasant colors and lustres
To recommend them.
Also the scent from them fills the room
With sweetness of flowers and crushed grasses.

When I shall have given you the last one,
You will have the whole of me,
But I shall be dead.

THE SHADOW

Paul Jannes was working very late,
For this watch must be done by eight
To-morrow or the Cardinal
Would certainly be vexed. Of all
His customers the old prelate
Was the most important, for his state
Descended to his watches and rings,
And he gave his mistresses many things
To make them forget his age and smile
When he paid visits, and they could while
The time away with a diamond locket
Exceedingly well. So they picked his pocket,
And he paid in jewels for his slobbering kisses.
This watch was made to buy him blisses
From an Austrian countess on her way
Home, and she meant to start next day.

Paul worked by the pointed, tulip-flame
Of a tallow candle, and became
So absorbed, that his old clock made him wince
Striking the hour a moment since.
Its echo, only half apprehended,
Lingered about the room. He ended
Screwing the little rubies in,
Setting the wheels to lock and spin,
Curling the infinitesimal springs,
Fixing the filigree hands. Chippings
Of precious stones lay strewn about.
The table before him was a rout
Of splashes and sparks of colored light.
There was yellow gold in sheets, and quite
A heap of emeralds, and steel.
Here was a gem, there was a wheel.
And glasses lay like limpid lakes
Shining and still, and there were flakes
Of silver, and shavings of pearl,
And little wires all awhirl
With the light of the candle. He took the watch
And wound its hands about to match
The time, then glanced up to take the hour
From the hanging clock.

Good, Merciful Power!

How came that shadow on the wall,
No woman was in the room! His tall
Chiffonier stood gaunt behind
His chair. His old cloak, rabbit-lined,
Hung from a peg. The door was closed.
Just for a moment he must have dozed.
He looked again, and saw it plain.
The silhouette made a blue-black stain
On the opposite wall, and it never wavered
Even when the candle quavered
Under his panting breath. What made
That beautiful, dreadful thing, that shade
Of something so lovely, so exquisite,
Cast from a substance which the sight

Had not been tutored to perceive?
Paul brushed his eyes across his sleeve.

Clear-cut, the Shadow on the wall
Gleamed black, and never moved at all.

Paul's watches were like amulets,
Wrought into patterns and rosettes;
The cases were all set with stones,
And wreathing lines, and shining zones.
He knew the beauty in a curve,
And the Shadow tortured every nerve
With its perfect rhythm of outline
Cutting the whitewashed wall. So fine
Was the neck he knew he could have spanned
It about with the fingers of one hand.
The chin rose to a mouth he guessed,
But could not see, the lips were pressed
Loosely together, the edges close,
And the proud and delicate line of the nose
Melted into a brow, and there
Broke into undulant waves of hair.
The lady was edged with the stamp of race.
A singular vision in such a place.

He moved the candle to the tall
Chiffonier; the Shadow stayed on the wall.
He threw his cloak upon a chair,
And still the lady's face was there.
From every corner of the room
He saw, in the patch of light, the gloom
That was the lady. Her violet bloom
Was almost brighter than that which came
From his candle's tulip-flame.
He set the filigree hands; he laid
The watch in the case which he had made;
He put on his rabbit cloak, and snuffed
His candle out. The room seemed stuffed
With darkness. Softly he crossed the floor,
And let himself out through the door.

The sun was flashing from every pin
And wheel, when Paul let himself in.
The whitewashed walls were hot with light.
The room was the core of a chrysolite,
Burning and shimmering with fiery might.
The sun was so bright that no shadow could fall
From the furniture upon the wall.
Paul sighed as he looked at the empty space
Where a glare usurped the lady's place.
He settled himself to his work, but his mind
Wandered, and he would wake to find
His hand suspended, his eyes grown dim,
And nothing advanced beyond the rim
Of his dreaming. The Cardinal sent to pay
For his watch, which had purchased so fine a day.
But Paul could hardly touch the gold,
It seemed the price of his Shadow, sold.
With the first twilight he struck a match
And watched the little blue stars hatch
Into an egg of perfect flame.
He lit his candle, and almost in shame
At his eagerness, lifted his eyes.
The Shadow was there, and its precise
Outline etched the cold, white wall.
The young man swore, "By God! You, Paul,
There's something the matter with your brain.
Go home now and sleep off the strain."

The next day was a storm; the rain
Whispered and scratched at the window-pane.
A grey and shadowless morning filled
The little shop. The watches, chilled,
Were dead and sparkless as burnt-out coals.
The gems lay on the table like shoals
Of stranded shells, their colors faded,
Mere heaps of stone, dull and degraded.
Paul's head was heavy, his hands obeyed
No orders, for his fancy strayed.
His work became a simple round

Of watches repaired and watches wound.
The slanting ribbons of the rain
Broke themselves on the window-pane,
But Paul saw the silver lines in vain.
Only when the candle was lit
And on the wall just opposite
He watched again the coming of IT,
Could he trace a line for the joy of his soul
And over his hands regain control.
Paul lingered late in his shop that night
And the designs which his delight
Sketched on paper seemed to be
A tribute offered wistfully
To the beautiful shadow of her who came
And hovered over his candle flame.
In the morning he selected all
His perfect jacinths. One large opal
Hung like a milky, rainbow moon
In the centre, and blown in loose festoon
The red stones quivered on silver threads
To the outer edge, where a single, fine
Band of mother-of-pearl the line
Completed. On the other side,
The creamy porcelain of the face
Bore diamond hours, and no lace
Of cotton or silk could ever be
Tossed into being more airily
Than the filmy golden hands; the time
Seemed to tick away in rhyme.
When, at dusk, the Shadow grew
Upon the wall, Paul's work was through.
Holding the watch, he spoke to her:
"Lady, Beautiful Shadow, stir
Into one brief sign of being.
Turn your eyes this way, and seeing
This watch, made from those sweet curves
Where your hair from your forehead swerves,
Accept the gift which I have wrought
With your fairness in my thought.

Grant me this, and I shall be
Honored overwhelmingly."

The Shadow rested black and still,
And the wind sighed over the window-sill.

Paul put the despised watch away
And laid out before him his array
Of stones and metals, and when the morning
Struck the stones to their best adorning,
He chose the brightest, and this new watch
Was so light and thin it seemed to catch
The sunlight's nothingness, and its gleam.
Topazes ran in a foamy stream
Over the cover; the hands were studded
With garnets, and seemed red roses, budded.
The face was of crystal, and engraved
Upon it the figures flashed and waved
With zircons, and beryls, and amethysts.
It took a week to make, and his trysts
At night with the Shadow were his alone.
Paul swore not to speak till his task was done.
The night that the jewel was worthy to give,
Paul watched the long hours of daylight live
To the faintest streak; then lit his light,
And sharp against the walls pure white
The outline of the Shadow started
Into form. His burning-hearted
Words so long imprisoned swelled
To tumbling speech. Like one compelled,
He told the lady all his love,
And holding out the watch above
His head, he knelt, imploring some
Littlest sign.
The Shadow was dumb.

Weeks passed, Paul worked in fevered haste,
And everything he made he placed
Before his lady. The Shadow kept
Its perfect passiveness. Paul wept.

He wooed her with the work of his hands,
He waited for those dear commands
She never gave. No word, no motion,
Eased the ache of his devotion.
His days passed in a strain of toil,
His nights burnt up in a seething coil.
Seasons shot by; uncognisant
He worked. The Shadow came to haunt
Even his days. Sometimes quite plain
He saw on the wall the blackberry stain
Of his lady's picture. No sun was bright
Enough to dazzle that from his sight.

There were moments when he groaned to see
His life spilled out so uselessly,
Begging for boons the Shade refused,
His finest workmanship abused,
The iridescent bubbles he blew
Into lovely existence, poor and few
In the shadowed eyes. Then he would curse
Himself and her! The Universe!
And more, the beauty he could not make,
And give her, for her comfort's sake!
He would beat his weary, empty hands
Upon the table, would hold up strands
Of silver and gold, and ask her why
She scorned the best which he could buy.
He would pray as to some high-niched saint,
That she would cure him of the taint
Of failure. He would clutch the wall
With his bleeding fingers, if she should fall
He could catch, and hold her, and make her live!
With sobs he would ask her to forgive
All he had done. And broken, spent,
He would call himself impertinent;
Presumptuous; a tradesman; a nothing; driven
To madness by the sight of Heaven.
At other times he would take the things
He had made, and winding them on strings,

Hang garlands before her, and burn perfumes,
Chanting strangely, while the fumes
Wreathed and blotted the shadow face,
As with a cloudy, nacreous lace.
There were days when he wooed as a lover, sighed
In tenderness, spoke to his bride,
Urged her to patience, said his skill
Should break the spell. A man's sworn will
Could compass life, even that, he knew.
By Christ's Blood! He would prove it true!

The edge of the Shadow never blurred.
The lips of the Shadow never stirred.

He would climb on chairs to reach her lips,
And pat her hair with his finger-tips.
But instead of young, warm flesh returning
His warmth, the wall was cold and burning
Like stinging ice, and his passion, chilled,
Lay in his heart like some dead thing killed
At the moment of birth. Then, deadly sick,
He would lie in a swoon for hours, while thick
Phantasmagoria crowded his brain,
And his body shrieked in the clutch of pain.
The crisis passed, he would wake and smile
With a vacant joy, half-imbecile
And quite confused, not being certain
Why he was suffering; a curtain
Fallen over the tortured mind beguiled
His sorrow. Like a little child
He would play with his watches and gems, with glee
Calling the Shadow to look and see
How the spots on the ceiling danced prettily
When he flashed his stones. "Mother, the green
Has slid so cunningly in between
The blue and the yellow. Oh, please look down!"
Then, with a pitiful, puzzled frown,
He would get up slowly from his play
And walk round the room, feeling his way
From table to chair, from chair to door,

Stepping over the cracks in the floor,
Till reaching the table again, her face
Would bring recollection, and no solace
Could balm his hurt till unconsciousness
Stifled him and his great distress.

One morning he threw the street door wide
On coming in, and his vigorous stride
Made the tools on his table rattle and jump.
In his hands he carried a new-burst clump
Of laurel blossoms, whose smooth-barked stalks
Were pliant with sap. As a husband talks
To the wife he left an hour ago,
Paul spoke to the Shadow. "Dear, you know
To-day the calendar calls it spring,
And I woke this morning gathering
Asphodels, in my dreams, for you.
So I rushed out to see what flowers blew
Their pink-and-purple-scented souls
Across the town-wind's dusty scrolls,
And made the approach to the Market Square
A garden with smells and sunny air.
I feel so well and happy to-day,
I think I shall take a holiday.
And to-night we will have a little treat.
I am going to bring you something to eat!"
He looked at the Shadow anxiously.
It was quite grave and silent. He
Shut the outer door and came
And leant against the window-frame.
"Dearest," he said, "we live apart
Although I bear you in my heart.
We look out each from a different world.
At any moment we may be hurled
Asunder. They follow their orbits, we
Obey their laws entirely.
Now you must come, or I go there,
Unless we are willing to live the flare
Of a lighted instant and have it gone."

A bee in the laurels began to drone.
A loosened petal fluttered prone.

"Man grows by eating; if you eat
You will be filled with our life; sweet
Will be our planet in your mouth.
If not, I must parch in death's wide drouth
Until I gain to where you are,
And give you myself in whatever star
May happen. O You Beloved of Me!
Is it not ordered cleverly?"

The Shadow, bloomed like a plum, and clear,
Hung in the sunlight. It did not hear.

Paul slipped away as the dusk began
To dim the little shop. He ran
To the nearest inn, and chose with care
As much as his thin purse could bear.
As rapt-souled monks watch over the baking
Of the sacred wafer, and through the making
Of the holy wine whisper secret prayers
That God will bless this labor of theirs;
So Paul, in a sober ecstasy,
Purchased the best which he could buy.
Returning, he brushed his tools aside,
And laid across the table a wide
Napkin. He put a glass and plate
On either side, in duplicate.
Over the lady's, excellent
With loveliness, the laurels bent.
In the centre the white-flaked pastry stood,
And beside it the wine flask. Red as blood
Was the wine which should bring the lustihood
Of human life to his lady's veins.
When all was ready, all which pertains
To a simple meal was there, with eyes
Lit by the joy of his great emprise,
He reverently bade her come,

And forsake for him her distant home.
He put meat on her plate and filled her glass,
And waited what should come to pass.

The Shadow lay quietly on the wall.
From the street outside came a watchman's call:
"A cloudy night. Rain beginning to fall."

And still he waited. The clock's slow tick
Knocked on the silence. Paul turned sick.
He filled his own glass full of wine;
From his pocket he took a paper. The twine
Was knotted, and he searched a knife
From his jumbled tools. The cord of life
Snapped as he cut the little string.
He knew that he must do the thing
He feared. He shook powder into the wine,
And holding it up so the candle's shine
Sparked a ruby through its heart,
He drank it. "Dear, never apart
Again! You have said it was mine to do.
It is done, and I am come to you!"

Paul Jannes let the empty wine-glass fall,
And held out his arms. The insentient wall
Stared down at him with its cold, white glare
Unstained! The Shadow was not there!
Paul clutched and tore at his tightening throat.
He felt the veins in his body bloat,
And the hot blood run like fire and stones
Along the sides of his cracking bones.
But he laughed as he staggered towards the door,
And he laughed aloud as he sank on the floor.

The Coroner took the body away,
And the watches were sold that Saturday.
The Auctioneer said one could seldom buy
Such watches, and the prices were high.

PURPLE GRACKLES

The grackles have come.
The smoothness of the morning is puckered with their incessant chatter.
A sociable lot, these purple grackles,
Thousands of them strung across a long run of wind,
Thousands of them beating the air-ways with quick wing-jerks,
Spinning down the currents of the South.
Every year they come;
My garden is a place of solace and recreation evidently,
For they always pass a day with me.
With high good nature they tell me what I do not want to hear.
The grackles have come.

I am persuaded that grackles are birds;
But when they are settled in the trees,
I am inclined to declare them fruits
And the trees turned hybrid blackberry vines.
Blackness shining and bulging under leaves,
Does not that mean blackberries, I ask you?
Nonsense! The grackles have come.

Nonchalant highwaymen, pickpockets, second-story burglars,
Stealing away my little hope of summer.
There is no stealthy robbing in this.
Who ever heard such a gabble of thieves' talk!
It seems they delight in unmasking my poor pretence.
Yes, now I see that the hydrangea blooms are rusty;
That the hearts of the golden glow are ripening to lustreless seeds;
That the garden is dahlia-colored,
Flaming with its last over-hot hues;
That the sun is pale as a lemon too small to fill the picking-ring.
I did not see this yesterday,
But to-day the grackles have come.

They drop out of the trees
And strut in companies over the lawn,
Tired of flying, no doubt;
A grand parade to limber legs and give wings a rest.
I should build a great fish-pond for them,
Since it is evident that a bird-bath, meant to accommodate
two goldfinches at most,
Is slight hospitality for these hordes.
Scarcely one can get in,
They all peck and scrabble so.
Crowding, pushing, chasing one another up the bank with
spread wings.
"Are we ducks, you, owner of such inadequate comforts,
That you offer us lily-tanks where one must swim or
drown,
Not stand and splash like a gentleman?"
I feel the reproach keenly, seeing them perch on the edges of
the tanks, trying the depth with a chary foot,
And hardly able to get their wings under water in the bird-
bath.
But there are resources I had not considered,
If I am bravely ruled out of count.
What is that thudding against the eaves just beyond my
window?
What is that spray of water blowing past my face?
Two—three—grackles bathing in the gutter,
The gutter providentially choked with leaves.
I pray they think I put the leaves there on purpose;
I would be supposed thoughtful and welcoming
To all guests, even thieves.
But considering that they are going South and I am not,
I wish they would bathe more quietly;
It is unmannerly to flaunt one's good fortune.

They rate me of no consequence,
But they might reflect that it is my gutter.
I know their opinion of me,
Because one is drying himself on the window-sill
Not two feet from my hand.

His purple neck is sleek with water,
And the fellow preens his feathers for all the world as if I
were a fountain statue.
If it were not for the window,
I am convinced he would light on my head.
Tyrian-feathered freebooter,
Appropriating my delightful gutter with so extravagant an
ease,
You are as cool a pirate as ever scuttled a ship,
And are you not scuttling my summer with every peck of
your sharp bill?

But there is a cloud over the beech-tree,
A quenching cloud for lemon-livered suns.
The grackles are all swinging in the tree-tops,
And the wind is coming up, mind you.
That boom and reach is no summer gale;
I know that wind;
It blows the equinox over seeds and scatters them;
It rips petals from petals, and tears off half-turned leaves.
There is rain on the back of that wind.
Now I would keep the grackles,
I would plead with them not to leave me.
I grant their coming, but I would not have them go.
It is a milestone, this passing of grackles.
A day of them, and it is a year gone by.
There is magic in this and terror,
But I only stare stupidly out of the window.
The grackles have come.

Come! Yes, they surely came.
But they have gone.
A moment ago the oak was full of them;
They are not there now.
Not a speck of a black wing,
Not an eye-peep of a purple head.
The grackles have gone.

And I watch an autumn storm
Stripping the garden,
Shouting black rain challenges
To an old, limp summer
Laid down to die in the flower-beds.

PATTERNS

I walk down the garden paths,
And all the daffodils
Are blowing, and the bright blue squills.
I walk down the patterned garden-paths
In my stiff, brocaded gown.
With my powdered hair and jewelled fan,
I too am a rare
Pattern. As I wander down
The garden paths.

My dress is richly figured,
And the train
Makes a pink and silver stain
On the gravel, and the thrift
Of the borders.
Just a plate of current fashion,
Tripping by in high-heeled, ribboned shoes.
Not a softness anywhere about me,
Only whalebone and brocade.
And I sink on a seat in the shade
Of a lime tree. For my passion
Wars against the stiff brocade.
The daffodils and squills
Flutter in the breeze
As they please.
And I weep;
For the lime tree is in blossom
And one small flower has dropped upon my bosom.

And the plashing of waterdrops
In the marble fountain

Comes down the garden-paths.
The dripping never stops.
Underneath my stiffened gown
Is the softness of a woman bathing in a marble basin,
A basin in the midst of hedges grown
So thick, she cannot see her lover hiding,
But she guesses he is near,
And the sliding of the water
Seems the stroking of a dear
Hand upon her.
What is summer in a fine brocaded gown!
I should like to see it lying in a heap upon the ground.
All the pink and silver crumpled up on the ground.

I would be the pink and silver as I ran along the paths,
And he would stumble after,
Bewildered by my laughter.
I should see the sun flashing from his sword-hilt and the buckles on his shoes.
I would choose
To lead him in a maze along the patterned paths,
A bright and laughing maze for my heavy-booted lover.
Till he caught me in the shade,
And the buttons of his waistcoat bruised my body as he clasped me,
Aching, melting, unafraid.
With the shadows of the leaves and the sundrops,
And the plopping of the waterdrops,
All about us in the open afternoon—
I am very like to swoon
With the weight of this brocade,
For the sun sifts through the shade.

Underneath the fallen blossom
In my bosom,
Is a letter I have hid.
It was brought to me this morning by a rider from the Duke.
"Madam, we regret to inform you that Lord Hartwell
Died in action Thursday se'nnight."

As I read it in the white, morning sunlight,
The letters squirmed like snakes.
"Any answer, Madam," said my footman.
"No," I told him.
"See that the messenger takes some refreshment.
No, no answer."
And I walked into the garden,
Up and down the patterned paths,
In my stiff, correct brocade.
The blue and yellow flowers stood up proudly in the sun,
Each one.
I stood upright too,
Held rigid to the pattern
By the stiffness of my gown.
Up and down I walked,
Up and down.

In a month he would have been my husband.
In a month, here, underneath this lime,
We would have broke the pattern;
He for me, and I for him,
He as Colonel, I as Lady,
On this shady seat.
He had a whim
That sunlight carried blessing.
And I answered, "It shall be as you have said."
Now he is dead.

In summer and in winter I shall walk
Up and down
The patterned garden-paths
In my stiff, brocaded gown.
The squills and daffodils
Will give place to pillared roses, and to asters, and to snow.
I shall go
Up and down,
In my gown.
Gorgeously arrayed,
Boned and stayed.

And the softness of my body will be guarded from embrace
By each button, hook, and lace.
For the man who should loose me is dead,
Fighting with the Duke in Flanders,
In a pattern called a war.
Christ! What are patterns for?

THE DINNER-PARTY

FISH

"So . . ." they said,
With their wine-glasses delicately poised,
Mocking at the thing they cannot understand.
"So . . ." they said again,
Amused and insolent.
The silver on the table glittered,
And the red wine in the glasses
Seemed the blood I had wasted
In a foolish cause.

GAME

The gentleman with the grey-and-black whiskers
Sneered languidly over his quail.
Then my heart flew up and labored,
And I burst from my own holding
And hurled myself forward.
With straight blows I beat upon him,
Furiously, with red-hot anger, I thrust against him.
But my weapon slithered over his polished surface,
And I recoiled upon myself,
Panting.

DRAWING-ROOM

In a dress all softness and half-tones,
Indolent and half-reclined,
She lay upon a couch,
With the firelight reflected in her jewels.

But her eyes had no reflection,
They swam in a grey smoke,
The smoke of smoldering ashes,
The smoke of her cindered heart.

COFFEE

They sat in a circle with their coffee-cups.
One dropped in a lump of sugar,
One stirred with a spoon.
I saw them as a circle of ghosts
Sipping blackness out of beautiful china,
And mildly protesting against my coarseness
In being alive.

TALK

They took dead men's souls
And pinned them on their breasts for ornament;
Their cuff-links and tiaras
Were gems dug from a grave;
They were ghouls battening on exhumed thoughts;
And I took a green liqueur from a servant
So that he might come near me
And give me the comfort of a living thing.

ELEVEN O'CLOCK

The front door was hard and heavy,
It shut behind me on the house of ghosts.
I flattened my feet on the pavement
To feel it solid under me;
I ran my hand along the railings
And shook them,
And pressed their pointed bars
Into my palms.
The hurt of it reassured me,
And I did it again and again
Until they were bruised.
When I woke in the night
I laughed to find them aching,
For only living flesh can suffer.

MADONNA OF THE EVENING FLOWERS

All day long I have been working,
Now I am tired.
I call: "Where are you?"
But there is only the oak-tree rustling in the wind.
The house is very quiet,
The sun shines in on your books,
On your scissors and thimble just put down,
But you are not there.
Suddenly I am lonely:
Where are you?
I go about searching.

Then I see you,
Standing under a spire of pale blue larkspur,
With a basket of roses on your arm.
You are cool, like silver,
And you smile.
I think the Canterbury bells are playing little tunes.

You tell me that the peonies need spraying,
That the columbines have overrun all bounds,
That the pyrus japonica should be cut back and rounded.
You tell me these things.
But I look at you, heart of silver,
White heart-flame of polished silver,
Burning beneath the blue steeples of the larkspur,
And I long to kneel instantly at your feet,
While all about us peal the loud, sweet *Te Deums* of the
Canterbury bells.

A DECADE

When you came, you were like red wine and honey,
And the taste of you burnt my mouth with its sweetness.
Now you are like morning bread,
Smooth and pleasant.
I hardly taste you at all for I know your savor,
But I am completely nourished.

FRIMAIRE

Dearest, we are like two flowers
Blooming last in a yellowing garden,
A purple aster flower and a red one
Standing alone in a withered desolation.

The garden plants are shattered and seeded
One brittle leaf scrapes against another,
Fiddling echoes of a rush of petals.
Now only you and I nodding together.

Many were with us; they have all faded.
Only we are purple and crimson,
Only we in the dew-clear mornings,
Smarten into color as the sun rises.

When I scarcely see you in the flat moonlight,
And later when my cold roots tighten,
I am anxious for the morning,
I cannot rest in fear of what may happen.

You or I—and I am a coward.
Surely frost should take the crimson.
Purple is a finer color,
Very splendid in isolation.

So we nod above the broken
Stems of flowers almost rotted.
Many mornings there cannot be now
For us both. Ah, Dear, I love you!

APPULDURCOMBE PARK

I am a woman, sick for passion,
Sitting under the golden beech-trees.
I am a woman, sick for passion,
Crumbling the beech leaves to powder in my fingers.

The servants say: "Yes, my Lady," and "No, my Lady."
And all day long my husband calls me
From his invalid chair:
"Mary, Mary, where are you, Mary? I want you."
Why does he want me?
When I come, he only pats my hand
And asks me to settle his cushions.
Poor little beech leaves,
Slowly falling,
Crumbling,
In the great park.
But there are many golden beech leaves
And I am alone.

I am a woman, sick for passion,
Walking between rows of painted tulips.
Parrot flowers, toucan-feathered flowers,
How bright you are!
You hurt me with your colors;
Your reds and yellows lance at me like flames.
Oh, I am sick—sick—
And your darting loveliness hurts my heart.
You burn me with your parrot-tongues.
Flame!
Flame!
My husband taps on the window with his stick:
"Mary, come in. I want you. You will take cold."

I am a woman, sick for passion,
Gazing at a white moon hanging over tall lilies.
The lilies sway and darken,
And a wind ruffles my hair.
There is a scrape of gravel behind me,
A red coat crashes scarlet against the lilies.
"Cousin-Captain!
I thought you were playing piquet with Sir Kenelm."
"Piquet, Dear Heart! And such a moon!"
Your red coat chokes me, Cousin-Captain.
Blood-color, your coat:

I am sick—sick—for your heart.
Keep away from me, Cousin-Captain.
Your scarlet coat dazzles and confuses me.
O heart of red blood, what shall I do!
Even the lilies blow for the bee.
Does your heart beat so loud, Beloved?
No, it is the tower-clock chiming eleven.
I must go in and give my husband his posset.
I hear him calling:
"Mary, where are you? I want you."

I am a woman, sick for passion,
Waiting in the long, black room for the funeral procession
to pass.
I sent a messenger to town last night.
When will you come?
Under my black dress a rose is blooming.
A rose?—a heart?—it rustles for you with open petals.
Come quickly, Dear,
For the corridors are full of noises.
In this fading light I hear whispers,
And the steady, stealthy purr of the wind.
What keeps you, Cousin-Captain? . . .
What was that?
"Mary, I want you."
Nonsense, he is dead,
Buried by now.
Oh, I am sick of these long, cold corridors!
Sick—for what?
Why do you not come?

I am a woman, sick—sick—
Sick of the touch of cold paper,
Poisoned with the bitterness of ink.
Snowflakes hiss, and scratch the windows.
"Mary, where are you?"
That voice is like water in my ears;
I cannot empty them.
He wanted me, my husband,

But these stone parlors do not want me.
You do not want me either, Cousin-Captain.
Your coat lied;
Only your white sword spoke the truth.
"Mary! Mary!"
Will nothing stop the white snow
Sifting,
Sifting?
Will nothing stop that voice,
Drifting through the wide, dark halls?
The tower-clock strikes eleven dully, stifled with snow.
Softly over the still snow,
Softly over the lonely park,
Softly . . .
Yes, I have only my slippers, but I shall not take cold.
A little dish of posset.
Do the dead eat?
I have done it so long,
So strangely long.

FOUR SIDES TO A HOUSE

Peter, Peter, along the ground,
Is it wind I hear, or your shoes' sound?
Peter, Peter, across the air,
Do dead leaves fall, or is it your hair?
Peter, Peter, North and South,
They have stopped your mouth
With water, Peter.

The long road runs, and the long road runs,
Who comes over the long road, Peter?
Who knocks at the door in the cold twilight,
And begs a heap of straw for the night,
And a bit of a sup, and a bit of a bite—
Do you know the face, Peter?

He lays him down on the floor and sleeps.
Must you wind the clock, Peter?

It will strike and strike the dark night through.
He will sleep past one, he will sleep past two,
But when it strikes three what will he do?
        He will rise and kill you, Peter.

He will open the door to one without.
        Do you hear that voice, Peter?
Two men prying and poking about,
Is it here, is it there, is it in, is it out?
Cover his staring eyes with a clout.
        But you're dead, dead, Peter.

They have ripped up the boards, they have pried up the
                stones,
        They have found your gold, dead Peter.
Ripe, red coins to itch a thief's hand,
But you drip ripe red on the floor's white sand,
You burn their eyes like a firebrand.
        They must quench you, Peter.

It is dark in the North, it is dark in the South.
        The wind blows your white hair, Peter.
One at your feet and one at your head.
A soft bed, a smooth bed,
Scarcely a splash, you sink like lead.
        Sweet water in your well, Peter.

Along the road and along the road,
        The next house, Peter.
Four-square to the bright and the shade of the moon.
The North winds shuffle, the South winds croon,
Water with white hair over-strewn.
        The door, the door, Peter!
Water seeps under the door.

They have risen up in the morning grey.
        What will they give to Peter?
The sorrel horse with the tail of gold,
Fastest pacer ever was foaled.

Shoot him, skin him, blanch his bones,
Nail up his skull with a silver nail
Over the door; it will not fail.
No ghostly thing can ever prevail
Against a horse's skull, Peter.

Over the lilacs, gazing down,
Is a window, Peter.
The North winds call, and the South winds cry.
Silver white hair in a bitter blowing,
Eel-green water washing by,
A red mouth floating and flowing.
Do you come, Peter?

They rose as the last star sank and set.
One more for Peter.
They slew the black mare at the flush of the sun,
And nailed her skull to the window-stone.
In the light of the moon how white it shone—
And your breathing mouth, Peter!

Around the house, and around the house,
With a wind that is North, and a wind that is South,
Peter, Peter.
Mud and ooze and a dead man's wrist
Wrenching the shutters apart, like mist
The mud and the ooze and the dead man twist.
They are praying, Peter.

Three in stable a week ago.
This is the last, Peter.
"My strawberry roan in the morning clear,
Lady heart and attentive ear,
Foot like a kitten, nose like a deer,
But the fear! The fear!"
Three skulls, Peter.

The sun goes down, and the night draws in.
Toward the hills, Peter.
What lies so stiff on the hill-room floor,

When the gusty wind claps to the door?
They have paid three horses and two men more.
Gather your gold, Peter.

Softly, softly, along the ground
Lest your shoes sound,
Gently, gently, across the air
Lest it stream, your hair.
North and South
For your aching mouth.
But the moon is old, Peter,
And death is long, and the well is deep.
Can you sleep, sleep, Peter?

THE DAY THAT WAS THAT DAY

The wind rose, and the wind fell,
And the day that was that day
Floated under a high Heaven.

"Home! Home! Home!"
Sang a robin in a spice-bush.
"Sun on a roof-tree! Sun on a roof-tree!"
Rang thin clouds
In a chord of silver across a placid sky.

Rachel Gibbs stepped up the path
To pass the time of day
With Haywood Green's Minnie.
My, ef she ain't shut th' door!
An' all th' breeze this side th' house too.
She must like to stew.
"Minnie,
Minnie,
You ain't gone out, have yer?
I'll skin my knuckles ef I knock agin.
I wonder did she lock th' door—

Well, I never!
Have you gone hard o' hearin'?
Have you—
Minnie, child, what's th' matter?
Why do you look like that?
What you doin'?
Speak, I tell yer,
What you hidin' that cup fer?
God A'mighty, girl, what you doin' with wood-alcohol
In a drinkin'-cup?
Here, give it ter me,
An' I'll set it on th' table.
Set down, Minnie, dear,
Set right here in th' rocker
An' tell me
What ails yer to be wantin'
To drink stuff like that?
There, there, you poor lamb,
Don't look so scared.
Jest tell me all about it,
An' ease your heart.
Minnie, I'll have to shake yer
Ef you don't stop starin'
In that dretful way.
Poor Dear,
You just lay your head up agin me
An' let me soothe yer.
Poor little thing.
Poor little thing."

"Don't, don't, Rachel,
I can't bear it.
I'm a wicked woman,
But I jest couldn't stand no more."

"No more o' what?
Ain't yer Pa good to yer?
What's come over yer, Minnie?
My! I'm jest as sorry as I can be."

"Oh, it ain't nothin' like that.
An' don't be so good to me,
You'll make me want to cry agin,
An' I can't cry.
I'm all dried up,
An' it's like squeezin' my heart sick
To want to cry, an' can't."

"But what is it?
Ain't yer never goin' ter tell me?"

"Why ther' ain't nothin' to tell
'Cept that I'm tired."

"Now, look-a-here, Minnie,
No one don't drink poison jest 'cause they're tired."

"I didn't drink it, as it happens."

"No, you didn't, 'cause I come in an' stopped yer.
But I'm mighty afeered you would have.
Lord, it makes me shudder!"

"I guess yer right,
I would have.
An' I wish you'd ha' let me be.
Now it's all to do over agin,
An' I don't know as I'll git th' courage
A second time.
I guess you ain't never been right down tired, Rachel."

"Well, never to th' poison point, no, I haven't,
But what's gone wrong to wear yer out so?"

"The cat's sick."

"Minnie Green, was you takin' poison
'Cause you got a sick cat?
That's down-right foolishness."

"Yes, it does sound so.
But I couldn't face nussin' her.
Look here, Rachel,

I may be foolish, or mad, or jest plain bad,
But I couldn't stan' another thing.
I'm all fretted now
An' more's one too many.
I can't go on!
Oh, God! I can't go on!
I ain't got no more'n most women,
I know that,
But I fuss a lot more.
There's al'ays th' same things
Goin' roun' like th' spokes to a cart-wheel,
Ef one ain't a-top it's another,
An' th' next comin' up all th' time.
It's breakfast, an' dinner, an' supper,
Every day.
An' th' same dishes to wash.
I hate them dishes.
I smashed a plate yesterday
'Cause I couldn't bear to see it
Settin' on th' sink waitin' fer me.
An' when I go up to make father's bed
I git seasick
Thinkin' I'll have to see that old check spread agin.
I've settled it,
An' twitched it this way an' that,
For thirty year,
An' I hate th' sight o' th' thing.
Sometimes I've set an hour on th' stair
Ruther'n go in an' touch it.
Oh, my God! Why couldn't yer let me be?
Why'd you have to come interferin'?
Why?
Why?"

"Thank th' Everlastin' Mercy I did!
But, Minnie, how long's this been goin' on?
I never had no idea anythin' was wrong."

"I don't know.
For ever an' ever, I guess.

Rachel, you can't think how hard it is fer me
To set one foot after th' other sometimes.
I hate lookin' out th' winder,
I'm so tired o' seein' th' path to th' barn.
An' I can't hardly bear
To hear father talkin' to th' horses.
He loves 'em.
But I don't love nothin'
'Cept th' cat,
An' cats is cold things to cling to,
An' now mine's sick!"

"Don't take on so, Minnie.
She'll get well.
There, you rest awhile,
You can tell me afterwards."

A wind rose, and a wind fell,
And the day that was that day
Hung against a turning sun.

The robin sang "Home! Home! Home!"
In an up-and-down scale of small, bright notes.
The clouds rang silver arpeggios
Stretched across a pleasant sky.

"I wish I loved somethin', Rachel."

"Bless your heart, Child, don't you love yer father?"

"I suppose so. But he don't mean nothin' ter me.
He don't say nothin' I want ter hear.
My ears is achin' to hear words,
Words like what's written in books,
Words that would make me all bright like a spring day.
I lay awake nights
Thinkin' o' hearin' things,
An' seein' things.
I'm awful tired o' these hills,
They crowd in so.
Seems sometimes ef I could see th' ocean,
Or a real big city,

'Twould help.
Kind o' lay my eyes out straight fer a while;
Everythin's so short here
My eyes feels pushed in,
An' it hurts 'em.
I love laylocks,
But I git so tired o' watchin'
Th' leaves come an' th' flowers
Every year th' same,
I'd like to root 'em up.
I've set an' set in th' kitchen evenin's
Awful late,
Fer not bein' able to git up an' light th' lamp
To go ter bed.
I'm all lead somehow.
I guess ef anybody did say anythin'
I'd be deaf
Jest with listenin' so long.
I'm plumb tired out."

"Look-a-here, Minnie,
Why don't you go away
Fer a spell?"

"Me go away!
Oh, no, I couldn't never do that.
I couldn't go no place.
I can't hardly git over to Dicksville
Fer my week with Aunt Abby now.
I'm all wrong away from home.
I can't do nothin'!
Nothin' at all.
I'm so awful tired."

"Minnie, did you ever love anybody?
Any man, I mean?"

"No, Rachel, I never did.
I know that sounds queer, but it's a fact.
I've tried to think I did,
But 'twarn't true.

I hadn't hardly no time fer men-folks,
Mother was sick so long,
An' then ther' was father.
I never was much account with 'em anyway,
But I s'pose I might ha' had one
Ef I'd fixed my mind so.
But I al'ays waited.
An' now I'm through waitin',
I'm through waitin' fer anything, Rachel.
It's jest go, go, go,
With never no end,
And nothin' done that ain't to do over agin.
Ther' now it's six o'clock,
An' I must be gittin' supper.
You needn't move that cup, Rachel.
I ain't a-goin' to touch it.
I'll jest keep on now till th' Lord takes me,
An' I only hope he'll do it soon."

The robin flew down from the spice-bush
And pecked about for worms.
The clouds were brazen trumpets
Tumbled along the edge of an apple-colored sky.
The shadow of the house
Fell across the path to the barn,
Confusing it with the grass and the daisies.

A wind rose, and a wind fell,
And the day that was that day
Vanished in the darkness.

THORN PIECE

Cliffs,
Cliffs,
And a twisted sea
Beating under a freezing moon.
Why should I,
Sitting peaceful and warm,
Cut my heart on so sharp a tune?

Liquid lapping of seething fire
Eating the heart of an old beech-tree.
Crack of icicles under the eaves,
Dog-wind whining eerily.

The oaks are red, and the asters flame,
And the sun is warm on bark and stones.
There's a Hunter's Moon abroad to-night—
The twigs are snapping like brittle bones.

You carry a lantern of rose-green glass,
Your dress is red as a Cardinal's cloak.
I kneel at the trace of your feet on the grass,
But when I would sing you a song, I choke.

Choke for the fragile careless years
We have scattered so easily from our hands.
They flutter like leaves through an autumn sun,
One by one, one by one.

I have lived in a place,
I shall die in a place,
I have no craving for distant lands.
But a place is nothing, not even space,
Unless at its heart a figure stands

Swinging a rose-green lantern for me.
I fear the fall of a rose-green gate,
And the cry of a cliff-driven, haunted sea,
And the crackle of ice while I wait—wait!

Your face is flowers and singing sun,
Your hands are the cool of waters falling.
If the rose-green bars should drop between
Would you know that I was calling?

For the stars I see in that sky are black.
The kind earth holds me and laughs in my ear.
I have nothing to do with the planet's track,
I only want you, my Dear.

Beyond is a glaze, but here is fire,
And love to comfort, and speech to bind,
And the common things of morning and evening,
And the light of your lantern I always find.

One or the other—then let it be me,
For I fear the whirl of the cliff-wrung sea,
And the biting night. You smile at my fears,
But the years—years—
Like leaves falling.

ROBERT FROST

Robert Lee Frost was born in San Francisco, March 26, 1875. He was a lineal descendant of Nicholas Frost, who in 1634 came on the *Wulfrana* from Plymouth to New England, where for eight generations the Frost family continued to reside, until the poet's father, William Prescott Frost, Jr., who had attended Harvard, left to teach school in Lewiston, Pennsylvania. In this town he met and married Belle Moody, also a school teacher, who at the age of fifteen had come from lowland Scotland to make her home in America. Although too young to take a part in the Civil War, William Frost had been sympathetic with the Southern cause, and being still an ardent states' rights man, he decided not to settle down in New England, where his ideas were unpopular, but to try his fortunes in the West. Going to San Francisco, he obtained work on a Democratic newspaper, *The Bulletin,* and a little later was joined by his wife. Here presently a son was born and christened Robert Lee after the Southern military leader. During the next ten years, the father was engaged in journalism and politics; but in 1885 he died of tuberculosis, leaving his family without means of support, having even allowed his life insurance to lapse. In this extremity the widow took her children and returned east to the home of their grandfather, in Lawrence, Massachusetts.

In San Francisco, Robert had shown no especial aptitude for learning, but in Lawrence he went ahead rapidly, graduating from high school in 1892 as valedictorian, his only near rival being the girl whom he later married. In the following autumn he entered Dartmouth College, but remained only a few months. Returning to Lawrence, he worked for a while as a bobbin boy in a mill, went on a tramping trip through the South, taught Latin in a school which his mother was conducting in Lawrence, and became reporter-editor of the Lawrence *Sentinel,* a weekly newspaper. Meanwhile his former classmate, Elinor Miriam White, the daughter of a retired Universalist clergyman, completed her education at St. Lawrence University, which she had attended since graduating from high school; and on December 28, 1895, she and Frost were married. In 1897 Frost moved his family to Cambridge and matriculated at Harvard University, where he studied for two years, giving particular attention to Latin and Greek. At the end of that time he withdrew from college, and moved to a farm which his grandfather had bought for him near Derry, New Hampshire. There he lived for eleven years. Farming, however, proved for him a losing game, and in 1905 he obtained an instructorship in English at Pinkerton Academy, in Derry, a position which he held until 1911, when his principal left to become head of the New Hampshire State Normal School, at Plymouth, and took Frost with him. During the school year 1911-12 Frost taught psychology at Plymouth.

Encouraged perhaps by his mother, who in the old San Francisco days had written poems for her husband's newspaper, Frost early began to write verse. In his fifteenth year he sold a poem to *The Independent* for fifteen dollars, and later disposed of others to *The Forum* and *The Youth's Companion.* On the whole, however, American magazines were unreceptive to his writings, and when in 1912 he had a chance to sell his farm at Derry, he did so, and taking the proceeds, sailed in September of that year for England, where poetry was just then receiving much attention. Frost settled with his family at Beaconsfield, in Buckinghamshire, and in the two succeeding years brought out two volumes of poetry. In 1914 he moved to a small farm near Ledbury, Herefordshire, where he had for neighbors the English poets W. W. Gibson and Lascelles Abercrombie. The war brought such changes, however, that Frost deemed it advisable to return to America, and in March, 1915, he came back and moved to a farm just outside Franconia, New Hampshire.

His first year at home he spent in farming, writing, and lecturing. From 1916 to 1920 he taught English at Amherst College, and in 1921 went for two years to the University of Michigan on a newly established fellowship in the creative arts. He was at Amherst again during the school year of 1924-25, but returned in 1925 to Michigan as permanent university fellow in letters. After holding this fellowship for a year, however, he resigned, and is now connected with Amherst.

Since his return to America, Frost has received many honors. In 1916 he was Phi Beta Kappa poet at Harvard. In 1917 Amherst conferred upon him the degree of Master of Arts. In 1922 the International P. E. N. Club elected him an honorary member, the Women's Clubs of Vermont named him Poet Laureate of that state, and the University of Michigan made him a Master of Arts. In the following year the University of Vermont gave him the honorary degree of L.H.D., and Yale University that of Litt.D. In 1924 he was awarded the Pulitzer prize for poetry for his volume *New Hampshire*.

Frost has a family of four children, a son and three daughters. In 1920 he bought a large farm at South Shaftsbury, Vermont, where he lives when not engaged in academic duties.

THE PASTURE

I'm going out to clean the pasture spring;
I'll only stop to rake the leaves away
(And wait to watch the water clear, I may):
I sha'n't be gone long.—You come too.

I'm going out to fetch the little calf
That's standing by the mother. It's so young,
It totters when she licks it with her tongue.
I sha'n't be gone long.—You come too.

MENDING WALL

Something there is that doesn't love a wall,
That sends the frozen-ground-swell under it,
And spills the upper boulders in the sun;
And makes gaps even two can pass abreast.
The work of hunters is another thing:
I have come after them and made repair
Where they have left not one stone on a stone,
But they would have the rabbit out of hiding,
To please the yelping dogs. The gaps I mean,
No one has seen them made or heard them made,
But at spring mending-time we find them there.
I let my neighbor know beyond the hill;
And on a day we meet to walk the line
And set the wall between us once again.
We keep the wall between us as we go.
To each the boulders that have fallen to each.
And some are loaves and some so nearly balls
We have to use a spell to make them balance:
"Stay where you are until our backs are turned!"
We wear our fingers rough with handling them.
Oh, just another kind of out-door game,
One on a side. It comes to little more:

There where it is we do not need the wall:
He is all pine and I am apple orchard.
My apple trees will never get across
And eat the cones under his pines, I tell him.
He only says, "Good fences make good neighbors."
Spring is the mischief in me, and I wonder
If I could put a notion in his head:
"*Why* do they make good neighbors? Isn't it
Where there are cows? But here there are no cows.
Before I built a wall I'd ask to know
What I was walling in or walling out,
And to whom I was like to give offence.
Something there is that doesn't love a wall,
That wants it down." I could say "Elves" to him,
But it's not elves exactly, and I'd rather
He said it for himself. I see him there
Bringing a stone grasped firmly by the top
In each hand, like an old-stone savage armed.
He moves in darkness as it seems to me,
Not of woods only and the shade of trees.
He will not go behind his father's saying,
And he likes having thought of it so well
He says again, "Good fences make good neighbors."

THE DEATH OF THE HIRED MAN

Mary sat musing on the lamp-flame at the table
Waiting for Warren. When she heard his step,
She ran on tip-toe down the darkened passage
To meet him in the doorway with the news
And put him on his guard. "Silas is back."
She pushed him outward with her through the door
And shut it after her. "Be kind," she said.
She took the market things from Warren's arms
And set them on the porch, then drew him down
To sit beside her on the wooden steps.

"When was I ever anything but kind to him?
But I'll not have the fellow back," he said.

"I told him so last haying, didn't I?
'If he left then,' I said, 'that ended it.'
What good is he? Who else will harbor him
At his age for the little he can do?
What help he is there's no depending on.
Off he goes always when I need him most.
'He thinks he ought to earn a little pay,
Enough at least to buy tobacco with,
So he won't have to beg and be beholden.'
'All right,' I say, 'I can't afford to pay
Any fixed wages, though I wish I could.'
'Someone else can.' 'Then someone else will have to.'
I shouldn't mind his bettering himself
If that was what it was. You can be certain,
When he begins like that, there's someone at him
Trying to coax him off with pocket-money,—
In haying time, when any help is scarce.
In winter he comes back to us. I'm done."

"Sh! not so loud: he'll hear you," Mary said.

"I want him to: he'll have to soon or late."

"He's worn out. He's asleep beside the stove.
When I came up from Rowe's I found him here,
Huddled against the barn-door fast asleep,
A miserable sight, and frightening, too—
You needn't smile—I didn't recognize him—
I wasn't looking for him—and he's changed.
Wait till you see."

"Where did you say he'd been?"

"He didn't say. I dragged him to the house,
And gave him tea and tried to make him smoke.
I tried to make him talk about his travels.
Nothing would do: he just kept nodding off."

"What did he say? Did he say anything?"

"But little."

"Anything? Mary, confess
He said he'd come to ditch the meadow for me."

"Warren!"

"But did he? I just want to know."

"Of course he did. What would you have him say?
Surely you wouldn't grudge the poor old man
Some humble way to save his self-respect.
He added, if you really care to know,
He meant to clear the upper pasture, too.
That sounds like something you have heard before?
Warren, I wish you could have heard the way
He jumbled everything. I stopped to look
Two or three times—he made me feel so queer—
To see if he was talking in his sleep.
He ran on Harold Wilson—you remember—
The boy you had in haying four years since.
He's finished school, and teaching in his college.
Silas declares you'll have to get him back.
He says they two will make a team for work:
Between them they will lay this farm as smooth!
The way he mixed that in with other things.
He thinks young Wilson a likely lad, though daft
On education—you know how they fought
All through July under the blazing sun,
Silas up on the cart to build the load,
Harold along beside to pitch it on."

"Yes, I took care to keep well out of earshot."

"Well, those days trouble Silas like a dream.
You wouldn't think they would. How some things linger!
Harold's young college boy's assurance piqued him.
After so many years he still keeps finding
Good arguments he sees he might have used.
I sympathize. I know just how it feels

To think of the right thing to say too late.
Harold's associated in his mind with Latin.
He asked me what I thought of Harold's saying
He studied Latin like the violin
Because he liked it—that an argument!
He said he couldn't make the boy believe
He could find water with a hazel prong—
Which showed how much good school had ever done him.
He wanted to go over that. But most of all
He thinks if he could have another chance
To teach him how to build a load of hay—"

"I know, that's Silas' one accomplishment.
He bundles every forkful in its place,
And tags and numbers it for future reference,
So he can find and easily dislodge it
In the unloading. Silas does that well.
He takes it out in bunches like big birds' nests.
You never see him standing on the hay
He's trying to lift, straining to lift himself."

"He thinks if he could teach him that, he'd be
Some good perhaps to someone in the world.
He hates to see a boy the fool of books.
Poor Silas, so concerned for other folk,
And nothing to look backward to with pride,
And nothing to look forward to with hope,
So now and never any different."

Part of a moon was falling down the west,
Dragging the whole sky with it to the hills.
Its light poured softly in her lap. She saw
And spread her apron to it. She put out her hand
Among the harp-like morning-glory strings,
Taut with the dew from garden bed to eaves,
As if she played unheard the tenderness
That wrought on him beside her in the night.
"Warren," she said, "he has come home to die:
You needn't be afraid he'll leave you this time."

"Home," he mocked gently.

"Yes, what else but home?
It all depends on what you mean by home.
Of course he's nothing to us, any more
Than was the hound that came a stranger to us
Out of the woods, worn out upon the trail."

"Home is the place where, when you have to go there,
They have to take you in."

"I should have called it
Something you somehow haven't to deserve."

Warren leaned out and took a step or two,
Picked up a little stick, and brought it back
And broke it in his hand and tossed it by.
"Silas has better claim on us you think
Than on his brother? Thirteen little miles
As the road winds would bring him to his door.
Silas has walked that far no doubt to-day.
Why didn't he go there? His brother's rich,
A somebody—director in the bank."

"He never told us that."

"We know it though."

"I think his brother ought to help, of course.
I'll see to that if there is need. He ought of right
To take him in, and might be willing to—
He may be better than appearances.
But have some pity on Silas. Do you think
If he'd had any pride in claiming kin
Or anything he looked for from his brother,
He'd keep so still about him all this time?"

"I wonder what's between them."

"I can tell you.
Silas is what he is—we wouldn't mind him—
But just the kind that kinsfolk can't abide.

He never did a thing so very bad.
He don't know why he isn't quite as good
As anyone. He won't be made ashamed
To please his brother, worthless though he is."

"I can't think Si ever hurt anyone."

"No, but he hurt my heart the way he lay
And rolled his old head on that sharp-edged chair-back.
He wouldn't let me put him on the lounge.
You must go in and see what you can do.
I made the bed up for him there to-night.
You'll be surprised at him—how much he's broken.
His working days are done; I'm sure of it."

"I'd not be in a hurry to say that."

"I haven't been. Go, look, see for yourself.
But, Warren, please remember how it is:
He's come to help you ditch the meadow.
He has a plan. You mustn't laugh at him.
He may not speak of it, and then he may.
I'll sit and see if that small sailing cloud
Will hit or miss the moon."

It hit the moon.
Then there were three there, making a dim row,
The moon, the little silver cloud, and she.
Warren returned—too soon, it seemed to her,
Slipped to her side, caught up her hand and waited.

"Warren," she questioned.

"Dead," was all he answered.

THE ROAD NOT TAKEN

Two roads diverged in a yellow wood,
And sorry I could not travel both
And be one traveler, long I stood
And looked down one as far as I could
To where it bent in the undergrowth;

Then took the other, as just as fair,
And having perhaps the better claim,
Because it was grassy and wanted wear;
Though as for that the passing there
Had worn them really about the same,

And both that morning equally lay
In leaves no step had trodden black.
Oh, I kept the first for another day!
Yet knowing how way leads on to way,
I doubted if I should ever come back.

I shall be telling this with a sigh
Somewhere ages and ages hence:
Two roads diverged in a wood, and I—
I took the one less traveled by,
And that has made all the difference.

A PATCH OF OLD SNOW

There's a patch of old snow in a corner
  That I should have guessed
Was a blow-away paper the rain
  Had brought to rest.

It is speckled with grime as if
  Small print overspread it,
The news of a day I've forgotten—
  If I ever read it.

BIRCHES

When I see birches bend to left and right
Across the lines of straighter darker trees,
I like to think some boy's been swinging them.
But swinging doesn't bend them down to stay.
Ice-storms do that. Often you must have seen them
Loaded with ice a sunny winter morning
After a rain. They click upon themselves

As the breeze rises, and turn many-colored
As the stir cracks and crazes their enamel.
Soon the sun's warmth makes them shed crystal shells
Shattering and avalanching on the snow-crust—
Such heaps of broken glass to sweep away
You'd think the inner dome of heaven had fallen.
They are dragged to the withered bracken by the load,
And they seem not to break; though once they are bowed
So low for long, they never right themselves:
You may see their trunks arching in the woods
Years afterwards, trailing their leaves on the ground
Like girls on hands and knees that throw their hair
Before them over their heads to dry in the sun.
But I was going to say when Truth broke in
With all her matter-of-fact about the ice-storm
(Now am I free to be poetical?)
I should prefer to have some boy bend them
As he went out and in to fetch the cows—
Some boy too far from town to learn baseball,
Whose only play was what he found himself,
Summer or winter, and could play alone.
One by one he subdued his father's trees
By riding them down over and over again
Until he took the stiffness out of them,
And not one but hung limp, not one was left
For him to conquer. He learned all there was
To learn about not launching out too soon
And so not carrying the tree away
Clear to the ground. He always kept his poise
To the top branches, climbing carefully
With the same pains you use to fill a cup
Up to the brim, and even above the brim.
Then he flung outward, feet first, with a swish,
Kicking his way down through the air to the ground.
So was I once myself a swinger of birches.
And so I dream of going back to be.
It's when I'm weary of considerations,
And life is too much like a pathless wood
Where your face burns and tickles with the cobwebs

Broken across it, and one eye is weeping
From a twig's having lashed across it open.
I'd like to get away from earth awhile
And then come back to it and begin over.
May no fate willfully misunderstand me
And half grant what I wish and snatch me away
Not to return. Earth's the right place for love:
I don't know where it's likely to go better.
I'd like to go by climbing a birch tree,
And climb black branches up a snow-white trunk
Toward heaven, till the tree could bear no more,
But dipped its top and set me down again.
That would be good both going and coming back.
One could do worse than be a swinger of birches.

THE HILL WIFE

LONELINESS

(*Her Word*)

One ought not to have to care
  So much as you and I
Care when the birds come round the house
  To seem to say good-bye;

Or care so much when they come back
  With whatever it is they sing;
The truth being we are as much
  Too glad for the one thing

As we are too sad for the other here—
  With birds that fill their breasts
But with each other and themselves
  And their built or driven nests.

HOUSE FEAR

Always—I tell you this they learned—
Always at night when they returned
To the lonely house from far away

To lamps unlighted and fire gone gray,
They learned to rattle the lock and key
To give whatever might chance to be
Warning and time to be off in flight:
And preferring the out- to the in-door night,
They learned to leave the house-door wide
Until they had lit the lamp inside.

THE SMILE

(Her Word)

I didn't like the way he went away.
That smile! It never came of being gay.
Still he smiled—did you see him?—I was sure!
Perhaps because we gave him only bread
And the wretch knew from that that we were poor.
Perhaps because he let us give instead
Of seizing from us as he might have seized.
Perhaps he mocked at us for being wed,
Or being very young (and he was pleased
To have a vision of us old and dead).
I wonder how far down the road he's got.
He's watching from the woods as like as not.

THE OFT-REPEATED DREAM

She had no saying dark enough
  For the dark pine that kept
Forever trying the window-latch
  Of the room where they slept.

The tireless but ineffectual hands
  That with every futile pass
Made the great tree seem as a little bird
  Before the mystery of glass!

It never had been inside the room,
  And only one of the two
Was afraid in an oft-repeated dream
  Of what the tree might do.

THE IMPULSE

It was too lonely for her there,
    And too wild,
And since there were but two of them,
    And no child,

And work was little in the house,
    She was free,
And followed where he furrowed field,
    Or felled tree.

She rested on a log and tossed
    The fresh chips,
With a song only to herself
    On her lips.

And once she went to break a bough
    Of black alder.
She strayed so far she scarcely heard
    When he called her—

And didn't answer—didn't speak—
    Or return.
She stood, and then she ran and hid
    In the fern.

He never found her, though he looked
    Everywhere,
And he asked at her mother's house
    Was she there.

Sudden and swift and light as that
    The ties gave,
And he learned of finalities
    Besides the grave.

THE SOUND OF THE TREES

I wonder about the trees.
Why do we wish to bear
Forever the noise of these
More than another noise
So close to our dwelling place?
We suffer them by the day
Till we lose all measure of pace,
And fixity in our joys,
And acquire a listening air.
They are that that talks of going
But never gets away;
And that talks no less for knowing,
As it grows wiser and older,
That now it means to stay.
My feet tug at the floor
And my head sways to my shoulder
Sometimes when I watch trees sway,
From the window or the door.
I shall set forth for somewhere,
I shall make the reckless choice
Some day when they are in voice
And tossing so as to scare
The white clouds over them on.
I shall have less to say,
But I shall be gone.

THE STAR-SPLITTER

"You know Orion always comes up sideways.
Throwing a leg up over our fence of mountains,
And rising on his hands, he looks in on me
Busy outdoors by lantern-light with something
I should have done by daylight, and indeed,
After the ground is frozen, I should have done
Before it froze, and a gust flings a handful

Of waste leaves at my smoky lantern chimney
To make fun of my way of doing things,
Or else fun of Orion's having caught me.
Has a man, I should like to ask, no rights
These forces are obliged to pay respect to?"
So Brad McLaughlin mingled reckless talk
Of heavenly stars with hugger-mugger farming,
Till having failed at hugger-mugger farming,
He burned his house down for the fire insurance
And spent the proceeds on a telescope
To satisfy a life-long curiosity
About our place among the infinities.

"What do you want with one of those blame things?"
I asked him well beforehand. "Don't you get one!"
"Don't call it blamed; there isn't anything
More blameless in the sense of being less
A weapon in our human fight," he said.
"I'll have one if I sell my farm to buy it."
There where he moved the rocks to plow the ground
And plowed between the rocks he couldn't move
Few farms changed hands; so rather than spend years
Trying to sell his farm and then not selling,
He burned his house down for the fire insurance
And bought the telescope with what it came to.
He had been heard to say by several:
"The best thing that we're put here for's to see;
The strongest thing that's given us to see with's
A telescope. Someone in every town
Seems to me owes it to the town to keep one.
In Littleton it may as well be me."
After such loose talk it was no surprise
When he did what he did and burned his house down.

Mean laughter went about the town that day
To let him know we weren't the least imposed on,
And he could wait—we'd see to him to-morrow.
But the first thing next morning we reflected
If one by one we counted people out

For the least sin, it wouldn't take us long
To get so we had no one left to live with.
For to be social is to be forgiving.
Our thief, the one who does our stealing from us,
We don't cut off from coming to church suppers,
But what we miss we go to him and ask for.
He promptly gives it back, that is if still
Uneaten, unworn out, or undisposed of.
It wouldn't do to be too hard on Brad
About his telescope. Beyond the age
Of being given one's gift for Christmas,
He had to take the best way he knew how
To find himself in one. Well, all we said was
He took a strange thing to be roguish over.
Some sympathy was wasted on the house,
A good old-timer dating back along;
But a house isn't sentient; the house
Didn't feel anything. And if it did,
Why not regard it as a sacrifice,
And an old-fashioned sacrifice by fire,
Instead of a new-fashioned one at auction?

Out of a house and so out of a farm
At one stroke (of a match), Brad had to turn
To earn a living on the Concord railroad,
As under-ticket-agent at a station
Where his job, when he wasn't selling tickets,
Was setting out up track and down, not plants
As on a farm, but planets, evening stars
That varied in their hue from red to green.

He got a good glass for six hundred dollars.
His new job gave him leisure for star-gazing.
Often he bid me come and have a look
Up the brass barrel, velvet black inside,
At a star quaking in the other end.
I recollect a night of broken clouds
And underfoot snow melted down to ice,
And melting further in the wind to mud.

Bradford and I had out the telescope.
We spread our two legs as we spread its three,
Pointed our thoughts the way we pointed it,
And standing at our leisure till the day broke,
Said some of the best things we ever said.
That telescope was christened the Star-splitter,
Because it didn't do a thing but split
A star in two or three the way you split
A globule of quicksilver in your hand
With one stroke of your finger in the middle.
It's a star-splitter if there ever was one
And ought to do some good if splitting stars
'S a thing to be compared with splitting wood.

We've looked and looked, but after all where are we?
Do we know any better where we are,
And how it stands between the night to-night
And a man with a smoky lantern chimney?
How different from the way it ever stood?

FIRE AND ICE

Some say the world will end in fire,
Some say in ice.
From what I've tasted of desire
I hold with those who favor fire.
But if it had to perish twice,
I think I know enough of hate
To say that for destruction ice
Is also great
And would suffice.

STOPPING BY WOODS ON A SNOWY EVENING

Whose woods these are I think I know.
His house is in the village though;
He will not see me stopping here
To watch his woods fill up with snow.

My little horse must think it queer
To stop without a farmhouse near
Between the woods and frozen lake
The darkest evening of the year.

He gives his harness bells a shake
To ask if there is some mistake.
The only other sound's the sweep
Of easy wind and downy flake.

The woods are lovely, dark and deep.
But I have promises to keep,
And miles to go before I sleep,
And miles to go before I sleep.

DUST OF SNOW

The way a crow
Shook down on me
The dust of snow
From a hemlock tree

Has given my heart
A change of mood
And saved some part
Of a day I had rued.

CARL SANDBURG

Carl Sandburg, journalist, writer of children's stories, biographer, and poet, was born in Galesburg, Illinois, January 6, 1878. His parents, August and Clara Anderson Sandburg, were Swedish immigrants, and possessed scarcely the rudiments of a formal education, the former having attended school for but three months, and the latter for but two. Sandburg's father was named August Johnson, but because there were several other August Johnsons in the railroad construction gang with which he worked, in consequence of which the pay envelopes sometimes became mixed, he changed his name to Sandburg. During Carl's youth, his father worked in the railroad blacksmith shops at Galesburg.

As a boy, Sandburg attended school when he could, and worked hard at many kinds of jobs. Between the ages of thirteen and seventeen he was successively a driver of a milk wagon, porter in a barber shop, scene-shifter in a theatre, and truck operator at a brick kiln. At seventeen he went west, riding freight cars and blind baggage. There among other jobs he pitched wheat in the Kansas wheatfields, washed dishes at hotels in Kansas City, Omaha, and Denver, and worked as carpenter's helper in Kansas. Returning to Galesburg, he worked for a while at his old job of delivering milk, and then started what but for the Spanish-American war might have been his lifework—the trade of house painter. But with the outbreak of the war, Sandburg enlisted in Company C of the Sixth Illinois Infantry, and was sent to Porto Rico, where he served for eight months. In the army he met a student from Lombard College, Galesburg, who so interested him in college that when the war was ended, and Sandburg was mustered out with a hundred dollars, he went back home and entered Lombard as a special student.

He attended college from 1898 to 1902, making his way by working as janitor of the gymnasium, ringing the college bell, and tutoring. In college he was captain of the basketball team, and editor of both the college monthly magazine and the college annual. There, too, he came into contact with Philip Green Wright, one of the teachers of the college, and became a member of the Poor Writers' Club, which Wright formed, and in which the members read their prose and verse, and criticized one another's work.

Upon completing his college work, Sandburg traveled for a while, selling films for Underwood and Underwood. In 1907-08 he was a district organizer for the Social-Democrat party of Wisconsin. Next he did newspaper work at Milwaukee, and there on June 15, 1908, he married Lillian Steichen. From 1910 to 1912 he was secretary to Emil Seidel, the first Socialist mayor of Milwaukee. Going to Chicago, he was associated for a while with the magazine *System*, and then assisted N. D. Cochran in the experiment of running a newspaper, *The Daybook*, without advertising. When this journal ceased publication in 1917, Sandburg joined the staff of *The Chicago Daily News*. In 1918 he traveled in Norway and Sweden as a reporter for the Newspaper Enterprise Association. Since his return from this trip he has been on the staff of *The Daily News*.

After college, Sandburg continued to write poetry, and in 1904 he issued privately his first volume, a paper bound pamphlet entitled *In Reckless Ecstasy*, its sponsor being his old college professor, Philip Green Wright. It was not until 1914, however, that he received any recognition as a poet. In that year, *Poetry: a Magazine of Verse* published a number of his poems, including "Chicago," for which he received the Levinson prize, offered by that magazine. In 1916 he published his first full volume, *Chicago Poems,* and has followed it with several others. All of his poetry of recent years is written in free verse.

For a number of years Sandburg has traveled across the United States, lecturing and giving readings from his works, singing folk songs, and collecting material for his *American Songbag,* a volume of ballads which he published in 1927. He has written two books of children's stories, entitled *Rootabaga Stories* (1922), and *Rootabaga Pigeons* (1923); and in 1926 published a biography of Abraham Lincoln, entitled *The Prairie Years.*

In 1919 and again in 1921 Sandburg shared half the award of the Poetry Society of America. In 1923 Lombard College conferred upon him the honorary degree of Doctor of Literature. In 1928 he was Phi Beta Kappa poet at Harvard University. He is the father of three children, all daughters, and lives at Elmhurst, Illinois.

CHICAGO

Hog Butcher for the World,
Tool Maker, Stacker of Wheat,
Player with Railroads and the Nation's Freight Handler;
Stormy, husky, brawling,
City of the Big Shoulders:

They tell me you are wicked and I believe them, for I have seen your painted women under the gas lamps luring the farm boys.
And they tell me you are crooked and I answer: Yes, it is true I have seen the gunman kill and go free to kill again.
And they tell me you are brutal and my reply is: On the faces of women and children I have seen the marks of wanton hunger.
And having answered so I turn once more to those who sneer at this my city, and I give them back the sneer and say to them:
Come and show me another city with lifted head singing so proud to be alive and coarse and strong and cunning.
Flinging magnetic curses amid the toil of piling job on job, here is a tall bold slugger set vivid against the little soft cities;
Fierce as a dog with tongue lapping for action, cunning as a savage pitted against the wilderness,
Bareheaded,
Shoveling,
Wrecking,
Planning,
Building, breaking, rebuilding,
Under the smoke, dust all over his mouth, laughing with white teeth,

Under the terrible burden of destiny laughing as a young man laughs,
Laughing even as an ignorant fighter laughs who has never lost a battle,
Bragging and laughing that under his wrist is the pulse, and under his ribs the heart of the people,
Laughing!
Laughing the stormy, husky, brawling laughter of Youth, half-naked, sweating, proud to be Hog Butcher, Tool Maker, Stacker of Wheat, Player with Railroads and Freight Handler to the Nation.

LOST

Desolate and lone
All night long on the lake
Where fog trails and mist creeps,
The whistle of a boat
Calls and cries unendingly,
Like some lost child
In tears and trouble
Hunting the harbor's breast
And the harbor's eyes.

AT A WINDOW

Give me a hunger,
O you gods that sit and give
The world its orders.
Give me hunger, pain and want,
Shut me out with shame and failure
From your doors of gold and fame,
Give me your shabbiest, weariest hunger!

But leave me a little love,
A voice to speak to me in the day end,
A hand to touch me in the dark room

Breaking the long loneliness.
In the dusk of day-shapes
Blurring the sunset,
One little wandering, western star
Thrust out from the changing shores of shadow.
Let me go to the window,
Watch there the day-shapes of dusk
And wait and know the coming
Of a little love.

MONOTONE

The monotone of the rain is beautiful,
And the sudden rise and slow relapse
Of the long multitudinous rain.

The sun on the hills is beautiful,
Or a captured sunset sea-flung,
Bannered with fire and gold.

A face I know is beautiful—
With fire and gold of sky and sea,
And the peace of long warm rain.

PRAIRIE

I was born on the prairie and the milk of its wheat, the red of its clover, the eyes of its women, gave me a song and a slogan.

Here the water went down, the icebergs slid with gravel, the gaps and the valleys hissed, and the black loam came, and the yellow sandy loam.
Here between the sheds of the Rocky Mountains and the Appalachians, here now a morning star fixes a fire sign over the timber claims and cow pastures, the corn belt, the cotton belt, the cattle ranches.

Here the gray geese go five hundred miles and back with a
wind under their wings honking the cry for a new home.
Here I know I will hanker after nothing so much as one more
sunrise or a sky moon of fire doubled to a river moon
of water.

The prairie sings to me in the forenoon and I know in the
night I rest easy in the prairie arms, on the prairie heart.

. . .

After the sunburn of the day
handling a pitchfork at a hayrack,
after the eggs and biscuit and coffee,
the pearl-gray haystacks
in the gloaming
are cool prayers
to the harvest hands.

In the city among the walls the overland passenger train is
choked and the pistons hiss and the wheels curse.
On the prairie the overland flits on phantom wheels and the
sky and the soil between them muffle the pistons and
cheer the wheels.

. . .

I am here when the cities are gone.
I am here before the cities come.
I nourished the lonely men on horses.
I will keep the laughing men who ride iron.
I am dust of men.

The running water babbled to the deer, the cottontail, the
gopher.
You came in wagons, making streets and schools,
Kin of the ax and rifle, kin of the plow and horse,
Singing *Yankee Doodle, Old Dan Tucker, Turkey in the
Straw,*
You in the coonskin cap at a log house door hearing a lone
wolf howl,
You at a sod house door reading the blizzards and chinooks
let loose from Medicine Hat,

I am dust of your dust, as I am brother and mother
To the copper faces, the worker in flint and clay,
The singing women and their sons a thousand years ago
Marching single file the timber and the plain.

I hold the dust of these amid changing stars.
I last while old wars are fought, while peace broods mother-like,
While new wars arise and the fresh killings of young men.
I fed the boys who went to France in great dark days.
Appomattox is a beautiful word to me and so is Valley Forge and the Marne and Verdun,
I who have seen the red births and the red deaths
Of sons and daughters, I take peace or war, I say nothing and wait.

Have you seen a red sunset drip over one of my cornfields, the shore of night stars, the wave lines of dawn up a wheat valley?
Have you heard my threshing crews yelling in the chaff of a strawpile and the running wheat of the wagonboards, my cornhuskers, my harvest hands hauling crops, singing dreams of women, worlds, horizons?

. . .

Rivers cut a path on flat lands.
The mountains stand up.
The salt oceans press in
And push on the coast lines.
The sun, the wind, bring rain
And I know what the rainbow writes across the east or west in a half-circle:
A love-letter pledge to come again.

. . .

Towns on the Soo Line,
Towns on the Big Muddy,
Laugh at each other for cubs
And tease as children.

Omaha and Kansas City, Minneapolis and St. Paul, sisters
in a house together, throwing slang, growing up.
Towns in the Ozarks, Dakota wheat towns, Wichita, Peoria,
Buffalo, sisters throwing slang, growing up.

. . .

Out of prairie-brown grass crossed with a streamer of
wigwam smoke—out of a smoke pillar, a blue promise
—out of wild ducks woven in greens and purples—
Here I saw a city rise and say to the peoples round world:
Listen, I am strong, I know what I want.
Out of log houses and stumps—canoes stripped from tree-
sides—flatboats coaxed with an ax from the timber
claims—in the years when the red and the white men
met—the houses and streets rose.

A thousand red men cried and went away to new places for
corn and women: a million white men came and put up
skyscrapers, threw out rails and wires, feelers to the
salt sea: now the smokestacks bite the skyline with stub
teeth.

In an early year the call of a wild duck woven in greens and
purples: now the riverter's chatter, the police patrol, the
song-whistle of the steamboat.

To a man across a thousand years I offer a handshake.
I say to him: Brother, make the story short, for the stretch
of a thousand years is short.

. . .

What brothers these in the dark?
What eaves of skyscrapers against a smoke moon?
These chimneys shaking on the lumber shanties
When the coal boats plow by on the river—
The hunched shoulders of the grain elevators—
The flame sprockets of the sheet steel mills
And the men in the rolling mills with their shirts off
Playing their flesh arms against the twisting wrists of steel:

what brothers these
in the dark
of a thousand years?

. . .

A headlight searches a snowstorm.
A funnel of white light shoots from over the pilot of the Pioneer Limited crossing Wisconsin.

In the morning hours, in the dawn,
The sun puts out the stars of the sky
And the headlight of the Limited train.

The fireman waves his hand to a country school teacher on a bobsled.
A boy, yellow hair, red scarf and mittens, on the bobsled, in his lunch box a pork chop sandwich and a V of gooseberry pie.

The horses fathom a snow to their knees.
Snow hats are on the rolling prairie hills.
The Mississippi bluffs wear snow hats.

. . .

Keep your hogs on changing corn and mashes of grain,
O farmerman.
Cram their insides till they waddle on short legs
Under the drums of bellies, hams of fat.
Kill your hogs with a knife slit under the ear.
Hack them with cleavers.
Hang them with hooks in the hind legs.

. . .

A wagonload of radishes on a summer morning.
Sprinkles of dew on the crimson-purple balls.
The farmer on the seat dangles the reins on the rumps of dapple-gray horses.
The farmer's daughter with a basket of eggs dreams of a new hat to wear to the country fair.

. . .

On the left- and right-hand side of the road,
Marching corn—
I saw it knee high weeks ago—now it is head high—tassels of red silk creep at the ends of the ears.

. . .

I am the prairie, mother of men, waiting.
They are mine, the threshing crews eating beeksteak, the farm-boys driving steers to the railroad cattle pens.
They are mine, the crowds of people at a Fourth of July basket picnic, listening to a lawyer read the Declaration of Independence, watching the pinwheels and Roman candles at night, the young men and women two by two hunting the bypaths and kissing bridges.
They are mine, the horses looking over a fence in the frost of late October, saying good-morning to the horses hauling wagons of rutabaga to market.
They are mine, the old zigzag rail fences, the new barb wire.

. . .

The cornhuskers wear leather on their hands.
There is no let-up to the wind.
Blue bandannas are knotted at the ruddy chins.
Falltime and winter apples take on the smolder of the five-o'clock November sunset: falltime, leaves, bonfires, stubble, the old things go, and the earth is grizzled.
The land and the people hold memories, even among the anthills and the angleworms, among the toads and woodroaches—among gravestone writings rubbed out by the rain—they keep old things that never grow old.

The frost loosens corn husks.
The sun, the rain, the wind
loosen corn husks.
The men and women are helpers.
They are all cornhuskers together.
I see them late in the western evening
in a smoke-red dust.

. . .

The phantom of a yellow rooster flaunting a scarlet comb, on top of a dung pile crying hallelujah to the streaks of daylight,
The phantom of an old hunting dog nosing in the underbrush for muskrats, barking at a coon in a treetop at midnight, chewing a bone, chasing his tail round a corncrib,
The phantom of an old workhorse taking the steel point of a plow across a forty-acre field in spring, hitched to a harrow in summer, hitched to a wagon among cornshocks in fall,
These phantoms come into the talk and wonder of people on the front porch of a farmhouse late summer nights.
"The shapes that are gone are here," said an old man with a cob pipe in his teeth one night in Kansas with a hot wind on the alfalfa.

. . .

Look at six eggs
In a mockingbird's nest.

Listen to six mockingbirds
Flinging follies of O-be-joyful
Over the marshes and uplands.

Look at songs
Hidden in eggs.

. . .

When the morning sun is on the trumpet-vine blossoms, sing at the kitchen pans: *Shout All Over God's Heaven.*
When the rain slants on the potato hills and the sun plays a silver shaft on the last shower, sing to the bush at the backyard fence: *Mighty Lak a Rose.*
When the icy sleet pounds on the storm windows and the house lifts to a great breath, sing for the outside hills: *The Ole Sheep Done Know the Road, the Young Lambs Must Find the Way.*
Spring slips back with a girl face calling always: "Any new songs for me? Any new songs?"

O prairie girl, be lonely, singing, dreaming, waiting—your lover comes—your child comes—the years creep with toes of April rain on new-turned sod.
O prairie girl, whoever leaves you only crimson poppies to talk with, whoever puts a good-by kiss on your lips and never comes back—
There is a song deep as the falltime red haws, long as the layer of black loam we go to, the shine of the morning star over the corn belt, the wave line of dawn up a wheat valley.

. . .

O prairie mother, I am one of your boys.
I have loved the prairie as a man with a heart shot full of pain over love.
Here I know I will hanker after nothing so much as one more sunrise or a sky moon of fire doubled to a river moon of water.

. . .

I speak of new cities and new people.
I tell you the past is a bucket of ashes.
I tell you yesterday is a wind gone down,
a sun dropped in the west.
I tell you there is nothing in the world
only an ocean of to-morrows,
a sky of to-morrows.

I am a brother of the cornhuskers who say
at sundown:
To-morrow is a day.

CABOOSE THOUGHTS

It's going to come out all right—do you know?
The sun, the birds, the grass—they know.
They get along—and we'll get along.

Some days will be rainy and you will sit waiting
And the letter you wait for won't come,
And I will sit watching the sky tear off gray and gray
And the letter I wait for won't come.

There will be ac-ci-dents.
I know ac-ci-dents are coming.
Smash-ups, signals wrong, washouts, trestles rotten,
Red and yellow ac-ci-dents.
But somehow and somewhere the end of the run
The train gets put together again
And the caboose and the green tail lights
Fade down the right of way like a new white hope.

I never heard a mockingbird in Kentucky
Spilling its heart in the morning.

I never saw the snow on Chimborazo.
It's a high white Mexican hat, I hear.

I never had supper with Abe Lincoln,
Nor a dish of soup with Jim Hill.

But I've been around.
I know some of the boys here who can go a little.
I know girls good for a burst of speed any time.

I heard Williams and Walker
Before Walker died in the bughouse.

I knew a mandolin player
Working in a barber shop in an Indiana town,
And he thought he had a million dollars.

I knew a hotel girl in Des Moines.
She had eyes; I saw her and said to myself
The sun rises and the sun sets in her eyes.

I was her steady and her heart went pit-a-pat.
We took away the money for a prize waltz at a Brotherhood dance.
She had eyes; she was safe as the bridge over the Mississippi at Burlington; I married her.

Last summer we took the cushions going west.
Pike's Peak is a big old stone, believe me.
It's fastened down; something you can count on.

It's going to come out all right—do you know?
The sun, the birds, the grass—they know.
They get along—and we'll get along.

LOAM

In the loam we sleep,
In the cool moist loam,
To the lull of years that pass
And the break of stars,

From the loam, then,
The soft warm loam,
We rise:
To shape of rose leaf,
Of face and shoulder.

We stand, then,
To a whiff of life,
Lifted to the silver of the sun
Over and out of the loam
A day.

COOL TOMBS

When Abraham Lincoln was shoveled into the tombs,
he forgot the copperheads and the assassin . . .
in the dust, in the cool tombs.

And Ulysses Grant lost all thought of con men and Wall
Street, cash and collateral turned ashes . . . in the
dust, in the cool tombs.

Pocahontas' body, lovely as a poplar, sweet as a red haw
in November or a pawpaw in May, did she wonder?
does she remember? . . . in the dust, in the cool tombs?

Take any streetful of people buying clothes and groceries,
cheering a hero or throwing confetti and blowing tin
horns . . . tell me if the lovers are losers . . . tell
me if any get more than the lovers . . . in the dust . . .
in the cool tombs.

PRAYERS OF STEEL

Lay me on an anvil, O God.
Beat me and hammer me into a crowbar.
Let me pry loose old walls.
Let me lift and loosen old foundations.

Lay me on an anvil, O God.
Beat me and hammer me into a steel spike.
Drive me into the girders that hold a skyscraper together.
Take red-hot rivets and fasten me into the central girders.
Let me be the great nail holding a skyscraper through blue
nights into white stars.

HOUSE

Two Swede families live downstairs and an Irish policeman
upstairs, and an old soldier, Uncle Joe.
Two Swede boys go upstairs and see Joe. His wife is dead,
his only son is dead, and his two daughters in Missouri
and Texas don't want him around.
The boys and Uncle Joe crack walnuts with a hammer on
the bottom of a flatiron while the January wind howls
and the zero air weaves laces on the window glass.

Joe tells the Swede boys all about Chickamauga and Chattanooga, how the Union soldiers crept in rain somewhere a dark night and ran forward and killed many Rebels, took flags, held a hill, and won a victory told about in the histories in school.
Joe takes a piece of carpenter's chalk, draws lines on the floor and piles stove wood to show where six regiments were slaughtered climbing a slope.
"Here they went" and "Here they went," says Joe, and the January wind howls and the zero air weaves laces on the window glass.
The two Swede boys go downstairs with a big blur of guns, men, and hills in their heads. They eat herring and potatoes and tell the family war is a wonder and soldiers are a wonder.
One breaks out with a cry at supper: I wish we had a war now and I could be a soldier.

RED-HEADED RESTAURANT CASHIER

Shake back your hair, O red-headed girl.
Let go your laughter and keep your two proud freckles on your chin.
Somewhere is a man looking for a red-headed girl and some day maybe he will look into your eyes for a restaurant cashier and find a lover, maybe.
Around and around go ten thousand men hunting a red-headed girl with two freckles on her chin.
I have seen them hunting, hunting.
Shake back your hair; let go your laughter.

BOY AND FATHER

The boy Alexander understands his father to be a famous lawyer.
The leather law books of Alexander's father fill a room like hay in a barn.

Alexander has asked his father to let him build a house like bricklayers build, a house with walls and roofs made of big leather law books.

The rain beats on the windows
And the raindrops run down the window glass
And the raindrops slide off the green blinds down the siding.

The boy Alexander dreams of Napoleon in John C. Abbott's history, Napoleon the grand and lonely man wronged, Napoleon in his life wronged and in his memory wronged.
The boy Alexander dreams of the cat Alice saw, the cat fading off into the dark and leaving the teeth of its Cheshire smile lighting the gloom.

Buffaloes, blizzards, way down in Texas, in the panhandle of Texas snuggling close to New Mexico,
These creep into Alexander's dreaming by the window when his father talks with strange men about land down in Deaf Smith County.
Alexander's father tells the strange men: Five years ago we ran a Ford out on the prairie and chased antelopes.

Only once or twice in a long while has Alexander heard his father say "my first wife" so-and-so and such-and-such.
A few times softly the father has told Alexander, "Your mother . . . was a beautiful woman . . . but we won't talk about her."
Always Alexander listens with a keen listen when he hears his father mention "my first wife" or "Alexander's mother."

Alexander's father smokes a cigar and the Episcopal rector smokes a cigar and the words come often: mystery of life, mystery of life.
These two come into Alexander's head blurry and gray while the rain beats on the windows and the raindrops run down the window glass and the raindrops slide off the green blinds and down the siding.

These and: There is a God, there must be a God, how can there be rain or sun unless there is a God?

So from the wrongs of Napoleon and the Cheshire cat smile on to the buffaloes and blizzards of Texas and on to his mother and to God, so the blurry gray rain dreams of Alexander have gone on five minutes, maybe ten, keeping slow easy time to the raindrops on the window glass and the raindrops sliding off the green blinds and down the siding.

THE HANGMAN AT HOME

What does the hangman think about
When he goes home at night from work?
When he sits down with his wife and
Children for a cup of coffee and a
Plate of ham and eggs, do they ask
Him if it was a good day's work
And everything went well, or do they
Stay off some topics and talk about
The weather, baseball, politics
And the comic strips in the papers
And the movies? Do they look at his
Hands when he reaches for the coffee
Or the ham and eggs? If the little
Ones say, Daddy, play horse, here's
A rope—does he answer like a joke:
I seen enough rope for to-day?
Or does his face light up like a
Bonfire of joy and does he say:
It's a good and dandy world we live
In. And if a white face moon looks
In through a window where a baby girl
Sleeps and the moon gleams mix with
Baby ears and baby hair—the hangman—
How does he act then? It must be easy
For him. Anything is easy for a hangman,
I guess.

DEATH SNIPS PROUD MEN

Death is stronger than all the governments because the governments are men and men die and then death laughs: Now you see 'em, now you don't.

Death is stronger than all proud men and so death snips proud men on the nose, throws a pair of dice and says: Read 'em and weep.

Death sends a radiogram every day: When I want you I'll drop in—and then one day he comes with a master-key and lets himself in and says: We'll go now.

Death is a nurse mother with big arms: 'Twon't hurt you at all; it's your time now; you just need a long sleep, child; what have you had anyhow better than sleep?

LOSERS

If I should pass the tomb of Jonah
I would stop there and sit for awhile;
Because I was swallowed one time deep in the dark
And came out alive after all.

If I pass the burial spot of Nero
I shall say to the wind, "Well, well!"—
I who have fiddled in a world on fire,
I who have done so many stunts not worth doing.

I am looking for the grave of Sinbad too.
I want to shake his ghost-hand and say,
"Neither of us died very early, did we?"

And the last sleeping-place of Nebuchadnezzar—
When I arrive there I shall tell the wind:
"You ate grass; I have eaten crow—
Who is better off now or next year?"

Jack Cade, John Brown, Jesse James,
There too I could sit down and stop for awhile.
I think I could tell their headstones:
"God, let me remember all good losers."

I could ask people to throw ashes on their heads
In the name of that sergeant at Belleau Woods,
Walking into the drumfires, calling his men,
"Come on, you . . . Do you want to live forever?"

STARS, SONGS, FACES

Gather the stars if you wish it so.
Gather the songs and keep them.
Gather the faces of women.
Gather for keeping years and years.
And then . . .
Loosen your hands, let go and say good-by.
Let the stars and songs go.
Let the faces and years go.
Loosen your hands and say good-by.

HELGA

The wishes on this child's mouth
Came like snow on marsh cranberries;
The tamarack kept something for her;
The wind is ready to help her shoes.
The north has loved her; she will be
A grandmother feeding geese on frosty
Mornings; she will understand
Early snow on the cranberries
Better and better then.

SANDHILL PEOPLE

I took away three pictures.
One was a white gull forming a half-mile arch from the pines toward Waukegan.
One was a whistle in the little sandhills, a bird crying either to the sunset gone or the dusk come.
One was three spotted waterbirds, zigzagging, cutting scrolls and jags, writing a bird Sanscrit of wing points, half over the sand, half over the water, a half-love for the sea, a half-love for the land.

I took away three thoughts.
One was a thing my people call "love," a shut-in river hunting the sea, breaking white falls between tall clefs of hill country.
One was a thing my people call "silence," the wind running over the butter faced sand-flowers, running over the sea, and never heard of again.
One was a thing my people call "death," neither a whistle in the little sandhills, nor a bird Sanscrit of wing points, yet a coat all the stars and seas have worn, yet a face the beach wears between sunset and dusk.

MIST FORMS

The sheets of night mist travel a long valley.
I know why you came at sundown in a scarf mist.

What was it we touched asking nothing and asking all?
How many times can death come and pay back what we saw?

In the oath of the sod, the lips that swore,
In the oath of night mist, nothing at all,
A riddle is here no man tells, no woman.

NIGHT STUFF

Listen a while, the moon is a lovely woman, a lonely woman, lost in a silver dress, lost in a circus rider's silver dress.

Listen a while, the lake by night is a lonely woman, a lovely woman, circled with birches and pines mixing their green and white among stars shattered in spray clear nights.

I know the moon and the lake have twisted the roots under my heart the same as a lonely woman, a lovely woman, in a silver dress, in a circus rider's silver dress.

WASHINGTON MONUMENT BY NIGHT

I

The stone goes straight.
A lean swimmer dives into night sky,
Into half-moon mist.

II

Two trees are coal black.
This is a great white ghost between.
It is cool to look at.
Strong men, strong women, come here.

III

Eight years is a long time
To be fighting all the time.

IV

The republic is a dream.
Nothing happens unless first a dream.

V

The wind bit hard at Valley Forge one Christmas.
Soldiers tied rags on their feet.
Red footprints wrote on the snow . . .
. . . and stone shoots into stars here
. . . into half-moon mist to-night.

VI

Tongues wrangled dark at a man.
He buttoned his overcoat and stood alone.
In a snowstorm, red hollyberries, thoughts,
    he stood alone.

VII

Women said: He is lonely
. . . fighting . . . fighting . . . eight years . . .

VIII

The name of an iron man goes over the world.
It takes a long time to forget an iron man.

IX

. . . .
. . . .

FOR YOU

The peace of great doors be for you.
Wait at the knobs, at the panel oblongs.
Wait for the great hinges.

The peace of great churches be for you,
Where the players of loft pipe organs
Practice old lovely fragments, alone.

The peace of great books be for you,
Stains of pressed clover leaves on pages,
Bleach of the light of years held in leather.

The peace of great prairies be for you.
Listen among windplayers in cornfields,
The wind learning over its oldest music.

The peace of great seas be for you.
Wait on a hook of land, a rock footing
For you, wait in the salt wash.

The peace of great mountains be for you,
The sleep and the eyesight of eagles,
Sheet mist shadows and the long look across.

The peace of great hearts be for you,
Valves of the blood of the sun,
Pumps of the strongest wants we cry.

The peace of great silhouettes be for you,
Shadow dancers alive in your blood now,
Alive and crying, "Let us out, let us out."

The peace of great changes be for you.
Whisper, Oh beginners in the hills.
Tumble, Oh cubs—to-morrow belongs to you.

The peace of great loves be for you.
Rain, soak these roots; wind, shatter the dry rot.
Bars of sunlight, grips of the earth, hug these.

The peace of great ghosts be for you,
Phantoms of night-gray eyes, ready to go
To the fog-star dumps, to the fire-white doors.

Yes, the peace of great phantoms be for you,
Phantom iron men, mothers of bronze,
Keepers of the lean clean breeds.

EXPLANATIONS OF LOVE

There is a place where love begins and a place where love ends.

There is a touch of two hands that foils all dictionaries.

There is a look of eyes fierce as a big Bethlehem open hearth furnace or a little green-fire acetylene torch.

There are single careless bywords portentous as a big bend in the Mississippi River.

Hands, eyes, bywords—out of these love makes battle-grounds and workshops.

There is a pair of shoes love wears and the coming is a mystery.

There is a warning love sends and the cost of it is never written till long afterward.

There are explanations of love in all languages and not one found wiser than this:

There is a place where love begins and a place where love ends—and love asks nothing.

VACHEL LINDSAY

Nicholas Vachel Lindsay came of Southern stock, his ancestors having moved across Virginia into Kentucky, and thence up into Illinois. He was born in Springfield, Illinois, November 10, 1879. His parents were Thomas and Catherine Frazee Lindsay.

He graduated from the Springfield High School in 1897, and in the autumn entered Hiram College, Ohio, which he attended for three years, leaving at the end of that time to take up the study of art. From 1900 to 1903 he studied at the Chicago Art Institute, but when his pictures failed to sell, he took a job for a time as salesman in a department store. In 1904 he went to New York, and pursued his studies at the New York School of Art, lecturing in the evenings during the winters of 1905-08 for the West Side Y. M. C. A. In 1908 he returned home, and in 1908-09 lectured for the Springfield Y. M. C. A., and in 1909-10 for the Anti-Saloon League in central Illinois.

In the spring of 1906 Lindsay tramped through the Blue Ridge Mountains from Florida to Tennessee, a trip which he described in a prose volume, *A Handy Guide for Beggars* (1916). He next went to Europe, where he studied in more than a score of museums. Later he made several other walking tours of the United States, at one time going as far west as New Mexico, and stopping on the way to work in the Kansas wheatfields; at another time going through the coal mine country of Pennsylvania; and at still another time walking through the Rocky Mountains. The former of these trips, taken in the summer of 1912, and the Pennsylvania trip, taken in 1908, he described in a prose volume, *Adventures While Preaching the Gospel of Beauty* (1914); and the latter is described in a volume, *Tramping with a Poet in the Rockies* (1922), written by the English explorer and poet Stephen Graham, who accompanied him. On all his early tours he took along paper bound pamphlets of his poems, which he traded for food and lodging. His mission on these walks was to preach the gospel of beauty, and to induce men to set about making their communities more attractive in appearance and in spirit.

Lindsay began writing verse as early as 1897, but for many years he published only pamphlets, none of which attracted much notice. In January, 1913, however, his poem *General William Booth Enters into Heaven* appeared in *Poetry: a Magazine of Verse*, and at once established him as a poet of significance. In the same year he published a full-sized volume, *General William Booth Enters into Heaven, and Other Poems*. Since then he has published a number of volumes of poetry—some of which he himself illustrated—and several books of prose, among the latter being *The Art of the Moving Picture* (1915) and *The Golden Book of Springfield* (1920). During the last ten years he has traveled extensively, reading his poetry and lecturing at various colleges and universities in the United States, and in the summer of 1920 in England at Oxford, Cambridge, and London.

On May 19, 1925, he married Elizabeth Conner, of Spokane, Washington, and is now living in Spokane. They have two children.

THE CHINESE NIGHTINGALE

(A SONG IN CHINESE TAPESTRIES)

"How, how," he said. "Friend Chang," I said,
"San Francisco sleeps as the dead—
Ended license, lust and play:
Why do you iron the night away?
Your big clock speaks with a deadly sound,
With a tick and a wail till dawn comes round.
While the monster shadows glower and creep,
What can be better for man than sleep?"

"I will tell you a secret," Chang replied;
"My breast with vision is satisfied,
And I see green trees and fluttering wings,
And my deathless bird from Shanghai sings."
Then he lit five firecrackers in a pan.
"Pop, pop," said the firecrackers, "cra-cra-crack."
He lit a joss stick long and black.
Then the proud gray joss in the corner stirred;
On his wrist appeared a gray small bird,
And this was the song of the gray small bird:
"Where is the princess, loved forever,
Who made Chang first of the kings of men?"

And the joss in the corner stirred again;
And the carved dog, curled in his arms, awoke,
Barked forth a smoke-cloud that whirled and broke
It piled in a maze round the ironing-place,
And there on the snowy table wide
Stood a Chinese lady of high degree,
With a scornful, witching, tea-rose face. . . .
Yet she put away all form and pride,
And laid her glimmering veil aside
With a childlike smile for Chang and for me.

The walls fell back, night was aflower,
The table gleamed in a moonlit bower,
While Chang, with a countenance carved of stone,
Ironed and ironed, all alone.
And thus she sang to the busy man Chang:
"Have you forgotten . . .
Deep in the ages, long, long ago,
I was your sweetheart, there on the sand—
Storm-worn beach of the Chinese land?
We sold our grain in the peacock town—
Built on the edge of the sea-sands brown—
Built on the edge of the sea-sands brown. . . .

When all the world was drinking blood
From the skulls of men and bulls
And all the world had swords and clubs of stone,
We drank our tea in China beneath the sacred spice-trees,
And heard the curled waves of the harbor moan.
And this gray bird, in Love's first spring,
With a bright-bronze breast and a bronze-brown wing,
Captured the world with his carolling.
Do you remember, ages after,
At last the world we were born to own?
You were the heir of the yellow throne—
The world was the field of the Chinese man
And we were the pride of the Sons of Han?
We copied deep books and we carved in jade,
And wove blue silks in the mulberry shade. . . ."

"I remember, I remember
That Spring came on forever,
That Spring came on forever,"
Said the Chinese nightingale.

My heart was filled with marvel and dream,
Though I saw the western street-lamps gleam,
Though dawn was bringing the western day,
Though Chang was a laundryman ironing away. . . .

Mingled there with the streets and alleys,
The railroad-yard and the clock-tower bright,
Demon clouds crossed ancient valleys;
Across wide lotus-ponds of light
I marked a giant firefly's flight.

And the lady, rosy-red,
Flourished her fan, her shimmering fan,
Stretched her hand toward Chang, and said:
"Do you remember,
Ages after,
Our palace of heart-red stone?
Do you remember
The little doll-faced children
With their lanterns full of moon-fire,
That came from all the empire
Honoring the throne?—
The loveliest fête and carnival
Our world had ever known?
The sages sat about us
With their heads bowed in their beards,
With proper meditation on the sight.
Confucius was not born;
We lived in those great days
Confucius later said were lived aright. . . .
And this gray bird, on that day of spring,
With a bright-bronze breast, and a bronze-brown wing,
Captured the world with his carolling.
Late at night his tune was spent.
Peasants,
Sages,
Children,
Homeward went,
And then the bronze bird sang for you and me.
We walked alone. Our hearts were high and free.
I had a silvery name, I had a silvery name,
I had a silvery name—do you remember
The name you cried beside the tumbling sea?"

Chang turned not to the lady slim—
He bent to his work, ironing away;
But she was arch, and knowing and glowing,
For the bird on his shoulder spoke for him.

"Darling . . . darling . . . darling . . . darling . . ."
Said the Chinese nightingale.

The great gray joss on the rustic shelf,
Rakish and shrewd, with his collar awry,
Sang impolitely, as though by himself,
Drowning with his bellowing the nightingale's cry:
"Back through a hundred, hundred years
Hear the waves as they climb the piers,
Hear the howl of the silver seas,
Hear the thunder.
Hear the gongs of holy China,
How the waves and tunes combine
In a rhythmic clashing wonder,
Incantation old and fine:

> 'Dragons, dragons, Chinese dragons,
> Red firecrackers, and green firecrackers
> And dragons, dragons, Chinese dragons.' "

Then the lady, rosy-red,
Turned to her lover Chang and said:
"Dare you forget that turquoise dawn
When we stood in our mist-hung velvet lawn,
And worked a spell this great joss taught
Till a God of the Dragons was charmed and caught?
From the flag high over our palace home
He flew to our feet in rainbow-foam—
A king of beauty and tempest and thunder
Panting to tear our sorrows asunder.
A dragon of fair adventure and wonder.
We mounted the back of that royal slave
With thoughts of desire that were noble and grave.
We swam down the shore to the dragon-mountains,
We whirled to the peaks and the fiery fountains.

To our secret ivory house we were borne.
We looked down the wonderful wing-filled regions
Where the dragons darted in glimmering legions.
Right by my breast the nightingale sang;
The old rhymes rang in the sunlit mist
That we this hour regain—
Song-fire for the brain.
When my hands and my hair and my feet you kissed,
When you cried for your heart's new pain,
What was my name in the dragon-mist,
In the rings of rainbowed rain?"

"Sorrow and love, glory and love,"
Said the Chinese nightingale.
"Sorrow and love, glory and love,"
Said the Chinese nightingale.

And now the joss broke in with his song:
"Dying ember, bird of Chang,
Soul of Chang, do you remember?—
Ere you returned to the shining harbor
There were pirates by ten thousand
Descended on the town
In vessels mountain-high and red and brown,
Moon-ships that climbed the storms and cut the skies.
On their prows were painted terrible bright eyes.
But I was then a wizard and a scholar and a priest;
I stood upon the sand;
With lifted hand I looked upon them
And sunk their vessels with my wizard eyes,
And the stately lacquer-gate made safe again.
Deep, deep below the bay, the seaweed, and the spray,
Embalmed in amber every pirate lies,
Embalmed in amber every pirate lies."

Then this did the noble lady say:
"Bird, do you dream of our home-coming day
When you flew like a courier on before
From the dragon-peak to our palace-door,

And we drove the steed in your singing path—
The ramping dragon of laughter and wrath:
And found our city all aglow,
And knighted this joss that decked it so?
There were golden fishes in the purple river
And silver fishes and rainbow fishes.
There were golden junks in the laughing river,
And silver junks and rainbow junks:
There were golden lilies by the bay and river,
And silver lilies and tiger-lilies,
And tinkling wind-bells in the gardens of the town
By the black-lacquer gate
Where walked in state
The kind king Chang
And his sweetheart mate. . . .
With his flag-born dragon
And his crown of pearl . . . and . . . jade,
And his nightingale reigning in the mulberry shade,
And sailors and soldiers on the sea-sands brown,
And priests who bowed them down to your song—
By the city called Han, the peacock town,
By the city called Han, the nightingale town,
The nightingale town."

Then sang the bird, so strangely gay,
Fluttering, fluttering, ghostly and gray,
A vague, unravelling, final tune,
Like a long unwinding silk cocoon;
Sang as though for the soul of him
Who ironed away in that bower dim:—
"I have forgotten
Your dragons great,
Merry and mad and friendly and bold.
Dim is your proud lost palace-gate.
I vaguely know
There were heroes of old,
Troubles more than the heart could hold,
There were wolves in the woods
Yet lambs in the fold,

Nests in the top of the almond tree. . . .
The evergreen tree . . . and the mulberry tree . . .
Life and hurry and joy forgotten,
Years on years I but half-remember . . .
Man is a torch, then ashes soon,
May and June, then dead December,
Dead December, then again June.
Who shall end my dream's confusion?
Life is a loom, weaving illusion . . .
I remember, I remember
There were ghostly veils and laces . . .
In the shadowy bowery places . . .
With lovers' ardent faces
Bending to one another,
Speaking each his part.
They infinitely echo
In the red cave of my heart.
'Sweetheart, sweetheart, sweetheart,'
They said to one another.
They spoke, I think, of perils past.
They spoke, I think, of peace at last.
One thing I remember:
Spring came on forever,
Spring came on forever,"
Said the Chinese nightingale.

A NET TO SNARE THE MOONLIGHT

(WHAT THE MAN OF FAITH SAID)

The dew, the rain and moonlight
All prove our Father's mind.
The dew, the rain and moonlight
Descend to bless mankind.

Come, let us see that all men
Have land to catch the rain,
Have grass to snare the spheres of dew,
And fields spread for the grain.

Yea, we would give to each poor man
Ripe wheat and poppies red,—
A peaceful place at evening
With the stars just overhead:

A net to snare the moonlight,
A sod spread to the sun,
A place of toil by daytime,
Of dreams when toil is done.

THE MOON'S THE NORTH WIND'S COOKY

(WHAT THE LITTLE GIRL SAID)

The Moon's the North Wind's cooky.
He bites it, day by day,
Until there's but a rim of scraps
That crumble all away.

The South Wind is a baker.
He kneads clouds in his den,
And bakes a crisp new moon *that . . . greedy*
North . . . Wind . . . eats . . . again!

ALADDIN AND THE JINN

"Bring me soft song," said Aladdin.
"This tailor-shop sings not at all.
Chant me a word of the twilight,
Of roses that mourn in the fall.
Bring me a song like hashish
That will comfort the stale and the sad,
For I would be mending my spirit,
Forgetting these days that are bad,
Forgetting companions too shallow,
Their quarrels and arguments thin,
Forgetting the shouting Muezzin:"—
"I AM YOUR SLAVE," said the Jinn.

"Bring me old wines," said Aladdin.
"I have been a starved pauper too long.
Serve them in vessels of jade and of shell,
Serve them with fruit and with song:—
Wines of pre-Adamite Sultans
Digged from beneath the black seas:—
New-gathered dew from the heavens
Dripped down from Heaven's sweet trees,
Cups from the angels' pale tables
That will make me both handsome and wise,
For I have beheld her, the princess,
Firelight and starlight her eyes.
Pauper I am, I would woo her.
And—let me drink wine, to begin,
Though the Koran expressly forbids it."
"I AM YOUR SLAVE," said the Jinn.

"Plan me a dome," said Aladdin,
"That is drawn like the dawn of the MOON,
When the sphere seems to rest on the mountains,
Half-hidden, yet full-risen soon.
Build me a dome," said Aladdin,
"That shall cause all young lovers to sigh,
The fullness of life and of beauty,
Peace beyond peace to the eye—
A palace of foam and of opal,
Pure moonlight without and within,
Where I may enthrone my sweet lady."
"I AM YOUR SLAVE," said the Jinn.

THE LEADEN-EYED

Let not young souls be smothered out before
They do quaint deeds and fully flaunt their pride.
It is the world's one crime its babes grow dull,
Its poor are ox-like, limp and leaden-eyed.

Not that they starve, but starve so dreamlessly,
Not that they sow, but that they seldom reap,
Not that they serve, but have no gods to serve,
Not that they die, but that they die like sheep.

THE BRONCHO THAT WOULD NOT BE BROKEN

A little colt—broncho, loaned to the farm
To be broken in time without fury or harm,
Yet black crows flew past you, shouting alarm,
Calling "Beware," with lugubrious singing . . .
The butterflies there in the bush were romancing,
The smell of the grass caught your soul in a trance,
So why be a-fearing the spurs and the traces,
O broncho that would not be broken of dancing?

You were born with the pride of the lords great and olden
Who danced, through the ages, in corridors golden.
In all the wide farm-place the person most human.
You spoke out so plainly with squealing and capering,
With whinnying, snorting, contorting and prancing,
As you dodged your pursuers, looking askance,
With Greek-footed figures, and Parthenon paces,
O broncho that would not be broken of dancing.

The grasshoppers cheered. "Keep whirling," they said.
The insolent sparrows called from the shed,
"If men will not laugh, make them wish they were dead."
But arch were your thoughts, all malice displacing,
Though the horse-killers came, with snake-whips advancing.
You bantered and cantered away your last chance.
And they scourged you, with Hell in their speech and their
faces,
O broncho that would not be broken of dancing.

"Nobody cares for you," rattled the crows,
As you dragged the whole reaper, next day, down the rows.
The three mules held back, yet you danced on your toes.
You pulled like a racer, and kept the mules chasing.
You tangled the harness with bright eyes side-glancing,
While the drunk driver bled you—a pole for a lance—
And the giant mules bit at you—keeping their places,
O broncho that would not be broken of dancing.

In that last afternoon your boyish heart broke.
The hot wind came down like a sledge-hammer stroke.
The blood-sucking flies to a rare feast awoke.
And they searched out your wounds, your death-warrant tracing.
And the merciful men, their religion enhancing,
Stopped the red reaper, to give you a chance.
Then you died on the prairie, and scorned all disgraces,
O broncho that would not be broken of dancing.

THE EAGLE THAT IS FORGOTTEN

John P. Altgeld. Born December 30, 1847; died March 12, 1902.

Sleep softly . . . eagle forgotten . . . under the stone.
Time has its way with you there, and the clay has its own.

"We have buried him now," thought your foes, and in secret rejoiced.
They made a brave show of their mourning, their hatred unvoiced.
They had snarled at you, barked at you, foamed at you day after day.
Now you were ended. They praised you, . . . and laid you away.

The others that mourned you in silence and terror and truth,
The widow bereft of her crust, and the boy without youth,
The mocked and the scorned and the wounded, the lame and the poor
That should have remembered forever, . . . remember no more.

Where are those lovers of yours, on what name do they call
The lost, that in armies wept over your funeral pall?
They call on the names of a hundred high-valiant ones;
A hundred white eagles have risen the sons of your sons;
The zeal in their wings is a zeal that your dreaming began,
The valor that wore out your soul in the service of man.

Sleep softly, . . . eagle forgotten, . . . under the stone,
Time has its way with you there, and the clay has its own.
Sleep on, O brave-hearted, O wise man, that kindled the flame—
To live in mankind is far more than to live in a name,
To live in mankind, far, far more . . . than to live in a name.

GENERAL WILLIAM BOOTH ENTERS INTO HEAVEN

(To be sung to the tune of "The Blood of the Lamb" with indicated instrument.)

I

(Bass drum beaten loudly.)

Booth led boldly with his big bass drum—
(Are you washed in the blood of the Lamb?)
The Saints smiled gravely and they said: "He's come."
(Are you washed in the blood of the Lamb?)
Walking lepers followed, rank on rank,
Lurching bravos from the ditches dank,
Drabs from the alleyways and drug fiends pale—
Minds still passion-ridden, soul-powers frail:—
Vermin-eaten saints with moldy breath,
Unwashed legions with the ways of Death—
(Are you washed in the blood of the Lamb?)

(Banjos.)

Every slum had sent its half-a-score
The round world over. (Booth had groaned for more.)
Every banner that the wide world flies
Bloomed with glory and transcendent dyes.
Big-voiced lasses made their banjos bang;
Tranced, fanatical they shrieked and sang:—
"Are you washed in the blood of the Lamb?"
Hallelujah! It was queer to see
Bull-necked convicts with that land make free.

Loons with trumpets blowed a blare, blare, blare
On, on upward thro' the golden air!
(Are you washed in the blood of the Lamb?)

II

(Bass drum slower and softer.)
Booth died blind and still by faith he trod,
Eyes still dazzled by the ways of God.
Booth led boldly, and he looked the chief,
Eagle countenance in sharp relief,
Beard a-flying, air of high command
Unabated in that holy land.

(Sweet flute music.)
Jesus came from out the court-house door,
Stretched his hands above the passing poor.
Booth saw not, but led his queer ones there
Round and round the mighty court-house square.
Then, in an instant all that blear review
Marched on spotless, clad in raiment new.
The lame were straightened, withered limbs uncurled
And blind eyes opened on a new, sweet world.

(Bass drum louder.)
Drabs and vixens in a flash made whole!
Gone was the weasel-head, the snout, the jowl!
Sages and sibyls now, and athletes clean,
Rulers of empires, and of forests green!

(Grand chorus of all instruments. Tambourines to the foreground.)
The hosts were sandalled, and their wings were fire!
(Are you washed in the blood of the Lamb?)
But their noise played havoc with the angel-choir.
(Are you washed in the blood of the Lamb?)
Oh, shout Salvation! It was good to see
Kings and Princes by the Lamb set free.
The banjos rattled and the tambourines
Jing-jing-jingled in the hands of Queens.

(*Reverently sung, no instruments.*)
And when Booth halted by the curb for prayer
He saw his Master thro' the flag-filled air.
Christ came gently with a robe and crown
For Booth the soldier, while the throng knelt down.
He saw King Jesus. They were face to face,
And he knelt a-weeping in that holy place.
Are you washed in the blood of the Lamb?

DANIEL

Beginning with a strain of "Dixie."

Darius the Mede was a king and a wonder.
His eye was proud, and his voice was thunder.
He kept bad lions in a monstrous den.
He fed up the lions on Christian men.

With a touch of "Alexander's Ragtime Band."

Daniel was the chief hired man of the land.
He stirred up the music in the palace band.
He whitewashed the cellar. He shovelled in the coal.
And Daniel kept a-praying:—"Lord save my soul."
Daniel kept a-praying:—"Lord save my soul."
Daniel kept a-praying:—"Lord save my soul."

Daniel was the butler, swagger and swell.
He ran up stairs. He answered the bell.
And *he* would let in whoever came a-calling:—
Saints so holy, scamps so appalling.
"Old man Ahab leaves his card.
Elisha and the bears are a-waiting in the yard.
Here comes Pharaoh and his snakes a-calling.
Here comes Cain and his wife a-calling.
Shadrach, Meshach and Abednego for tea.
Here comes Jonah and the whale,
And the *Sea!*
Here comes St. Peter and his fishing pole.
Here comes Judas and his silver a-calling.
Here comes old Beelzebub a-calling."

And Daniel kept a-praying:—"Lord save my soul."
Daniel kept a-praying:—"Lord save my soul."
Daniel kept a-praying:—"Lord save my soul."

His sweetheart and his mother were Christian and meek.
They washed and ironed for Darius every week.
One Thursday he met them at the door:—
Paid them as usual, but acted sore.

He said:—"Your Daniel is a dead little pigeon.
He's a good hard worker, but he talks religion."
And he showed them Daniel in the lions' cage.
Daniel standing quietly, the lions in a rage.
His good old mother cried:—
"Lord save him."
And Daniel's tender sweetheart cried:—
"Lord save him."

And she was a golden lily in the dew.
And she was as sweet as an apple on the tree,
And she was as fine as a melon in the corn-field,
Gliding and lovely as a ship on the sea,
Gliding and lovely as a ship on the sea.

This to be repeated three times, very softly and slowly.

And she prayed to the Lord:—
"Send Gabriel. Send Gabriel."

King Darius said to the lions:—
"Bite Daniel. Bite Daniel.
Bite him. Bite him. Bite him!"

Thus roared the lions:—
"We want Daniel, Daniel, Daniel,
We want Daniel, Daniel, Daniel."

Here the audience roars with the leader.

And Daniel did not frown,
Daniel did not cry.
He kept on looking at the sky.
And the Lord said to Gabriel:—

"Go chain the lions down.
Go chain the lions down.
Go chain the lions down.
Go chain the lions down."

The audience sings this with the leader, to the old negro tune.

And *Gabriel* chained the lions,
And *Gabriel* chained the lions,
And *Gabriel* chained the lions,
And Daniel got out of the den,
And Daniel got out of the den,
And Daniel got out of the den.
And Darius said:—"You're a Christian child,"
Darius said:—"You're a Christian child,"
Darius said:—"You're a Christian child,"
And gave him his job again,
And gave him his job again,
And gave him his job again.

THE CONGO

A STUDY OF THE NEGRO RACE

I. THEIR BASIC SAVAGERY

Fat black bucks in a wine-barrel room,
Barrel-house kings, with feet unstable,
Sagged and reeled and pounded on the table,
Pounded on the table,

A deep rolling bass.

Beat an empty barrel with the handle of a broom,
Hard as they were able,
Boom, boom, BOOM.
With a silk umbrella and the handle of a broom,
Boomlay, boomlay, boomlay, BOOM.
THEN I had religion, THEN I had a vision.
I could not turn from their revel in derision.
THEN I SAW THE CONGO, CREEPING THROUGH THE BLACK,
CUTTING THROUGH THE FOREST WITH A GOLDEN TRACK.

More deliberate. Solemnly chanted.

Then along that riverbank
A thousand miles
Tattooed cannibals danced in files;
Then I heard the boom of the blood-lust song
And a thigh-bone beating on a tin-pan gong.
And "BLOOD" screamed the whistles and the fifes
of the warriors,
"BLOOD" screamed the skull-faced, lean witch-
doctors,
"Whirl ye the deadly voo-doo rattle,
Harry the uplands,
Steal all the cattle,
Rattle-rattle, rattle-rattle,
Bing.
Boomlay, boomlay, boomlay, BOOM,"
A roaring, epic, rag-time tune
From the mouth of the Congo
To the Mountains of the Moon.
Death is an Elephant,
Torch-eyed and horrible,
Foam-flanked and terrible.
BOOM, steal the pygmies,
BOOM, kill the Arabs,
BOOM, kill the white men,
HOO, HOO, HOO.
Listen to the yell of Leopold's ghost
Burning in Hell for his hand-maimed host.
Hear how the demons chuckle and yell
Cutting his hands off, down in Hell.
Listen to the creepy proclamation,
Blown through the lairs of the forest-nation,
Blown past the white-ants' hill of clay,
Blown past the marsh where the butterflies play:
"Be careful what you do,
Or Mumbo-Jumbo, God of the Congo,
And all of the other
Gods of the Congo,
Mumbo-Jumbo will hoo-doo you,
Mumbo-Jumbo will hoo-doo you,
Mumbo-Jumbo will hoo-doo you."

A rapidly piling climax of speed and racket.

With a philosophic pause.

Shrilly and with a heavily accented metre.

Like the wind in the chimney.

All the "o" sounds very golden. Heavy accents very heavy. Light accents very light. Last line whispered.

II. THEIR IRREPRESSIBLE HIGH SPIRITS

Wild crap-shooters with a whoop and a call
Danced the juba in their gambling hall
And laughed fit to kill, and shook the town,
And guyed the policemen and laughed them down
With a boomlay, boomlay, boomlay, BOOM.
THEN I SAW THE CONGO, CREEPING
THROUGH THE BLACK,
CUTTING THROUGH THE FOREST WITH
A GOLDEN TRACK.
A negro fairyland swung into view,
A minstrel river
Where dreams come true.
The ebony palace soared on high
Through the blossoming trees to the evening sky.
The inlaid porches and casements shone
With gold and ivory and elephant-bone.
And the black crowd laughed till their sides were sore
At the baboon butler in the agate door,
And the well-known tunes of the parrot band
That trilled on the bushes of that magic land.

Rather shrill and high.

Read exactly as in first section.

Lay emphasis on the delicate ideas. Keep as light-footed as possible.

A troupe of skull-faced witch-men came
Through the agate doorway in suits of flame,
Yea, long-tailed coats with a gold-leaf crust
And hats that were covered with diamond-dust.
And the crowd in the court gave a whoop and a call
And danced the juba from wall to wall.
But the witch-men suddenly stilled the throng
With a stern cold glare, and a stern old song:—
"Mumbo-Jumbo will hoo-doo you." . . .
Just then from the doorway, as fat as shotes,
Came the cake-walk princes in their long
red coats,
Canes with a brilliant lacquer shine,
And tall silk hats that were red as wine.
And they pranced with their butterfly part-
ners there,

With pomposity.

With a great deliberation and ghostliness.

With overwhelming assurance, good cheer, and pomp.

Coal-black maidens with pearls in their hair,
Knee-skirts trimmed with the jassamine sweet,
And bells on their ankles and little black feet.
And the couples railed at the chant and the frown
Of the witch-men lean, and laughed them down.
(Oh, rare was the revel, and well worth while
That made those glowering witch-men smile.)

With growing speed and sharply marked dance-rhythm.

The cake-walk royalty then began
To walk for a cake that was tall as a man
To the tune of "Boomlay, boomlay, BOOM,"
While the witch-men laughed, with a sinister air,
And sang with the scalawags prancing there:—
"Walk with care, walk with care,
Or Mumbo-Jumbo, God of the Congo,
And all of the other Gods of the Congo,
Mumbo-Jumbo will hoo-doo you.
Beware, beware, walk with care,
Boomlay, boomlay, boomlay, boom.
Boomlay, boomlay, boomlay, boom.
Boomlay, boomlay, boomlay, boom.
Boomlay, boomlay, boomlay,
BOOM."

With a touch of negro dialect, and as rapidly as possible toward the end.

(Oh, rare was the revel, and well worth while
That made those glowering witch-men smile.)

Slow philosophic calm.

III. THE HOPE OF THEIR RELIGION

A good old negro in the slums of the town
Preached at a sister for her velvet gown.
Howled at a brother for his low-down ways,
His prowling, guzzling, sneak-thief days.
Beat on the Bible till he wore it out
Starting the jubilee revival shout.
And some had visions, as they stood on chairs,
And sang of Jacob, and the golden stairs,
And they all repented, a thousand strong,
From their stupor and savagery and sin and wrong,

Heavy bass. With a literal imitation of camp-meeting racket, and trance.

And slammed with their hymn books till they
 shook the room
With "Glory, glory, glory,"
And "Boom, boom, BOOM."
THEN I SAW THE CONGO, CREEPING
 THROUGH THE BLACK,
CUTTING THROUGH THE JUNGLE WITH
 A GOLDEN TRACK.
And the gray sky opened like a new-rent veil
And showed the Apostles with their coats of
 mail.
In bright white steel they were seated round
And their fire-eyes watched where the Congo
 wound.
And the twelve Apostles, from their thrones on
 high,
Thrilled all the forest with their heavenly cry:—
"Mumbo-Jumbo will die in the jungle;
Never again will he hoo-doo you,
Never again will he hoo-doo you."

Exactly as in the first section. Begin with terror and power, end with joy.

Sung to the tune of "Hark, ten thousand harps and voices."

Then along that river, a thousand miles,
The vine-snared trees fell down in files.
Pioneer angels cleared the way
For a Congo paradise, for babes at play,
For sacred capitals, for temples clean.
Gone were the skull-faced witch-men lean.
There, where the wild ghost-gods had wailed
A million boats of the angels sailed
With oars of silver, and prows of blue
And silken pennants that the sun shone through.
'Twas a land transfigured, 'twas a new creation.
Oh, a singing wind swept the negro nation
And on through the backwoods clearing flew:—
"Mumbo-Jumbo is dead in the jungle.
Never again will he hoo-doo you.
Never again will he hoo-doo you."

With growing deliberation and joy.

In a rather high key—as delicately as possible.

To the tune of "Hark, ten thousand harps and voices."

Redeemed were the forests, the beasts and the men,
And only the vulture dared again

By the far, lone mountains of the moon
To cry, in the silence, the Congo tune:—
Mumbo-Jumbo will hoo-doo you,
"Mumbo-Jumbo will hoo-doo you.
Mumbo . . . Jumbo . . . will . . . hoo-doo
. . . you."

Dying down into a penetrating, terrified whisper.

WHEN THE MISSISSIPPI FLOWED IN INDIANA

Inscribed to Bruce Campbell, who read "Tom Sawyer" with me in the old house.

Beneath Time's roaring cannon
Many walls fall down.
But though the guns break every stone,
Level every town:—
Within our Grandma's old front hall
Some wonders flourish yet:—
The Pavement of Verona,
Where stands young Juliet;
The roof of Blue-beard's palace,
And Kubla Khan's wild ground;
The cave of young Aladdin,
Where the jewel-flowers were found;
And the garden of old Sparta
Where little Helen played;
The grotto of Miranda
That Prospero arrayed;
And the cave, by the Mississippi,
Where Becky Thatcher strayed.

On that Indiana stairway
Gleams Cinderella's shoe.
Upon that mighty mountainside
Walks Snow-white in the dew.
Upon that grassy hillside
Trips shining Nicolette:—
That stairway of remembrance
Time's cannon will not get—
That chattering slope of glory
Our little cousins made,
That hill by the Mississippi

Where Becky Thatcher strayed.

Spring beauties on that cliffside,
Love in the air,
While the soul's deep Mississippi
Sweeps on, forever fair.
And he who enters in the cave,
Nothing shall make afraid,
The cave by the Mississippi
Where Tom and Becky strayed.

THE MOUSE THAT GNAWED THE OAK-TREE DOWN

The mouse that gnawed the oak-tree down
Began his task in early life.
He kept so busy with his teeth
He had no time to take a wife.

He gnawed and gnawed through sun and rain
When the ambitious fit was on,
Then rested in the sawdust till
A month of idleness had gone.

He did not move about to hunt
The coteries of mousie-men.
He was a snail-paced, stupid thing
Until he cared to gnaw again.

The mouse that gnawed the oak-tree down,
When that tough foe was at his feet—
Found in the stump no angel-cake
Nor buttered bread, nor cheese nor meat—

The forest-roof let in the sky.
"This light is worth the work," said he.
"I'll make this ancient swamp more light,"
And started on another tree.

MY LADY IS COMPARED TO A YOUNG TREE

When I see a young tree
In its white beginning,
With white leaves
And white buds
Barely tipped with green,
In the April weather,
In the weeping sunshine—
Then I see my lady,
My democratic queen,
Standing free and equal
With the youngest woodland sapling
Swaying, singing in the wind,
Delicate and white:
Soul so near to blossom,
Fragile, strong as death;
A kiss from far-off Eden,
A flash of Judgment's trumpet—
April's breath.

PROLOGUE TO "RHYMES TO BE TRADED FOR BREAD"

Even the shrewd and bitter,
Gnarled by the old world's greed,
Cherished the stranger softly
Seeing his utter need.
Shelter and patient hearing,
These were their gifts to him,
To the minstrel chanting, begging,
As the sunset-fire grew dim.
The rich said, "You are welcome."
Yea, even the rich were good.
How strange that in their feasting
His songs were understood!
The doors of the poor were open,

The poor who had wandered too,
Who slept with never a roof-tree
Under the wind and dew.
The minds of the poor were open,
There dark mistrust was dead:
They loved his wizard stories,
They bought his rhymes with bread.

Those were his days of glory,
Of faith in his fellow-men.
Therefore, to-day the singer
Turns beggar once again.

I HEARD IMMANUEL SINGING

The poem shows the Master with his work done, singing to free his heart in Heaven.

This poem is intended to be half said, half sung, very softly, to the well-known tune:..

"Last night I lay a-sleeping,
There came a dream so fair,
I stood in Old Jerusalem
Beside the temple there,"— etc.

Yet this tune is not to be fitted on, arbitrarily. It is here given to suggest the manner of handling rather than determine it.

I heard Immanuel singing *To be sung.*
Within his own good lands;
I saw him bend above his harp.
I watched his wandering hands
Lost amid the harp-strings;
Sweet, sweet I heard him play.
His wounds were altogether healed.
Old things had passed away.

All things were new, but music.
The blood of David ran
Within the Son of David,

Our God, the Son of Man.
He was ruddy like a shepherd.
His bold young face, how fair.
Apollo of the silver bow
Had not such flowing hair.

I saw Immanuel singing
On a tree-girdled hill.
The glad remembering branches
Dimly echoed still
The grand new song proclaiming
The Lamb that had been slain.
New-built, the Holy City
Gleamed in the murmuring plain.

To be read very softly, but in spirited response.

The crowning hours were over.
The pageants all were past.
Within the many mansions
The hosts, grown still at last,
In homes of holy mystery
Slept long by crooning springs
Or waked to peaceful glory,
A universe of Kings.

He left his people happy.
He wandered free to sigh
Alone in lowly friendship
With the green grass and the sky.
He murmured ancient music
His red heart burned to sing
Because his perfect conquest
Had grown a weary thing.

To be sung.

No chant of gilded triumph—
His lonely song was made
Of Art's deliberate freedom;
Of minor chords arrayed
In soft and shadowy colors
That once were radiant flowers:—
The Rose of Sharon, bleeding
In Olive-shadowed bowers:—

And all the other roses
In the songs of East and West
Of love and war and worshipping,
And every shield and crest
Of thistle or of lotus
Or sacred lily wrought
In creeds and psalms and palaces
And temples of white thought:—

All these he sang, half-smiling
And weeping as he smiled,
Laughing, talking to his harp
As to a new-born child:—
As though the arts forgotten
But bloomed to prophecy
These careless, fearless harp-strings,
New-crying in the sky.

To be read very softly, yet in spirited response.

"When this his hour of sorrow
For flowers and Arts of men
Has passed in ghostly music,"
I asked my wild heart then—
What will he sing to-morrow,
What wonder, all his own
Alone, set free, rejoicing
With a green hill for his throne?
What will he sing to-morrow,
What wonder all his own
Alone, set free, rejoicing,
With a green hill for his throne?

To be sung.

THE UNPARDONABLE SIN

This is the sin against the Holy Ghost:—
To speak of bloody power as right divine,
And call on God to guard each vile chief's house,
And for such chiefs, turn men to wolves and swine:—

To go forth killing in White Mercy's name,
Making the trenches stink with spattered brains,
Tearing the nerves and arteries apart,
Sowing with flesh the unreaped golden plains.

In any Church's name, to sack fair towns,
And turn each home into a screaming sty,
To make the little children fugitive,
And have their mothers for a quick death cry,—

This is the sin against the Holy Ghost:
This is the sin no purging can atone:—
To send forth rapine in the name of Christ:—
To set the face, and make the heart a stone.

THE COMET OF GOING-TO-THE-SUN

On the mountain peak, called "Going-To-The-Sun,"
A comet stopped to drink from a cool spring
And like a spirit-harp began to sing
To us, then hurried on to reach the sun.
We called him "Homer's soul," and "Milton's wing."
The harp-sound stayed, though he went up and on.
It turned to thunder, when he had quite gone—
And yet was like a soft voice of the sea,
And every whispering root and every blade of grass
And every tree
In the whole world, and brought thoughts of old songs
That blind men sang ten thousand years ago,
And all the springtime hearts of every nation know.

RAIN

Each storm-soaked flower has a beautiful eye.
And this is the voice of the stone-cold sky:
"Only boys keep their cheeks dry.
Only boys are afraid to cry.
Men thank God for tears,
Alone with the memory of their dead,
Alone with lost years."

NANCY HANKS, MOTHER OF ABRAHAM LINCOLN

Out of the eater came forth meat; and out of the strong came forth sweetness.

Judges 14: 14.

A sweet girl graduate, lean as a fawn,
The very whimsy of time,
Read her class poem Commencement Day—
A trembling filigree rhyme.

The pansy that blooms on the window sill,
Blooms in exactly the proper place;
And she nodded just like a pansy there,
And her poem was all about bowers and showers,
Sugary streamlet and mossy rill,
All about daisies on dale and hill—
And she was the mother of Buffalo Bill.

Another girl, a cloud-drift sort,
Dreamlit, moonlit, marble-white,
Light-footed saint on the pilgrim shore,
The best since New England fairies began,
Was the mother of Barnum, the circus man.

A girl from Missouri, snippy and vain,
As frothy a miss as any you know,
A wren, a toy, a pink silk bow,
The belle of the choir, she drove insane
Missouri deacons and all the sleek,
Her utter tomfoolery made men weak,
Till they could not stand and they could not speak.
Oh, queen of fifteen and sixteen,
Missouri sweetened beneath her reign—
And she was the mother of bad Mark Twain.

Not always are lions born of lions,
Roosevelt sprang from a palace of lace;
On the other hand is the dizzy truth:
Not always is beauty born of beauty.

Some treasures wait in a hidden place.
All over the world were thousands of belles.
In far-off eighteen hundred and nine,
Girls of fifteen, girls of twenty,
Their mammas dressed them up a-plenty—
Each garter was bright, each stocking fine,
But for all their innocent devices,
Their cheeks of fruit and their eyes of wine,
And each voluptuous design,
And all soft glories that we trace
In Europe's palaces of lace,
A girl who slept in dust and sorrow,
Nancy Hanks, in a lost log cabin,
Nancy Hanks had the loveliest face!

THE GAMBLERS

Life's a jail where men have common lot.
Gaunt the one who has, and who has not.
All our treasures neither less nor more,
Bread alone comes through the guarded door.
Cards are foolish in this jail, I think,
Yet they play for shoes, for drabs and drink.
She, my lawless, sharp-tongued gypsy maid,
Will not scorn with me this jail-bird trade,
Pets some fox-eyed boy who turns the trick,
Though he win a button or a stick,
Pencil, garter, ribbon, corset-lace—
His the glory, *mine* is the disgrace.

Sweet, I'd rather lose than win despite
Love of hearty words and maids polite.
"Love's a gamble," say you. I deny.
Love's a gift. I love you till I die.
Gamblers fight like rats. I will not play.
All I ever had I gave away.
All I ever coveted was peace
Such as comes if we have jail release.

Cards are puzzles, though the prize be gold;
Cards help not the bread that tastes of mold;
Cards dye not your hair to black more deep;
Cards make not the children cease to weep.

Scorned, I sit with half-shut eyes all day—
Watch the cataract of sunshine play
Down the wall, and dance upon the floor.
Sun, come down and break the dungeon door!
Of such gold dust could I make a key,—
Turn the bolt—how soon we would be free!
Over borders we would hurry on
Safe by sunrise farms, and springs of dawn,
Wash our wounds and jail stains there at last,
Azure rivers flowing, flowing past.
God has great estates just past the line,
Green farms for all, and meat and corn and wine.

SARA TEASDALE

Sara Teasdale, the youngest child of John Warren and Mary Elizabeth Willard Teasdale, was born at St. Louis, Missouri, on August 8, 1884. She came of an old and distinguished American family, one ancestor, Major Simon Willard, being the founder of Concord, Massachusetts. Her ancestors on both sides fought in the Revolutionary War, and both emigrated west about the middle of the nineteenth century. Her maternal grandfather owned steamboats on the Mississippi River; her paternal grandfather was a Baptist minister.

As a child she was not strong; consequently she received her earliest education at home. Later, however, she attended Hosmer Hall, a private school for girls, from which she graduated in 1903. Ill health prevented her from carrying her formal education farther, but by a habit of wide reading, which she had formed in childhood, she continued her mental growth. In 1905 she went to Europe, and remained for some time in Egypt, Palestine, and Greece. In 1912 she spent a summer in Italy and Switzerland in company with the poet Jessie B. Rittenhouse. She also traveled a great deal in the United States, spending several winters in California and Arizona. On December 19, 1914, she married Ernst B. Filsinger, of St. Louis, an authority on international trade, and author of books on South American commerce. Since 1916 they have lived in New York City, but Mrs. Filsinger spends much of her time in Europe and in the Southwest.

Her interest in poetry began early, being first aroused by the reading of Christina Rossetti. While at school she made translations in verse from Heine and other German poets. After graduation she continued writing, and with some of her friends issued a monthly magazine, *The Potter's Wheel,* which was limited to one copy a month, and was in manuscript. In it from time to time her early work appeared. Her first recognition came in 1907 with the acceptance by *Reedy's Mirror* of her poem *Guenevere.* In the same year she published her first volume, *Sonnets to Duse and Other Poems.* Since then she has written five volumes of poetry, and has edited two collections, *The Answering Voice* (1917), which contains a hundred love lyrics by women, and *Rainbow Gold* (1922), a book of poems for children.

In 1916 her group of poems, *Songs out of Sorrow,* won the prize offered by the Poetry Society of America; and in 1918 she was awarded the Columbia University Poetry Prize of five hundred dollars for the best book of poetry produced by an American in 1917.

THE WAYFARER

Love entered in my heart one day,
  A sad, unwelcome guest;
But when he begged that he might stay,
  I let him wait and rest.

He broke my sleep with sorrowing,
  And shook my dreams with tears,
And when my heart was fain to sing,
  He stilled its joy with fears.

But now that he has gone his way,
  I miss the old sweet pain,
And sometimes in the night I pray
  That he may come again.

THE METROPOLITAN TOWER

We walked together in the dusk
  To watch the tower grow dimly white,
And saw it lift against the sky
  Its flower of amber light.

You talked of half a hundred things,
  I kept each hurried word you said;
And when at last the hour was full,
  I saw the light turn red.

You did not know the time had come,
  You did not see the sudden flower,
Nor know that in my heart Love's birth
  Was reckoned from that hour.

THE KISS

I hoped that he would love me,
   And he has kissed my mouth,
But I am like a stricken bird
   That cannot reach the south.

For though I know he loves me,
   To-night my heart is sad;
His kiss was not so wonderful
   As all the dreams I had.

CENTRAL PARK AT DUSK

Buildings above the leafless trees
   Loom high as castles in a dream,
While one by one the lamps come out
   To thread the twilight with a gleam.

There is no sign of leaf or bud,
   A hush is over everything—
Silent as women wait for love,
   The world is waiting for the spring.

THE PRAYER

My answered prayer came up to me,
And in the silence thus spake he:
"O you who prayed for me to come,
Your greeting is but cold and dumb."

My heart made answer: "You are fair,
But I have prayed too long to care.
Why came you not when all was new,
And I had died for joy of you."

SPRING NIGHT

The park is filled with night and fog,
The veils are drawn about the world,
The drowsy lights along the paths
Are dim and pearled.

Gold and gleaming the empty streets,
Gold and gleaming the misty lake,
The mirrored lights like sunken swords,
Glimmer and shake.

Oh, is it not enough to be
Here with this beauty over me?
My throat should ache with praise, and I
Should kneel in joy beneath the sky.
Oh, beauty are you not enough?
Why am I crying after love
With youth, a singing voice and eyes,
To take earth's wonder with surprise?
Why have I put off my pride,
Why am I unsatisfied,
I for whom the pensive night
Binds her cloudy hair with light,
I for whom all beauty burns
Like incense in a million urns?
Oh, beauty, are you not enough?
Why am I crying after love?

LONGING

I am not sorry for my soul
That it must go unsatisfied,
For it can live a thousand times;
Eternity is deep and wide.

I am not sorry for my soul,
But oh, my body that must go
Back to a little drift of dust
Without the joy it longed to know.

THE POOR HOUSE

Hope went by and Peace went by
And would not enter in;
Youth went by and Health went by
And Love that is their kin.

Those within the house shed tears
On their bitter bread;
Some were old and some were mad,
And some were sick a-bed.

Gray Death saw the wretched house
And even he passed by—
"They have never lived," he said,
"They can wait to die."

THE INN OF EARTH

I came to the crowded Inn of Earth,
And called for a cup of wine,
But the Host went by with averted eye
From a thirst as keen as mine.

Then I sat down with weariness
And asked a bit of bread,
But the Host went by with averted eye
And never a word he said.

While always from the outer night
The waiting souls came in
With stifled cries of sharp surprise
At all the light and din.

"Then give me a bed to sleep," I said,
"For midnight comes apace"—
But the Host went by with averted eye
And I never saw his face.

"Since there is neither food nor rest,
I go where I fared before"—
But the Host went by with averted eye
And barred the outer door.

THOUGHTS

When I can make my thoughts come forth
To walk like ladies up and down,
Each one puts on before the glass
Her most becoming hat and gown.

But oh, the shy and eager thoughts
That hide and will not get them dressed,
Why is it that they always seem
So much more lovely than the rest?

"I AM NOT YOURS"

I am not yours, not lost in you,
Not lost, although I long to be
Lost as a candle lit at noon,
Lost as a snow-flake in the sea.

You love me, and I find you still
A spirit beautiful and bright,
Yet I am I, who long to be
Lost as a light is lost in light.

Oh, plunge me deep in love—put out
My senses, leave me deaf and blind,
Swept by the tempest of your love,
A taper in a rushing wind.

TO E.

I have remembered beauty in the night;
Against black silences I waked to see
A shower of sunlight over Italy
And green Ravello dreaming on her height;

I have remembered music in the dark,
  The clean swift brightness of a fugue of Bach's,
  And running water singing on the rocks
When once in English woods I heard a lark.

But all remembered beauty is no more
  Than a vague prelude to the thought of you—
  You are the rarest soul I ever knew,
    Lover of beauty, knightliest and best;
My thoughts seek you as waves that seek the shore,
    And when I think of you, I am at rest.

BARTER

Life has loveliness to sell,
  All beautiful and splendid things,
Blue waves whitened on a cliff,
  Soaring fire that sways and sings,
And children's faces looking up,
Holding wonder like a cup.

Life has loveliness to sell,
  Music like a curve of gold,
Scent of pine trees in the rain,
  Eyes that love you, arms that hold,
And for your spirit's still delight,
Holy thoughts that star the night.

Spend all you have for loveliness,
  Buy it and never count the cost;
For one white singing hour of peace
  Count many a year of strife well lost,
And for a breath of ecstasy
Give all you have been, or could be.

NIGHT SONG AT AMALFI

I asked the heaven of stars
  What I should give my love—
It answered me with silence,
  Silence above.

I asked the darkened sea
Down where the fishers go—
It answered me with silence,
Silence below.

Oh, I could give him weeping,
Or I could give him song—
But how can I give silence,
My whole life long?

THE LOOK

Strephon kissed me in the spring,
Robin in the fall,
But Colin only looked at me
And never kissed at all.

Strephon's kiss was lost in jest,
Robin's lost in play,
But the kiss in Colin's eyes
Haunts me night and day.

GIFTS

I gave my first love laughter,
I gave my second tears,
I gave my third love silence
Through all the years.

My first love gave me singing,
My second eyes to see,
But oh, it was my third love
Who gave my soul to me.

SONG AT CAPRI

When beauty grows too great to bear
How shall I ease me of its ache,
For beauty more than bitterness
Makes the heart break.

Now while I watch the dreaming sea
With isles like flowers against her breast,
Only one voice in all the world
Could give me rest.

PIERROT

Pierrot stands in the garden
Beneath a waning moon,
And on his lute he fashions
A fragile silver tune.

Pierrot plays in the garden,
He thinks he plays for me,
But I am quite forgotten
Under the cherry tree.

Pierrot plays in the garden,
And all the roses know
That Pierrot loves his music,—
But I love Pierrot.

THE SONG FOR COLIN

I sang a song at dusking time
Beneath the evening star,
And Terence left his latest rhyme
To answer from afar.

Pierrot laid down his lute to weep,
And sighed, "She sings for me."
But Colin slept a careless sleep
Beneath an apple tree.

FAULTS

They came to tell your faults to me,
They named them over one by one;
I laughed aloud when they were done,
I knew them all so well before;—
Oh, they were blind, too blind to see
Your faults had made me love you more.

I SHALL NOT CARE

When I am dead and over me bright April
  Shakes out her rain-drenched hair,
Though you should lean above me broken-hearted,
  I shall not care.

I shall have peace, as leafy trees are peaceful
  When rain bends down the bough,
And I shall be more silent and cold-hearted
  Than you are now.

BURIED LOVE

I have come to bury Love
  Beneath a tree,
In the forest tall and black
  Where none can see.

I shall put no flowers at his head,
  Nor stone at his feet,
For the mouth I loved so much
  Was bittersweet.

I shall go no more to his grave,
  For the woods are cold.
I shall gather as much of joy
  As my hands can hold.

I shall stay all day in the sun
  Where the wide winds blow,—
But oh, I shall cry at night
  When none will know.

MASTERY

I would not have a god come in
To shield me suddenly from sin,
And set my house of life to rights;
Nor angels with bright burning wings
Ordering my earthly thoughts and things;
Rather my own frail guttering lights
Wind blown and nearly beaten out;
Rather the terror of the nights
And long, sick groping after doubt;
Rather be lost than let my soul
Slip vaguely from my own control—
Of my own spirit let me be
In sole though feeble mastery.

BECAUSE

Oh, because you never tried
To bow my will or break my pride,
And nothing of the cave-man made
You want to keep me half afraid,
Nor ever with a conquering air
You thought to draw me unaware—
Take me, for I love you more
Than I ever loved before.

And since the body's maidenhood
Alone were neither rare nor good
Unless with it I gave to you
A spirit still untrammeled, too,
Take my dreams and take my mind
That were masterless as wind;
And "Master!" I shall say to you
Since you never asked me to.

COME

Come, when the pale moon like a petal
  Floats in the pearly dusk of spring,
Come with arms outstretched to take me,
  Come with lips pursed up to cling.

Come, for life is a frail moth flying,
  Caught in the web of the years that pass,
And soon we two, so warm and eager,
  Will be as the gray stones in the grass.

DOUBT

My soul lives in my body's house,
  And you have both the house and her—
But sometimes she is less your own
  Than a wild, gay adventurer;
A restless and an eager wraith,
  How can I tell what she will do—
Oh, I am sure of my body's faith,
  But what if my soul broke faith with you?

THE LAMP

If I can bear your love like a lamp before me,
When I go down the long steep Road of Darkness,
I shall not fear the everlasting shadows,
    Nor cry in terror.

If I can find out God, then I shall find Him;
If none can find Him, then I shall sleep soundly,
Knowing how well on earth your love sufficed me,
    A lamp in darkness.

BLUE SQUILLS

How many million Aprils came
  Before I ever knew
How white a cherry bough could be,
  A bed of squills, how blue!

And many a dancing April
  When life is done with me,
Will lift the blue flame of the flower
  And the white flame of the tree.

Oh, burn me with your beauty, then,
  Oh, hurt me, tree and flower,
Lest in the end death try to take
  Even this glistening hour.

O shaken flowers, O shimmering trees,
  O sunlit white and blue,
Wound me, that I, through endless sleep,
  May bear the scar of you.

"I HAVE LOVED HOURS AT SEA"

I have loved hours at sea, gray cities,
  The fragile secret of a flower,
Music, the making of a poem
  That gave me heaven for an hour;

First stars above a snowy hill,
  Voices of people kindly and wise,
And the great look of love, long hidden,
  Found at last in meeting eyes.

I have loved much and been loved deeply—
  Oh, when my spirit's fire burns low,
Leave me the darkness and the stillness;
  I shall be tired and glad to go.

THE VOICE

Atoms as old as stars,
Mutation on mutation,
Millions and millions of cells
Dividing, yet still the same,
From air and changing earth,
From ancient Eastern rivers,
From turquoise tropic seas,
Unto myself I came.

My spirit like my flesh
Sprang from a thousand sources,
From cave-man, hunter and shepherd,
From Karnak, Cyprus, Rome;
The living thoughts in me
Spring from dead men and women,
Forgotten time out of mind
And many as bubbles of foam.

Here for a moment's space
Into the light out of darkness,
I come and they come with me,
Finding words with my breath;
From the wisdom of many life-times
I hear them cry: "Forever
Seek for Beauty; she only
Fights with man against Death!"

"THERE WILL COME SOFT RAINS"

(WAR TIME)

There will come soft rains and the smell of the ground,
And swallows circling with their shimmering sound;

And frogs in the pools singing at night,
And wild plum-trees in tremulous white;

Robins will wear their feathery fire
Whistling their whims on a low fence-wire;

And not one will know of the war, not one
Will care at last when it is done.

Not one would mind, neither bird nor tree,
If mankind perished utterly;

And Spring herself, when she woke at dawn,
Would scarcely know that we were gone.

THE UNCHANGING

Sun-swept beaches with a light wind blowing
From the immense blue circle of the sea,
And the soft thunder where long waves whiten—
These were the same for Sappho as for me.

Two thousand years—much has gone by forever;
Change takes the gods and ships and speech of men—
But here on the beaches that time passes over
The heart aches now as then.

IF DEATH IS KIND

Perhaps if Death is kind, and there can be returning,
We will come back to earth some fragrant night,
And take these lanes to find the sea, and bending
Breathe the same honeysuckle, low and white.

We will come down at night to these resounding beaches
And the long gentle thunder of the sea,
Here for a single hour in the wide starlight
We shall be happy, for the dead are free.

THE LONG HILL

I must have passed the crest a while ago
And now I am going down—
Strange to have crossed the crest and not to know,
But the brambles were always catching the hem of my gown.

All the morning I thought how proud I should be
To stand there straight as a queen,
Wrapped in the wind and the sun with the world under me—
But the air was dull; there was little I could have seen.

It was nearly level along the beaten track
And the brambles caught in my gown—
But it's no use now to think of turning back,
The rest of the way will be only going down.

SEPTEMBER DAY

(PONT DE NEUILLY)

The Seine flows out of the mist
And into the mist again;
The trees lean over the water,
The small leaves fall like rain.

The leaves fall patiently;
Nothing remembers or grieves;
The river takes to the sea
The yellow drift of the leaves.

Milky and cold is the air,
The leaves float with the stream,
The river comes out of a sleep
And goes away in a dream.

THE FOUNTAIN

Fountain, fountain, what do you say
  Singing at night alone?
"It is enough to rise and fall
  Here in my basin of stone."

But are you content as you seem to be
So near the freedom and rush of the sea?
  "I have listened all night to its laboring sound,
  It heaves and sags, as the moon runs round;
Ocean and fountain, shadow and tree,
Nothing escapes, nothing is free."

DAY'S ENDING

(TUCSON)

Aloof as aged kings,
Wearing like them the purple,
The mountains ring the mesa
Crowned with a dusky light;
Many a time I watched
That coming-on of darkness
Till stars burned through the heavens
Intolerably bright.

It was not long I lived there,
But I became a woman
Under those vehement stars,
For it was there I heard
For the first time my spirit
Forging an iron rule for me,
As though with slow cold hammers
Beating out word by word:

"Only yourself can heal you;
Only yourself can lead you;
The road is heavy going

And ends where no man knows;
Take love when love is given,
But never think to find it
A sure escape from sorrow
Or a complete repose."

"I HAVE SEEN THE SPRING"

Nothing is new; I have seen the spring too often;
There have been other plum-trees white as this one
Like a silvery cloud tethered beside the road;
I have been waked from sleep too many times
By birds at dawn boasting their love is beautiful.
The grass-blades gleam in the wind; nothing is changed.
Nothing is lost; it is all as it used to be;
Unopened lilacs are still as deep a purple;
The boughs of the elm are dancing still in a veil of tiny
leaves;
Nothing is lost but a few years from my life.

WINTER NIGHT SONG

Will you come as of old with singing,
And shall I hear as of old?
Shall I rush to open the window
In spite of the arrowy cold?

Ah no, my dear, ah no,
I shall sit by the fire reading,
Though you sing half the night in the snow
I shall not be heeding.

Though your voice remembers the forest,
The warm green light and the birds,
Though you gather the sea in your singing
And pour its sound into words,

Even so, my dear, even so,
  I shall not heed you at all;
Though your shoulders are white with snow,
  Though you strain your voice to a call,
I shall drowse and the fire will drowse,
  The draught will be cold on the floor,
The clock running down,
  Snow banking the door.

THE FLIGHT

We are two eagles
Flying together
Under the heavens,
Over the mountains,
Stretched on the wind.
Sunlight heartens us,
Blind snow baffles us,
Clouds wheel after us
Ravelled and thinned.

We are like eagles,
But when Death harries us,
Human and humbled
When one of us goes,
Let the other follow,
Let the flight be ended,
Let the fire blacken,
Let the book close.

EZRA POUND

Ezra Loomis Pound, poet and critic, was born at Hailey, Idaho, October 30, 1885. His parents, Homer Loomis and Isabel Weston Pound, were descendants of early English settlers in New England. His mother was distantly related to Longfellow.

Pound attended Hamilton College, graduating in 1905 with the degree of Ph.B. In the same year he entered the University of Pennsylvania on a fellowship in the romance languages, and received the degree of A.M. in 1906. He then went to Europe in search of further material for a thesis on Lope de Vega, and during 1906-07 traveled in Spain, Italy, and Provence, settling for a while in Venice, and then moving on to London. Here he settled, and for some years occupied himself with translating, lecturing on the arts, writing poetry, and contributing to *The Fortnightly Review, The Dial,* and *Poetry: a Magazine of Verse.* From 1917 to 1919 he was London editor of *The Little Review.*

Pound published his first volume of poetry, *A Lume Spento,* while living in Venice in 1908. Upon going to London, he brought out there in 1909 a second volume, *Personae,* which included most of the poems in his former book. Since then he has written a number of volumes of poetry. It was as a pioneer in the new poetic forms, however, that he became best known in America. Largely through his efforts the Imagists emerged as a group in 1913, and he has constantly written and lectured in the interests of the "new poetry."

In 1914 he married Dorothy Shakespear. For some years Pound has made his home in Paris.

THE TREE

I stood still and was a tree amid the wood,
Knowing the truth of things unseen before;
Of Daphne and the laurel bow
And that god-feasting couple old
That grew elm-oak amid the wold.
'Twas not until the gods had been
Kindly entreated, and been brought within
Unto the hearth of their heart's home
That they might do this wonder thing;
Nathless I have been a tree amid the wood
And many a new thing understood
That was rank folly to my head before.

HISTRION

No man hath dared to write this thing as yet,
And yet I know, how that the souls of all men great
At times pass through us,
And we are melted into them, and are not
Save reflexions of their souls.
Thus am I Dante for a space and am
One François Villon, ballad-lord and thief,
Or am such holy ones I may not write,
Lest blasphemy be writ against my name;
This for an instant and the flame is gone.

'Tis as in midmost us there glows a sphere
Translucent, molten gold, that is the "I,"
And into this some form projects itself:
Christus, or John, or eke the Florentine;
And as the clear space is not if a form's
Imposed thereon,
So cease we from all being for the time,
And these, the Masters of the Soul, live on.

A VIRGINAL

No, no! Go from me. I have left her lately.
I will not spoil my sheath with lesser brightness,
For my surrounding air hath a new lightness;
Slight are her arms, yet they have bound me straitly
And left me cloaked as with a gauze of æther:
As with sweet leaves; as with subtle clearness.
Oh, I have picked up magic in her nearness
To sheathe me half in half the things that sheathe her.
No, no! Go from me. I have still the flavor,
Soft as spring wind that's come from birchen bowers.
Green come the shoots, aye April in the branches,
As winter's wound with her sleight hand she staunches,
Hath of the trees a likeness of the savor:
As white their bark, so white this lady's hours.

BALLAD OF THE GOODLY FERE [1]

Simon Zelotes speaketh it somewhile after the Crucifixion.

Ha' we lost the goodliest fere o' all
For the priests and the gallows tree?
Aye lover he was of brawny men,
O' ships and the open sea.

When they came wi' a host to take Our Man
His smile was good to see;
"First let these go!" quo' our Goodly Fere,
"Or I'll see ye damned," says he.

Aye, he sent us out through the crossed high spears,
And the scorn of his laugh rang free;
"Why took ye not me when I walked about
Alone in the town?" says he.

Oh, we drunk his "Hale" in the good red wine
When we last made company;

[1] Fere = mate, companion.

No capon priest was the Goodly Fere
But a man o' men was he.

I ha' seen him drive a hundred men
Wi' a bundle o' cords swung free,
That they took the high and holy house
For their pawn and treasury.

They'll no' get him a' in a book I think,
Though they write it cunningly;
No mouse of the scrolls was the Goodly Fere
But aye loved the open sea.

If they think they ha' snared our Goodly Fere
They are fools to the last degree.
"I'll go to the feast," quo' our Goodly Fere,
"Though I go to the gallows tree."

"Ye ha' seen me heal the lame and blind,
And wake the dead," says he;
"Ye shall see one thing to master all:
'Tis how a brave man dies on the tree."

A son of God was the Goodly Fere
That bade us his brothers be.
I ha' seen him cow a thousand men.
I have seen him upon the tree.

He cried no cry when they drave the nails
And the blood gushed hot and free;
The hounds of the crimson sky gave tongue
But never a cry cried he.

I ha' seen him cow a thousand men
On the hills o' Galilee;
They whined as he walked out calm between,
Wi' his eyes like the grey o' the sea,

Like the sea that brooks no voyaging
With the winds unleashed and free,
Like the sea that he cowed at Genseret
Wi' twey words spoke' suddently.

A master of men was the Goodly Fere,
A mate of the wind and sea;
If they think they ha' slain our Goodly Fere
They are fools eternally.

I ha' seen him eat o' the honey-comb
Sin' they nailed him to the tree.

AN IMMORALITY

Sing we for love and idleness,
Naught else is worth the having.

Though I have been in many a land,
There is naught else in living.

And I would rather have my sweet,
Though rose-leaves die of grieving,

Than do high deeds in Hungary
To pass all men's believing.

THE EYES

Rest, Master, for we be a-weary, weary
And would feel the fingers of the wind
Upon these lids that lie over us
Sodden and lead-heavy.

Rest, brother, for lo! the dawn is without!
The yellow flame paleth
And the wax runs low.

Free us, for without be goodly colors,
Green of the wood-moss and flower colors,
And coolness beneath the trees.

Free us, for we perish
In this ever-flowing monotony
Of ugly print marks, black
Upon white parchment.

Free us, for there is one
Whose smile more availeth
Than all the age-old knowledge of thy books:
And we would look thereon.

NIGHT LITANY

O Dieu, purifiez nos cœurs!
Purifiez nos cœurs!

Yea, the lines hast thou laid unto me
in pleasant places,
And the beauty of this thy Venice
hast thou shown unto me
Until is its loveliness become unto me
a thing of tears.

O God, what great kindness
have we done in times past
and forgotten it,
That thou givest this wonder unto us,
O God of waters?

O God of the night,
What great sorrow
Cometh unto us,
That thou thus repayest us
Before the time of its coming?

O God of silence,
Purifiez nos cœurs,
Purifiez nos cœurs,
For we have seen
The glory of the shadow of the
likeness of thine handmaid,

Yea, the glory of the shadow
of thy Beauty hath walked
Upon the shadow of the waters
in this thy Venice.
And before the holiness
Of the shadow of thy handmaid
Have I hidden mine eyes,
O God of waters.

O God of silence,
Purifiez nos cœurs,
Purifiez nos cœurs,
O God of waters,
make clean our hearts within us
And our lips to show forth thy praise,
For I have seen the
Shadow of this thy Venice
Floating upon the waters,
And thy stars
Have seen this thing; out of their far courses
Have they seen this thing,
O God of waters;
Even as are thy stars
Silent unto us in their far-coursing,
Even so is mine heart
become silent within me.

Purifiez nos cœurs,
O God of the silence,
Purifiez nos cœurs,
O God of waters.

DANCE FIGURE

For the Marriage in Cana of Galilee.

Dark-eyed,
O woman of my dreams,
Ivory-sandaled,
There is none like thee among the dancers,
None with swift feet.

I have not found thee in the tents,
In the broken darkness.
I have not found thee at the well-head
Among the women with pitchers.

Thine arms are as a young sapling under the bark;
Thy face as a river with lights.

White as an almond are thy shoulders;
As new almonds stripped from the husk.

They guard thee not with eunuchs;
Not with bars of copper.

Gilt, turquoise and silver are in the place of thy rest.
A brown robe, with threads of gold woven in patterns, hast
thou gathered about thee,
O Nathat-Ikanaie, "Tree-at-the-river."

As a rillet among the sedge are thy hands upon me;
Thy fingers a frosted stream.

Thy maidens are white like pebbles;
Their music about thee!

There is none like thee among the dancers;
None with swift feet.

THE STUDY IN ÆSTHETICS

The very small children in patched clothing,
Being smitten with an unusual wisdom,
Stopped in their play as she passed them
And cried up from their cobbles:
Guarda! Ahi, guarda! ch' è be'a!

But three years after this
I heard the young Dante, whose last name I do not know—
For there are, in Sirmione, twenty-eight young Dantes and
thirty-four Catulli;
And there had been a great catch of sardines,

And his elders
Were packing them in the great wooden boxes
For the market in Brescia, and he
Leapt about, snatching at the bright fish
And getting in both of their ways;
And in vain they commanded him to *sta fermo!*
And when they would not let him arrange
The fish in the boxes
He stroked those which were already arranged,
Murmuring for his own satisfaction
This identical phrase:
Ch' è be'a.

And at this I was mildly abashed.

ENVOI (1919)

Go, dumb-born book,
Tell her that sang me once that song of Lawes:
Hadst thou but song
As thou hast subjects known,
Then were there cause in thee that should condone
Even my faults that heavy upon me lie,
And build her glories their longevity.

Tell her that sheds
Such treasure in the air,
Recking naught else but that her graces give
Life to the moment,
I would bid them live
As roses might, in magic amber laid,
Red overwrought with orange and all made
One substance and one color
Braving time.

Tell her that goes
With song upon her lips
But sings not out the song, nor knows
The maker of it, some other mouth

May be as fair as hers,
Might, in new ages, gain her worshippers,
When our two dusts with Waller's shall be laid,
Siftings on siftings in oblivion,
Till change hath broken down
All things save Beauty alone.

JOHN GOULD FLETCHER

John Gould Fletcher was born on January 3, 1886, at Little Rock, Arkansas. His father was Scotch-Irish, and came of pioneer stock, the family having lived in Tennessee from pre-Revolutionary days until the early nineteenth century, when the poet's grandfather moved westward across the Mississippi River. John Gould Fletcher, Sr., enlisted in the Southern army at the beginning of the Civil War, and was made captain after the battle of Chickamauga, serving with distinction until he was wounded at the battle of Murfreesboro. He had little formal education, but possessed excellent business sense, and as cotton buyer and owner of a general store in Little Rock was able to amass considerable wealth. In 1877 he married Adolphine Krause, a talented woman of Danish and German descent, her father having come from Denmark in 1839 and her mother from Hanover in 1835.

When the future poet was four years old, he moved with his parents and two sisters into a large square white house of Colonial design, and this became the background of his childhood. His mother began his training herself, but when he was eight, teachers were employed to instruct him in Latin and German. At eleven he entered school, and at about this age wrote his first verse. He attended high school in Little Rock from 1899 to 1902, and Phillips Academy, Andover, in 1902-03. In 1903 he matriculated at Harvard, remaining there until his senior year, when he came into a small competence through the death of his father; whereupon he left college and moved to Boston to devote all his time to writing.

In August, 1908, Fletcher sailed for Europe, and going first to Italy, lived in Venice till November, and in Rome till the following May, when he went to England. Finding London a congenial place in which to work, he settled there at Adelphi Terrace. In 1910 he went for a while to Paris, where he read much French literature. Soon, however, he was back in London, working hard. In 1913 he published in rapid succession five volumes of poetry, but these brought him little recognition. His first book to receive much attention was *Irradiations—Sand and Spray* (1915), for which Amy Lowell secured an American publisher. It was written in free verse, and indicated that Fletcher had definitely broken with the conventional forms of poetry. About this time he became identified with the Imagist group, and has since been an ardent advocate of the newer poetic forms.

He came back to the United States in December, 1914, and after short stays in New York and Little Rock, settled in Boston, where, except for a summer in northern Michigan and trips to the West, he lived till May, 1916, when he returned to England. He revisited America in 1920, 1923, and 1926, traveling from coast to coast, lecturing and gathering material for such typically American works as *Breakers and Granite* (1921).

On July 5, 1916, Fletcher was married to Florence Emily Arbuthnot, of England, and they have two children. He is now living in London.

IRRADIATIONS

X

The trees, like great jade elephants,
Chained, stamp and shake 'neath the gadflies of the breeze;
The trees lunge and plunge, unruly elephants:
The clouds are their crimson howdah-canopies,
The sunlight glints like the golden robe of a Shah.
Would I were tossed on the wrinkled backs of those trees.

IRRADIATIONS

XVIII

Blue, brown, blue: sky, sand, sea:
I swell to your immensity.
I will run over the endless beach,
I will shout to the breaking spray,
I will touch the sky with my fingers.
My happiness is like this sand:
I let it run out of my hand.

THE GULLS

(*Molto Allegro*)

White stars scattering,
Pale rain of spray-drops,
Delicate flash of smoke wind-drifted low and high.
Silver upon dark purple,
The gulls quiver
In a noiseless flight, far out across the sky.

THE GROUNDSWELL

(*Marcia Funebre*)

With heavy doleful clamor, hour on hour, and day on day,
The muddy groundswell lifts and breaks and falls and slides
away.

The cold and naked wind runs shivering over the sands,
Salt are its eyes, open its mouth, its brow wet, blue its hands.

It finds naught but a starving gull whose wings trail at its
side,
And the dull battered wreckage, grey jetsam of the tide.

The lifeless chilly slaty sky with no blue hope is lit,
A rusty waddling steamer plants a smudge of smoke on it.

Stupidly stand the factory chimneys staring over all,
The grey grows ever denser, and soon the night will fall:

The wind runs sobbing over the beach and touches with its
hands
Straw, chaff, old bottles, broken crates, the litter of the sands.

Sometimes the bloated carcase of a dog or fish is found,
Sometimes the rumpled feathers of a sea-gull shot or drowned.

Last year it was an unknown man who came up from the sea,
There is his grave hard by the dunes under a stunted tree.

With heavy doleful clamor, hour on hour, and day on day,
The muddy groundswell lifts and breaks and falls and
slides away.

SNOW AT SEA

(*Andante*)

Silently fell
The snow on the waters
In the grey dusk
Of the winter evening:
Swirling and falling,
Sucked into the oily
Blue-black surface
Of the sea.

We pounded on slowly;
From our bows sheeted
A shuddering mass of heavy foam:
Night closed about us,
But ere we were darkened,
We saw close in
A great gaunt schooner
Beating to southward.

Silently fell
The snow on the waters,
As we pounded north
In the winter evening.

THE FRONT DOOR

[*From* THE HOUSE]

It was always the place where our farewells were taken,
When we travelled to the north.

I remember there was one who made some journey,
But did not come back.
Many years they waited for him;
At last the one who wished the most to see him
Was carried out of this selfsame door in death.

Since then all our family partings
Have been at another door.

BLUE SYMPHONY

I

The darkness rolls upward.
The thick darkness carries with it
Rain and a ravel of cloud.
The sun comes forth upon earth.

Palely the dawn
Leaves me facing timidly
Old gardens sunken:
And in the gardens is water.

Sombre wreck—autumnal leaves;
Shadowy roofs
In the blue mist,
And a willow-branch that is broken.

Oh, old pagodas of my soul, how you glittered across
green trees!

Blue and cool:
Blue, tremulously,
Blow faint puffs of smoke
Across sombre pools.
The damp green smell of rotted wood;
And a heron that cries from out the water.

II

Through the upland meadows
I go alone.
For I dreamed of someone last night
Who is waiting for me.

Flower and blossom, tell me, do you know of her?

Have the rocks hidden her voice?
They are very blue and still.

Long upward road that is leading me,
Light-hearted I quit you,

For the long loose ripples of the meadow-grass
Invite me to dance upon them.

Quivering grass
Daintily poised
For her foot's tripping.

Oh, blown clouds, could I only race up like you,
Oh, the last slopes that are sun-drenched and steep!

Look, the sky!
Across black valleys
Rise blue-white aloft
Jagged unwrinkled mountains, ranges of death.

Solitude. Silence.

III

One chuckles by the brook for me:
One rages under the stone.
One makes a spout of his mouth,
One whispers—one is gone.

One over there on the water
Spreads cold ripples
For me
Enticingly.

The vast dark trees
Flow like blue veils
Of tears
Into the water.

Sour sprites,
Moaning and chuckling,
What have you hidden from me?

"In the palace of the blue stone she lies forever
Bound hand and foot."

Was it the wind
That rattled the reeds together?

Dry reeds,
A faint shiver in the grasses.

IV

On the left hand there is a temple:
And a palace on the right-hand side.
Foot passengers in scarlet
Pass over the glittering tide.

Under the bridge
The old river flows
Low and monotonous
Day after day.

I have heard and have seen
All the news that has been:
Autumn's gold and spring's green!

Now in my palace
I see foot passengers
Crossing the river:
Pilgrims of autumn
In the afternoons.

Lotus pools:
Petals in the water.
These are my dreams.

For me silks are outspread.
I take my ease, unthinking.

V

And now the lowest pine-branch
Is drawn across the disk of the sun.
Old friends who will forget me soon,
I must go on,
Towards those blue death-mountains
I have forgot so long.

In the marsh grasses
There lies forever
My last treasure,
With the hopes of my heart.

The ice is glazing over,
Torn lanterns flutter,
On the leaves is snow.
In the frosty evening
Toll the old bell for me
Once, in the sleepy temple.

Perhaps my soul will hear.

Afterglow:
Before the stars peep
I shall creep out into darkness.

WHITE SYMPHONY

I

Forlorn and white,
Whorls of purity about a golden chalice,
Immense the peonies
Flare and shatter their petals over my face.

They slowly turn paler,
They seem to be melting like blue-grey flakes of ice,
Thin greyish shivers
Fluctuating mid the dark green lance-thrust of the leaves.

Like snowballs tossed,
Like soft white butterflies,
The peonies poise in the twilight.
And their narcotic insinuating perfume
Draws me into them
Shivering with the coolness,
Aching with the void.

They kiss the blue chalice of my dreams
Like a gesture seen for an instant and then lost forever.

* *
*

Outwards the petals
Thrust to embrace me,
Pale daggers of coldness
Run through my aching breast.

Outwards, still outwards,
Till on the brink of twilight
They swirl downwards silently,
Flurry of snow in the void.

Outwards, still outwards,
Till the blue walls are hidden,
And in the blinding white radiance
Of a whirlpool of clouds, I awake.

* *
*

Like spraying rockets
My peonies shower
Their glories on the night.

Wavering perfumes,
Drift about the garden;
Shadows of the moonlight,
Drift and ripple over the dew-gemmed leaves.

Soar, crash, and sparkle,
Shoal of stars drifting
Like silver fishes,
Through the black sluggish boughs.

Towards the impossible,
Towards the inaccessible,
Towards the ultimate,
Towards the silence,

Towards the eternal,
These blossoms go.

The peonies spring like rockets in the twilight,
And out of them all I rise.

II

Downwards through the blue abyss it slides,
The white snow-water of my dreams,
Downwards crashing from slippery rock
Into the boiling chasm:
In which no eye dare look, for it is the chasm of death.

Upwards from the blue abyss it rises,
The chill water-mist of my dreams;
Upwards to greyish weeping pines,
And to skies of autumn ever about my heart,
It is blue at the beginning,
And blue-white against the grey-greenness;
It wavers in the upper air,
Catching unconscious sparkles, a rainbow-glint of sunlight,
And fading in the sad depths of the sky.

Outwards rush the strong pale clouds,
Outwards and ever outwards;
The blue-grey clouds indistinguishable one from another:
Nervous, sinewy, tossing their arms and brandishing,
Till on the blue serrations of the horizon
They drench with their black rain a great peak of changeless snow.

* *
*

As evening came on, I climbed the tower,
To gaze upon the city far beneath:
I was not weary of day; but in the evening
A white mist assembled and gathered over the earth
And blotted it from sight.

But to escape:
To chase with the golden clouds galloping over the horizon:
Arrows of the northwest wind
Singing amid them,
Ruffling up my hair!

As evening came on the distance altered,
Pale wavering reflections rose from out the city,
Like sighs or the beckoning of half-invisible hands.
Monotonously and sluggishly they crept upwards
A river that had spent itself in some chasm,
And dwindled and foamed at last at my weary feet.

Autumn! Golden fountains,
And the winds neighing
Amid the monotonous hills:
Desolation of the old gods,
Rain that lifts and rain that moves away;
In the green-black torrent
Scarlet leaves.

It was now perfectly evening:
And the tower loomed like a gaunt peak in mid-air
Above the city: its base was utterly lost.
It was slowly coming on to rain,
And the immense columns of white mist
Wavered and broke before the faint-hurled spears.

I will descend the mountains like a shepherd,
And in the folds of tumultuous misty cities,
I will put all my thoughts, all my old thoughts, safely to sleep.
For it is already autumn,
O whiteness of the pale southwestern sky!
O wavering dream that was not mine to keep!

* * *

In midnight, in mournful moonlight,
By paths I could not trace,
I walked in the white garden;
Each flower had a white face.

Their perfume intoxicated me: thus I began my dream.

I was alone; I had no one to guide me,
But the moon was like the sun:
It stooped and kissed each waxen petal,
One after one.

Green and white was that garden: diamond rain hung in the
branches;
You will not believe it!

In the morning, at the dayspring,
I wakened, shivering; lo,
The white garden that blossomed at my feet
Was a garden hidden in snow.

It was my sorrow to see that all this was a dream.

III

Blue, clogged with purple,
Mists uncoil themselves:
Sparkling to the horizon,
I see the snow alone.

In the deep blue chasm,
Boats sleep under gold thatch;
Icicle-like trees fret
Faintly rose-touched sky.

Under their heaped snow-eaves,
Leaden houses shiver.
Through thin blue crevasses
Trickles an icy stream.

The pines groan white-laden,
The waves shiver, struck by the wind;
Beyond from treeless horizons,
Broken snow-peaks crawl to the sea.

* *
*

Wearily the snow glares,
Through the grey silence, day after day,
Mocking the colorless, cloudless sky
With the reflection of death.

There is no smoke through the pine tops,
No strong red boatmen in pale green reeds,
No herons to flicker an instant,
No lanterns to glow with gay ray.

No sails beat up to the harbor,
With creaking cordage and sailor's song.
Somnolent, bare-poled, indifferent,
They sleep, and the city sleeps.

Mid-winter about them casts
Its dreary fortifications:
Each day is a gaunt grey rock,
And death is the last of them all.

* *
*

Over the sluggish snow,
Drifts now a pallid weak shower of bloom;
Boredom of fresh creation,
Death-weariness of old returns.

White, white blossom,
Fall of the shattered cups day on day:
Is there anything here that is not ancient,
That has not bloomed a thousand years ago?

Under the glare of the white-hot day,
Under the restless wind-rakes of the winter,
White blossom or white snow scattered,
And beneath them, dark, the graves.

Dark graves never changing,
White dream drifting, never changing above them:
O that the white scroll of heaven might be rolled up,
And the naked red lightning thrust at the smouldering earth!

COURT LADY STANDING UNDER CHERRY TREE

She is an iris,
Dark purple, pale rose,
Under the gnarled boughs
That shatter their stars of bloom.
She waves delicately
With the movement of the tree.

Of what is she dreaming?

Of long nights lit with orange lanterns,
Of wine cups and compliments and kisses of the two-sword
    men.
And of dawn when weary sleepers
Lie outstretched on the mats of the palace,
And of the iris stalk that is broken in the fountain.

TWO WAYS OF LOVE

The wind half blows her robes,
That subside
Listlessly
As swaying pines.

The wind tosses hers
In circles
That recoil upon themselves:
How should I love—as the swaying or tossing wind?

A WOMAN STANDING BY A GATE WITH AN UMBRELLA

Late summer changes to autumn:
Chrysanthemums are scattered
Behind the palings.

Gold and vermilion
The afternoon.

I wait here dreaming of vermilion sunsets:
In my heart is a half fear of the chill autumn rain.

SPRING LOVE

Through the weak spring rains
Two lovers walk together,
Holding together the parasol.

But the laughing rains of spring
Will break the weak green shoots of their love.

His will grow a towering stalk,
Hers, a cowering flower under it.

A LIFE

Her life was like a swiftly rushing stream
Green and scarlet,
Falling into darkness.

The seasons passed for her,
Like pale iris wilting,
Or peonies flying to ribbons before the storm-gusts.
The sombre pine-tops waited until the seasons had passed.

Then in her heart they grew
The snows of changeless winter
Stirred by the bitter winds of unsatisfied desire.

MUTABILITY

The wind shakes the mists,
Making them quiver
With faint drum-tones of thunder.

Out of the crane-haunted mists of autumn,
Blue and brown
Rolls the moon.

There was a city living here long ago;
Of all that city
There is only one stone left half-buried in the marsh,
With characters upon it which no one now can read.

FUGITIVE BEAUTY

As the fish that leaps from the river,
As the dropping of a November leaf at twilight,
As the faint flicker of lightning down the southern sky,
So I saw beauty, far away.

MEMORY: THE WALK ON THE BEACH

The evening, blue, voluptuous, of June
Settled slowly on the beach with pulsating wings,
Like a sea-gull come to rest: far, far-off twinkled
Gold lights from the towers of a city and a passing ship.
The dark sea rolled its body at the end of the beach,
The warm soft beach which it was too tired to climb,
And we two walked together there
Arm in arm, having nothing in our souls but love.

Your face shaded by the hat looked up at me;
Your pale face framed in the dark gold of your hair,
Your face with its dumb unforgetable look in the eyes,
A look I have only once seen, that I shall see never again.
Our steps were lost on the long vast carpet of sand;
Our souls were lost in the sky where the stars came out;
Our bodies clung together: time was not.
Love came and passed: our lives were cleaned and changed.

The winter will spill upon us soon its dark cruse laden with
rain,
Time has broken our moorings; we have drifted apart; love
is done.

I can only dream in the long still nights that we rest heart to heart;
I can only wake to the knowledge that my love is lost and won.
We were as two weak swallows, together to southward set,
Blown apart, vainly crying to each other while at strife with the seas.
We go out in the darkness; we speak but in memories;
But I have never forgotten and I shall never forget.

THE ORDEAL

I have humbled my proud soul into the dust for your sake,
Give me my soul again!
In torment and in suffering I have pressed from me my soul,
Give me my soul again!
My travail and my anguish have not been as the travail of women,
But a self-consuming annihilation:
Give me my soul again.
Ah, now you give me my soul again,
You give, you give utterly,
My soul transformed, exalted, made more perfect,
Filled with the love that is greater to-day than the love of yesterday.

FAITH

The dark clouds gather around my path, they bar me in every way,
Every way but westward, where is the great sun's death;
But I do not fear those great dark clouds, nor the tragic death of a day;
My heart beats fully and steadily; faith is new-born with each breath,
Faith in that part of me which was not mine, which was given to me to use,

Which shall live on though all the suns fall dead into the
night;
Faith in a love which rules all things: for though I fall and
lose,
I shall live on for ever, for I have held with the light.

IN THE OPEN AIR

It is only in the open air
That our love can be given to us:
We must be free each instant,
And over our heads see the sky.
The roystering cry of the vagabond wind
Wakens the gipsy song in our hearts;
The sun on the black horizon
Is the camp-fire at which we may sleep.

I am the wind,
And you are the slender birch for me;
Over the hilltops I shall seek you;
You will wait drooping at last.
You caress me with eager fingers;
I breathe into your entangled boughs:
In the sunlight we laugh together,
And breathe side by side in the night.

Golden clouds we have seen racing
Full-bellied up the blue waveless sky;
All of our hearts have soared on to them
Like skylarks striving in flight.
We have taken the old green earth
For our great lawless adventure,
And seen in the white-thorn blossoming
The pale smile of the Crucified.

It is only in the open air
That our love may be given to us;
No house may for long time hold us,
Love does not dwell in houses.

Freely over the pathless earth
Rove our two hearts together:
Joy and song in the morning,
At nightfall kisses and sleep.

EBB-TIDE

Ebb-tide at ending of the sea,
Which wrecked our castles on the sands;
We drift apart mysteriously,
With empty eyes, with open hands,
Knowing not what could make us so,
Not able to check the current's might;
The force that set our hearts aglow,
Now dwindling down to endless night.

It is as if we never met:
Was't I who loved, and I who lost?
Were yours the lips on which I set
That kiss which, lit with passion, cost
Half life, half reason? Now, alas,
The vision fades, the glory's gone,
The image shatters with the glass,
The empty frame is all I own.

Ebb-tide, the dying of the sea;
A weedy stretch of gloomy beach
Torn by the gale—and, mystery,
A wave that sparkles out of reach.
All we have left is rubbish now,
Mere wrecks of glory, lifeless, wet;
The chalice spoilt, the broken vow,
Bury them together, let's forget!

The year is whirling withered leaves;
The last one falls soon—when 'tis gone,
No matter who suffers or who grieves,
Time blows a truce, our love is done.

The dream of summer far-off stands;
Its hours are spent beyond recall,
Only the dull and lifeless sands,
And darkness rising as we fall.

Ebb-tide, the waning of the light;
I cannot hope, I cannot weep.
Only at middle of the night
Shall rise the dream that conquers sleep;
And that, too, fails soon, like false light.
We could not keep love, 'twas too fair;
Within each empty heart to-night
Only the ashes of despair!

Perhaps the tide will rise once more;
Perhaps ere death will call us in,
We'll hear again its fading roar,
But then too old, too cold to win.
The sparkling glimmering mystery
That swept us on, is gone from sight.
Ebb-tide at ending of the sea,
My love, my lost, good-night, good-night.

SKYSCRAPERS

What are these, angels or demons,
Or steel and stone?
Soaring, alert,
Striped with diversified windows,
These sweep aloft
And the multitude crane their necks to them:—
Are they angels, or demons,
Or stone?

If the grey sapless people,
Moving along the street, thought them angels,
They too would be beautiful,
Erect and laughing to the sky for joy.

If as demons they feared them,
They would smite with fierce hatred
These brown haughty foreheads:
They would not suffer them to hold the sun in trust.

What are they, then, angels, or demons,
Or stone?
Deaf sightless towers
Unendowed yet with life;
Soaring vast effort
Spent in the sky till it breaks there.
You men of my country
Who shaped these proud visions,
You have yet to find godhead
Not here, but in the human heart.

EMBARKATION

[*From* DOWN THE MISSISSIPPI]

Dull masses of dense green,
The forests range their sombre platforms;
Between them silently, like a spirit,
The river finds its own mysterious path.

Loosely the river sways out, backward, forward,
Always fretting the outer side;
Shunning the invisible focus of each crescent,
Seeking to spread into shining loops over fields.

Like an enormous serpent, dilating, uncoiling,
Displaying a broad scaly back of earth-smeared gold;
Swaying out sinuously between the dull motionless forests,
As molten metal might glide down the lip of a vase of dark
bronze;

It goes, while the steamboat drifting out upon it,
Seems now to be floating not only outwards but upwards;
In the flight of a petal detached and gradually moving sky-
ward
Above the pink explosion of the calyx of the dawn.

HEAT

[*From* DOWN THE MISSISSIPPI]

As if the sun had trodden down the sky,
Until no more it holds living air, but only humid vapor,
Heat pressing upon earth with irresistible languor,
Turns all the solid forest into half-liquid smudge.

The heavy clouds like cargo-boats strain slowly against its
current;
And the flickering of the haze is like the thunder of ten
thousand paddles
Against the heavy wall of the horizon, pale-blue and utterly
windless,
Whereon the sun hangs motionless, a brassy disc of flame.

THE STEVEDORES

[*From* DOWN THE MISSISSIPPI]

Frieze of warm bronze that glides with catlike movements
Over the gangplank poised and yet awaiting,
The sinewy thudding rhythm of forty shuffling feet
Falling like muffled drumbeats on the stillness.
O roll the cotton down,
Roll, roll the cotton down,
From the further side of Jordan,
O roll the cotton down!

And the river waits,
The river listens,
Chuckling little banjo-notes that break with a flop on the
stillness;
And by the low dark shed that holds the heavy freights,
Two lonely cypress trees stand up and point with stiffened
fingers
Far southward where a single chimney stands out aloof in the
sky.

THE GRAND CANYON OF THE COLORADO

I

I have seen that which is mysterious,
Aloof, divided, silent;
Something not of this earth.

Suddenly the endless dark green piney uplands
Stopped.
Yellow, red, grey-green, purple-black chasms fell swiftly below each other.

On the other side,
Strong-built, arose
Towers whose durable terraces were hammered from red sandstone,
Purple granite, and gold.

Beyond
A golden wall,
Aloof, inscrutable.

It was hidden
Behind layers of white silence.
No voice might reach it;
It was not of this earth.

II

When the free thunder-spirit
Had built and carved these terraced walls,
Completing his task of ages,
He wrote upon them
In dark invisible words,
"It is finished."

Silent and windless,
The forever completed
Is never broken but by clouds.

Sometimes dark eagles slow-sailing
Rise out of it, like spirits,
Wheeling away.

Now in the steady glare,
Some will moves darkly,
Driving the clouds, piling them,
Shaping masses of shadow
That move slowly forward
Over the array of towers.

Yet still behind them,
Unscarred, unaltered,
The work stands finished.
Without a cry of protest, for protest is uncompletion,
Moulded and fashioned forever in durable ageless stone,
And on every surface is written
In strong invisible words:
"It is finished."

III

Should I by chance deserve some last reward from earth,—
The rewards of earth are usually unwholesome;—
One single thing I would ask for,
Burn my body here.

Kindle the pyre
Upon this jutting point:
Dry aromatic juniper,
Lean flame, blue smoke,
Ashes and dust.

The winds would drift the ash
Outwards across the canyon,
To the rose-purple rim of the desert
Beyond the red-barred towers.

The rabbits in the morning
Would come and snuff at the embers,
While the chasm, rekindling,
Would build up its silent poem of color to the sun.

IV

Shadows of clouds
March across the canyon,
Shadows of blue hands passing
Over a curtain of flame.

Clutching, staggering, upstriking,
Darting in blue-black fury,
To where the pinnacles, green and orange,
Await.

The winds are battling and striving to break them;
Thin lightnings spit and flicker;
The peaks seem a dance of scarlet demons
Flitting amid the shadows.

Grey rain-curtains wave afar off;
Wisps of vapor curl and vanish:
The sun throws soft shafts of golden light
Over rose-buttressed palisades.

Now the clouds are a lazy procession:
Blue balloons bobbing solemnly
Over black-dappled walls:

Where rise sharp-fretted, golden-roofed cathedrals
Exultantly, and split the sky with light.

MEXICAN QUARTER

By an alley lined with tumble-down shacks,
And street-lamps askew, half-sputtering,
Feebly glimmering on gutters choked with filth and dogs
Scratching their mangy backs:
Half-naked children are running about,

Women puff cigarettes in black doorways,
Crickets are crying.
Men slouch sullenly
Into the shadows:
Behind a hedge of cactus,
The smell of a dead horse
Mingles with the smell of tortillas frying.

And a girl in a black lace shawl
Sits in a rickety chair by the square of an unglazed window,
And sees the explosion of the stars
Softly poised on a velvet sky,
And she is humming to herself:—
"Stars, if I could reach you,
(You are so very clear that it seems as if I could reach you)
I would give you all to the Madonna's image,
On the grey-plastered altar behind the paper flowers,
So that Juan would come back to me,
And we could live again those lazy burning hours,
Forgetting the tap of my fan and my sharp words.
And I would only keep four of you,
Those two blue-white ones overhead,
To hang in my ears;
And those two orange ones yonder,
To fasten on my shoe-buckles."

A little further along the street
A man sits stringing a brown guitar.
The smoke of his cigarette curls 'round his head,
And he too is humming, but other words:
"Think not that at your window I wait;
New love is better, the old is turned to hate.
Fate! Fate! All things pass away;
Life is forever, youth is for a day.
Love again if you may
Before the stars are blown out of the sky,
And the crickets die!
Babylon and Samarkand
Are mud walls in a waste of sand."

LINCOLN

I

Like a gaunt, scraggly pine
Which lifts its head above the mournful sandhills;
And patiently, through dull years of bitter silence,
Untended and uncared for, starts to grow.

Ungainly, laboring, huge,
The wind of the north has twisted and gnarled its branches;
Yet in the heat of mid-summer days, when thunder clouds
ring the horizon,
A nation of men shall rest beneath its shade.

And it shall protect them all,
Hold everyone safe there, watching aloof in silence;
Until at last, one mad stray bolt from the zenith
Shall strike it in an instant down to earth.

II

There was a darkness in this man; an immense and hollow
darkness,
Of which we may not speak, nor share with him nor enter;
A darkness through which strong roots stretched downwards
into the earth,
Towards old things;

Towards the herdman-kings who walked the earth and spoke
with God,
Towards the wanderers who sought for they knew not what,
and found their goal at last;
Towards the men who waited, only waited patiently when
all seemed lost,
Many bitter winters of defeat;

Down to the granite of patience,
These roots swept, knotted fibrous roots, prying, piercing,
seeking,

And drew from the living rock and the living waters about it,
The red sap to carry upwards to the sun.

Not proud, but humble,
Only to serve and pass on, to endure to the end through
service,
For the axe is laid at the roots of the trees, and all that
bring not forth good fruit
Shall be cut down on the day to come and cast into the fire.

III

There is a silence abroad in the land to-day,
And in the hearts of men, a deep and anxious silence;
And, because we are still at last, those bronze lips slowly
open,
Those hollow and weary eyes take on a gleam of light.

Slowly a patient, firm-syllabled voice cuts through the end-
less silence,
Like laboring oxen that drag a plough through the chaos of
rude clay-fields,
"I went forward as the light goes forward in early spring,
But there were also many things which I left behind.

"Tombs that were quiet;
One, of a mother, whose brief light went out in the darkness,
One of a loved one, the snow on whose grave is long falling,
One only of a child, but it was mine.

"Have you forgotten your graves? Go, question them in
anguish,
Listen long to their unstirred lips. From your hostages to
silence
Learn there is no life without death, no dawn without sun-
setting,
No victory but to him who has given all."

The clamor of cannon dies down, the furnace-mouth of the
battle is silent,

The midwinter sun dips and descends, the earth takes on
afresh its bright colors.
But he whom we mocked and obeyed not, he whom we
scorned and mistrusted,
He has descended, like a god, to his rest.

Over the uproar of cities,
Over the million intricate threads of life weaving and crossing,
In the midst of problems we know not, tangling, perplexing,
ensnaring,
Rises one white tomb alone.

Beam over it, stars,
Wrap it 'round, stripes—stripes red for the pain that he
bore for you—
Enfold it forever, O flag, rent, soiled, but repaired through
your anguish;
Long as you keep him there safe, the nations shall bow to
your law.

Strew over him flowers:
Blue forget-me-nots from the north and the bright pink
arbutus
From the east, and from the west rich orange blossom,
But from the heart of the land take the passion-flower;

Rayed, violet, dim,
With the nails that pierced, the cross that he bore and the
circlet,
And beside it there lay also one lonely snow-white magnolia,
Bitter for remembrance of the healing which has passed.

HILDA DOOLITTLE (H. D.)

Hilda Doolittle Aldington, whose pen name is "H. D.," was born on September 10, 1886, at Bethlehem, Pennsylvania. She was a daughter of Charles L. Doolittle, professor of mathematics and astronomy at Lehigh University, and his second wife, Helen Eugenia Wolle. When she was nine, her father moved to Philadelphia to become director of the Flower Astronomical Observatory at the University of Pennsylvania, a position which he held until he retired in 1912.

She attended a public school in Bethlehem, but in Philadelphia she entered the Gordon School, where she stayed until 1902, when she went to the Friends' Central School to prepare for entrance to Bryn Mawr College. She entered Bryn Mawr in 1904, but in her sophomore year ill health forced her to withdraw.

Soon after leaving Bryn Mawr she began writing stories, and some of these, designed for children, were published in a Presbyterian paper in Philadelphia. In 1911 she went to Europe, intending to stay only for the summer, but after a trip through Italy and France she reached London, and becoming interested in the literary movements there, decided to remain. To Ezra Pound, who at the time was a leader of the Imagist group, she showed some poetry that she had written, and he sent it to *Poetry: a Magazine of Verse*. The January, 1913, number of that magazine contained a group of her poems, her first verse to be published. She joined the Imagists, and was presently writing for a number of periodicals. In 1916 her first book, *Sea Garden*, was published in England.

On October 18, 1913, she married Richard Aldington, an English poet and member of the Imagist group. During the following winter they made a number of translations of Greek and Latin poets. When her husband entered the army, "H. D." took over his editorial duties on *The Egoist,* a London magazine. She remained in England until 1920, when she came back for a few months to America, settling in California. In 1921, however, she returned to Europe, and went to live in Switzerland, on the shore of Lake Geneva.

SEA ROSE

Rose, harsh rose,
marred and with stint of petals,
meagre flower, thin,
sparse of leaf,

more precious
than a wet rose
single on a stem—
you are caught in the drift.

Stunted, with small leaf,
you are flung on the sand,
you are lifted
in the crisp sand
that drives in the wind.

Can the spice-rose
drip such acrid fragrance
hardened in a leaf?

EVENING

The light passes
from ridge to ridge,
from flower to flower—
the hypaticas, wide-spread
under the light
grow faint—
the petals reach inward,
the blue tips bend
toward the bluer heart
and the flowers are lost.

The cornel-buds are still white,
but shadows dart
from the cornel-roots—
black creeps from root to root,
each leaf
cuts another leaf on the grass,
shadow seeks shadow,
then both leaf
and leaf-shadow are lost.

SEA GODS

I

They say there is no hope—
sand—drift—rocks—rubble of the sea—
the broken hulk of a ship,
hung with shreds of rope,
pallid under the cracked pitch.

They say there is no hope
to conjure you—
no whip of the tongue to anger you—
no hate of words
you must rise to refute.

They say you are twisted by the sea,
you are cut apart
by wave-break upon wave-break,
that you are misshapen by the sharp rocks,
broken by the rasp and after-rasp.

That you are cut, torn, mangled,
torn by the stress and beat,
no stronger than the strips of sand
along your ragged beach.

II

But we bring violets,
great masses—single, sweet,
wood-violets, stream violets,
violets from a wet marsh.

Violets in clumps from hills,
tufts with earth at the roots,
violets tugged from rocks,
blue violets, moss, cliff, river-violets.

Yellow violets' gold,
burnt with a rare tint—
violets like red ash
among tufts of grass.

We bring deep-purple
bird-foot violets.

We bring the hyacinth-violet,
sweet, bare, chill to the touch—
And violets whiter than the in-rush
of your own white surf.

III

For you will come,
you will yet haunt men in ships,
you will trail across the fringe of strait
and circle the jagged rocks.

You will trail across the rocks
and wash them with your salt,
you will curl between sand-hills—
you will thunder along the cliff—
break—retreat—get fresh strength—
gather and pour weight upon the beach.

You will draw back,
and the ripple on the sand-shelf
will be witness of your track.
O privet-white, you will paint
the lintel of wet sand with froth.

You will bring myrrh-bark
and drift laurel-wood from hot coasts!
when you hurl high—high—
we will answer with a shout.

For you will come,
you will come,
you will answer our taut hearts,
you will break the lie of men's thoughts,
and cherish and shelter us.

CITIES

Can we believe—by an effort
comfort our hearts:
it is not waste, all this,
not placed here in disgust,
street after street,
each patterned alike,
no grace to lighten
a single house of the hundred
crowded into one garden-space.

Crowded—can we believe,
not in utter disgust,
in ironical play—
but the maker of cities grew faint
with the beauty of temple
and space before temple,
arch upon perfect arch,
of pillars and corridors that led out

to strange court-yards and porches
where sun-light stamped
hyacinth-shadows
black on the pavement.

That the maker of cities grew faint
with the splendor of palaces,
paused while the incense-flowers
from the incense-trees
dropped on the marble-walk,
thought anew, fashioned this—
street after street alike.

For alas,
he had crowded the city so full
that men could not grasp beauty,
beauty was over them,
through them, about them,
no crevice unpacked with the honey,
rare, measureless.

So he built a new city,
ah, can we believe, not ironically,
but for new splendor,
constructed new people
to lift through slow growth
to a beauty unrivalled yet—
and created new cells,
hideous first, hideous now—
spread larvæ across them,
not honey but seething life;

And in these dark cells,
packed street after street,
souls live, hideous yet—
O disfigured, defaced,
with no trace of the beauty
men once held so light.

Can we think a few old cells
were left—we are left—
grains of honey,
old dust of stray pollen
dull on our torn wings,
we are left to recall the old streets?

Is our task the less sweet
that the larvæ still sleep in their cells?
Or crawl out to attack our frail strength:
You are useless. We live.
We await great events.
We are spread through this earth.
We protect our strong race.
You are useless.
Your cell takes the place
of our young future strength.

Though they sleep or wake to torment
and wish to displace our old cells—
thin rare gold—
that their larvæ grow fat—
is our task the less sweet?
Though we wander about,
find no honey of flowers in this waste,
is our task the less sweet—
who recall the old splendor,
await the new beauty of cities?

The city is peopled
with spirits, not ghosts, O my love:

Though they crowded between
and usurped the kiss of my mouth
their breath was your gift,
their beauty, your life.

"WHERE LOVE IS KING"

[*From* HYMEN]

Where love is king,
Ah, there is little need
To dance and sing,
With bridal-torch to flare
Amber and scatter light
Across the purple air,
To sing and dance
To flute-note and to reed.

Where love is come
(Ah, love is come indeed!)
Our limbs are numb
Before his fiery need;
With all their glad
Rapture of speech unsaid,
Before his fiery lips
Our lips are mute and dumb.

Ah, sound of reed,
Ah, flute and trumpet wail,
Ah, joy decreed—
The fringes of her veil
Are seared and white;
Across the flare of light,
Blinded the torches fail.
(Ah, love is come indeed!)

CUCKOO SONG

Ah, bird,
our love is never spent
with your clear note,
nor satiate our soul;
not song, not wail, not hurt,

but just a call summons us
with its simple top-note
and soft fall;

not to some rarer heaven
of lilies over-tall,
nor tuberose set against
some sun-lit wall,
but to a gracious
cedar-palace hall;

not marble set with purple
hung with roses and tall
sweet lilies—such
as the nightingale
would summon for us
with her wail—
(surely only unhappiness
could thrill
such a rich madrigal!)
not she, the nightingale
can fill our souls
with such a wistful joy as this:

nor, bird, so sweet
was ever a swallow note—
not hers, so perfect
with the wing of lazuli
and bright breast—
nor yet the oriole
filling with melody
from her fiery throat
some island-orchard
in a purple sea.

Ah, dear, ah, gentle bird,
you spread warm length
of crimson wool
and tinted woven stuff

for us to rest upon,
nor numb with ecstasy
nor drown with death:

only you soothe, make still
the throbbing of our brain:
so through her forest trees,
when all her hope was gone
and all her pain,
Calypso heard your call—
across the gathering drift
of burning cedar-wood,
across the low-set bed
of wandering parsley and violet,
when all her hope was dead.

"WASH OF COLD RIVER"

Wash of cold river
in a glacial land,
Ionian water,
chill, snow-ribbed sand,
drift of rare flowers,
clear, with delicate shell—
like leaf enclosing
frozen lily-leaf,
camellia texture,
colder than a rose;

wind-flower
that keeps the breath
of the north-wind—
these and none other;

intimate thoughts and kind
reach out to share
the treasure of my mind,
intimate hands and dear

draw garden-ward and sea-ward
all the sheer rapture
that I would take
to mould a clear
and frigid statue;

rare, of pure texture,
beautiful space and line,
marble to grace
your inaccessible shrine.

HELIODORA

He and I sought together,
over the spattered table,
rhymes and flowers,
gifts for a name.

He said, among others,
I will bring
(and the phrase was just and good,
but not as good as mine,)
"the narcissus that loves the rain."

We strove for a name,
while the light of the lamps burnt thin
and the outer dawn came in,
a ghost, the last at the feast
or the first,
to sit within
with the two that remained
to quibble in flowers and verse
over a girl's name.

He said, "the rain, loving,"
I said, "the narcissus, drunk,
drunk with the rain."

Yet I had lost
for he said,
"the rose, the lover's gift,
is loved of love,"
he said it,
"loved of love";
I waited, even as he spoke,
to see the room filled with a light,
as when in winter
the embers catch in a wind
when a room is dank;
so it would be filled, I thought,
our room with a light
when he said
(and he said it first,)
"the rose, the lover's delight,
is loved of love,"
but the light was the same.

Then he caught,
seeing the fire in my eyes,
my fire, my fever, perhaps,
for he leaned
with the purple wine
stained on his sleeve,
and said this:
"did you ever think
a girl's mouth
caught in a kiss,
is a lily that laughs?"

I had not.
I saw it now
as men must see it forever afterwards;
no poet could write again,
"the red-lily,
a girl's laugh caught in a kiss";
it was his to pour in the vat
from which all poets dip and quaff,
for poets are brothers in this.

So I saw the fire in his eyes,
it was almost my fire,
(he was younger,)
I saw the face so white,
my heart beat,
it was almost my phrase;
I said, "surprise the muses,
take them by surprise;
it is late,
rather it is dawn-rise,
those ladies sleep, the nine,
our own king's mistresses."

A name to rhyme,
flowers to bring to a name,
what was one girl faint and shy,
with eyes like the myrtle,
(I said: "her underlids
are rather like myrtle,")
to vie with the nine?

Let him take the name,
he had the rhymes,
"the rose, loved of love,
the lily, a mouth that laughs,"
he had the gift,
"the scented crocus,
the purple hyacinth,"
what was one girl to the nine?

He said:
"I will make her a wreath";
he said:
"I will write it thus:

I will bring you the lily that laughs.
I will twine

with soft narcissus, the myrtle,
sweet crocus, white violet,
the purple hyacinth, and last,
the rose, loved-of-love,
that these may drip on your hair
the less soft flowers,
may mingle sweet with the sweet
of Heliodora's locks,
myrrh-curled."
(He wrote myrrh-curled,
I think, the first.)

I said:
"they sleep, the nine,"
when he shouted swift and passionate:
"*that* for the nine!
above the hills
the sun is about to wake,
and to-day white violets
shine beside white lilies
adrift on the mountain side;
to-day the narcissus opens
that loves the rain."

I watched him to the door,
catching his robe
as the wine-bowl crashed to the floor,
spilling a few wet lees,
(ah, his purple hyacinth!)
I saw him out of the door,
I thought:
there will never be a poet
in all the centuries after this,
who will dare write,
after my friend's verse,
"a girl's mouth
is a lily kissed."

FRAGMENT THIRTY-SIX

I know not what to do: my mind is divided.
Sappho.

I know not what to do,
my mind is reft:
is song's gift best?
is love's gift loveliest?
I know not what to do,
now sleep has pressed
weight on your eyelids.

Shall I break your rest,
devouring, eager?
is love's gift best?
nay, song's the loveliest:
yet were you lost,
what rapture
could I take from song?
what song were left?

I know not what to do:
to turn and slake
the rage that burns,
with my breath burn
and trouble your cool breath?
so shall I turn and take
snow in my arms?
(is love's gift best?)
yet flake on flake
of snow were comfortless,
did you lie wondering,
wakened yet unawake.

Shall I turn and take
comfortless snow within my arms?
press lips to lips
that answer not,
press lips to flesh
that shudders not nor breaks?

Is love's gift best?
shall I turn and slake
all the wild longing?
O I am eager for you!
as the Pleiads shake
white light in whiter water
so shall I take you?

My mind is quite divided,
my minds hesitate,
so perfect matched,
I know not what to do:
each strives with each
as two white wrestlers
standing for a match,
ready to turn and clutch
yet never shake muscle nor nerve nor tendon;
so my mind waits
to grapple with my mind,
yet I lie quiet,
I would seem at rest.

I know not what to do:
strain upon strain,
sound surging upon sound
makes my brain blind;
as a wave-line may wait to fall
yet (waiting for its falling)
still the wind may take
from off its crest,
white flake on flake of foam,
that rises,
seeming to dart and pulse
and rend the light,
so my mind hesitates
above the passion
quivering yet to break,
so my mind hesitates
above my mind,
listening to song's delight.

I know not what to do:
will the sound break,
rending the night
with rift on rift of rose
and scattered light?
will the sound break at last
as the wave hesitant,
or will the whole night pass
and I lie listening awake?

LETHE

Nor skin nor hide nor fleece
  Shall cover you,
Nor curtain of crimson nor fine
Shelter of cedar-wood be over you,
  Nor the fir-tree
  Nor the pine.

Nor sight of whin nor gorse
  Nor river-yew,
Nor fragrance of flowering bush,
Nor wailing of reed-bird to waken you,
  Nor of linnet,
  Nor of thrush.

Nor word nor touch nor sight
  Of lover; you
Shall long through the night but for this:
The roll of the full tide to cover you
  Without question,
  Without kiss.

CONRAD AIKEN

Conrad Potter Aiken, critic, short story writer, novelist, and poet, was born on August 5, 1889, at Savannah, Georgia. His parents were William Ford and Anna Potter Aiken. He attended Middlesex School, Concord, Massachusetts, and in 1907 entered Harvard University, receiving his A. B. degree from there in 1912, as of the class of 1911.

While an undergraduate at Harvard, Aiken wrote poetry of such merit that he was chosen class poet. His first book, *Earth Triumphant and Other Tales in Verse,* appeared in 1914; and for the next few years he published on an average of a volume a year, besides writing much criticism. From 1917 to 1919 he was contributing editor of *The Dial,* most of his articles in that magazine being collected and published as a volume, *Scepticisms,* in 1919. Of late years Aiken has turned to prose, publishing in 1925 a volume of short stories, *Bring! Bring! and Other Stories,* and in 1927 a novel, *Blue Voyage.* He has edited a number of volumes, has made a collection of poetry, *Modern American Poets* (1922), and is a frequent contributor to such magazines as *Scribner's* and *The Dial.*

On August 25, 1912, he was married to Jessie McDonald, of Montreal, Canada; they have three children, a son and two daughters. Aiken lived for a number of years at South Yarmouth, Massachusetts; but in 1921 he went to Europe, and after living for a while in Rome, settled at Rye, on the coast of Sussex. In 1926 he returned to America, and is now an instructor in English at Harvard. His home is in Cambridge, Massachusetts.

"MUSIC I HEARD WITH YOU"

Music I heard with you was more than music,
And bread I broke with you was more than bread;
Now that I am without you, all is desolate;
All that was once so beautiful is dead.

Your hands once touched this table and this silver,
And I have seen your fingers hold this glass.
These things do not remember you, belovèd,—
And yet your touch upon them will not pass.

For it was in my heart you moved among them,
And blessed them with your hands and with your eyes;
And in my heart they will remember always,—
They knew you once, O beautiful and wise.

"DEAD CLEOPATRA LIES IN A CRYSTAL CASKET"

Dead Cleopatra lies in a crystal casket,
Wrapped and spiced by the cunningest of hands.
Around her neck they have put a golden necklace,
Her tatbebs, it is said, are worn with sands.

Dead Cleopatra was once revered in Egypt,
Warm-eyed she was, this princess of the South.
Now she is very old and dry and faded,
With black bitumen they have sealed up her mouth.

Grave-robbers pulled the gold rings from her fingers,
Despite the holy symbols across her breast;
They scared the bats that quietly whirled above her.
Poor lady! she would have been long since at rest,

If she had not been wrapped and spiced so shrewdly,
Preserved, obscene, to mock black flights of years. . . .
What would her lover have said,—had he forseen it?
Had he been moved to ecstasy,—or tears?

O sweet clean earth, from whom the green blade cometh!
When we are dead, my best belovèd and I,
Close well above us, that we may rest forever,
Sending up grass and blossoms to the sky.

"ALL LOVELY THINGS WILL HAVE AN ENDING"

All lovely things will have an ending,
All lovely things will fade and die,
And youth, that's now so bravely spending,
Will beg a penny by and by.

Fine ladies all are soon forgotten,
And goldenrod is dust when dead,
The sweetest flesh and flowers are rotten
And cobwebs tent the brightest head.

Come back, true love! Sweet youth, return!—
But time goes on, and will, unheeding,
Though hands will reach, and eyes will yearn,
And the wild days set true hearts bleeding.

Come back, true love! Sweet youth, remain!—
But goldenrod and daisies wither,
And over them blows autumn rain,
They pass, they pass, and know not whither.

WHITE NOCTURNE

I

The first soft snowflakes hovering down the night,
From one white cloud that hurries beneath the stars,—
Whispering over the black unfrozen pool,
Silently falling on withered leaves,

Eddying slowly among bare boughs of trees,—
The music you are to me is as ghostly as these,
Softly falling, softly passing;
The first soft snowflakes slanting down this night
Melt on the lifted palms of your hands;
One of them finds your lip, and you quietly laugh,
A laugh that means to say,
"This was the kiss you gave me yesterday,
Or the ghost of it—ah, yes, the ghost of it,
For the ghost of it is all we have to-day."
The first slow snowflakes pass,
Leaving a sprinkled whiteness on leaves and grass,
The cloud turns ghostlike against the cold bright stars,
Over the long black boughs that seem to reach
Forlornly after it,
And now it is gone, and suddenly we seem
To walk in silence where before we walked in speech.
But the silence itself is exquisite,
Like a pause in music, ghostly with overtones,
And, silent, we seem to hear
The echoes of words we spoke and heard last year.
Clearly our footsteps sound on the moistened stones,
Clearly the lamplit hill-street gleams before us;
And silently we climb,
Climbing our tragic destiny together,
From lamp to lamp up the bright street of time.

II

You sit beneath the lamp and talk to me,
With dark hair somehow turned to fire,
Your white hands lie in your lap, or touch your lips,
And your talk, like music, weaving intricately,
Plays upon me. It is a magic of white
Touching and changing all familiar things;
It flows in the windy night,
It quietly opens secret doors, it sings,
It returns upon itself, repeats, denies,
Or takes sweet pleasure in silence. And all the while

You sit beneath the lamp, and smile,
Or turn away your eyes.
"We remember," you seem to say,—
Choosing strange words to say it, in another way,—
"How slowly and how inevitably we change,
How what was then familiar now grows strange."
White valleys fall between us;
Your words become a wind, and heavily blow;
We seem to be crying across a chasm of snow,
Trying to hear the half-remembered words,
Trying to guess what we no longer know.
Yes, life changes, we are never the same.
Your eyes grow dark with a tiny flame,
You say the words, and wait;
And a terror seizes me, for I fear
That you have divined the things that I have forgotten,
Things that still shine before you white and clear.
Yes, it is strange. You sigh, your talk flows on,
You touch your hair with your hands, and sigh,
And suddenly it seems to me that this word,
This word so quietly said, was a terrible cry.
And I am confused; I desire to touch your hand,
But again white chasms open, the night flows chill,
And something freezes within me, and I am still.

III

The snowflakes tick the frosted windowpane,
The night is mad with the senseless dance of flakes,
The coal fire sinks and shakes;
I wait by the window, and look along the street,
To where in the snow, beneath a lamp,
A man and a woman stand:
He is leaning close to her face, he takes her hand,
He pleads with her, she tries to turn away.
What is it he leans to say?
What is the savage music he plays upon her?
What chords profound with memories?
She lifts her face in the sombre light,

And together, slowly, they walk away,
Whirled about by the mad dance of snow;
Down the white silent street from lamp to lamp they go,
Into the immortal night.
Where have they gone? Where will the white streets lead
them?
To what tempestuous or ignoble end?
To what faint peace, or dazzling pain?
The snowflakes whirl and madden my brain,
They whirl in patterns before my eyes.
And I see them at last in a small and sombre room,
In the yellow lamplight I see them rise;
She smiles, and lifts white hands to touch her hair:
And he waits wearily in the eternal chair.

IV

I would like to touch this snow with the wind of a dream,
And turn it all
To petals of roses. Why is it that I recall
Your two pale hands holding a bowl of roses,
Wide open like lotos flowers, floating in water?
I would like to touch this snow with the wind of a dream;
To hold the world in my hands and let it fall.
We have walked together through snow for a long, long
way;
We have walked among the hills immortally white,
Golden by noon and blue by night.
I would like to touch this snow with the wind of a dream:
And hear you singing again by a starlight wall.

V

You talk to me—what is it that you are saying?
April . . . April . . .. the soft sun falls between
The deep white chasm; the gorge of the frozen river
Flashes with white and green;
And we are walking there by the blue river,
By the blue river scaled with golden fire,

Our feet move pace for pace through the tall grasses,
And the earth is light with desire.
A great cloud crosses the sky,
Wind shakes the leaves, you fall in the grass and cry;
Crying silently, hiding your face with your hands;
And you are crying, I know,
Because this day, this youth, this beauty, must go,
Go down into the dust.
The golden river is dark with a sudden gust,
The green of the willows is ruffled grey,
A great cloud crosses the sky,
Wind shakes the leaves, you fall in the grass and cry.
Youth . . . April . . . we clamor to them to stay,
And a shadow is on us, for we know that love must die.
And rising, then, we see white peaks in the distance.
White peaks. Quiet. Peace. Eternity.

VI

Yes, we have changed, slowly and silently changed;
We are the hungry ghosts of the selves we knew;
We sit on each other's tombs and stare at death,
We scarcely believe it true—
And only then with a pang that is almost a cry,—
That once, long ago, we were the "I" and the "you"
Who stood bewildered under an April sky.
White night of snow, and a thousand nights like this;
Snow on our lips like the ghost of a kiss;
And a thousand nights in a hollow second of time
We will return again,
Silently, or with trivial speech, to climb
From lamp to lamp up the white street of pain.
Yet, is it better (you say,
Painfully turning your darkened eyes away)
To lend our souls to a quieter music at last,—
Remembering, when we will,
The sudden and gorgeous clashings of the past? . . .
Snow falls about us, the hills immortally white
Wait far off in the undisturbing night.

MORNING SONG OF SENLIN

It is morning, Senlin says, and in the morning
When the light drips through the shutters like the dew,
I arise, I face the sunrise,
And do the things my fathers learned to do.
Stars in the purple dusk above the rooftops
Pale in a saffron mist and seem to die,
And I myself on a swiftly tilting planet
Stand before a glass and tie my tie.

Vine leaves tap my window,
Dew-drops sing to the garden stones,
The robin chirps in the chinaberry tree
Repeating three clear tones.

It is morning. I stand by the mirror
And tie my tie once more.
While waves far off in a pale rose twilight
Crash on a white sand shore.
I stand by a mirror and comb my hair:
How small and white my face!—
The green earth tilts through a sphere of air
And bathes in a flame of space.

There are houses hanging above the stars
And stars hung under a sea . . .
And a sun far off in a shell of silence
Dapples my walls for me . . .

It is morning, Senlin says, and in the morning
Should I not pause in the light to remember god?
Upright and firm I stand on a star unstable,
He is immense and lonely as a cloud.
I will dedicate this moment before my mirror
To him alone; for him I will comb my hair.
Accept these humble offerings, cloud of silence!
I will think of you as I descend the stair.

Vine leaves tap my window,
The snail-track shines on the stones,
Dew-drops flash from the chinaberry tree
Repeating two clear tones.

It is morning, I awake from a bed of silence,
Shining I rise from the starless waters of sleep.
The walls are about me still as in the evening,
I am the same, and the same name still I keep.
The earth revolves with me, yet makes no motion,
The stars pale silently in a coral sky.
In a whistling void I stand before my mirror,
Unconcerned, and tie my tie.

There are horses neighing on far-off hills
Tossing their long white manes,
And mountains flash in the rose-white dusk,
Their shoulders black with rains . . .
It is morning. I stand by the mirror
And surprise my soul once more;
The blue air rushes above my ceiling,
There are suns beneath my floor . . .

. . . It is morning, Senlin says, I ascend from darkness
And depart on the winds of space for I know not where,
My watch is wound, a key is in my pocket,
And the sky is darkened as I descend the stair.
There are shadows across the windows, clouds in heaven,
And a god among the stars; and I will go
Thinking of him as I might think of daybreak
And humming a tune I know . . .

Vine leaves tap at the window,
Dew-drops sing to the garden stones,
The robin chirps in the chinaberry tree
Repeating three clear tones.

"WIND IN THE OLD TREES"

Wind, wind, wind in the old trees,
Whispering prophecies all night long . . .
What do the grey leaves sing to the wind,
What do they say in their whispered song?

We were all young once, and green as the sea,
We all loved beauty, the maiden of white.
But now we are old. O wind, have mercy
And let us remember our youth this night!

The wind is persuasive, it turns through the trees
And sighs of a miracle under its breath . . .
Beauty the dream will die with the dreamer,
None shall have mercy, but all shall have death.

PORTRAIT OF ONE DEAD

This is the house. On one side there is darkness,
On one side there is light.
Into the darkness you may lift your lanterns—
Oh, any number—it will still be night.
And here are echoing stairs to lead you downward
To long sonorous halls.
And here is spring forever at these windows,
With roses on the walls.

This is her room. On one side there is music—
On one side not a sound.
At one step she could move from love to silence,
Feel myriad darkness coiling round.
And here are balconies from which she heard you,
Your steady footsteps on the stair.
And here the glass in which she saw your shadow
As she unbound her hair.

Here is the room—with ghostly walls dissolving—
The twilight room in which she called you "lover";
And the floorless room in which she called you "friend."
So many times, in doubt, she ran between them!—
Through windy corridors of darkening end.

Here she could stand with one dim light above her
And hear far music, like a sea in caverns,
Murmur away at hollowed walls of stone.
And here, in a roofless room where it was raining,
She bore the patient sorrow of rain alone.

Your words were walls which suddenly froze around her.
Your words were windows,—large enough for moonlight,
Too small to let her through.
Your letters—fragrant cloisters faint with music.
The music that assuaged her there was you.

How many times she heard your step ascending
Yet never saw your face!
She heard them turn again, ring slowly fainter,
Till silence swept the place.
Why had you gone? . . . The door, perhaps, mistaken . . .
You would go elsewhere. The deep walls were shaken.

A certain rose-leaf—sent without intention—
Became, with time, a woven web of fire—
She wore it, and was warm.
A certain hurried glance, let fall at parting,
Became, with time, the flashings of a storm.

Yet, there was nothing asked, no hint to tell you
Of secret idols carved in secret chambers
From all you did and said.
Nothing was done, until at last she knew you.
Nothing was known, till, somehow, she was dead.

How did she die?—You say, she died of poison.
Simple and swift. And much to be regretted.
You did not see her pass
So many thousand times from light to darkness,
Pausing so many times before her glass;

You did not see how many times she hurried
To lean from certain windows, vainly hoping,
Passionate still for beauty, remembered spring.
You did not know how long she clung to music,
You did not hear her sing.

Did she, then, make the choice, and step out bravely
From sound to silence,—close, herself, those windows?
Or was it true, instead,
That darkness moved,—for once,—and so possessed her? . . .
We'll never know, you say, for she is dead.

PALIMPSEST: A DECEITFUL PORTRAIT

Well, as you say, we live for small horizons:
We move in crowds, we flow and talk together,
Seeing so many eyes and hands and faces,
So many mouths, and all with secret meanings,—
Yet know so little of them; only seeing
The small bright circle of our consciousness,
Beyond which lies the dark. Some few we know,—
Or think we know. . . . Once, on a sun-bright morning,
I walked in a certain hallway, trying to find
A certain door: I found one, tried it, opened,
And there in a spacious chamber, brightly lighted,
A hundred men played music, loudly, swiftly,
While one tall woman sent her voice above them
In powerful sweetness. . . . Closing then the door
I heard it die behind me, fade to whisper,—
And walked in a quiet hallway as before.
Just such a glimpse, as through that opened door,
Is all we know of those we call our friends. . . .

We hear a sudden music, see a playing
Of ordered thoughts—and all again is silence.
The music, we suppose, (as in ourselves)
Goes on forever there, behind shut doors,—
As it continues after our departure,
So, we divine, it played before we came . . .
What do you know of me, or I of you? . . .
Little enough. . . . We set these doors ajar
Only for chosen movements of the music:
This passage, (so I think—yet this is guesswork)
Will please him,—it is in a strain he fancies,—
More brilliant, though, than his; and while he likes it
He will be piqued . . . He looks at me bewildered
And thinks (to judge from self—this too is guesswork)
The music strangely subtle, deep in meaning,
Perplexed with implications; he suspects me
Of hidden riches, unexpected wisdom. . . .
Or else I let him hear a lyric passage,—
Simple and clear; and all the while he listens
I make pretence to think my doors are closed.
This too bewilders him. He eyes me sidelong
Wondering "Is he such a fool as this?
Or only mocking?"—There I let it end. . . .
Sometimes, of course, and when we least suspect it—
When we pursue our thoughts with too much passion,
Talking with too great zeal—our doors fly open
Without intention; and the hungry watcher
Stares at the feast, carries away our secrets,
And laughs . . . but this, for many counts, is seldom.
And for the most part we vouchsafe our friends,
Our lovers too, only such few clear notes
As we shall deem them likely to admire:
"Praise me for this" we say, or "laugh at this,"
Or "marvel at my candor" . . . all the while
Withholding what's most precious to ourselves,—
Some sinister depth of lust or fear or hatred,
The sombre note that gives the chord its power;
Or a white loveliness—if such we know—
Too much like fire to speak of without shame.

Well, this being so, and we who know it being
So curious about those well-locked houses,
The minds of those we know,—to enter softly,
And steal from floor to floor up shadowy stairways,
From room to quiet room, from wall to wall,
Breathing deliberately the very air,
Pressing our hands and nerves against warm darkness
To learn what ghosts are there,—
Suppose for once I set my doors wide open
And bid you in. . . . Suppose I try to tell you
The secrets of this house, and how I live here;
Suppose I tell you who I am, in fact. . . .
Deceiving you—as far as I may know it—
Only so much as I deceive myself.

If you are clever you already see me
As one who moves forever in a cloud
Of warm bright vanity: a luminous cloud
Which falls on all things with a quivering magic,
Changing such outlines as a light may change,
Brightening what lies dark to me, concealing
Those things that will not change . . . I walk sustained
In a world of things that flatter me: a sky
Just as I would have had it; trees and grass
Just as I would have shaped and colored them;
Pigeons and clouds and sun and whirling shadows,
And stars that brightening climb through mist at nightfall,—
In some deep way I am aware these praise me:
Where they are beautiful, or hint of beauty,
They point, somehow, to me. . . . This water says,—
Shimmering at the sky, or undulating
In broken gleaming parodies of clouds,
Rippled in blue, or sending from cool depths
To meet the falling leaf the leaf's clear image,—
This water says, there is some secret in you
Akin to my clear beauty, beauty swaying
To mirror beauty, silently responsive

To all that circles you. This bare tree says,—
Austere and stark and leafless, split with frost,
Resonant in the wind, with rigid branches
Flung out against the sky,—this tall tree says,
There is some cold austerity in you,
A frozen strength, with long roots gnarled on rocks,
Fertile and deep; you bide your time, are patient,
Serene in silence, bare to outward seeming,
Concealing what reserves of power and beauty!
What teeming Aprils!—chorus of leaves on leaves!
These houses say, such walls in walls as ours,
Such streets of walls, solid and smooth of surface,
Such hills and cities of walls, walls upon walls;
Motionless in the sun, or dark with rain;
Walls pierced with windows, where the light may enter;
Walls windowless where darkness is desired;
Towers and labyrinths and domes and chambers,—
Amazing deep recesses, dark on dark,—
All these are like the walls which shape your spirit:
You move, are warm, within them, laugh within them,
Proud of their depth and strength; or sally from them,
When you are bold, to blow great horns at the world. . . .
This deep cool room, with shadowed walls and ceiling,
Tranquil and cloistral, fragrant of my mind,
This cool room says,—just such a room have you,
It waits you always at the tops of stairways,
Withdrawn, remote, familiar to your uses,
Where you may cease pretence and be yourself. . . .
And this embroidery, hanging on this wall,
Hung there forever,—these so soundless glidings
Of dragons golden-scaled, sheer birds of azure,
Coilings of leaves in pale vermilion, griffins
Drawing their rainbow wings through involutions
Of mauve chrysanthemums and lotus flowers,—
This goblin wood where someone cries enchantment,—
This says, just such an involuted beauty
Of thought and coiling thought, dream linked with dream,
Image to image gliding, wreathing fires,
Soundlessly cries enchantment in your mind:

You need but sit and close your eyes a moment
To see these deep designs unfold themselves.

And so, all things discern me, name me, praise me—
I walk in a world of silent voices, praising;
And in this world you see me like a wraith
Blown softly here and there, on silent winds.
"Praise me"—I say; and look, not in a glass,
But in your eyes, to see my image there—
Or in your mind; you smile, I am contented;
You look at me, with interest unfeigned,
And listen—I am pleased; or else, alone,
I watch thin bubbles veering brightly upward
From unknown depths,—my silver thoughts ascending;
Saying now this, now that, hinting of all things,—
Dreams, and desires, velleities, regrets,
Faint ghosts of memory, strange recognitions,—
But all with one deep meaning: this is I,
This is the glistening secret holy I,
This silver-wingèd wonder, insubstantial,
This singing ghost. . . . And hearing, I am warmed.

* * * * * *

You see me moving, then, as one who moves
Forever at the centre of his circle:
A circle filled with light. And into it
Come bulging shapes from darkness, loom gigantic,
Or huddle in dark again. . . . A clock ticks clearly,
A gas-jet steadily whirs, light streams across me;
Two church bells, with alternate beat, strike nine;
And through these things my pencil pushes softly
To weave grey webs of lines on this clear page.
Snow falls and melts; the eaves make liquid music;
Black wheel-tracks line the snow-touched street; I turn
And look one instant at the half-dark gardens,
Where skeleton elm-trees reach with frozen gesture
Above unsteady lamps,—with black boughs flung
Against a luminous snow-filled grey-gold sky.

"Beauty!" I cry. . . . My feet move on, and take me
Between dark walls, with orange squares for windows.
Beauty; beheld like someone half-forgotten,
Remembered, with slow pang, as one neglected . . .
Well, I am frustrate; life has beaten me,
The thing I strongly seized has turned to darkness,
And darkness rides my heart. . . . These skeleton elm-
trees—
Leaning against that grey-gold snow filled sky—
Beauty! they say, and at the edge of darkness
Extend vain arms in a frozen gesture of protest . . .
A clock ticks softly; a gas-jet steadily whirs:
The pencil meets its shadow upon clear paper,
Voices are raised, a door is slammed. The lovers,
Murmuring in an adjacent room, grow silent,
The eaves make liquid music. . . . Hours have passed,
And nothing changes, and everything is changed.
Exultation is dead, Beauty is harlot,—
And walks the streets. The thing I strongly seized
Has turned to darkness, and darkness rides my heart.
If you could solve this darkness you would have me.
This causeless melancholy that comes with rain,
Or on such days as this when large wet snowflakes
Drop heavily, with rain . . . whence rises this?
Well, so-and-so, this morning when I saw him,
Seemed much preoccupied, and would not smile;
And you, I saw too much; and you, too little;
And the word I chose for you, the golden word,
The word that should have struck so deep in purpose,
And set so many doors of wish wide open,
You let it fall, and would not stoop for it,
And smiled at me, and would not let me guess
Whether you saw it fall. . . . These things, together,
With other things, still slighter, wove to music,
And this in time drew up dark memories;
And there I stand. This music breaks and bleeds me,
Turning all frustrate dreams to chords and dischords,
Faces and griefs, and words, and sunlit evenings,
And chains self-forged that will not break nor lengthen,

And cries that none can answer, few will hear.
Have these things meaning? Or would you see more clearly
If I should say "My second wife grows tedious,
Or, like gay tulip, keeps no perfumed secret"?
Or "one day dies eventless as another,
Leaving the seeker still unsatisfied,
And more convinced life yields no satisfaction"?
Or "seek too hard, the sight at length grows callous,
And beauty shines in vain"?—

These things you ask for,
These you shall have. . . . So, talking with my first wife,
At the dark end of evening, when she leaned
And smiled at me, with blue eyes weaving webs
Of finest fire, revolving me in scarlet,—
Calling to mind remote and small successions
Of countless other evenings ending so,—
I smiled, and met her kiss, and wished her dead;
Dead of a sudden sickness, or by my hands
Savagely killed; I saw her in her coffin,
I saw her coffin borne downstairs with trouble,
I saw myself alone there, palely watching,
Wearing a masque of grief so deeply acted
That grief itself possessed me. Time would pass,
And I should meet this girl,—my second wife—
And drop the masque of grief for one of passion.
Forward we move to meet, half hesitating,
We drown in each other's eyes, we laugh, we talk,
Looking now here, now there, faintly pretending
We do not hear the powerful pulsing prelude
Roaring beneath our words . . . The time approaches.
We lean unbalanced. The mute last glance between us,
Profoundly searching, opening, asking, yielding,
Is steadily met: our two lives draw together . . .
. . . "What are you thinking of?" . . . My first wife's voice
Scattered these ghosts. "Oh, nothing—nothing much—
Just wondering where we'd be two years from now,

And what we might be doing . . ." And then remorse
Turned sharply in my mind to sudden pity,
And pity to echoed love. And one more evening
Drew to the usual end of sleep and silence.

And, as it is with this, so too with all things.
The pages of our lives are blurred palimpsest:
New lines are wreathed on old lines half-erased,
And those on older still; and so forever.
The old shines through the new, and colors it.
What's new? What's old? All things have double meanings,—
All things return. I write a line with passion
(Or touch a woman's hand, or plumb a doctrine)
Only to find the same thing, done before,—
Only to know the same thing comes to-morrow. . . .
This curious riddled dream I dreamed last night,—
Six years ago I dreamed it just as now;
The same man stooped to me; we rose from darkness,
And broke the accustomed order of our days,
And struck for the morning world, and warmth, and freedom. . . .
What does it mean? Why is this hint repeated?
What darkness does it spring from, seek to end?

You see me, then, pass up and down these stairways,
Now through a beam of light, and now through shadow,—
Pursuing silent ends. No rest there is,—
No more for me than you. I move here always,
From quiet room to room, from wall to wall,
Searching and plotting, weaving a web of days.
This is my house, and now, perhaps, you know me. . . .
Yet I confess, for all my best intentions,
Once more I have deceived you. . . . I withhold
The one thing precious, the one dark thing that guides me;
And I have spread two snares for you, of lies.

CLIFF MEETING

Met on the westworn cliff, where the short grass
Blew on the sea-rock edge, with crowded sea-pinks
And heather, she and I stood face to face,
Strangers, and stared. What's in a face or eye
That gives its secret, when the moment comes,
For nothing, less than nothing? We but looked,
Looked once, looked hard, looked deep; the sea-wind spared
The blue still waters of her soul; far down
I saw the ghost I loved. Did she see also,
In my wan eyes, a depth, and a swimming ghost?
Tranced so at cliff's-edge, stood and stared; then laughed;
Then sat together in chilly sunlight, watching
The moving brows of foam come round the headland,
And rabbits daring the cliff.

Her hand, in grass—
(A sea-pink nodded betwixt thumb and finger)
I touched and lifted: she but smiled. Her arm
I scratched with a tiny fork of heather, drawing
A pair of furrows from elbow down to wrist,
White and sharp; she smiled at first, then frowned.
Her mouth, which said no word and gave no name,
I kissed; and as I kissed it, with eyes open,
I saw the sea-pink (caught 'twixt thumb and finger)
Plucked up unmercifully.

The sun went down
Between two waves; and as it went, she rose,
Shaking her dress. To-morrow (so she said)
Here by the cliff's-edge we might meet again.
What's in a face or eye that gives its secret
So lightly, when the moment comes? She saw
Weariness in me, love gone down like the sun,
The fleet ghost gone; and as she saw, she drooped.
Beauty waned out of her; the light drained out
From her deep eyes; pathetic seemed she; I

Discomfited, leering upon her, angry
That I had thought I loved her. So, she went:
Miserable, small, self-pitying, down to darkness.
I watched her go, thinking it strange that she—
Meagre, unlovely—should have captured me.

And on the morrow, when she did not come,
There by the cliff's-edge, staked, I found a letter
Mystic, insoluble, with few words written,
Saying—(and it was strange, and like a dream,
For, as I read, the words seemed only marks
Of bird-claws in the sand)—that she was gone
Down to the village, darkness, gone forever;
But left this bird for me, that I might know—
What I should know. And in the short grass lay,
There with the sea-pinks, a blue cormorant,
White eyelids closed, and dying. Her I lifted
Between my hands, and laid against my breast,
Striving to warm her heart. The bird was starved;
The eyes drooped open, and the livid beak
Opened a little; and I gave my hands
To her to eat, having no other food;
Thrusting a finger in the beak, that she
Might eat my flesh and live. But she was dying,
And could not move the purple beak, falling
Against my hand, inert; and then I thought
That, seeking to make her eat, I did but hasten
Her death. For in a moment, then, she died.

Along the cliff I walked, taking the bird,
Holding it in my hands. . . . What had she meant
In leaving this blue cormorant for me?
Was she not coming? Everywhere I looked;
By rock and tree; in coigns of heather; even
Down where the moving brows of foam came in.
Nowhere—nowhere. The sun went west behind
Two waves. It was the hour of parting. Would
She come not now for that?

The darkness gathered.
The sea-pinks lost their color. And I walked
Along the cliff's-edge, losing all power of thought,
Taking the cormorant into the dark with me.

TETÉLESTAI

I

How shall we praise the magnificence of the dead,
The great man humbled, the haughty brought to dust?
Is there a horn we should not blow as proudly
For the meanest of us all, who creeps his days,
Guarding his heart from blows, to die obscurely?
I am no king, have laid no kingdoms waste,
Taken no princes captive, led no triumphs
Of weeping women through long walls of trumpets;
Say rather, I am no one, or an atom;
Say rather, two great gods, in a vault of starlight,
Play ponderingly at chess, and at the game's end
One of the pieces, shaken, falls to the floor
And runs to the darkest corner; and that piece
Forgotten there, left motionless, is I. . . .
Say that I have no name, no gifts, no power,
Am only one of millions, mostly silent;
One who came with eyes and hands and a heart,
Looked on beauty, and loved it, and then left it.
Say that the fates of time and space obscured me,
Led me a thousand ways to pain, bemused me,
Wrapped me in ugliness; and like great spiders
Dispatched me at their leisure. . . . Well, what then?
Should I not hear, as I lie down in dust,
The horns of glory blowing above my burial?

II

Morning and evening opened and closed above me:
Houses were built above me; trees let fall
Yellowing leaves upon me, hands of ghosts;
Rain has showered its arrows of silver upon me

Seeking my heart; winds have roared and tossed me;
Music in long blue waves of sound has borne me
A helpless weed to shores of unthought silence;
Time, above me, within me, crashed its gongs
Of terrible warning, sifting the dust of death;
And here I lie. Blow now your horns of glory
Harshly over my flesh, you trees, you waters!
You stars and suns, Canopus, Deneb, Rigel,
Let me, as I lie down, here in this dust,
Hear, far off, your whispered salutation!
Roar now above my decaying flesh, you winds,
Whirl out your earth-scents over this body, tell me
Of ferns and stagnant pools, wild roses, hillsides!
Anoint me, rain, let crash your silver arrows
On this hard flesh! I am the one who named you,
I lived in you, and now I die in you.
I your son, your daughter, treader of music,
Lie broken, conquered . . . Let me not fall in silence.

III

I, the restless one; the circler of circles;
Herdsman and roper of stars, who could not capture
The secret of self; I who was tyrant to weaklings,
Striker of children; destroyer of women; corrupter
Of innocent dreamers, and laugher at beauty; I,
Too easily brought to tears and weakness by music,
Baffled and broken by love, the helpless beholder
Of the war in my heart of desire with desire, the struggle
Of hatred with love, terror with hunger; I
Who laughed without knowing the cause of my laughter,
who grew
Without wishing to grow, a servant to my own body;
Loved without reason the laughter and flesh of a woman,
Enduring such torments to find her! I who at last
Grow weaker, struggle more feebly, relent in my purpose,
Choose for my triumph an easier end, look backward
At earlier conquests; or, caught in the web, cry out
In a sudden and empty despair, "Tetélestai!"
Pity me, now! I, who was arrogant, beg you!

Tell me, as I lie down, that I was courageous.
Blow horns of victory now, as I reel and am vanquished.
Shatter the sky with trumpets above my grave.

IV

. . . Look! this flesh how it crumbles to dust and is blown!
These bones, how they grind in the granite of frost and are nothing!
This skull, how it yawns for a flicker of time in the darkness,
Yet laughs not and sees not! It is crushed by a hammer of sunlight,
And the hands are destroyed. . . . Press down through the leaves of the jasmine,
Dig through the interlaced roots—nevermore will you find me;
I was no better than dust, yet you cannot replace me. . . .
Take the soft dust in your hand—does it stir: does it sing?
Has it lips and a heart? Does it open its eyes to the sun?
Does it run, does it dream, does it burn with a secret, or tremble
In terror of death? Or ache with tremendous decisions? . . .
Listen! . . . It says: "I lean by the river. The willows
Are yellowed with bud. White clouds roar up from the south
And darken the ripples; but they cannot darken my heart,
Nor the face like a star in my heart! . . . Rain falls on the water
And pelts it, and rings it with silver. The willow trees glisten,
The sparrows chirp under the eaves; but the face in my heart
Is a secret of music. . . . I wait in the rain and am silent."
Listen again! . . . It says: "I have worked, I am tired,
The pencil dulls in my hand: I see through the window
Walls upon walls of windows with faces behind them,
Smoke floating up to the sky, an ascension of sea-gulls.
I am tired. I have struggled in vain, my decision was fruitless,
Why then do I wait? with darkness, so easy, at hand! . . .
But to-morrow, perhaps . . . I will wait and endure till to-morrow!" . . .

Or again: "It is dark. The decision is made. I am vanquished
By terror of life. The walls mount slowly about me
In coldness. I had not the courage. I was forsaken.
I cried out, was answered by silence . . . Tetélestai! . . ."

V

Hear how it babbles!—Blow the dust out of your hand,
With its voices and visions, tread on it, forget it, turn home-
ward
With dreams in your brain. . . . This, then, is the humble,
the nameless,—
The lover, the husband and father, the struggler with
shadows,
The one who went down under shoutings of chaos, the
weakling
Who cried his "forsaken!" like Christ on the darkening hill-
top! . . .
This, then, is the one who implores, as he dwindles to silence,
A fanfare of glory. . . . And which of us dares to deny
him?

"THIS IS THE SHAPE OF THE LEAF"

[*From* PRIAPUS AND THE POOL]

This is the shape of the leaf, and this of the flower,
And this the pale bole of the tree
Which watches its bough in a pool of unwavering water
In a land we never shall see.

The thrush on the bough is silent, the dew falls softly,
In the evening is hardly a sound.
And the three beautiful pilgrims who come here together
Touch lightly the dust of the ground,

Touch it with feet that trouble the dust but as wings do,
Come shyly together, are still,
Like dancers who wait, in a pause of the music, for music
The exquisite silence to fill.

This is the thought of the first, and this of the second,
And this the grave thought of the third:
"Linger we thus for a moment, palely expectant,
And silence will end, and the bird

"Sing the pure phrase, sweet phrase, clear phrase in the twilight
To fill the blue bell of the world;
And we, who on music so leaflike have drifted together,
Leaflike apart shall be whirled

"Into what but the beauty of silence, silence forever?" . . .
. . . This is the shape of the tree,
And the flower, and the leaf, and the three pale beautiful pilgrims:
This is what you are to me.

"THERE IS NOTHING MOVING"

[*From* PRIAPUS AND THE POOL]

There is nothing moving there, in that desert of silence,
Nothing living there, not even a blade of grass.
The morning there is as silent as the evening;
The nights and days with an equal horror pass.

Nothing moving except the cold, slow shadow
Thrown on sand by a boulder, or by the cliff
Whose rock not even a lichen comes to cover,
To hide—from what?—time's ancient hieroglyph.

The sun, at noon, sings like a flaming cymbal
Above that waste: but the waste makes no reply.
In all that desolation of rock and gravel
There is no water, no answer to the sky.

Sometimes, perhaps, from other lands more happy,
A faint wind, slow, exhausted, ventures there,
And loses itself in silence, like a music.
And then—who knows?—beneath that alien air,

Which moves mysteriously as memory over
Forlorn abysms and peaks of stone and sand,
Ghosts of delight awake for a shining moment,
And all is troubled, and that desolate land

Remembers grass and flowers, and birds that sang there
Their miracles of song in lovely trees,
And waters that poured, or stood, in dreaming azure,
Praising the sky. Perhaps once more it sees

The rose, the moon, the pool, in the blue evening,
And knows that silence in which one bird will sing
Slowly and sleepily his praise of gardens.
Perhaps once more, for a moment, it remembers spring.

"THERE WAS AN ISLAND IN THE SEA"

[*From* PRIAPUS AND THE POOL]

There was an island in the sea
That out of immortal chaos reared
Towers of topaz, trees of pearl,
For maidens adored and warriors feared.

Long ago it sank in the sea;
And now, a thousand fathoms deep,
Sea-worms above it whirl their lamps,
Crabs on the pale mosaic creep.

Voyagers over that haunted sea
Hear from the waters under the keel
A sound that is not wave or foam;
Nor do they only hear, but feel

The timbers quiver, as eerily comes
Up from the dark an elfin singing
Of voices happy as none can be,
And bells an ethereal anthem ringing.

Thereafter, where they go or come,
They will be silent; they have heard
Out of the infinite of the soul
An incommunicable word;

Thereafter, they are as lovers who
Over an infinite brightness lean:
"It is Atlantis!" all their speech;
"To lost Atlantis have we been."

EDNA ST. VINCENT MILLAY

Edna St. Vincent Millay, a daughter of Henry Tolman and Cora Buzzelle Millay, was born on February 22, 1892, at Rockland, Maine. She spent her childhood in Maine, attending school there, and early acquired an interest in poetry. At the age of fourteen she showed promise as a poet. In 1912 she submitted *Renascence* to *The Lyric Year,* an anthology, in competition for a prize offered by Mitchell Kennerley, publisher of the volume. Although failing to win one of the three prizes offered, her poem was placed first by one of the judges, and attracted considerable notice among critics.

In 1913 she entered Vassar College, where she continued to write poetry. While in college she also wrote, and acted in, two plays, *The Princess Marries the Page* and *Two Slatterns and a King*. Upon receiving her degree of A. B. from Vassar in 1917, she went to New York, and settled in a tiny room in Waverly Place, Greenwich Village, with the avowed intention of winning recognition for herself as a poet. In the same year she brought out her first volume, *Renascence*.

For some time she had a difficult struggle in New York, and it became necessary to supplement her meager income from writing by engaging in other work. For a while she was connected with the Provincetown Players, acting in a number of comedies, and having some of her own plays produced; but since with them she received no salary, she presently took a small part in a Literary Guild production. Her acting and such work as translating songs enabled her to remain in New York. During these years, also, she wrote a number of short stories, using the pseudonym Nancy Boyd. In the five years following the publication of *Renascence,* she issued three volumes of lyric poetry and three plays. By 1922 her reputation was established, and in this year she was awarded the Pulitzer prize for poetry.

In 1922 she went to Europe for several months, returning in January, 1923, in poor health. On July 19, 1923, she married Eugen Jan Boissevain, a wealthy importer, the ceremony taking place at the home of Boardman Robinson, the artist, at Croton-on-the-Hudson.

In 1924 she published a volume of short stories, *Distressing Dialogues,* under the name Nancy Boyd. Since her marriage she has written one other volume of lyric poetry, and has contributed to various magazines. Her most noted recent work, however, was *The King's Henchman,* the libretto for Deems Taylor's opera, produced at the Metropolitan Opera House, New York, on February 17, 1927.

Tufts College in 1925 conferred upon her the degree of Doctor of Literature. She now lives with her husband at their home in Greenwich Village, but spends much of her time in travel.

RENASCENCE

All I could see from where I stood
Was three long mountains and a wood;
I turned and looked another way,
And saw three islands in a bay.
So with my eyes I traced the line
Of the horizon, thin and fine,
Straight around till I was come
Back to where I'd started from;
And all I saw from where I stood
Was three long mountains and a wood.
Over these things I could not see:
These were the things that bounded me;
And I could touch them with my hand,
Almost, I thought, from where I stand.
And all at once things seemed so small
My breath came short, and scarce at all.
But, sure, the sky is big, I said;
Miles and miles above my head;
So here upon my back I'll lie
And look my fill into the sky.
And so I looked, and, after all,
The sky was not so very tall.
The sky, I said, must somewhere stop,
And—sure enough!—I see the top!
The sky, I thought, is not so grand;
I 'most could touch it with my hand!
And reaching up my hand to try,
I screamed to feel it touch the sky.
I screamed, and—lo!—Infinity
Came down and settled over me;

Forced back my scream into my chest,
Bent back my arm upon my breast,
And, pressing of the Undefined
The definition on my mind,
Held up before my eyes a glass
Through which my shrinking sight did pass
Until it seemed I must behold
Immensity made manifold;
Whispered to me a word whose sound
Deafened the air for worlds around,
And brought unmuffled to my ears
The gossiping of friendly spheres,
The creaking of the tented sky,
The ticking of Eternity.
I saw and heard and knew at last
The How and Why of all things, past,
And present, and forevermore.
The Universe, cleft to the core,
Lay open to my probing sense
That, sick'ning, I would fain pluck thence
But could not,—nay! But needs must suck
At the great wound, and could not pluck
My lips away till I had drawn
All venom out.—Ah, fearful pawn!
For my omniscience paid I toll
In infinite remorse of soul.
All sin was of my sinning, all
Atoning mine, and mine the gall
Of all regret. Mine was the weight
Of every brooded wrong, the hate
That stood behind each envious thrust,
Mine every greed, mine every lust.
And all the while for every grief,
Each suffering, I craved relief
With individual desire,—
Craved all in vain! And felt fierce fire
About a thousand people crawl;
Perished with each,—then mourned for all!
A man was starving in Capri;

He moved his eyes and looked at me;
I felt his gaze, I heard his moan,
And knew his hunger as my own.
I saw at sea a great fog-bank
Between two ships that struck and sank;
A thousand screams the heavens smote;
And every scream tore through my throat.
No hurt I did not feel, no death
That was not mine; mine each last breath
That, crying, met an answering cry
From the compassion that was I.
All suffering mine, and mine its rod;
Mine, pity like the pity of God.
Ah, awful weight! Infinity
Pressed down upon the finite Me!
My anguished spirit, like a bird,
Beating against my lips I heard;
Yet lay the weight so close about
There was no room for it without.
And so beneath the weight lay I
And suffered death, but could not die.

Long had I lain thus, craving death,
When quietly the earth beneath
Gave way, and inch by inch, so great
At last had grown the crushing weight,
Into the earth I sank till I
Full six feet under ground did lie,
And sank no more,—there is no weight
Can follow here, however great.
From off my breast I felt it roll,
And as it went my tortured soul
Burst forth and fled in such a gust
That all about me swirled the dust.

Deep in the earth I rested now;
Cool is its hand upon the brow
And soft its breast beneath the head
Of one who is so gladly dead.

And all at once, and over all
The pitying rain began to fall;
I lay and heard each pattering hoof
Upon my lowly, thatchèd roof,
And seemed to love the sound far more
Than ever I had done before.
For rain it hath a friendly sound
To one who's six feet under ground;
And scarce the friendly voice or face:
A grave is such a quiet place.

The rain, I said, is kind to come
And speak to me in my new home.
I would I were alive again
To kiss the fingers of the rain,
To drink into my eyes the shine
Of every slanting silver line,
To catch the freshened, fragrant breeze
From drenched and dripping apple-trees.
For soon the shower will be done,
And then the broad face of the sun
Will laugh above the rain-soaked earth
Until the world with answering mirth
Shakes joyously, and each round drop
Rolls, twinkling, from its grass-blade top.
How can I bear it; buried here,
While overhead the sky grows clear
And blue again after the storm?
O, multi-colored, multiform,
Belovèd beauty over me,
That I shall never, never see
Again! Spring-silver, autumn-gold,
That I shall never more behold!
Sleeping your myriad magics through,
Close-sepulchred away from you!
O God, I cried, give me new birth,
And put me back upon the earth!

Upset each cloud's gigantic gourd
And let the heavy rain, down-poured
In one big torrent, set me free,
Washing my grave away from me!

I ceased; and through the breathless hush
That answered me, the far-off rush
Of herald wings came whispering
Like music down the vibrant string
Of my ascending prayer, and—crash!
Before the wild wind's whistling lash
The startled storm-clouds reared on high
And plunged in terror down the sky,
And the big rain in one black wave
Fell from the sky and struck my grave.
I know not how such things can be;
I only know there came to me
A fragrance such as never clings
To aught save happy living things;
A sound as of some joyous elf
Singing sweet songs to please himself,
And, through and over everything,
A sense of glad awakening.
The grass, a-tiptoe at my ear,
Whispering to me I could hear;
I felt the rain's cool finger-tips
Brushed tenderly across my lips,
Laid gently on my sealèd sight,
And all at once the heavy night
Fell from my eyes and I could see,—
A drenched and dripping apple-tree,
A last long line of silver rain,
A sky grown clear and blue again.
And as I looked a quickening gust
Of wind blew up to me and thrust
Into my face a miracle
Of orchard-breath, and with the smell,—
I know not how such things can be!—
I breathed my soul back into me.

Ah! Up then from the ground sprang I
And hailed the earth with such a cry
As is not heard save from a man
Who has been dead, and lives again.
About the trees my arms I wound;
Like one gone mad I hugged the ground;
I raised my quivering arms on high;
I laughed and laughed into the sky,
Till at my throat a strangling sob
Caught fiercely, and a great heart-throb
Sent instant tears into my eyes;
O God, I cried, no dark disguise
Can e'er hereafter hide from me
Thy radiant identity!
Thou canst not move across the grass
But my quick eyes will see Thee pass,
Nor speak, however silently,
But my hushed voice will answer Thee.
I know the path that tells Thy way
Through the cool eve of every day;
God, I can push the grass apart
And lay my finger on Thy heart!

The world stands out on either side
No wider than the heart is wide;
Above the world is stretched the sky,—
No higher than the soul is high.
The heart can push the sea and land
Farther away on either hand;
The soul can split the sky in two,
And let the face of God shine through.
But East and West will pinch the heart
That can not keep them pushed apart;
And he whose soul is flat—the sky
Will cave in on him by and by.

"THOU ART NOT LOVELIER THAN LILACS"

Thou are not lovelier than lilacs,—no,
Nor honeysuckle; thou art not more fair
Than small white single poppies,—I can bear
Thy beauty; though I bend before thee, though
From left to right, not knowing where to go,
I turn my troubled eyes, nor here nor there
Find any refuge from thee, yet I swear
So has it been with mist,—with moonlight so.

Like him who day by day unto his draught
Of delicate poison adds him one drop more
Till he may drink unharmed the death of ten,
Even so, inured to beauty, who have quaffed
Each hour more deeply than the hour before,
I drink—and live—what has destroyed some men.

"OH, THINK NOT I AM FAITHFUL TO A VOW!"

Oh, think not I am faithful to a vow!
Faithless am I save to love's self alone.
Were you not lovely I would leave you now:
After the feet of beauty fly my own.
Were you not still my hunger's rarest food,
And water ever to my wildest thirst,
I would desert you—think not but I would!—
And seek another as I sought you first.
But you are mobile as the veering air,
And all your charms more changeful than the tide,
Wherefore to be inconstant is no care:
I have but to continue at your side.
So wanton, light and false, my love, are you,
I am most faithless when I most am true.

"I KNOW I AM BUT SUMMER TO YOUR HEART"

I know I am but summer to your heart,
And not the full four seasons of the year;
And you must welcome from another part
Such noble moods as are not mine, my dear.
No gracious weight of golden fruits to sell
Have I, nor any wise and wintry thing;
And I have loved you all too long and well
To carry still the high sweet breast of Spring.
Wherefore I say: O love, as summer goes,
I must be gone, steal forth with silent drums,
That you may hail anew the bird and rose
When I come back to you, as summer comes.
  Else will you seek, at some not distant time,
  Even your summer in another clime.

"EUCLID ALONE HAS LOOKED ON BEAUTY BARE"

Euclid alone has looked on Beauty bare.
Let all who prate of Beauty hold their peace,
And lay them prone upon the earth and cease
To ponder on themselves, the while they stare
At nothing, intricately drawn nowhere
In shapes of shifting lineage; let geese
Gabble and hiss, but heroes seek release
From dusty bondage into luminous air.

O blinding hour, O holy, terrible day,
When first the shaft into his vision shone
Of light anatomized! Euclid alone
Has looked on Beauty bare. Fortunate they
Who, though once only and then but far away,
Have heard her massive sandal set on stone.

BIBLIOGRAPHIES

BIBLIOGRAPHIES

PART ONE

THE ENGLISH AND IRISH POETS

THOMAS HARDY

A. POETICAL WORKS

Collected Poems. London: Macmillan & Co., Ltd., 1919. 540 pp. [New edition, London: Macmillan & Co., Ltd., 1928. 840 pp. New Complete American Edition, N. Y.: The Macmillan Co., 1926. 818 pp.]

The Poetical Works of Thomas Hardy. In Two Volumes. . . . [I. Lyrical, Narratory, & Reflective. II. *The Dynasts*, an Epic-Drama.] London: Macmillan & Co., Ltd., 1920-21. 521, 525 pp.

Wessex Poems and Other Verses. With 30 Illustrations by the Author. N. Y. and London: Harper & Brothers, 1898. 228 pp.

Poems of the Past and the Present. [N. Y. and London: Harper & Brothers, 1902.] 260 pp.

The Dynasts. A Drama of the Napoleonic Wars, in Three Parts, Nineteen Acts, & One Hundred and Thirty Scenes. Part First. London: Macmillan & Co., Ltd.; N. Y.: The Macmillan Co., 1903. 228 pp.

The Dynasts. . . . Part Second. London: Macmillan & Co., Ltd.; N. Y.: The Macmillan Co., 1906. 304 pp.

The Dynasts. . . . Part Third. London: Macmillan & Co., Ltd., 1908. 356 pp.

The Pocket Thomas Hardy: Being Selections from the Wessex Novels and Poems of Thomas Hardy. Made by A. H. Hyatt. London: Chatto & Windus, 1906. 312 pp.

Time's Laughingstocks and Other Verses. London: Macmillan & Co., Ltd., 1909. [208 pp.]

Satires of Circumstance: Lyrics and Reveries, with Miscellaneous Pieces. London: Macmillan & Co., Ltd., 1914. 230 pp.

Selected Poems. [Golden Treasury Series.] London: Macmillan & Co., Ltd., 1916. 214 pp.
[Also N. Y.: The Macmillan Co. 1927.]

The Fiddler's Story. A Jingle on the Times. [Privately printed, 1917.] [8 pp.]

Moments of Vision and Miscellaneous Verses. London: Macmillan & Co., Ltd., 1917. 256 pp.

Domicilium. [Privately printed, Chiswick Press, 1918.] [6 pp.]

Selected Poems. With Portrait and Title-Page Design Engraved on the Wood by William Nicholson. London: P. Lee Warner, 1921. 154 pp.

Late Lyrics and Earlier, with Many Other Verses. London: Macmillan & Co., Ltd., 1922. 288 pp.

The Famous Tragedy of the Queen of Cornwall at Tintagel in Lyonnesse. A New Version of an Old Story. Arranged as a Play for Mummers. In One Act. Requiring No Theatre or Scenery. London: Macmillan & Co., Ltd., 1923. [77 pp.]
[Also N. Y.: The Macmillan Co., 1923.]

Human Shows; Far Phantasies; Songs, and Trifles. London: Macmillan & Co., Ltd., 1925. 279 pp.
[Also N. Y.: The Macmillan Co., 1925.]

Yuletide in a Younger World. Drawings by Albert Rutherston. [Ariel Poems, No. 1.] London: Faber & Gwyer, 1927. [4 pp.]

Winter Words in Various Moods and Metres, N. Y.: The Macmillan Co., 1928. 184 pp.

B. BIOGRAPHICAL AND CRITICAL REFERENCES

I. BOOKS

ABERCROMBIE, LASCELLES. *Thomas Hardy. A Critical Study.* London: Martin Secker, 1912. [225 pp.]

BRENNECKE, ERNEST, JR. *The Life of Thomas Hardy.* N. Y.: Greenberg, 1925. [260 pp.]

BRENNECKE, ERNEST, JR. *Thomas Hardy's Universe. A Study of a Poet's Mind.* London: T. Fisher Unwin, Ltd. [1924]. 153 pp.

CHEW, SAMUEL C. *Thomas Hardy. Poet and Novelist.* [Bryn Mawr Notes and Monographs. III.] Bryn Mawr: Bryn Mawr College; N. Y., London [etc.]: Longmans, Green & Co., 1921. 257 pp.
[Contains some biographical information, though chiefly critical.]
[Revised edition, N. Y.: Alfred A. Knopf, 1928.]

CHILD, HAROLD. *Thomas Hardy.* [Writers of the Day.] N. Y.: Henry Holt & Co., [1916]. [128 pp.]
[Criticism.]

FREEMAN, JOHN, *The Moderns. Essays in Literary Criticism* (N. Y., 1917), pp. 103-60.

GOSSE, EDMUND, *Some Diversions of a Man of Letters* (N. Y., 1919), pp. 233-59.

HARDY, FLORENCE EMILY. *The Early Life of Thomas Hardy, 1840-1891. . . .* N. Y.: The Macmillan Co., 1928. 327 pp.

HEDGCOCK, F. A. *Thomas Hardy, Penseur et Artiste. Étudié dans les Romans du Wessex.* Paris: Hachette & Cie., [1911]. 508 pp.

[Contains an account of Hardy's life.]

JOHNSON, LIONEL. *The Art of Thomas Hardy.* [New Edition.] To Which Is Added a Chapter on the Poetry by J. E. Barton and a Bibliography by John Lane together with a New Portrait by Vernon Hill and the Etched Portrait by William Strang. London: John Lane, 1923. 357 pp.

LEA, HERMANN. *Thomas Hardy's Wessex.* Illustrated from Photographs by the Author. London: Macmillan & Co., Ltd., 1913. [318 pp.]

[Contains information bearing on the poetry.]

LYND, ROBERT, *Old and New Masters* (London, 1919), pp. 234-49.

MAIS, S. P. B., *From Shakespeare to O. Henry. Studies in Literature* [Rev. ed.] (London, 1923), pp. 282-300.

A Thomas Hardy Dictionary. The Characters and Scenes of the Novels and Poems Alphabetically Arranged and Described. By F. Outwin Saxelby. London: George Routledge & Sons, Ltd.; N. Y.: E. P. Dutton & Co.; Toronto: Musson Book Co., Ltd., 1911. 238 pp.

SQUIRE, J. C., *Essays on Poetry* (London, 1923), pp. 140-52.

STURGEON, MARY C., *Studies of Contemporary Poets* [Rev. ed.] (N. Y., 1920), pp. 368-81.

WEBB, A. P. *A Bibliography of the Works of Thomas Hardy—1865-1915.* London: Frank Hollings, 1916. [128 pp.]

WILLIAMS, HAROLD, *Modern English Writers: Being a Study of Imaginative Literature, 1890-1914* [Third ed.] (London, 1925), pp. 77-88.

II. MAGAZINE ARTICLES

CHEW, SAMUEL C., "Homage to Thomas Hardy," *New Republic,* XXIII (June 2, 1920), 22-26.

COURTNEY, W. L., "Mr. Thomas Hardy and Æschylus," *Fortnightly Rev.,* CVII (March 1, April 2, 1917), 464-78, 629-41.

FLETCHER, JOHN GOULD, "Thomas Hardy's Poetry," *Poetry,* XVI (April, 1920), 43-49.

FREEMAN, JOHN, "The Poetry of Thomas Hardy," *Bookman* (London), LVII (January, 1920), 139-41.

FREEMAN, JOHN, "Thomas Hardy," *London Mercury*, XVII (March, 1928), 532-45.
[Criticism.]

HONE, J. M., "The Poetry of Mr. Hardy," *London Mercury*, V (February, 1922), 396-406.

KING, R. W., "The Lyrical Poems of Thomas Hardy," *London Mercury*, XV (December, 1926), 157-71.

LOWES, JOHN LIVINGSTON, "Two Readings of Earth," *Yale Rev.*, n. s. XV (April, 1926), 515-40.

MARTIN, DOROTHY, "Thomas Hardy's Lyrics," *Freeman*, VIII (January 30, February 6, 1924), 490-92, 515-16.

MAYNARD, THEODORE, "The Poetry of Thomas Hardy," *Catholic World*, CXXIII (April, 1926), 46-55.

"Mr. Hardy's *Dynasts*," *Edinburgh Rev.*, CCVII (April, 1908), 421-40.

NOYES, ALFRED, "The Poetry of Thomas Hardy," *No. American Rev.*, CXCIV (July, 1911), 96-106.

ROBERT BRIDGES

A. POETICAL WORKS

Poetical Works. [6 vols.] London: Smith, Elder & Co., 1898-1905.

Poetical Works of Robert Bridges. Excluding the Eight Dramas. London: H. Froude; Oxford: Oxford University Press, 1912. 472 pp.

Poems. London: B. M. Pickering, 1873. 125 pp.

The Growth of Love. A Poem in Twenty-Four Sonnets. London: E. Bumpus, 1876. 28 pp.
[Enlarged edition, Oxford: H. Daniel, 1890. [79 pp.]]

Carmen Elegiacum Roberti Bridges. [London]: Impensis Eduardi Bumpus, 1877.

Poems. By the Author of "The Growth of Love." London: E. Bumpus, 1879. 51 pp.

Poems. By the Author of "The Growth of Love." [Third Series.] London: E. Bumpus, 1880.

Prometheus the Firegiver. Oxford: H. Daniel, 1883. 72 pp.

Poems. Oxford: Printed at the Private Press of H. Daniel, 1884. 52 pp.

Eight Plays. [*Nero I.* (1885), *Palicio* (1890), *Return of Ulysses* (1890), *Christian Captives* (1890), *Achilles in Scyros* (1890), *Humours of the Court* (1893), *Feast of Bacchus* (1894), *Nero II.* (1894).] [London: George Bell & Sons; E. Bumpus, 1885-94.]
[Each play published separately.]

Eros & Psyche . . . [Translated from the Latin of Apuleius.] London: George Bell & Sons, [1885]. 158 pp.

The Feast of Bacchus. Oxford: H. Daniel, 1889. 94 pp.

The Shorter Poems of Robert Bridges. London: George Bell & Sons, 1890. 91 pp.

Eden. An Oratorio . . . Set to Music by C. V. Stanford. London: George Bell & Sons, 1891. 40 pp.

Achilles in Scyros. London: George Bell & Sons, 1892. 68 pp.

The Humours of the Court, a Comedy, and Other Poems. N. Y.: The Macmillan Co.; London: George Bell & Sons, 1893. 185 pp.

Ode for the Bicentenary Commemoration of Henry Purcell. With Other Poems and a Preface on the Musical Setting of Poetry. [E. Mathews' Shilling Garland, No. 2.] [London: E. Mathews, 1896.] 43 pp.

Purcell Ode and Other Poems. Chicago: Way & Williams, 1896. [55 pp.]

Now in Wintry Delights. Oxford: H. Daniel, 1903. 23 pp.

Peace. An Ode Written on the Conclusion of the Three Years' War. [Oxford: H. Daniel, 1903.] [6 pp.]

Demeter, a Mask. Oxford: Clarendon Press, 1905. 67 pp.

Poems Written in the Year 1913. [Privately printed by St. John Hornby, Ashendene Press, 1914.]

Ibant Obscuri: an Experiment in the Classical Hexameter. Oxford: Clarendon Press, 1916. 158 pp.

Britannia Victrix. London: Oxford University Press, 1918. [4 pp.]

October and Other Poems, with Occasional Verses on the War. London: William Heinemann, 1920. 63 pp.
[Also N. Y.: Alfred A. Knopf, 1920.]

New Verse. Written in 1921 . . . with the Other Poems of That Year and a Few Earlier Pieces. Oxford: Clarendon Press, 1925. [89 pp.]

Robert Bridges. [Augustan Books of Modern Poetry.] London: E. Benn, Ltd., [1925]. 29 pp.

B. BIOGRAPHICAL AND CRITICAL REFERENCES

I. BOOKS

DOWDEN, EDWARD, *New Studies in Literature* (New ed., London, 1902), pp. 61-90.

FIGGIS, DARRELL, *Studies and Appreciations* (London, 1912), pp. 155-69.

FREEMAN, JOHN, *The Moderns. Essays in Literary Criticism* (N. Y., 1917), pp. 319-41.

HEARN, LAFCADIO, *Appreciations of Poetry* [Edited by John Erskine] (N. Y., 1916), pp. 385-403.

KELSHALL, T. M. *Robert Bridges (Poet Laureate)*. London: Robert Scott [1924]. 93 pp.
[Criticism, with a brief account of the poet's life.]

SQUIRE, J. C., *Essays on Poetry* (London, 1923), pp. 122-40.

SYMONS, ARTHUR, *Studies in Prose and Verse* (London, 1904), pp. 207-24.

WARREN, T. HERBERT. *Robert Bridges, Poet Laureate. Readings from His Poems*. A Public Lecture Delivered at the Examination Schools on November 8, 1913. Oxford: Clarendon Press, 1913. [39 pp.]
[Both biographical and critical.]

WILLIAMS, HAROLD, *Modern English Writers: Being a Study of Imaginative Literature, 1890-1914* [Third ed.] (London, 1925), pp. 29-31.

YOUNG, F. E. BRETT. *Robert Bridges. A Critical Study*. London: Martin Secker, 1914. [215 pp.]

II. MAGAZINE ARTICLES

BAILEY, JOHN, "The Poetry of Robert Bridges," *Quarterly Rev.*, CCXIX (July, 1913), 231-56.

BINYON, LAURENCE, "Robert Bridges and the Poetic Art," *Bookman* (London), LIV (August, 1918), 144-48.

BRAITHWAITE, WILLIAM STANLEY, "The Lyrical Poetry of the New Laureate," *Forum*, L (December, 1913), 877-91.

BRONNER, MILTON, "Robert Bridges as Lyrist," *Bookman*, XXXVIII (September, 1913), 42-46.

DAVISON, EDWARD, "Robert Bridges, Poet Laureate of England," *English Journal*, XIV (December, 1925), 749-60.
[Criticism.]

DAVISON, EDWARD, "In Praise of the Poet Laureate," *Fortnightly Rev.*, n. s. CXXIV (July, 1928), 66-80.
[Criticism.]

KELLETT, E. E., "The Poems of Robert Bridges," *London Quarterly Rev.*, CXXIV (October, 1915), 232-49.

MILES, LOUIS W., "The Poetry of Robert Bridges," *Sewanee Rev.*, XXIII (April, 1915), 129-40.

"The Poet Laureate," *New Statesman*, XV (April 24, 1920), 76-78.
[Criticism.]

RANSOM, JOHN CROWE, "The Poet Laureate," *Literary Rev.*, IV (March 29, 1924), 625-26.

A. E. HOUSMAN

A. POETICAL WORKS

A Shropshire Lad. London: Kegan Paul & Co., 1896. 96 pp.
[A number of subsequent editions, both in England and America. Authorized American Edition, N. Y.: Henry Holt & Co., 1922.]

Last Poems. London: Grant Richards, Ltd., 1922. [79 pp.]
[Also N. Y.: Henry Holt & Co., 1922.]

B. CRITICAL REFERENCES

I. BOOKS

ARCHER, WILLIAM, *Poets of the Younger Generation* (London, 1902), pp. 183-96.

COLLINS, H. P., *Modern Poetry* (London, 1925), pp. 67-78.

GOSSE, EDMUND, *More Books on the Table* (London, 1923), pp. 21-27.

PHELPS, WILLIAM LYON, *The Advance of English Poetry in the Twentieth Century* (N. Y., 1918), pp. 65-71.

PRIESTLEY, J. B., *Figures in Modern Literature* (N. Y., 1924), pp. 77-103.

SQUIRE, J. C., *Essays on Poetry* (London, 1923), pp. 152-60.

II. MAGAZINE ARTICLES

BENÉT, WILLIAM ROSE, "A. E. Housman's *Last Poems,*" *Bookman,* LVII (March, 1923), 83-86.

FERGUSON, J. DE LANCEY, "The Belligerent Don," *Sat. Rev. of Literature,* II (March 27, 1926), 657-59, 663.
[On Housman as man and scholar.]

FREEMAN, JOHN, "A. E. Housman," *Bookman* (London), LIX (November, 1920), 71-72.
[Criticism.]

JACKSON, HOLBROOK, "The Poetry of A. E. Housman," *Living Age,* CCCII (September 20, 1919), 728-32.

LUCAS, F. L., "Few, but Roses," *Dial,* LXXVII (September, 1924), 201-9.

"The Silent Singer," *Nation & Athenæum,* XXXII (October 28, 1922), 151-53.
[Criticism.]

W. B. YEATS

A. POETICAL WORKS

The Poetical Works of William B. Yeats. In Two Volumes. N. Y.: The Macmillan Co.; London: Macmillan & Co., Ltd., 1906-7.
[Several later editions.]

Mosada. A Dramatic Poem. Dublin: Sealy, Bryers & Walker, 1886.

The Wanderings of Oisin and Other Poems. London: K. Paul, Trench & Co., 1889. 156 pp.

The Countess Kathleen: an Irish Drama; and Various Legends and Lyrics. [Cameo Series.] London: T. Fisher Unwin, 1892. 141 pp.
[Also Boston: Roberts Brothers, 1893.]

The Land of Heart's Desire. London: T. F. Unwin; Chicago: Stone & Kimball, 1894.

Poems. London: T. F. Unwin; Boston: Copeland & Day, 1895. [286 pp.]
[A number of later editions of *Poems* published by T. F. Unwin.]

The Wind among the Reeds. N. Y. and London: John Lane, 1899. 108 pp.
[Both prose and verse.]

The Shadowy Waters. London: Hodder & Stoughton, 1900. 57 pp.
[Also N. Y.: Dodd, Mead & Co., 1901.]

In the Seven Woods. Being Poems Chiefly of the Irish Heroic Age. N. Y.: The Macmillan Co.; London: Macmillan & Co., Ltd., 1903. 87 pp.
[Also Dundrum: Dun Emer Press, 1903.]

The King's Threshold. A Play in Verse. N. Y.: [Printed for private circulation], 1904. 58 pp.

The King's Threshold: and On Baile's Strand. Being Volume Three of Plays for an Irish Theatre. London: A. H. Bullen, 1904. 117 pp.

Poems, 1899-1905. London: A. H. Bullen; Dublin: Maunsel & Co., Ltd., 1906. [280 pp.]

Deirdre. Being Volume Five of Plays for an Irish Theatre. London: A. H. Bullen; Dublin: Maunsel & Co., Ltd., 1907. [48 pp.]

The Golden Helmet. N. Y.: J. Quinn, 1908. 32 pp.

The Green Helmet and Other Poems. Churchtown, Dundrum: Cuala Press, 1910. 33 pp.
[Also N. Y.: The Macmillan Co., 1912. 91 pp.]

Poems Written in Discouragement. [Dundrum, Ireland: Cuala Press, 1913.]

A Selection from the Love Poetry of William Butler Yeats. Dundrum: Cuala Press, 1913. [30 pp.]

Responsibilities; Poems and a Play. Churchtown, Dundrum, Ireland: Cuala Press, 1914. [81 pp.]

Dramatic Poems. N. Y.: The Macmillan Co., 1916. 478 pp.

Easter, 1916. [Privately printed, 1916.]

Eight Poems. [Privately printed, 1916.]

Lyric Poems. N. Y.: The Macmillan Co., 1916. 338 pp.

Responsibilities and Other Poems. London: Macmillan & Co., Ltd., 1916. 188 pp.
[Also N. Y.: The Macmillan Co., 1916.]

The Wild Swans at Coole, Other Verses and a Play in Verse. Churchtown, Dundrum: Cuala Press, 1917. [47 pp.]

Nine Poems. [Privately printed: Clement Shorter, 1918.] [15 pp.]

Two Plays for Dancers. [Churchtown, Dundrum]: Cuala Press, 1919. 38 pp.

The Wild Swans at Coole. N. Y.: The Macmillan Co., 1919. [115 pp.]

Michael Robartes and the Dancer. Churchtown, Dundrum: Cuala Press. 1920. [35 pp.]

Four Plays for Dancers. London: Macmillan & Co., Ltd., 1921. 138 pp.

Selected Poems. N. Y.: The Macmillan Co., 1921. 308 pp.

Later Poems. London: Macmillan & Co., Ltd., 1922. 363 pp.
[Also N. Y.: The Macmillan Co., 1924.]

Plays in Prose and Verse. Written for an Irish Theatre, and Generally with the Help of a Friend. London: Macmillan & Co., Ltd., 1922. 447 pp.
[Also N. Y.: The Macmillan Co., 1924.]

Seven Poems and a Fragment. Dundrum, Ireland: Cuala Press, 1922. 24 pp.

Plays and Controversies. London: Macmillan & Co., Ltd., 1923. 461 pp.
[Both prose and verse.]

The Cat and the Moon and Certain Poems. Dublin: Cuala Press, 1924. 41 pp.

The Lake Isle of Innisfree. . . . [With facsimile in Yeats's handwriting.] [San Francisco: J. H. Nash], 1924. [8 pp.]

Early Poems and Stories. London: Macmillan & Co., Ltd., 1925. 528 pp.
[Also N. Y.: The Macmillan Co., 1925.]

October Blast. Dublin, Ireland: Cuala Press, 1927. [25 pp.]

W. B. Yeats. [Augustan Books of Modern Poetry.] London: E. Benn, Ltd., 1927. 29 pp.

The Tower. London: Macmillan & Co., Ltd., 1928. 110 pp.
[Also N. Y.: The Macmillan Co., 1928.]

B. BIOGRAPHICAL AND CRITICAL REFERENCES

I. BOOKS

ARCHER, WILLIAM, *Poets of the Younger Generation* (London, 1902), pp. 531-60.

BOYD, ERNEST A., *Ireland's Literary Renaissance* (N. Y., 1916), pp. 122-45.

BOYD, ERNEST, *Portraits: Real and Imaginary* . . . (N. Y., 1924), pp. 236-46.
[Of biographical value.]

ERVINE, ST. JOHN G., *Some Impressions of My Elders* (N. Y., 1922), pp. 264-305.
[About Yeats as a man.]

FIGGIS, DARRELL, *Studies and Appreciations* (London, 1912), pp. 119-38.

GURD, PATTY. *The Early Poetry of William Butler Yeats* . . . [Doctoral dissertation, Zurich.] Lancaster, Pa., 1916. 101 pp.

HONE, J. M. *William Butler Yeats. The Poet in Contemporary Ireland.* [Irishmen of To-day.] Dublin and London: Maunsel & Co., Ltd., [1916]. 134 pp.
[Chiefly biographical.]

JONES, LLEWELLYN, *First Impressions. Essays on Poetry, Criticism, and Prosody* (N. Y., 1925), pp. 137-49.

KRANS, HORATIO SHEAFE. *William Butler Yeats and the Irish Literary Revival.* [Contemporary Men of Letters Series.] N. Y.: McClure, Phillips & Co., 1904. 196 pp.
[Contains two chapters on Yeats's poetry.]

LYND, ROBERT, *Old and New Masters* (London, 1919), pp. 156-71.

MARBLE, ANNIE RUSSELL, *The Nobel Prize Winners in Literature* (N. Y., 1925), pp. 253-64.

MAYNARD, THEODORE, *Our Best Poets. English and American* (N. Y., 1922), pp. 67-84.

MOORE, GEORGE. *Hail and Farewell.* [3 vols. I. *Ave.* II. *Salve.* III. *Vale.*] N. Y.: D. Appleton & Co., 1912-14.
[Much information on Yeats in the three volumes.]

MORRIS, LLOYD R., *The Celtic Dawn. A Survey of the Renascence in Ireland—1889-1916* (N. Y., 1917), pp. 38-60.

REID, FORREST. *W. B. Yeats. A Critical Study.* N. Y.: Dodd, Mead & Co., 1915. [258 pp.]

SQUIRE, J. C., *Essays on Poetry* (London, 1923), pp. 160-71.

STURGEON, MARY C., *Studies of Contemporary Poets* [Rev. ed.] (N. Y., 1920), pp. 419-33.

SYMONS, ARTHUR, *Studies in Prose and Verse* (London, 1904), pp. 230-42.

SYMONS, A. J. A. *A Bibliography of the First Editions of Books by William Butler Yeats.* London: First Edition Club, 1924. 46 pp.

TYNAN, KATHARINE [Mrs. H. A. Hinkson], *Twenty-five Years: Reminiscences* (London, 1913), pp. 254-74.

[Contains some first hand biographical information.]

WADE, ALLEN. *A Bibliography of the Writings of William Butler Yeats.* Stratford-on-Avon: Shakespeare Head Press, 1908. [96 pp.]

WEYGANDT, CORNELIUS, *Irish Plays and Playwrights* (London, 1913), pp. 37-72.

WILLIAMS, HAROLD, *Modern English Writers: Being a Study of Imaginative Literature, 1890-1914* [Third ed.] (London, 1925), pp. 183-94.

YEATS, W. B. *Autobiographies: Reveries over Childhood and Youth and The Trembling of the Veil.* N. Y.: The Macmillan Co., 1927. 477 pp.

II. MAGAZINE ARTICLES

A. E., "Yeats's Early Poetry," *Living Age,* CCCXXVII (November 28, 1925), 464-67.

BINYON, LAURENCE, "William Butler Yeats," *Bookman* (London), LXIII (January, 1923), 196-99.

[Criticism.]

BROWN, FORMAN G., "Mr. Yeats and the Supernatural," *Sewanee Rev.,* XXXIII (July, 1925), 323-31.

COLUM, MARY M., "The Later Yeats," *Poetry,* VII (February, 1916), 258-60.

[Criticism.]

EGLINTON, JOHN, "Yeats and His Story," *Dial,* LXXX (May, 1926), 357-67.

[Chiefly criticism.]

JACKSON, SCHUYLER, "William Butler Yeats," *London Mercury,* XI (February, 1925), 396-411.

[Criticism.]

MACLEOD, FIONA [William Sharp], "The Later Work of W. B. Yeats," *No. American Rev.,* CLXXV (October, 1902), 473-86.

"A School of Irish Poetry," *Edinburgh Rev.,* CCIX (January, 1909), 94-119.

WILSON, EDMUND, "W. B. Yeats," *New Republic,* XLII: supplement (April 15, 1925), 8-11.

GEORGE W. RUSSELL (Æ)

A. POETICAL WORKS

Collected Poems. London: Macmillan & Co., Ltd., 1913. 275 pp.
[Enlarged edition, London: Macmillan & Co., Ltd., 1926. 373 pp.]

Homeward, Songs by the Way. London: John Lane, 1894. 64 pp.
[Also *Homeward: Songs by the Way.* Portland, Me.: Thomas B. Mosher, 1904. 75 pp.]

The Earth Breath and Other Poems. N. Y. and London: John Lane, 1897. 94 pp.

The Nuts of Knowledge. Lyrical Poems Old and New. [Dundrum, Ireland: Dun Emer Press, 1903.] 32 pp.

The Divine Vision and Other Poems. N. Y.: The Macmillan Co.; London: Macmillan & Co., Ltd., 1904. 123 pp.

By Still Waters. Lyrical Poems Old and New. Dundrum, Ireland: Dun Emer Press, 1906. [33 pp.]

Gods of War and Other Poems. [Dundrum, Ireland: Cuala Press, 1915.]

The Interpreters. London: Macmillan & Co., Ltd., 1922. 180 pp.
[Also N. Y.: The Macmillan Co., 1923.]
[Prose with some verse included.]

Voices of the Stones. London: Macmillan & Co., Ltd., 1925. 61 pp.
[Also N. Y.: The Macmillan Co., 1925.]

B. BIOGRAPHICAL AND CRITICAL REFERENCES

I. BOOKS

BOYD, ERNEST A., *Appreciations and Depreciations. Irish Literary Studies* (N. Y., 1918), pp. 25-49.

BOYD, ERNEST A., *Ireland's Literary Renaissance* (N. Y., 1916), pp. 219-39.

BOYD, ERNEST, *Portraits: Real and Imaginary* . . . (N. Y., 1924), pp. 255-65.
[Of biographical value.]

FIGGIS, DARRELL. *Æ (George W. Russell). A Study of a Man and a Nation.* [Irishmen of To-day.] Dublin and London: Maunsel & Co., Ltd., 1916. 159 pp.
[Criticism, with some biographical matter.]

HARRIS, FRANK, *Latest Contemporary Portraits* (N. Y., 1927), pp. 75-95.

MOORE, GEORGE. *Hail and Farewell.* [3 vols. I. *Ave.* II. *Salve.* III. *Vale.*] N. Y.: D. Appleton & Co., 1912-14.
[Much information on Russell in the three volumes.]

MORRIS, LLOYD R., *The Celtic Dawn. A Survey of the Renascence in Ireland—1889-1916* (N. Y., 1917), pp. 25-38.

WEYGANDT, CORNELIUS, *Irish Plays and Playwrights* (London, 1913), pp. 114-38.

WILLIAMS, HAROLD, *Modern English Writers: Being a Study of Imaginative Literature, 1890-1914* [Third ed.] (London, 1925), pp. 194-96.

II. MAGAZINE ARTICLES

COLUM, PADRAIC, " 'A.E.', Poet, Painter and Economist," *New Republic,* XV (June 8, 1918), 172-74.

DAVISON, EDWARD, "Three Irish Poets—A. E., W. B. Yeats, and James Stephens," *English Journal,* XV (May, 1926), 329-32.

EGLINTON, JOHN, " 'A. E.' and His Story," *Dial,* LXXXII (April, 1927), 271-81.
[About the man and his theories.]

FREEMAN, JOHN, "The Poetry of A. E.," *Bookman* (London), LXVIII (August, 1925), 243-44.

"George William Russell—'A. E.'," *Irish Book Lover,* VII (October, 1915), 37-38.

MORRIS, LLOYD R., "Four Irish Poets," *Columbia University Quarterly,* XVIII (September, 1916), 332-36.

W. H. DAVIES

A. POETICAL WORKS

Collected Poems. With a Portrait in Collotype from a Pencil Sketch by Will Rothenstein, and Facsimile of Author's Script. London: A. C. Fifield [1916]. 160 pp.
[Also N. Y.: Alfred A. Knopf, 1916.]

Collected Poems: First Series. London: J. Cape [1923]. 160 pp.

Collected Poems: Second Series. London: J. Cape [1923]. 157 pp.
[Also N. Y.: Harper & Bros., 1923.]

Collected Poems. London: J. Cape, 1928. 416 pp.

The Soul's Destroyer and Other Poems. [London, Farmhouse, Marshalsea Road, S. E.: Printed for the Author by Watts & Co., 1905.] [108 pp.]

New Poems. London: Elkin Mathews, 1907. 75 pp.
Nature Poems and Others. London: A. C. Fifield, 1908. 62 pp.
Farewell to Poesy and Other Pieces. London: A. C. Fifield, 1910. 60 pp.
Songs of Joy and Others. London: A. C. Fifield, 1911. 94 pp.
Foliage. Various Poems. London: Elkin Mathews, 1913. 63 pp.
The Bird of Paradise and Other Poems. London: Methuen & Co. [1914]. 86 pp.
Child Lovers and Other Poems. London: A. C. Fifield, 1916. 29 pp.
Forty New Poems. London: A. C. Fifield, 1918. 53 pp.
Raptures. A Book of Poems. [London: William Beaumont, 1918.] 39 pp.
The Song of Life and Other Poems. With a Frontispiece from a Portrait by Laura Knight. London: A. C. Fifield, 1920. 61 pp.
The Captive Lion & Other Poems. New Haven: Yale University Press, 1921. 99 pp.
The Hour of Magic and Other Poems. Decorated by William Nicholson. N. Y. and London: Harper & Brothers, 1922. 34 pp.
[Also London: J. Cape, [1922].]
Selected Poems. Decorated with Woodcuts by Stephen Bone. London: J. Cape [1923]. 76 pp.
[Also N. Y.: Harcourt, Brace & Co., 1925.]
True Travellers. A Tramp's Opera in Three Acts. With Decorations by William Nicholson. London: J. Cape, [1923]. 52 pp.
[Prose, with songs included.]
Secrets. London: J. Cape, [1924]. 48 pp.
[Also N. Y.: Harcourt, Brace & Co., [1924].]
W. H. Davies. [Augustan Books of Modern Poetry.] London: E. Benn, Ltd., [1925]. 30 pp.
A Poet's Alphabet. [With Decorations by Dora M. Batty.] London: J. Cape, [1925]. 63 pp.
The Song of Love. [With Decorations by Dora M. Batty.] London: J. Cape, [1926]. 61 pp.
A Poet's Calendar. London: J. Cape, [1927]. 61 pp.

B. BIOGRAPHICAL AND CRITICAL REFERENCES

I. BOOKS

DAVIES, W. H. *The Autobiography of a Super-Tramp.* With a Preface by Bernard Shaw. London: A. C. Fifield, 1908. 295 pp.
DAVIES, W. H. *Later Days.* London: J. Cape, Ltd., [1925]. 223 pp.
[A sequel to *The Autobiography.*]

FIGGIS, DARRELL, *Studies and Appreciations* (London, 1912), pp. 138-48.

MAYNARD, THEODORE, *Our Best Poets. English and American* (N. Y., 1922), pp. 107-16.

MONRO, HAROLD, *Some Contemporary Poets (1920)* (London, 1920), pp. 70-75.

STURGEON, MARY C., *Studies of Contemporary Poets* [Rev. ed.] (N. Y., 1920), pp. 53-72.

WILLIAMS, HAROLD, *Modern English Writers: Being a Study of Imaginative Literature, 1890-1914* [Third ed.] (London, 1925), pp. 151-52.

II. MAGAZINE ARTICLES

ARMSTRONG, MARTIN D., "Recent English Poetry," *Fortnightly Rev.*, CI (March 2, 1914), 501-4.

"Bibliographies of Modern Authors," *London Mercury*, XVII (November, 1927; January, April, 1928), 76-80, 301-5, 684-89.

GWYNN, STEPHEN, "The Making of a Poet," *Nineteenth Century*, LXVII (January, 1910), 71-79.

POUND, EZRA, "William H. Davies, Poet," *Poetry*, XI (November, 1917), 99-103.

SCOTT-JAMES, R. A., "Living English Poets," *North American Rev.*, CXCVIII (September, 1913), 379-83.

TROMBLY, A. E., "The Poems of William H. Davies," *Sewanee Rev.*, XXVIII (July, 1920), 414-21.

RALPH HODGSON

A. POETICAL WORKS

The Last Blackbird and Other Lines. London: George Allen, 1907. 104 pp.

[Also N. Y.: The Macmillan Co., 1917.]

The Bull. London: Printed by A. T. Stevens for Flying Fame, 1913. 20 pp.

Eve, and Other Poems. Westminster: A. T. Stevens, 1913. 20 pp.

The Mystery and Other Poems. London: Printed by A. T. Stevens for Flying Fame, 1913. 20 pp.

The Song of Honour. London: Printed by A. T. Stevens for Flying Fame, 1913. 24 pp.

Poems. N. Y.: The Macmillan Co., 1917. 64 pp.

B. BIOGRAPHICAL AND CRITICAL REFERENCES

I. BOOKS

AIKEN, CONRAD, *Scepticisms. Notes on Contemporary Poetry* (N. Y., 1919), pp. 208-11.

DAVIES, W. H., *Later Days* (London, 1925), pp. 73-84.
[Biographical information.]

MAYNARD, THEODORE, *Our Best Poets. English and American* (N. Y., 1922), pp. 55-67.

MONRO, HAROLD, *Some Contemporary Poets (1920)* (London, 1920), pp. 65-70.

PHELPS, WILLIAM LYON, *The Advance of English Poetry in the Twentieth Century* (N. Y., 1918), pp. 114-23.

STURGEON, MARY C., *Studies of Contemporary Poets* [Rev. ed.] (N. Y., 1920), pp. 108-22.

II. MAGAZINE ARTICLES

CHESSON, W. H., "The Poetry of Ralph Hodgson," *Nineteenth Century*, LXXXVIII (July, 1920), 54-63.

"Contented if He Might Enjoy." *Athenæum*, II (August, 1917), 401-2.

LANDOR, GEORGE, "Ralph Hodgson," *Bookman* (London), LII (July, 1917), 108-10.
[Criticism.]

LUCAS, E. V., "Ralph Hodgson," *Nation*, XCIX (September 17, 1914), 341-43.
[Criticism, with some biographical material.]

WALTER DE LA MARE

A. POETICAL WORKS

Poems: 1901 to 1918. [2 vols.] London: Constable & Co., Ltd. [1920]. 251, 250 pp.
[Published as *Collected Poems: 1901-1918*. [2 vols.] N. Y.: Henry Holt & Co., 1920.]

Songs of Childhood. By Walter Ramal. With Frontispiece. London: Longmans, Green & Co., 1902. 106 pp.

Poems. London: John Murray, 1906. 127 pp.

The Listeners and Other Poems. London: Constable & Co., Ltd., 1912. 92 pp.
[Also N. Y.: Henry Holt & Co., 1916.]

A Child's Day. A Book of Rhymes. . . . To Pictures by Carine and Will Cadby. London: Constable & Co., Ltd., 1912. 57 pp.
[Also N. Y.: E. P. Dutton & Co., 1912.]

Peacock Pie. A Book of Rhymes. London: Constable & Co., Ltd., 1913. 122 pp.
[Also N. Y.: Henry Holt & Co., 1917.]

The Sunken Garden and Other Poems. [Limited Edition.] [London: Beaumont Press], [1917]. 40 pp.

Motley and Other Poems. London: Constable & Co., 1918. 75 pp.
[Also N. Y.: Henry Holt & Co., 1918.]

Flora. A Book of Drawings by Pamela Bianco. With Illustrative Poems by Walter de la Mare. London: William Heinemann, [1919]. 45 pp.

Crossings. A Fairy Play. With Music by C. Armstrong Gibbs. [London: Beaumont Press, 1921.] 132 pp.
[Also N. Y.: Alfred A. Knopf, 1923.]
[Prose text with lyrics included.]

Story and Rhyme. A Selection from the Writings of Walter de la Mare. Chosen by the Author. [King's Treasuries of Literature.] London: J. M. Dent & Co., [1921]. 160 pp.

The Veil and Other Poems. London: Constable & Co., Ltd., [1921]. [92 pp.]
[Also N. Y.: Henry Holt & Co., 1922.]

Down-adown-Derry. A Book of Fairy Poems. With Illustrations by Dorothy P. Lathrop. London: Constable & Co., Ltd., [1922]. 193 pp.
[Also N. Y.: Henry Holt & Co., [1922].]

Thus Her Tale. A Poem. Designs by William Ogilvie. Edinburgh: Porpoise Press, 1923. 8 pp.

Ding Dong Bell. London: Selwyn & Blount, Ltd., 1924. 76 pp.
[Also N. Y.: Alfred A. Knopf, 1924.]
[Prose and verse.]

A Ballad of Christmas. Decorated by Alec Buckles. London: Selwyn & Blount, [1924]. 8 pp.

Before Dawn. Decorated by Alec Buckles. London: Selwyn & Blount, 1924. 8 pp.

Walter de la Mare. [Augustan Books of Modern Poetry.] London: E. Benn, Ltd., [1926]. 31 pp.

Alone. Wood Engravings by Blair Hughes-Stanton. [Ariel Poems, No. 4.] London: Faber & Gwyer, 1927. [4 pp.]

Selected Poems. N. Y.: Henry Holt & Co., [1927]. 120 pp.

Stuff and Nonsense, and So On. With Woodcuts by Bold. London: Constable & Co., Ltd., 1927. 110 pp.
[Also N. Y.: Henry Holt & Co., [1927].]

B. BIOGRAPHICAL AND CRITICAL REFERENCES

I. BOOKS

DANIELSON, HENRY. *Bibliographies of Modern Authors.* London: Bookman's Journal; N. Y.: James F. Drake, Inc., 1921. [212 pp.]
["Walter de la Mare," pp. 25-39.]

JONES, LLEWELLYN, *First Impressions. Essays on Poetry, Criticism, and Prosody* (N. Y., 1925), pp. 125-37.

LYND, ROBERT, *The Art of Letters* (N. Y., 1921), pp. 190-96.

MAYNARD, THEODORE, *Our Best Poets. English and American* (N. Y., 1922), pp. 43-55.
[Criticism.]

MÉGROZ, R. L. *Walter de la Mare: A Biographical and Critical Study.* London: Hodder & Stoughton, 1924. 303 pp.

MURRY, JOHN MIDDLETON, *Countries of the Mind. Essays in Literary Criticism* (London, 1922), pp. 123-37.

PRIESTLEY, J. B. *Figures in Modern Literature* (N. Y., 1924), pp. 31-55.
[Criticism.]

STURGEON, MARY C., *Studies of Contemporary Poets* [Rev. ed.] (N. Y., 1920), pp. 72-87.

WILLIAMS-ELLIS, A., *An Anatomy of Poetry* (Oxford, 1922), pp. 252-57.

II. MAGAZINE ARTICLES

AIKEN, CONRAD, "Three English Poets," *Dial,* LXIII (August 30, 1917), 151-52.
[Criticism.]

BARFIELD, OWEN, "Walter de la Mare," *New Statesman,* XVI (November 6, 1920), 140-42.
[Criticism.]

"Bibliographies of Modern Authors," *London Mercury,* XV (March, April, 1927), 526-32, 635-40; XVI (May, 1927), 70-71.

BUCHAN, SUSAN, "Walter de la Mare for Children," *Spectator,* CXXI (August 24, 1918), 200-1.

COATS, R. H., "The World of Walter de la Mare," *Fortnightly Rev.,* CXXII (October, 1927), 483-92.

DAVISON, EDWARD, "Walter de la Mare," *English Journal*, XV (February, 1926), 89-99.
[Criticism.]

FREEMAN, JOHN, "Walter de la Mare," *Bookman* (London), LIX (December, 1920), 122-24.
[Criticism.]

FREEMAN, JOHN, "The Work of Walter de la Mare," *Quarterly Rev.*, CCXXXVIII (July, 1922), 32-48.

"A Poet of Beauty," *Nation* (London), XXVIII (October 16, 1920), 78-80.

SHANKS, EDWARD, "The Poetry of Walter de la Mare," *London Mercury*, III (March, 1921), 521-31.

JOHN MASEFIELD

A. POETICAL WORKS

The Collected Poems of John Masefield. London: William Heinemann, Ltd., 1923. 784 pp.

Poems. [2 vols.] N. Y.: The Macmillan Co., 1925. 446, 291 pp.

Verse Plays. N. Y.: The Macmillan Co., 1925. 313 pp.

Salt-Water Ballads. London: Grant Richards, 1902. 112 pp.
[Also N. Y.: The Macmillan Co., 1913.]

Ballads. [Vigo Cabinet Series.] London: Elkin Mathews, 1903. 56 pp.

Ballads and Poems. London: Elkin Mathews, 1910. 100 pp.

The Everlasting Mercy. London: Sidgwick & Jackson, Ltd., 1911. 91 pp.

The Widow in the Bye Street. London: Sidgwick & Jackson, Ltd., 1912. [98 pp.]

The Everlasting Mercy and The Widow in the Bye Street. N. Y.: The Macmillan Co., 1912. 230 pp.

The Story of a Round-House and Other Poems. N. Y.: The Macmillan Co., 1912. 324 pp.

The Daffodil Fields. London: William Heinemann, 1913. 111 pp.
[Also N. Y.: The Macmillan Co., 1913.]

Dauber. A Poem. London: William Heinemann, Ltd., 1913. [98 pp.]

Philip the King and Other Poems. With a Portrait by William Strang. London: William Heinemann, 1914. [119 pp.]
[Also N. Y.: The Macmillan Co., 1914.]

The Faithful. A Tragedy in Three Acts. London: William Heinemann, 1915. 131 pp.
[Also N. Y.: The Macmillan Co., 1915.]
[Prose, with a few lyrics.]

Good Friday. A Dramatic Poem. London: Macmillan & Co., Ltd., 1916. 64 pp.
[Also N. Y.: The Macmillan Co., 1916.]

Good Friday and Other Poems. N. Y.: The Macmillan Co., 1916. 131 pp.

Salt-Water Poems and Ballads. Illustrated by Chas. Pears. N. Y.: The Macmillan Co., 1916. 163 pp.

Sonnets and Poems. Letchworth: Garden City Press, Ltd., 1916. 51 pp.
[A different edition, Lollingdon, Cholsey, Berkshire: John Masefield, 1916.]

Lollingdon Downs and Other Poems. N. Y.: The Macmillan Co., 1917. 53 pp.

Lollingdon Downs and Other Poems, with Sonnets. London: William Heinemann, 1917. [93 pp.]

The Cold Cotswolds. [Reprinted from *The Cambridge Magazine.*] Cambridge: Express Printing Works, [1917]. [4 pp.]

Poems by John Masefield. Selected by Henry Seidel Canby, Frederick Erastus Pierce, Willard Higley Durham. [Published with the consent of Mr. Masefield.] N. Y.: The Macmillan Co., 1917. 313 pp.

Rosas. N. Y.: The Macmillan Co., 1918. 65 pp.

A Poem and Two Plays. London: William Heinemann, [1919]. [152 pp.]

Reynard the Fox, or The Ghost Heath Run. London: William Heinemann, 1919. 124 pp.
[Also N. Y.: The Macmillan Co., 1919.]

Enslaved and Other Poems. London: William Heinemann, [1920]. [125 pp.]
[Also N. Y.: The Macmillan Co., 1920.]

Right Royal. London: William Heinemann, 1920. 120 pp.
[Also N. Y.: The Macmillan Co., 1920.]

King Cole. With Drawings in Black and White by Judith Masefield. N. Y.: The Macmillan Co., 1921. 87 pp.

The Dream. Illustrated by Judith Masefield. London: William Heinemann, 1922. 13 pp.
[Also N. Y.: The Macmillan Co., 1922.]

Esther. A Tragedy. Adapted and Partially Translated from the French of Jean Racine. London: William Heinemann, 1922. 68 pp.

Esther and Berenice. Two Plays. [Adapted and translated from the French of Racine.] N. Y.: The Macmillan Co., 1922. 205 pp.

Selected Poems. London: William Heinemann, 1922. 244 pp.
[Also N. Y.: The Macmillan Co., 1923.]

Dauber; The Daffodil Fields. N. Y.: The Macmillan Co., 1923. 163 pp.

The Dream and Other Poems. Illustrated by Judith Masefield. N. Y.: The Macmillan Co., 1923. 63 pp.

King Cole and Other Poems. London: William Heinemann, Ltd., [1923]. 93 pp.
[Also N. Y.: The Macmillan Co., 1923.]

A King's Daughter. A Tragedy in Verse. London: William Heinemann, 1923. 127 pp.
[Also N. Y.: The Macmillan Co., 1923.]

Philip the King; Good Friday, a Play in Verse; Lollingdon Downs and Other Poems, with Sonnets. N. Y.: The Macmillan Co., 1923. 277 pp.

The Trial of Jesus. London: William Heinemann, Ltd., [1925]. 101 pp.
[Prose with some verse included.]

Tristan and Isolt. A Play in Verse. London: William Heinemann, Ltd., [1927]. 135 pp.
[Also N. Y.: The Macmillan Co., 1927.]

The Coming of Christ. N. Y.: The Macmillan Co., 1928. 57 pp.

Midsummer Night and Other Tales in Verse. N. Y.: The Macmillan Co., 1928. 164 pp.

B. BIOGRAPHICAL AND CRITICAL REFERENCES

I. BOOKS

American Criticism, 1926 [Edited by William A. Drake] (N. Y., 1926), pp. 231-43.
[An article, "In Behalf of John Masefield," by Stuart Sherman.]

BIGGANE, CECIL. *John Masefield. A Study*. Cambridge: W. Heffer & Sons, Ltd., 1924. 53 pp.
[Criticism only.]

DANIELSON, HENRY. *Bibliographies of Modern Authors*. London: Bookman's Journal; N. Y.: James F. Drake, Inc., 1921. [212 pp.]
[See pp. 129-57.]

HAMILTON, W. H. *John Masefield. A Critical Study*. London: George Allen & Unwin, Ltd.; N. Y.: The Macmillan Co., [1922]. 155 pp.
[Criticism.]

KERNAHAN, COULSON, *Six Famous Living Poets. Introductory Studies, Illustrated by Quotation and Comment* (London, 1922), pp. 13-51.

LYND, ROBERT, *Old and New Masters* (London, 1919), pp. 149-56.

MACY, JOHN, *The Critical Game* (N. Y., 1922), pp. 279-87.

MAIS, S. P. B., *From Shakespeare to O. Henry. Studies in Literature* [Rev. ed.] (London, 1923), pp. 234-58.

John Masefield. [Pamphlet.] [N. Y.: The Macmillan Co., n. d.] 37 pp. [Contains a biographical sketch, with comments of the critics.]

MAYNARD, THEODORE, *Our Best Poets. English and American* (N. Y., 1922), pp. 139-51.

MONRO, HAROLD, *Some Contemporary Poets (1920)* (London, 1920), pp. 51-60.

PHELPS, WILLIAM LYON, *The Advance of English Poetry in the Twentieth Century* (N. Y., 1918), pp. 71-98.

STURGEON, MARY C., *Studies of Contemporary Poets* [Rev. ed.] (N. Y., 1920), pp. 197-217.

WILLIAMS, HAROLD, *Modern English Writers: Being a Study of Imaginative Literature, 1890-1914* [Third ed.] (London, 1925), pp. 118-22.

WILLIAMS, I. A. . . . *John Masefield.* [Bibliographies of Modern Authors. No. 2.] London: L. Chaundy & Co., 1921. 12 pp.

WILLIAMS-ELLIS, A., *An Anatomy of Poetry* (Oxford, 1922), pp. 246-52.

II. MAGAZINE ARTICLES

ARMSTRONG, MARTIN D., "Recent English Poetry," *Fortnightly Rev.*, CI (March 2, 1914), 509-11.

CANBY, HENRY SEIDEL, "Noyes and Masefield," *Yale Rev.*, n. s. III (January, 1914), 294-303.

DAVISON, EDWARD, "The Poetry of John Masefield," *English Journal*, XV (January, 1926), 5-13.

FIRKINS, O. W., "Mr. Masefield's Poetry," *Nation*, CVIII (March 15, 1919), 389-91.

GOULD, GERALD, "The Poetry of John Masefield," *Bookman* (London), LXVI (May, 1924), 95-97.

LUCAS, F. L., "John Masefield," *New Statesman*, XIX (August 5, 1922), 489-91.

SHANKS, EDWARD, "Mr. Masefield: Some Characteristics," *London Mercury*, II (September, 1920), 578-89.
[Criticism.]

THOMAS, GILBERT, "Mr. Masefield's Poetry," *Fortnightly Rev.*, XCIX (June 2, 1913), 1154-65.

THORNDIKE, ASHLEY H., "The Great Tradition," *Dial*, LXVI (February 8, 1919), 118-21.

WHITE, NEWMAN I., "John Masefield—An Estimate," *So. Atlantic Quar.*, XXVI (April, 1927), 189-201.

W. W. GIBSON

A. POETICAL WORKS

Poems (1904-1917). N. Y.: The Macmillan Co., 1917. 552 pp.
Collected Poems. 1905-1925. London: Macmillan & Co., Ltd., 1926. 791 pp.
Urlyn the Harper and Other Song. [Vigo Cabinet Series.] London: Elkin Mathews, 1902. 64 pp.
The Queen's Vigil and Other Song. [Vigo Cabinet Series.] London: Elkin Mathews, 1902. 64 pp.
The Golden Helm and Other Verse. London: Elkin Mathews, 1903. 132 pp.
The Nets of Love. [Vigo Cabinet Series.] London: Elkin Mathews, 1905. 58 pp.
On the Threshold. [Cranleigh, Surrey: Samurai Press, 1907.] 33 pp.
The Stonefolds. [Cranleigh, Surrey: Samurai Press, 1907.] 32 pp.
The Web of Life. A Book of Poems. [Cranleigh, Surrey: Samurai Press, 1908.] 111 pp.
Akra the Slave. London: Elkin Mathews, 1910. [42 pp.]
Daily Bread. [3 vols.] London: Elkin Mathews, 1910.
[Also N. Y.: The Macmillan Co., 1912.]
Mates and Other Dramatic Poems. London: Elkin Mathews, 1910.
Fires. [3 vols.] London: Elkin Mathews, 1912. 64, 46, 45 pp.
[Also N. Y.: The Macmillan Co., 1912. 175 pp.]
Womankind. A Play in One Act. London: D. Nutt, 1912. 24 pp.
[Also N. Y.: The Macmillan Co., 1912.]
Borderlands. London: Elkin Mathews, 1914. 64 pp.
Thoroughfares. London: Elkin Mathews, 1914. 48 pp.
Borderlands and Thoroughfares. N. Y.: The Macmillan Co., 1914. 195 pp.
Battle. N. Y.: The Macmillan Co., 1915. 10 pp.
[Also *Battle*, N. Y.: The Macmillan Co., 1915. 54 pp.]
Battle and Other Poems. N. Y.: The Macmillan Co., 1916. 198 pp.
Friends. London: Elkin Mathews, 1916. 37 pp.
Livelihood: Dramatic Reveries. N. Y.: The Macmillan Co., 1917. 119 pp.
Hill-Tracks. With Portrait. N. Y.: The Macmillan Co., 1918. 65 pp.
Whin. London: Macmillan & Co., Ltd., 1918. [59 pp.]
[Same as *Hill-Tracks*.]
Home. A Book of Poems. [London: William Beaumont, 1920.] 41 pp.

Neighbors. N. Y.: The Macmillan Co., 1920. 169 pp.

Krindlesyke. London: Macmillan & Co., Ltd., 1922. [140 pp.]

Kestrel Edge and Other Plays. London: Macmillan & Co., Ltd., 1924. 150 pp.

I Heard a Sailor. London: Macmillan & Co., Ltd., 1925. 133 pp.

Sixty-Three Poems. Selected for Use in Schools and Colleges by E. A. Parker. With a Critical Introduction. London: Macmillan & Co., Ltd., 1926. 155 pp.

The Early Whistler. Drawings by John Nash. [Ariel Poems, No. 6.] London: Faber & Gwyer, 1927. [4 pp.]

The Golden Room and Other Poems. London: Macmillan & Co., Ltd., 1928. 190 pp.

B. BIOGRAPHICAL AND CRITICAL REFERENCES

I. BOOKS

AIKEN, CONRAD, *Scepticisms. Notes on Contemporary Poetry* (N. Y., 1919), pp. 199-202.

PHELPS, WILLIAM LYON, *The Advance of English Poetry in the Twentieth Century* (N. Y., 1918), pp. 98-114.

STURGEON, MARY C., *Studies of Contemporary Poets* [Rev. ed.] (N. Y., 1920), pp. 87-108.

WILLIAMS, HAROLD, *Modern English Writers: Being a Study of Imaginative Literature, 1890-1914* [Third ed.] (London, 1925), pp. 116-18.

II. MAGAZINE ARTICLES

ABERCROMBIE, LASCELLES, "The War and the Poets," *Quarterly Rev.*, CCXXIV (October, 1915), 401-4.

ARMSTRONG, MARTIN D., "Recent English Poetry," *Fortnightly Rev.*, CI (March 2, 1914), 498-503.

BRADLEY, W. A., "Wilfrid Wilson Gibson," *Dial*, LXII (March 22, 1917), 223-26.

BRONNER, MILTON, "A Panel of Poets," *Bookman*, XXXV (April, 1912), 159-61.

DILLA, GERALDINE P., "The Development of Wilfrid Wilson Gibson's Poetic Art," *Sewanee Rev.*, XXX (January, 1922), 39-57.
[Contains a biographical note.]

HOLMES, JOHN HAYNES, "Wilfrid Wilson Gibson. Poet of Tenement and Trench," *Survey*, XXXVII (January 6, 1917), 409-11.

SHAFER, ROBERT, "Two of the Newest Poets," *Atlantic Monthly*, CXI (April, 1913), 489-96.

HAROLD MONRO

A. POETICAL WORKS

Poems. [Vigo Cabinet Series.] London: Elkin Mathews, 1906. [64 pp.]

The Evolution of the Soul. [Cranleigh, Surrey: Samurai Press, 1907.]

Before Dawn (Poems and Impressions). London: Constable & Co., Ltd., 1911. 144 pp.

Judas. London: S. Low, Marston & Co., Ltd., [1911]. 31 pp.

Children of Love. London: Poetry Bookshop, 1914. 31 pp.

Trees. London: Poetry Bookshop, 1915. [15 pp.]

Strange Meetings. London: Poetry Bookshop, 1917. 63 pp.

Real Property. London: Poetry Bookshop, 1922. 63 pp.

. . . *Harold Monro.* [Augustan Books of English Poetry.] London: E. Benn, Ltd., [1927]. 30 pp.

The Earth for Sale. London: Chatto & Windus, 1928. [64 pp.]

B. CRITICAL REFERENCES

AIKEN, CONRAD, *Scepticisms. Notes on Contemporary Poetry* (N. Y., 1919), pp. 211-13.

STURGEON, MARY C., *Studies of Contemporary Poets* [Rev. ed.] (N. Y., 1920), pp. 217-35.

E[LIOT], T. S., "Reflections on Contemporary Poetry," *Egoist*, IV (September, 1917), p. 119.

ALFRED NOYES

A. POETICAL WORKS

Collected Poems. [2 vols.] Edinburgh and London: W. Blackwood & Sons, 1910. 344, 374 pp.

Collected Poems. [3 vols.] N. Y.: Frederick A. Stokes Co., [1913-1920]. 426, 451, 315 pp.

Collected Poems. [Vol. 4.] Edinburgh and London: W. Blackwood & Sons, 1927. 312 pp.

The Loom of Years. London: Grant Richards, 1902.

Poems. Edinburgh and London: W. Blackwood & Sons, 1902.

The Flower of Old Japan: A Dim Strange Tale for All Ages. London: Grant Richards, 1903.

The Forest of Wild Thyme. A Tale for Children under Ninety. Edinburgh and London: W. Blackwood & Sons, 1905.

Drake. An English Epic. Books I-III. Edinburgh and London: W. Blackwood & Sons, 1906.

Poems. With an Introduction by Hamilton W. Mabie. N. Y.: The Macmillan Co.; London: Macmillan & Co., Ltd., 1906. 193 pp.

The Flower of Old Japan and Other Poems. N. Y.: The Macmillan Co.; London: Macmillan & Co., Ltd., 1907. 175 pp.

Forty Singing Seamen and Other Poems. Edinburgh and London: W. Blackwood & Sons, 1907. 175 pp.

Drake. An English Epic. Books I-XII. Edinburgh and London: W. Blackwood & Sons, 1908. 504 pp.

[Also N. Y.: Frederick A. Stokes Co., [1909].]

The Golden Hynde and Other Poems. N. Y.: The Macmillan Co., 1908. 185 pp.

The Enchanted Island and Other Poems. Edinburgh and London: W. Blackwood & Sons, 1909. 209 pp.

Also N. Y.: Frederick A. Stokes Co., [1910].]

The Prayer for Peace. Cleveland, Ohio: [Printed for private distribution], 1911. 12 pp.

Sherwood, or Robin Hood and the Three Kings. A Play in Five Acts. N. Y.: Frederick A. Stokes Co., [1911]. [225 pp.]

The Carol of the Fir Tree. London: Burns & Oates, Ltd., 1912. 19 pp.

Peace Poems. N. Y.: Frederick A. Stokes Co., 1913. [3 pp.]

Tales of the Mermaid Tavern. Edinburgh and London: W. Blackwood & Sons, 1913. [216 pp.]

[Also N. Y.: Frederick A. Stokes Co., 1913.]

Two Christmas Poems. With a Drawing by Walter A. Heller . . . Cleveland, Ohio, [1913]. [11 pp.]

The Wine-Press. A Tale of War. Edinburgh and London: W. Blackwood & Sons, 1913. 95 pp.

[Also N. Y.: Frederick A. Stokes Co., [1913].]

Rada. A Drama of War in One Act. N. Y.: Frederick A. Stokes Co., 1914. 31 pp.

A Belgian Christmas Eve. Being *Rada* Rewritten and Enlarged as an Episode of the Great War. With Four Illustrations. N. Y.: Frederick A. Stokes Co., 1915. 71 pp.

[Also London: Methuen & Co., Ltd., 1915.]

The Lord of Misrule and Other Poems. With Frontispiece in Colours by Spencer Baird Nichols. N. Y.: Frederick A. Stokes Co., [1915]. 184 pp.

A Salute from the Fleet and Other Poems. London: Methuen & Co., Ltd., 1915. [208 pp.]

The New Morning. Poems. N. Y.: Frederick A. Stokes Co., [1919]. 172 pp.

The Elfin Artist and Other Poems. Edinburgh and London: W. Blackwood & Sons, 1920. 195 pp.
[Also N. Y.: Frederick A. Stokes Co., [1920].]

The Torch-Bearers. Edinburgh and London: W. Blackwood & Sons, 1922. 281 pp.
[Published as *Watchers of the Sky,* N. Y.: Frederick A. Stokes Co. [1922].]

Selected Poems. . . . Edinburgh and London: W. Blackwood & Sons, 1923. 91 pp.

Songs of Shadow-of-a-Leaf and Other Poems. Edinburgh and London: W. Blackwood & Sons, 1924. 127 pp.

The Book of Earth. [*The Torch-Bearers. II.*] N. Y.: Frederick A. Stokes Co., 1925. 328 pp.

Dick Turpin's Ride and Other Poems. N. Y.: Frederick A. Stokes Co., 1927. 142 pp.

B. CRITICAL REFERENCES

I. BOOKS

KERNAHAN, COULSON, *Six Famous Living Poets. Introductory Studies, Illustrated by Quotation and Comment* (London, 1922), pp. 159-216.

PHELPS, WILLIAM LYON, *The Advance of English Poetry in the Twentieth Century* (N. Y., 1918), pp. 56-65.

WILLIAMS, HAROLD, *Modern English Writers: Being a Study of Imaginative Literature, 1890-1914* [Third ed.] (London, 1925), pp. 139-43.

II. MAGAZINE ARTICLES

BETTANY, F. G., "Mr. Noyes's Collected Poems," *Bookman* (London), XXXIX (December, 1910), 149-50.

CANBY, HENRY SEIDEL, "Noyes and Masefield," *Yale Rev.,* n. s. III (January, 1914), 287-303.

COLBY, ELBRIDGE, "Who Is Alfred Noyes?", *Catholic World,* XCVII (June, 1913), 289-305.
[Criticism.]

DAVISON, EDWARD, "The Poetry of Alfred Noyes," *English Journal,* XV (April, 1926), 247-56.

GIVEN, PHILIP LOMBARD, "The Poetry of Alfred Noyes," *No. American Rev.*, CC (July, 1914), 85-97.

HAMILTON, CLAYTON, "The Youngest of the Epics," *Forum*, XLIII (May, 1910), 550-58.

HOOKER, BRIAN, "Alfred Noyes," *Century*, n. s. LXVI (July, 1914), 349-53.
[Criticism.]

MACFIE, RONALD CAMPBELL, "The Poems of Alfred Noyes," *Bookman* (London), LXXIII (November, 1927), 112-14.

THOMAS, GILBERT, "Alfred Noyes," *Bookman* (London), XLVIII (May, 1915), 41-44.
[Criticism.]

JAMES STEPHENS

A. POETICAL WORKS

Collected Poems. London: Macmillan & Co., Ltd., 1926, 268 pp.
[Also N. Y.: The Macmillan Co., 1926.]

Insurrections. Dublin: Maunsel & Co.; N. Y.: The Macmillan Co., 1909. 55 pp.

The Lonely God and Other Poems. N. Y.: The Macmillan Co., 1909. 27 pp.

The Hill of Vision. Dublin and London: Maunsel & Co., Ltd., [1912]. 131 pp.
[Also N. Y.: The Macmillan Co., 1912.]

Five New Poems. London: Printed by A. T. Stevens for Flying Fame. 1913. 20 pp.

The Rocky Road to Dublin. The Adventures of Seumas Beg. N. Y.: The Macmillan Co., 1915. 94 pp.

Songs from the Clay. London: Macmillan & Co., Ltd., 1915. 106 pp.
[Also N. Y.: The Macmillan Co., 1915.]

The Adventures of Seumas Beg. The Rocky Road to Dublin. London: Macmillan & Co., Ltd., 1916. 86 pp.

Green Branches. Dublin: Maunsel & Co., Ltd., 1916. [19 pp.]
[Also N. Y.: The Macmillan Co., 1916. [40 pp.]]

Reincarnations. N. Y.: The Macmillan Co., 1918. 76 pp.

A Poetry Recital. N. Y.: The Macmillan Co., 1925. 41 pp.

B. BIOGRAPHICAL AND CRITICAL REFERENCES

I. BOOKS

BOYD, ERNEST A., *Ireland's Literary Renaissance* (N. Y., 1916), pp. 265-74.

BOYD, ERNEST, *Portraits: Real and Imaginary . . .* (N. Y., 1924), pp. 246-55.
[Of biographical value.]

MOORE, GEORGE, *Hail and Farewell* [Vol. 3—*Vale* (N. Y., 1914), pp. 251-53.]
[Account of Russell's discovery of Stephens.]

[RUSSELL, GEORGE W.], *Imaginations and Reveries* (N. Y., 1916), pp. 34-45.

STURGEON, MARY C., *Studies of Contemporary Poets* [Rev. ed.] (N. Y., 1920), pp. 282-301.

WILLIAMS, HAROLD, *Modern English Writers: Being a Study of Imaginative Literature, 1890-1914* [Third ed.] (London, 1925), pp. 199-200.

WILLIAMS, IOLA A., . . . *John Collings Squire and James Stephens.* [Bibliographies of Modern Authors, No. 4.] London: L. Chaundy & Co., 1922. 13 pp.

II. MAGAZINE ARTICLES

LAWRENCE, DAVID HERBERT, "Bibliographies of Modern Authors," *London Mercury,* IV (June, 1921), 193.

MARSHALL, H. P., "James Stephens," *London Mercury,* XII (September, 1925), 500-11.

SHAFER, ROBERT, "James Stephens and the Poetry of the Day," *Forum,* L (October, 1913), 560-70.

SIEGFRIED SASSOON

A. POETICAL WORKS

Twelve Sonnets. [Privately printed, 1911.]

Hyacinth. [Privately printed, 1912.]

Melodies. [Privately printed, 1912.]

An Ode for Music. [Privately printed, 1912.]

Apollo in Doelyrium. [Privately printed, 1913.]

Discoveries. [Privately printed, 1915.]

Morning Glory. [Privately printed, 1916.]

The Old Huntsman and Other Poems. London: William Heinemann, 1917. 118 pp.
[Also N. Y.: E. P. Dutton & Co., 1918.]

Counter-Attack and Other Poems. London: William Heinemann, 1918. [64 pp.]
[Also N. Y.: E. P. Dutton & Co., 1918.]

The War Poems of Siegfreid Sassoon. London: William Heinemann, Ltd., 1919. 95 pp.

Picture-Show. London: William Heinemann, 1919. 56 pp.
[Also N. Y.: E. P. Dutton & Co., [1920].]

Selected Poems. London: William Heinemann, 1925. 75 pp.

Satirical Poems. London: William Heinemann, 1926. 61 pp.
[Also N. Y.: Viking Press, 1926.]

. . . *Siegfried Sassoon.* [Augustan Books of Modern Poetry.] London: E. Benn, Ltd., 1926. 31 pp.

Nativity. Designs by Paul Nash. [Ariel Poems, No. 7.] London: Faber & Gwyer, Ltd., [1927]. [2 pp.]

The Heart's Journey. London: William Heinemann, Ltd.; N. Y.: Crosby Gage, 1928. 45 pp.

B. BIOGRAPHICAL AND CRITICAL REFERENCES

I. BOOKS

LYND, ROBERT, *The Art of Letters* (N. Y., 1921), pp. 201-3.

MAIS, S. P. B., *Books and Their Writers* (London, 1920), pp. 131-38.

MONRO, HAROLD, *Some Contemporary Poets (1920)* (London, 1920), pp. 130-36.

[See also the Introduction, by Robert Nichols, in the American edition of *Counter-Attack.*]

II. MAGAZINE ARTICLES

"A Poet's Horror of War," *Lit. Digest,* LX (February 1, 1919), 30-32. [Biographical and critical.]

UNTERMEYER, LOUIS, "Aftermath," *New Republic,* XXII (March 3, 1920), 37-38.

WILKINSON, MARGUERITE, "Siegfried Sassoon," *Touchstone,* VII (May, 1920), 142-45.

ROBERT GRAVES

A. POETICAL WORKS

Poems (1914-26). London: William Heinemann, Ltd., 1927. [218 pp.]

Over the Brazier. London: Poetry Bookshop, 1916. 32 pp.

Fairies and Fusiliers. London: William Heinemann, [1917]. [84 pp.]
[Also N. Y.: Alfred A. Knopf, 1918.]

Country Sentiment. London: Martin Secker, [1920]. 81 pp.
[Also N. Y.: Alfred A. Knopf, 1920.]

The Pier-Glass. London: Martin Secker, [1921]. 53 pp.
[Also N. Y.: Alfred A. Knopf, 1921.]

The Feather Bed. With a Cover Design by William Nicholson. Richmond: L. & V. Woolf, 1923. 28 pp.

Whipperginny. London: William Heinemann, [1923]. [72 pp.]
[Also N. Y.: Alfred A. Knopf, 1923.]

Mock Beggar Hall. With a Cover Design by William Nicholson. London: L. & V. Woolf, 1924. 79 pp.
[In prose and verse.]

John Kemp's Wager. A Ballad Opera. Oxford: Blackwell, 1925. 75 pp.
[Also N. Y.: S. French, 1925.]

Robert Graves. [Augustan Books of Modern Poetry.] London: E. Benn, Ltd., 1925. 31 pp.

B. CRITICAL REFERENCES

I. BOOKS

MONRO, HAROLD, *Some Contemporary Poets (1920)* (London, 1920), pp. 172-75.

MUIR, EDWIN, *Transition. Essays on Contemporary Literature* (N. Y., 1926), pp. 163-77.

II. MAGAZINE ARTICLES

J. M. M., "The Dignity of Poetry," *Athenæum*, I (1920), 472-4.

MUIR, EDWIN, "Robert Graves," *Nation*, CXXIII (September, 1926), 217-19.

Review of *Country Sentiment*, *Spectator*, CXXIV (April 10, 1920), 494-95.

PART TWO

THE AMERICAN POETS

EDWIN ARLINGTON ROBINSON

A. POETICAL WORKS

Collected Poems. N. Y.: The Macmillan Co., 1921. 591 pp.
[Also London: Cecil Palmer, 1922.]
[Also [in five volumes] N. Y.: The Macmillan Co., 1927.]

The Torrent and the Night Before. By Edwin Arlington Robinson, Gardiner, Maine, 1889-1896. [Cambridge: Riverside Press.] Printed for the Author, 1896. 44 pp.

The Children of the Night. A Book of Poems. Boston: R. G. Badger & Co., 1897. 121 pp.

Captain Craig. A Book of Poems. Boston: Houghton Mifflin, 1902. 171 pp.
[Also London: Gay & Bird, 1903.]

The Town down the River. A Book of Poems. N. Y.: Charles Scribner's Sons, 1910. 129 pp.

The Man against the Sky. A Book of Poems. N. Y.: The Macmillan Co., 1916. 149 pp.
[Also London: Macmillan & Co., Ltd., 1916.]

Merlin. A Poem. N. Y.: The Macmillan Co., 1917. 168 pp.

Lancelot. A Poem. N. Y.: Thomas Seltzer, 1920. 184 pp.
[Also published, 1919, N. Y.: Poetry Book Shop.]

The Three Taverns. A Book of Poems. N. Y.: The Macmillan Co., 1920. 120 pp.

Avon's Harvest. N. Y.: The Macmillan Co., 1921. 65 pp.
[Also London: Macmillan & Co., Ltd., 1921.]

Roman Bartholow. N. Y.: The Macmillan Co., 1923. 191 pp.
[Also London: Cecil Palmer, 1923.]

The Man Who Died Twice. N. Y.: The Macmillan Co., 1924. 79 pp.
[Also London: Cecil Palmer, 1924.]

Dionysus in Doubt. A Book of Poems. N. Y.: The Macmillan Co., 1925. 117 pp.

Tristram. N. Y.: The Macmillan Co., 1927. 210 pp.

Sonnets (1889-1927). N. Y.: The Macmillan Co., 1928.

B. BIOGRAPHICAL AND CRITICAL REFERENCES

I. BOOKS

BEEBE, LUCIUS MORRIS. *Aspects of the Poetry of Edwin Arlington Robinson*. Cambridge, Mass.: Dunster House, 1928.

BEEBE, LUCIUS MORRIS. *Edwin Arlington Robinson and the Arthurian Legend*. [Privately printed.] Cambridge, Mass.: For Sale at Dunster House Bookshop, 1927. 30 pp.

BOYNTON, PERCY H., *Some Contemporary Americans. The Personal Equation in Literature* (Chicago, 1924), pp. 16-33.
[Criticism, and a biographical note.]

JONES, LLEWELLYN, *First Impressions. Essays on Poetry, Criticism, and Prosody* (N. Y., 1925), pp. 13-37.

The Literary Spotlight . . . [Edited by John Farrar.] (N. Y., 1924), pp. 116-25.
[Chiefly biographical.]

Literature in the Making. By Some of Its Makers. Presented by Joyce Kilmer (N. Y., 1917), pp. 265-74.
[Account of a discussion, by Robinson, of poetry.]

LOWELL, AMY, *Tendencies in Modern American Poetry* (N. Y., 1917), pp. 10-76.
[Both biographical and critical.]

MAYNARD, THEODORE, *Our Best Poets. English and American* (N. Y., 1922), pp. 153-69.

MONROE, HARRIET, *Poets and Their Art* (N. Y., 1926), pp. 1-12.

MORRIS, LLOYD. *The Poetry of Edwin Arlington Robinson. An Essay in Appreciation*. With a Bibliography by W. Van R. Whitall. N. Y.: George H. Doran Co., [1923]. 116 pp.

REDMAN, BEN RAY. *Edwin Arlington Robinson*. [Modern American Writers. VI.] N. Y.: Robert M. MacBride & Co., 1926. [97 pp.]
[Biographical and critical.]

UNTERMEYER, LOUIS, *The New Era in American Poetry* (N. Y., 1919), pp. 111-36.
[See also Untermeyer's *American Poetry since 1900* (N. Y., 1923), pp. 42-67.]

VAN DOREN, MARK. *Edwin Arlington Robinson*. N. Y.: Literary Guild of America, 1927. 93 pp.
[Criticism, and a biographical chapter.]

WOOD, CLEMENT, *Poets of America* (N. Y., 1925), pp. 119-42.
[Biographical and critical.]

II. MAGAZINE ARTICLES

COLTON, ARTHUR W., "Edwin Arlington Robinson," *Literary Rev.*, III (June 23, 1923), 781-82.

DRINKWATER, JOHN, "Edwin Arlington Robinson," *Fortnightly Rev.*, CXVII (April 1, 1922), 649-61.

FLETCHER, JOHN GOULD, "Some Contemporary American Poets," *Chapbook*, II (May, 1920), 1-5.

LOWELL, AMY, "A Bird's-Eye View of E. A. Robinson," *Dial*, LXXII (February, 1922), 130-43.

MUNSON, GORHAM B., "Edwin Arlington Robinson," *Sat. Rev. of Literature*, III (May 21, 1927), 839-40.

SINCLAIR, MAY, "Three American Poets of To-day," *Atlantic Monthly*, XCVIII (September, 1906), 330-33.

SQUIRE, J. C., "Contemporary American Authors. IV: Edwin Arlington Robinson," *London Mercury*, XIII (February, 1926), 401-13.

THEIS, O. F., "Edwin Arlington Robinson," *Forum*, LI (February, 1914), 305-13.

WALDO, FULLERTON, "The Earlier E. A. R. Some Memories of a Poet in the Making," *Outlook*, CXXIX (November 30, 1921), 531-34.

WINTERS, YVOR, "A Cool Master," *Poetry*, XIX (February, 1922), 278-88.

AMY LOWELL

A. POETICAL WORKS

A Dome of Many-Coloured Glass. Boston: Houghton Mifflin, 1912. 139 pp.

[Also London: Constable & Co., Ltd., 1913.]

Sword Blades and Poppy Seed. N. Y.: The Macmillan Co., 1914. 246 pp.

[Also London: Macmillan & Co., Ltd., 1914.]

Men, Women and Ghosts. N. Y.: The Macmillan Co., 1916. 363 pp.

[Also London: Macmillan & Co., Ltd., 1916.]

Can Grande's Castle. N. Y.: The Macmillan Co., 1918. 232 pp.

[Also Oxford: Blackwell, 1920.]

Pictures of the Floating World. N. Y.: The Macmillan Co., 1919. 257 pp.

Fir-Flower Tablets. Poems Translated from the Chinese by Florence Ayscough. English Version by Amy Lowell. Boston: Houghton Mifflin, 1921. 227 pp.

Legends. Boston: Houghton Mifflin, 1921. 259 pp.

A Critical Fable . . . [Published anonymously.] Boston: Houghton Mifflin, 1922. 99 pp.

What's O'Clock? Boston: Houghton Mifflin, 1925. 240 pp.
[Also London: Jonathan Cape, 1926.]

East Wind. Boston: Houghton Mifflin, 1926. 240 pp.

Ballads for Sale. Boston: Houghton Mifflin, 1927. 311 pp.

Selected Poems of Amy Lowell. Edited by John Livingston Lowes. Boston: Houghton Mifflin, 1928. 240 pp.

B. BIOGRAPHICAL AND CRITICAL REFERENCES

I. BOOKS

AIKEN, CONRAD, *Scepticisms. Notes on Contemporary Poetry* (N. Y., 1919), pp. 115-26.

BOYNTON, PERCY H., *Some Contemporary Americans. The Personal Equation in Literature* (Chicago, 1924), pp. 72-89.
[Criticism, and a biographical note.]

BRYHER, W. *Amy Lowell. A Critical Appreciation.* [Second ed.] London: Eyre & Spottiswoode, Ltd., 1918. [48 pp.]

COLLINS, JOSEPH, *Taking the Literary Pulse. Psychological Studies of Life and Letters* (N. Y., 1924), pp. 60-68.

COOK, HOWARD WILLARD, *Our Poets of Today* (N. Y., 1918), pp. 2-12.
[Biographical and critical.]

ERSKINE, JOHN, *The Kinds of Poetry and Other Essays* (N. Y., 1920), pp. 126-30.

HUNT, RICHARD. *Amy Lowell. A Sketch of Her Life and Her Place in Contemporary American Literature.* [A pamphlet.] N. Y.: The Macmillan Co., n. d. 14 pp.

Literature in the Making, By Some of Its Makers. Presented by Joyce Kilmer (N. Y., 1917), pp. 253-62.
[Report of a discussion, by Amy Lowell, of the new poetry.]

The Literary Spotlight . . . [Edited by John Farrar.] (N. Y., 1924), pp. 51-65.
[Criticism.]

MONROE, HARRIET, *Poets and Their Art* (N. Y., 1926), pp. 78-86.

PHELPS, WILLIAM LYON, *The Advance of English Poetry in the Twentieth Century* (N. Y., 1918), pp. 245-56.

SERGEANT, ELIZABETH SHEPLEY, *Fire under the Andes. A Group of North American Portraits* (N. Y., 1927), pp. 11-33.
[Biographical material.]

UNTERMEYER, LOUIS, *The New Era in American Poetry* (N. Y., 1919), pp. 137-60.

[See also Untermeyer's *American Poetry Since 1900* (N. Y., 1923), pp. 135-57.]

WOOD, CLEMENT. *Amy Lowell.* N. Y.: Harold Vinal, 1926. 185 pp., [Biography and criticism.]

WOOD, CLEMENT, *Poets of America* (N. Y., 1925), pp. 214-29.

II. MAGAZINE ARTICLES

ALDINGTON, RICHARD, "The Poetry of Amy Lowell," *Egoist,* II (July 1, 1915), 109-10.

ALLEN, HERVEY, "The Passing of Amy Lowell," *Bookman,* LXI (July, 1925), 519-23.

ALLEN, HERVEY, "Amy Lowell as a Poet," *Sat. Rev. of Literature,* III (February 5, 1927), 557-59, 568.

AYSCOUGH, FLORENCE, "Amy Lowell and the Far East," *Bookman,* LXIII (March, 1926), 11-19.

[On Miss Lowell's translation of Oriental literature.]

CATEL, JEAN, "Amy Lowell," *Literary Rev.,* IV (July 26, 1924), 913-14.

CATEL, JEAN, "Mort d'Amy Lowell," *Mercure de France,* CLXXXI (August 1, 1925), 826-31.

COLUM, PADRAIC, "A World of High Visibility," *Freeman,* IV (September 14, 1921), 18-19.

FLETCHER, JOHN GOULD, "Some Contemporary American Poets," *Chapbook,* II (May, 1920), 8-11.

FLETCHER, JOHN GOULD, "The Poetry of Amy Lowell," *Egoist,* II (May 1, 1915), 81-82.

LOWES, JOHN LIVINGSTON, "The Poetry of Amy Lowell," *Sat. Rev. of Literature,* II (October 3, 1925), 169-71, 174-75.

MACLEISH, ARCHIBALD, "Amy Lowell and the Art of Poetry," *No. American Rev.,* CCXXI (March, 1925), 508-22.

PERKINS, ELIZABETH WARD, "Amy Lowell of New England," *Scribner's Mag.,* LXXXII (September, 1927), 329-35.

[Has some biographical value.]

TUPPER, JAMES W., "The Poetry of Amy Lowell," *Sewanee Rev.,* XXVIII (January, 1920), 37-54.

WILKINSON, MARGUERITE, "Poets of the People: Amy Lowell . . ." *Touchstone,* II (January, 1918), 416-20.

YEAMAN, VIRGINIA, "Amy Lowell at Sevenels," *Forum,* LXXIV (July, 1925), 76-80.

[Report of a visit to Amy Lowell's home.]

ROBERT FROST

A. POETICAL WORKS

A Boy's Will. London: David Nutt, 1913. 63 pp.
[Also N. Y.: Henry Holt & Co., 1915.]

North of Boston. London: David Nutt, 1914. 144 pp.
[Also N. Y.: Henry Holt & Co., 1915.]

Mountain Interval. N. Y.: Henry Holt & Co., [1916]. 99 pp.

New Hampshire. A Poem with Notes and Grace Notes by Robert Frost. With Woodcuts by J. J. Lankes. N. Y.: Henry Holt & Co., 1923. 113 pp.
[Also London: Grant Richards, 1924.]

Selected Poems. N. Y.: Henry Holt & Co., 1923. 143 pp.
[Also London: William Heinemann, 1923.]

West-Running Brook. N. Y.: Henry Holt & Co., [1928]. 64 pp.

B. BIOGRAPHICAL AND CRITICAL REFERENCES

I. BOOKS

BOYNTON, PERCY H., *Some Contemporary Americans. The Personal Equation in Literature* (Chicago, 1924), pp. 33-50.
[Criticism, with a biographical note.]

ERSKINE, JOHN, *The Kinds of Poetry and Other Essays* (N. Y., 1920), pp. 123-26.

GARNETT, EDWARD, *Friday Nights. Literary Criticisms and Appreciations. [First Series]* (London, 1922), pp. 221-43.

HOLLIDAY, ROBERT CORTES, *Literary Lanes and Other Byways* (N. Y., 1925), pp. 27-33.
[Report of conversation with Frost.]

JONES, LLEWELLYN, *First Impressions. Essays on Poetry, Criticism, and Prosody* (N. Y., 1925), pp. 37-53.

The Literary Spotlight . . . [Edited by John Farrar.] (N. Y., 1924), pp. 213-22.
[About Frost as a man.]

LOWELL, AMY, *Tendencies in Modern American Poetry* (N. Y., 1917), pp. 79-137.
[Both biographical and critical.]

MAYNARD, THEODORE, *Our Best Poets. English and American* (N. Y., 1922), pp. 169-81.

MONROE, HARRIET, *Poets and Their Art* (N. Y., 1926), pp. 56-63.

MUNSON, GORHAM B. *Robert Frost. A Study in Sensibility and Good Sense.* [The Murray Hill Biographies.] N. Y.: George H. Doran Co., [1927]. 135 pp.
[Biography and criticism.]

PHELPS, WILLIAM LYON, *The Advance of English Poetry in the Twentieth Century* (N. Y., 1918), pp. 235-45.

SERGEANT, ELIZABETH SHEPLEY, *Fire under the Andes. A Group of North American Portraits* (N. Y., 1927), pp. 285-304.
[Chiefly criticism.]

UNTERMEYER, LOUIS, *The New Era in American Poetry* (N. Y., 1919), pp. 15-40.
[See also Untermeyer's *American Poetry Since 1900* (N. Y., 1923), pp. 15-42.]

VAN DOREN, CARL, *Many Minds* (N. Y., 1924), pp. 50-67.

WEIRICK, BRUCE, *From Whitman to Sandburg in American Poetry* (N. Y., 1924), pp. 178-84.

WOOD, CLEMENT, *Poets of America* (N. Y., 1925), pp. 142-63.
[Biographical and critical.]

II. MAGAZINE ARTICLES

BENJAMIN, PAUL L., "Robert Frost—Poet of Neighborliness," *Survey*, XLV (November 27, 1920), 318-20.
[Criticism.]

CATEL, JEAN, "La Poésie Américaine d'Aujourd'hui," *Mercure de France*, CXXXVIII (March 15, 1920), 603-15.

COLUM, PADRAIC, "The Poetry of Robert Frost," *New Republic*, IX (December 23, 1916), 219-22.

COX, S. H., "The Sincerity of Robert Frost," *New Republic*, XII (August 25, 1917), 109-11.

ELLIOTT, G. R., "The Neighborliness of Robert Frost," *Nation*, CIX (December 6, 1919), 713-15.

FEUILLERAT, ALBERT, "Poètes Américains d'Aujourd'hui. M. Robert Frost," *Revue des Deux Mondes*, XVII (September, 1923), 185-211.
[Biographical and critical.]

FLETCHER, JOHN GOULD, "Some Contemporary American Poets," *Chapbook*, II (May, 1920), 5-8.

FREEMAN, JOHN, "Contemporary American Authors. II. Robert Frost," *London Mercury*, XIII (December, 1925), 176-88.

MUNSON, GORHAM B., "Robert Frost," *Sat. Rev. of Literature*, I (March 28, 1925), 625-26.

POUND, EZRA, "Modern Georgics," *Poetry*, V (December, 1914), 127-31.

WHIPPLE, T. H., "Robert Frost," *Literary Rev.*, IV (March 22, 1924), 605-6.

WILKINSON, MARGUERITE, "Poets of the People. No. V: Robert Frost," *Touchstone*, III (April, 1918), 71-75.
[Criticism.]

CARL SANDBURG

A. POETICAL WORKS

In Reckless Ecstasy. [Pamphlet.] [Galesburg: Asgard Press, 1904.]

Chicago Poems. N. Y.: Henry Holt & Co., 1916. 183 pp.

Cornhuskers. N. Y.: Henry Holt & Co., 1918. 147 pp.

Smoke and Steel. N. Y.: Harcourt, Brace & Co., 1920. 268 pp.
[Also London: J. Cape, 1922.]

Slabs of the Sunburnt West. N. Y.: Harcourt, Brace & Co., [1922]. 76 pp.

Selected Poems of Carl Sandburg. Edited by Rebecca West. London: J. Cape, 1926. 287 pp.
[Also N. Y.: Harcourt, Brace & Co., [1926].]

Carl Sandburg. [Pamphlet Poets.] N. Y.: Simon & Schuster [1926]. 30 pp.

Good Morning, America. N. Y.: Harcourt, Brace & Co., 1928. 251 pp.

B. BIOGRAPHICAL AND CRITICAL REFERENCES

I. BOOKS

AIKEN, CONRAD, *Scepticisms. Notes on Contemporary Poetry* (N. Y., 1919), pp. 143-49.

BOYNTON, PERCY H., *Some Contemporary Americans. The Personal Equation in Literature* (Chicago, 1924), pp. 62-72.

HANSEN, HARRY, *Midwest Portraits. A Book of Memories and Friendships* (N. Y., 1923), pp. 17-92.
[Contains first hand biographical information.]

JONES, LLEWELLYN, *First Impressions. Essays on Poetry, Criticism, and Prosody* (N. Y., 1925), pp. 53-69.

LOWELL, AMY, *Tendencies in Modern American Poetry* (N. Y., 1917), pp. 200-33.
[Biographical and critical.]

MONROE, HARRIET, *Poets and Their Art* (N. Y., 1926), pp. 29-39.

ROSENFELD, PAUL, *Port of New York. Essays on Fourteen American Moderns* (N. Y., 1924), pp. 65-82.

SHERMAN, STUART P., *Americans* (N. Y., 1922), pp. 239-46.

UNTERMEYER, LOUIS, *The New Era in American Poetry* (N. Y., 1919), pp. 95-110.

[See also Untermeyer's *American Poetry since 1900* (N. Y., 1923), pp. 67-88.]

VAN DOREN, CARL, *Many Minds* (N. Y., 1924), pp. 136-51.

WEIRICK, BRUCE, *From Whitman to Sandburg in American Poetry* (N. Y., 1924), pp. 210-20.

WOOD, CLEMENT, *Poets of America* (N. Y., 1925), pp. 246-62.

II. MAGAZINE ARTICLES

BENJAMIN, PAUL L., "A Poet of the Commonplace," *Survey*, XLV (October 2, 1920), 12-13.

CARNEVALI, EMANUEL, "Our Great Carl Sandburg," *Poetry*, XVII (February, 1921), 266-72.

CATEL, JEAN, "La Poésie Américaine d'Aujourd'hui," *Mercure de France*, CXXXVIII (March 15, 1920), 615-27.

FLETCHER, JOHN GOULD, "Some Contemporary American Poets," *Chapbook*, II (May, 1920), 15-19.

KREYMBORG, ALFRED, "Carl Sandburg's New Book," *Poetry*, XIII (December, 1918), 155-61.

RASCOE, BURTON, "Carl Sandburg," *Literary Rev.*, V (September 27, 1924), 1-2.

UNTERMEYER, LOUIS, "Strong Timber," *Dial*, LXV (October 5, 1918), 263-65.

YUST, WALTER, "Carl Sandburg, Human Being," *Bookman*, LII (January, 1921), 285-90.

[Account of an interview.]

VACHEL LINDSAY

A. POETICAL WORKS

Collected Poems. N. Y.: The Macmillan Co., 1923. 390 pp.

[Revised and Illustrated Edition, N. Y.: The Macmillan Co., 1925. 464 pp.]

The Tree of Laughing Bells. [Pamphlet. N. Y., 1905.]

Poems, Cartoons, Advertisements, and Miscellaneous Material. [15 pieces, illustrated.] [Springfield, Ill., 1905-15.]

God Help Us to Be Brave. [Pamphlet. N. Y., 1908.]

The Last Song of Lucifer. [Pamphlet. N. Y., 1908.]

The Tramp's Excuse and Other Poems. [Springfield, Ill., 1909.] [169 pp.]

The Village Magazine. [Privately printed.] [Springfield, Ill., 1910.] [75 pp.] [A second number, 1920.]

Rhymes to Be Traded for Bread. [Privately printed.] [Springfield, Ill., 1912.]

The Wedding of the Rose and the Lotus. A Poem Written on the Near-Completion of the Panama Canal. . . . Nicholas Vachel Lindsay, Rhymer and Designer, Springfield, Illinois, [1912]. [2 pp.]

General William Booth Enters into Heaven and Other Poems. N. Y.: M. Kennerley, 1913. 119 pp.

[Also London: Chatto & Windus, 1919.]

The Congo and Other Poems. With an Introduction by Harriet Monroe. N. Y.: The Macmillan Co., 1914. 159 pp.

The Chinese Nightingale and Other Poems. N. Y.: The Macmillan Co., 1917. 127 pp.

The Daniel Jazz and Other Poems. London: George Bell & Sons, 1920. 94 pp.

The Golden Whales of California and Other Rhymes in the American Language. N. Y.: The Macmillan Co., 1920. 181 pp.

I Know All This When Gipsy Fiddles Cry. [Pamphlet. San Francisco, 1922.]

Going-to-the-Sun. N. Y. and London: D. Appleton & Co., 1923. 101 pp.

The Candle in the Cabin. A Weaving together of Script and Singing. N. Y. and London: D. Appleton & Co., 1926. 130 pp.

Going-to-the-Stars. N. Y. and London: D. Appleton & Co., 1926. 102 pp.

B. BIOGRAPHICAL AND CRITICAL REFERENCES

I. BOOKS

COOK, HOWARD WILLARD, *Our Poets of Today* (N. Y., 1918), pp. 56-65.

[Biographical and critical.]

GRAHAM, STEPHEN. *Tramping with a Poet in the Rockies.* With Thirty-Eight Emblems by Vernon Hill. N. Y.: D. Appleton & Co., 1922. 279 pp.

JONES, LLEWELLYN, *First Impressions. Essays on Poetry, Criticism, and Prosody* (N. Y., 1925), pp. 85-97.

LINDSAY, VACHEL. *Adventures while Preaching the Gospel of Beauty.* N. Y.: M. Kennerley, 1914. 186 pp.

[Also N. Y.: The Macmillan Co., 1921.]

LINDSAY, VACHEL. *A Handy Guide for Beggars. Especially Those of the Poetic Fraternity. Being Sundry Explorations Made While Afoot and Penniless in Florida, Georgia,* [etc.]. [N. Y.]: The Macmillan Co., 1916. 205 pp.

LYND, ROBERT, *Books and Authors* (N. Y., 1923), pp. 237-44.

MAYNARD, THEODORE, *Our Best Poets. English and American* (N. Y., 1922), pp. 181-94.

MONROE, HARRIET, *Poets and Their Art* (N. Y., 1926), pp. 21-29.

PHELPS, WILLIAM LYON, *The Advance of English Poetry in the Twentieth Century* (N. Y., 1918), pp. 213-35.

UNTERMEYER, LOUIS, *The New Era in American Poetry* (N. Y., 1919), pp. 65-94.

[See also Untermeyer's *American Poetry since 1900* (N. Y., 1923), pp. 88-113.]

VAN DOREN, CARL, *Many Minds* (N. Y., 1924), pp. 151-67.

WILLIAMS-ELLIS, A., *An Anatomy of Poetry* (Oxford, 1922), pp. 233-40.

WOOD, CLEMENT, *Poets of America* (N. Y., 1925), pp. 229-46.

[Biographical and critical.]

II. MAGAZINE ARTICLES

BENJAMIN, PAUL L., "Vachel Lindsay—A Folk Poet," *Survey,* XLVII (October 15, 1921), 73-75.

DAVISON, EDWARD, "Contemporary American Authors. VIII. Vachel Lindsay," *London Mercury,* XVII (April, 1928), 652-66.

FLETCHER, JOHN GOULD, "Some Contemporary American Poets," *Chapbook,* II (May, 1920), 19-22.

GORMAN, HERBERT S., "Vachel Lindsay: Evangelist of Poetry," *No. American Rev.,* CCXIX (January, 1924), 123-29.

MASTERS, EDGAR LEE, "Vachel Lindsay," *Bookman,* LXIV (October, 1926), 156-61.

RITTENHOUSE, JESSIE B., "Contemporary Poetry. Notes and Reviews," *Bookman,* XLVI (January, 1918), 575-77.

WILKINSON, MARGUERITE, "Vachel Lindsay," *Spectator,* CXXV (September 18, 1920), 372-73.

WILKINSON, MARGUERITE, "Poets of the People. No. III.—Vachel Lindsay," *Touchstone,* II (February, 1918), 510-13, 519.

SARA TEASDALE

A. POETICAL WORKS

Poems. [*Flame and Shadow, Love Songs, Rivers to the Sea.*] [3 vols.] N. Y.: The Macmillan Co., 1923.

Sonnets to Duse and Other Poems. Boston: Poet Lore Co., 1907. 44 pp.

Helen of Troy and Other Poems. N. Y. and London: G. P. Putnam's Sons, 1911. 106 pp.

[New edition, revised, N. Y.: The Macmillan Co., 1922.]

Rivers to the Sea. N. Y.: The Macmillan Co., 1915. 148 pp.

Love Songs. N. Y.: The Macmillan Co., 1917. 91 pp.

Vignettes of Italy. A Cycle of Nine Songs for High Voice. Music by W. Watts. Boston: Ditson, 1919. 32 pp.

Flame and Shadow. N. Y.: The Macmillan Co., 1920. 144 pp.

[Also London: J. Cape, 1924.]

Dark of the Moon. N. Y.: The Macmillan Co., 1926. 92 pp.

B. BIOGRAPHICAL AND CRITICAL REFERENCES

I. BOOKS

COOK, HOWARD WILLARD, *Our Poets of Today* (N. Y., 1918), pp. 12-19.

[Biographical and critical.]

MONROE, HARRIET, *Poets and Their Art* (N. Y., 1926), pp. 72-78.

Sara Teasdale. [Pamphlet.] [N. Y.: The Macmillan Co., n. d.] 32 pp.

[Biographical sketch, with comments of the critics.]

UNTERMEYER, LOUIS, *The New Era in American Poetry* (N. Y., 1919), pp. 264-71.

[See also Untermeyer's *American Poetry since 1900* (N. Y., 1923), pp. 206-14.]

II. MAGAZINE ARTICLES

COLUM, PADRAIC, "Sara Teasdale's Poems," *New Republic*, XV (June 22, 1918), 239-41.

M[ONROE], H[ARRIET], review of *Rivers to the Sea*, *Poetry*, VII (December, 1915), 148-50.

RITTENHOUSE, JESSIE B., "Sara Teasdale," *Bookman*, LXV (May, 1927), 290-95.

T[IETJENS], E[UNICE], "A Singer," *Poetry*, XVII (February, 1921), 272-76.

WILKINSON, MARGUERITE, "Sara Teasdale's Poems," *Forum*, LXV (February, 1921), 229-36.

WILKINSON, MARGUERITE, "Poets of the People: Sara Teasdale. The First of the Series," *Touchstone*, II (December, 1917), 311-13.

EZRA POUND

A. POETICAL WORKS

Personae. The Collected Poems of Ezra Pound . . . N. Y.: Boni & Liveright, 1926. 231 pp.

A Lume Spento. Venice, Italy: Antonelli, 1908.

A Quinzaine for This Yule. Being Selected from a Venetian Sketch-Book, "San Trovaso," by Ezra Pound. London: Pollock & Co., 1908. 27 pp.

Exultations. London: E. Mathews, 1909. 51 pp.

Personae. London: E. Mathews, 1909. 59 pp.

Provença. Poems Selected from *Personae, Exultations,* and *Canzoniere* of Ezra Pound. Boston: Small, Maynard & Co., [1910]. 84 pp.

Canzoni. London: Elkin Mathews, 1911. 60 pp.

Ripostes of Ezra Pound. Whereto Are Appended the Complete Poetical Works of T. E. Hulme. With Prefatory Note. London: Stephen Swift & Co., Ltd., 1912. 64 pp.
[Also Boston: Small, Maynard & Co., 1913.]

Sonnets and Ballate of Guido Cavalcanti. [Translations.] Boston: Small, Maynard & Co.; London: Stephen Swift & Co., 1912.

Canzoni and Ripostes of Ezra Pound. . . . London: Elkin Mathews, 1913. 51, 63 pp.

Personae and Exultations. London: Elkin Mathews, 1913. 59, 51 pp.

Cathay. . . . [Translations from the Chinese, from notes by Ernest Fenollosa.] London: Elkin Mathews, 1915. 31 pp.

Certain Noble Plays of Japan: From the Manuscripts of Ernest Fenollosa, Chosen and Finished by Ezra Pound, with an Introduction by William Butler Yeats. Churchtown, Dundrum: Cuala Press, 1916. [50 pp.]
[Translations in prose and verse.]

Lustra of Ezra Pound. . . . London: Elkin Mathews, 1916. 115 pp.

Lustra of Ezra Pound, with Earlier Poems. N. Y.: Alfred A. Knopf, 1917. 202 pp.

'Noh' or Accomplishment. A Study of the Classical Stage of Japan. By Ernest Fenollosa and Ezra Pound. London: Macmillan & Co., Ltd., 1916. [268 pp.]

[Some verse translations included.]

Quia Pauper Amavi. London: Egoist Press, 1919. 51 pp.

Umbra. The Early Poems of Ezra Pound. . . . London: Elkin Mathews, 1920. 128 pp.

Poems—1918-21. Including Three Portraits and Four Cantos. N. Y.: Boni & Liveright, [1921]. 90 pp.

B. CRITICAL REFERENCES

I. BOOKS

AIKEN, CONRAD, *Scepticisms. Notes on Contemporary Poetry* (N. Y., 1919), pp. 136-43.

MONRO, HAROLD, *Some Contemporary Poets (1920)* (London, 1920), pp. 87-93.

MONROE, HARRIET, *Poets and Their Art* (N. Y., 1926), pp. 12-21.

UNTERMEYER, LOUIS, *The New Era in American Poetry* (N. Y., 1919), pp. 201-15.

[See also Untermeyer's *American Poetry since 1900* (N. Y., 1923), pp. 157-70.]

II. MAGAZINE ARTICLES

ALDINGTON, RICHARD, "The Poetry of Ezra Pound," *Egoist*, II (May 1, 1915), 71-72.

"Ezra Pound" [from the French of Jean de Bosschère], *Egoist*, IV (January, February, April, 1917), 7-9, 27-29, 44.

[On Pound as a translator.]

BRONNER, MILTON, "A Panel of Poets," *Bookman*, XXXV (April, 1912), 156-58.

[Criticism.]

FLETCHER, JOHN GOULD, "Some Contemporary American Poets," *Chapbook*, II (May, 1920), 23-25.

[Criticism.]

GORMAN, HERBERT S., "Bolingbroke of Bards," *No. American Rev.*, CCXIX (June, 1924), 855-66.

[Criticism.]

LESEMANN, MAURICE, "Mr. Pound and the Younger Generation," *Poetry*, XXX (July, 1927), 216-22.

MICHELSON, MAX, "A Glass-Blower of Time," *Poetry*, XI (March, 1918), 330-33.
[Criticism.]

RITTENHOUSE, JESSIE B., "Contemporary Poetry. Notes and Reviews," *Bookman*, XLVI (January, 1918), 577-78.

SANDBURG, CARL, "The Work of Ezra Pound," *Poetry*, VII (February, 1916), 249-58.

SINCLAIR, MAY, "The Reputation of Ezra Pound," *No. American Rev.*, CCXI (May, 1920), 658-69.
[Also in *English Rev.*, XXX (April, 1920), 326-36.]

THOMAS, EDWARD, "Two Poets," *English Rev.*, II (June, 1909), 627-30.

JOHN GOULD FLETCHER

A. POETICAL WORKS

The Book of Nature. London: Constable & Co., Ltd., 1913. 108 pp.

The Dominant City (1911-12). London: Max Goschen, Ltd., 1913. 75 pp.

Fire and Wine. London: Grant Richards, 1913.

Fool's Gold. London: Max Goschen, Ltd., 1913. 92 pp.

Visions of the Evening. London: Erskine MacDonald, 1913. 43 pp.

Irradiations—Sand and Spray. Boston: Houghton Mifflin, 1915. [60 pp.]
[Also London: Constable & Co., Ltd., 1915.]

Goblins and Pagodas. Boston: Houghton Mifflin, 1916. [99 pp.]
[Also London: Constable & Co., Ltd., 1918.]

Japanese Prints. Imagist Poems . . . Boston: Four Seas Co., 1917. 94 pp.

The Tree of Life. London: Chatto & Windus, 1918. 127 pp.
[Also N. Y.: The Macmillan Co., 1918.]

Breakers and Granite. N. Y.: The Macmillan Co., 1921. 163 pp.

Preludes and Symphonies. Boston: Houghton Mifflin, 1922. [60, 99 pp.]
[A reprint of *Irradiations—Sand and Spray* and of *Goblins and Pagodas*.]

Parables. With Woodcut Frontispiece by John J. A. Murphy. London: K. Paul, Trench, Trubner & Co., 1925. 143 pp.

Branches of Adam. London: Faber & Gwyer, [1926]. 81 pp.

The Black Rock. London: Faber & Gwyer, 1928. 176 pp.

B. BIOGRAPHICAL AND CRITICAL REFERENCES

I. BOOKS

AIKEN, CONRAD, *Scepticisms. Notes on Contemporary Poetry* (N. Y., 1919), pp. 105-15.

LOWELL, AMY, *Tendencies in Modern American Poetry* (N. Y., 1917), pp. 280-343.
[Both biographical and critical.]

MONROE, HARRIET, *Poets and Their Art* (N. Y., 1926), pp. 86-92.

UNTERMEYER, LOUIS, *The New Era in American Poetry* (N. Y., 1919), pp. 301-9.
[See also Untermeyer's *American Poetry since 1900* (N. Y., 1923), pp. 316-23.]

II. MAGAZINE ARTICLES

GREENSLET, FERRIS, "The Poetry of John Gould Fletcher," *Egoist*, II (May 1, 1915), 73.

H[ENDERSON], A[LICE] C., review of *Irradiations, Poetry*, VII (October, 1915), 44-47.

LOWELL, AMY, "Mr. Fletcher's Verse," *New Republic*, III (May 15, 1915), 48-49.

SHERRY, LAURA, "Fletcherian Colors," *Poetry*, XIX (December, 1921), 155-58.

E. W., "Faery-lands Forlorn," *New Republic*, IX: supplement (November 18, 1916), 11.

HILDA DOOLITTLE (H. D.)

A. POETICAL WORKS

Collected Poems of H. D. N. Y.: Boni & Liveright, 1925. 306 pp.

Sea Garden. London: Constable & Co., Ltd., 1916. 47 pp.
[Also Boston: Houghton Mifflin, 1916.]

Hymen. N. Y.: Henry Holt & Co., 1921. [47 pp.]

Heliodora and Other Poems. Boston: Houghton Mifflin, [1924]. 127 pp.

H. D. [Pamphlet Poets.] N. Y.: Simon & Schuster, 1926. 32 pp.

Hippolytus Temporizes. A Play in Three Acts. Boston: Houghton Mifflin, 1927. 139 pp.

B. BIOGRAPHICAL AND CRITICAL REFERENCES

I. BOOKS

COLLINS, H. P., *Modern Poetry* (London, 1925), pp. 154-203.

LOWELL, AMY, *Tendencies in Modern American Poetry* (N. Y., 1917), pp. 249-80.
[Includes both biographical and critical material.]

MONROE, HARRIET, *Poets and Their Art* (N. Y., 1926), pp. 92-100.

UNTERMEYER, LOUIS, *The New Era in American Poetry* (N. Y., 1919), pp. 297-301.
[See also Untermeyer's *American Poetry since 1900* (N. Y., 1923), pp. 309-16.]

II. MAGAZINE ARTICLES

FLINT, F. S., "H. D.," *Chapbook*, II (March, 1920), 22-24.
[Criticism.]

FLINT, F. S., "The Poetry of H. D.," *Egoist*, II (May, 1915), 72-73.

LOWELL, AMY, "Exquisite Cameos and Intaglios," *Poetry Journal*, VII (August, 1917), 171-81.

SINCLAIR, MAY, "On H. D.," *Egoist*, II (June, 1915), 88.
[Criticism.]

SINCLAIR, MAY, "The Poems of H. D.," *Dial*, LXXII (February, 1922), 203-8.

CONRAD AIKEN

A. POETICAL WORKS

Earth Triumphant and Other Tales in Verse. N. Y.: The Macmillan Co., 1914. 219 pp.

Turns and Movies and Other Tales in Verse. Boston: Houghton Mifflin, 1916. [91 pp.]
[Also London: Constable & Co., 1916.]

The Jig of Forslin. A Symphony. Boston: Four Seas Co., 1916. 127 pp.
[Also London: M. Secker, 1921.]

Nocturne of Remembered Spring and Other Poems. Boston: Four Seas Co., 1917. 140 pp.
[Also London: M. Secker, 1921.]

The Charnel Rose, Senlin: A Biography, and Other Poems. Boston: Four Seas Co., 1918. 156 pp.

The House of Dust. A Symphony. Boston: Four Seas Co., 1920. 148 pp.

Punch: the Immortal Liar. Documents in His History. N. Y.: Alfred A. Knopf, 1921. 80 pp.
[Also London: M. Secker, 1921.]

Priapus and the Pool. Cambridge: Dunster House, 1922. [63 pp.]

The Pilgrimage of Festus. N. Y.: Alfred A. Knopf, 1923. 75 pp.
[Also London: M. Secker, 1924.]

Priapus and the Pool and Other Poems. N. Y.: Boni & Liveright, 1925. 151 pp.

Senlin: a Biography. London: Hogarth Press, 1925. 36 pp.

Conrad Aiken . . . [Pamphlet Poets.] N. Y.: Simon & Schuster, [1927]. 31 pp.

B. BIOGRAPHICAL AND CRITICAL REFERENCES

I. BOOKS

AIKEN, CONRAD. *Scepticisms. Notes on Contemporary Poetry.* N. Y.: Alfred A. Knopf, 1919. 305 pp.
[Of some autobiographical value; incidentally throws light on Aiken's own poetry.]

UNTERMEYER, LOUIS, *The New Era in American Poetry* (N. Y., 1919), pp. 330-38.
[See also Untermeyer's *American Poetry since 1900* (N. Y., 1923), pp. 170-83.]

II. MAGAZINE ARTICLES

DEUTSCH, BABETTE, "Orchestral Poetry," *Dial,* LXX (March, 1921), 343-47.

FLETCHER, JOHN GOULD, "Some Contemporary American Poets," *Chapbook,* II (May, 1920), 26-28.
[Criticism.]

FLETCHER, JOHN GOULD, "The Poetry of Conrad Aiken," *Dial,* LXIV (March 28, 1918), 291-93.

FLETCHER, JOHN GOULD, "Conrad Aiken—Metaphysical Poet," *Dial,* LXVI (May 31, 1919), 558-59.

STROBEL, MARION, "Through a Glass Darkly," *Poetry,* XVII (January, 1921), 220-22.

EDNA ST. VINCENT MILLAY

A. POETICAL WORKS

Renascence and Other Poems. N. Y.: Mitchell Kennerley, 1917. 73 pp.
[Also N. Y. and London: Harper & Brothers, [1917].]

Aria da Capo. A Play in One Act. N. Y.: D. Appleton & Co., 1920. 51 pp.
[Also N. Y. and London: Harper & Brothers, [1920].]

A Few Figs from Thistles. Poems and Four Sonnets. N. Y.: Frank Shay, 1920. 20 pp.
[Also N. Y. and London: Harper & Brothers, 1923.]

The Lamp and the Bell. A Drama in Five Acts. N. Y.: Frank Shay, 1921. 71 pp.
[Also N. Y. and London: Harper & Brothers, [1923].]

Second April. N. Y.: Mitchell Kennerley, 1921. 112 pp.
[Also N. Y. and London: Harper & Brothers, [1921].]

Two Slatterns and a King. A Moral Interlude. [Stewart Kidd Modern Plays.] Cincinnati: Stewart Kidd Co., [1921]. 18 pp.

The Ballad of the Harp-Weaver. N. Y.: Frank Shay, 1922. 10 pp.

The Harp-Weaver and Other Poems. N. Y. and London: Harper & Brothers, 1923. 93 pp.
[Also London: M. Secker, 1924.]

Poems. London: Martin Secker, 1923. [146 pp.]

Three Plays. [*Two Slatterns and a King, Aria da Capo, The Lamp and the Bell.*] N. Y. and London: Harper & Brothers, 1926. 147 pp.
[Also London: J. Cape, 1927.]

Edna St. Vincent Millay. [Pamphlet Poets.] N. Y.: Simon & Schuster, [1927]. 31 pp.

The King's Henchman. A Play in Three Acts. N. Y. and London: Harper & Brothers, 1927. [132 pp.]
[Also London: J. Cape, 1927.]

The Buck in the Snow and Other Poems. N. Y. and London: Harper & Brothers, 1928. 69 pp.

B. BIOGRAPHICAL AND CRITICAL REFERENCES

I. BOOKS

The Literary Spotlight . . . [Edited by John Farrar.] (N. Y., 1924), pp. 77-91.
[Criticism, with some biographical information.]

MAYNARD, THEODORE, *Our Best Poets. English and American* (N. Y., 1922), pp. 226-32.

MONROE, HARRIET, *Poets and Their Art* (N. Y., 1926), pp. 63-72.

UNTERMEYER, LOUIS, *The New Era in American Poetry* (N. Y., 1919), pp. 271-75.

[See also Untermeyer's *American Poetry since 1900* (N. Y., 1923), pp. 214-21.]

VAN DOREN, CARL, *Many Minds* (N. Y., 1924), pp. 105-20.

WOOD, CLEMENT. *Poets of America* (N. Y., 1925), pp. 199-214.

II. MAGAZINE ARTICLES

COLUM, PADRAIC, "Miss Millay's Poems," *Freeman*, IV (November 2, 1921), 189-90.

DAVISON, EDWARD, "Edna St. Vincent Millay," *English Journal*, XVI (November, 1927), 671-82.

[Criticism.]

M[ONROE], H[ARRIET], "First Books of Verse," *Poetry*, XIII (December, 1918), 167-69.

INDEXES

INDEX OF AUTHORS

INDEX OF TITLES AND FIRST LINES

In the following index the titles of poems are printed in capitals, and first lines are printed in ordinary roman type.